YESTERDAYS WITH AUTHORS

"*The air is full of their voices. Their books are the world's holiday and playground, and into these neither care, nor the dun, nor despondency can follow the enfranchised man.*" — DREAMTHORP.

James T. Fields

YESTERDAYS WITH AUTHORS

BY

JAMES T. FIELDS

*ILLUSTRATED WITH PHOTOGRAVURE PORTRAITS
AUTOGRAPH LETTERS, ETC.*

Was it not yesterday we spoke together? — SHAKESPEARE.

AMS PRESS
NEW YORK

Reprinted from the edition of 1900, Boston
First AMS EDITION published 1970
Manufactured in the United States of America

Library of Congress Catalog Card Number: 79-100520
SBN: 404-00603-5

AMS PRESS, INC.
NEW YORK, N.Y. 10003

Inscribed

TO MY FELLOW-MEMBERS
OF THE SATURDAY CLUB

CONTENTS.

		PAGE
I.	INTRODUCTORY	1
II.	THACKERAY	11
III.	HAWTHORNE	39
IV.	DICKENS	125
V.	WORDSWORTH	251
VI.	MISS MITFORD	261
VII.	"BARRY CORNWALL" AND SOME OF HIS FRIENDS	353

LIST OF ILLUSTRATIONS.

	PAGE
JAMES T. FIELDS. From a photograph by Mrs. Cameron *Frontispiece*	
ALEXANDER POPE	4
FACSIMILE OF LETTER FROM JOHN RUSKIN	8
WILLIAM MAKEPEACE THACKERAY	24
DR. JOHN BROWN	34
ROBERT BURNS	42
FACSIMILE OF LETTER FROM NATHANIEL HAWTHORNE	52
THOMAS DE QUINCEY. From a portrait in the National Portrait Gallery by Sir J. Watson Gordon	76
LEIGH HUNT. Engraved by H. Wright Smith	80
TICKNOR, FIELDS, AND HAWTHORNE	96
FACSIMILE OF LETTER FROM HENRY D. THOREAU	110
NATHANIEL HAWTHORNE. From a photograph	120
CORNELIUS C. FELTON. From a photograph loaned by Miss Louisa C. Felton	130
FACSIMILE OF LETTER FROM WASHINGTON ALLSTON	146
CHARLES DICKENS	156
CHARLES DICKENS, HIS WIFE, AND HER SISTER, GEORGINA HOGARTH. After a drawing by Maclise in 1842	176
FACSIMILE OF LETTER FROM CHARLES DICKENS	184
HENRY W. LONGFELLOW. Engraved by J. J. Wilcox	192
KEEP OF ROCHESTER CASTLE. From photograph	218
GADSHILL FROM THE REAR, DICKENS'S HOME	228
WILLIAM WORDSWORTH. Engraved by Stuart	254
RYDAL MOUNT, WORDSWORTH'S HOME	258
MARY R. MITFORD	266

LIST OF ILLUSTRATIONS.

WALTER SAVAGE LANDOR. From painting by Dance	273
ROBERT BROWNING. From photograph	288
OLIVER WENDELL HOLMES	314
JAMES RUSSELL LOWELL. From photograph	332
FACSIMILE OF LETTER FROM JAMES RUSSELL LOWELL	344
CHARLES AND MARY LAMB. After portraits by Francis Stevens Cary in the National Portrait Gallery	358
B. W. PROCTER ("BARRY CORNWALL"). Engraved by Stuart	362
ELIZABETH BARRETT BROWNING. From a drawing by Field Talfourd in the National Portrait Gallery	368
ANNA JAMESON	376
FACSIMILE OF THE LAST PAGE OF A LETTER FROM LEIGH HUNT	382
SAMUEL ROGERS	390
JOHN FORSTER	396
FACSIMILE OF THE ORIGINAL POEM BY B. W. PROCTER ("BARRY CORNWALL")	412
FACSIMILE OF LETTER FROM MRS. PROCTER	416

The originals of these illustrations, excepting those noted, are from the library of Mrs. James T. Fields.

INTRODUCTORY.

"Some there are,
By their good works exalted, lofty minds
And meditative, authors of delight
And happiness, which to the end of time
Will live, and spread, and kindle."
                        WORDSWORTH.

I.

INTRODUCTORY.

SURROUNDED by the portraits of those I have long counted my friends, I like to chat with the people about me concerning these pictures, my companions on the wall, and the men and women they represent. These are my assembled guests, who dropped in years ago and stayed with me, without the form of invitation or demand on my time or thought. They are my eloquent silent partners for life, and I trust they will dwell here as long as I do. Some of them I have known intimately; several of them lived in other times; but they are all my friends and associates in a certain sense.

To converse with them and of them—

"When to the sessions of sweet silent thought
I summon up remembrance of things past"—

is one of the delights of existence, and I am never tired of answering questions about them, or gossiping of my own free will as to their every-day life and manners.

If I were to call the little collection in this diminutive house a *Gallery of Pictures*, in the usual sense of that title, many would smile and remind me of what Foote said with his characteristic sharpness of David Garrick, when he joined his brother Peter in the wine trade: "Davy lived with three quarts of vinegar in the cellar, calling himself a wine merchant."

My friends have often heard me in my "garrulous old age" discourse of things past and gone, and know what they bring down on their heads when they request me "to run over," as they call it, the faces looking out upon us from these plain unvarnished frames.

Let us begin, then, with the little man of Twickenham, for that is his portrait which hangs over the front fireplace. An original portrait of Alexander Pope I certainly never expected to possess, and I must relate how I came by it. Only a year ago I was strolling in my vagabond way up and down the London streets, and dropped in to see an old picture-shop, — kept by a man so thoroughly instructed in his calling that it is always a pleasure to talk with him and examine his collection of valuables, albeit his treasures are of such preciousness as to make the humble purse of a commoner seem to shrink into a still smaller compass from sheer inability to respond when prices are named. At No. 6 Pall Mall one is apt to find Mr. Graves "clipp'd round about" by first-rate canvas. When I dropped in upon him that summer morning he had just returned from the sale of the Marquis of Hastings's effects. The Marquis, it will be remembered, went wrong, and his debts swallowed up everything. It was a wretched stormy day when the pictures were sold, and Mr. Graves secured, at very moderate prices, five original portraits. All the paintings had suffered more or less decay, and some of them, with their frames, had fallen to the floor. One of the best preserved pictures inherited by the late Marquis was a portrait of Pope, painted from life by Richardson for the Earl of Burlington, and even that had been allowed to drop out of its oaken frame. Horace Walpole says, Jonathan Richardson was undoubtedly one of the best painters of a head that had appeared in England. He was pupil of the celebrated Riley, the master of Hudson, of whom Sir Joshua took lessons in his art and it was Richardson's "Treatise on Painting" which

A Pope.

INTRODUCTORY. 5

inflamed the mind of young Reynolds, and stimulated his ambition to become a great painter. Pope seems to have had a real affection for Richardson, and probably sat to him for this picture some time during the year 1732. In Pope's correspondence there is a letter addressed to the painter making an engagement with him for a several days' sitting, and it is quite probable that the portrait before us was finished at that time. One can imagine the painter and the poet chatting together day after day, in presence of that canvas. During the same year Pope's mother died, at the great age of ninety-three; and on the evening of June 10th, while she lay dead in the house, Pope sent off the following heart-touching letter from Twickenham to his friend the painter: —

"As you know you and I mutually desire to see one another, I hoped that this day our wishes would have met, and brought you hither. And this for the very reason which possibly might hinder your coming, that my poor mother is dead. I thank God, her death was as easy as her life was innocent; and as it cost her not a groan, or even a sigh, there is yet upon her countenance such an expression of tranquillity, nay, almost of pleasure, that it is even amiable to behold it. It would afford the finest image of a saint expired that ever painting drew; and it would be the greatest obligation which even that obliging art could ever bestow on a friend, if you could come and sketch it for me. I am sure, if there be no very prevalent obstacle, you will leave any common business to do this; and I hope to see you this evening, as late as you will, or to-morrow morning as early, before this winter flower is faded. I will defer her interment till tomorrow night. I know you love me, or I could not have written this; I could not (at this time) have written at all. Adieu! May you die as happily!"

Several eminent artists of that day painted the likeness of Pope, and among them Sir Godfrey Kneller and Jervas, but I like the expression of this one by Richardson best of all. The mouth, it will be observed, is very sensitive and the eyes almost painfully so. It is told of the poet, that when he was a boy "there was great sweetness in his look," and that his face was plump and pretty, and that he had a very fresh complexion. Continual study ruined his constitution and changed his form, it is said. Richardson has skilfully kept out of sight the poor little decrepit figure, and gives us only the beautiful head of a man of genius. I scarcely know a face on canvas that expresses the poetical sense in a higher degree than this one. The likeness must be perfect, and I can imagine the delight of the Rev. Joseph Spence hobbling into his presence on the 4th of September, 1735, after "a ragged boy of an ostler came in with a little scrap of paper not half an inch broad, which contained the following words : 'Mr. Pope would be very glad to see Mr. Spence at the Cross Inn just now.'"

English literature is full of eulogistic mention of Pope. Thackeray is one of the last great authors who has spoken golden words about the poet. "Let us always take into account," he says, "that constant tenderness and fidelity of affection which pervaded and sanctified his life."

What pluck and dauntless courage possessed the "gallant little cripple" of Twickenham! When all the dunces of England were aiming their poisonous barbs at him, he said, "I had rather die at once, than live in fear of those rascals." A vast deal that has been written about him is untrue. No author has been more elaborately slandered on principle, or more studiously abused through envy. Smarting dullards went about for years, with an ever-ready microscope, hunting for flaws in his character that might be injuriously exposed; but to-day his defamers are in bad repute. Excellence in a fellow-mortal is to many men worse than death; and great suffering fell upon a host of mediocre writers when Pope uplifted his sceptre and sat supreme above them all.

Pope's latest champion is John Ruskin. Open his Lectures on Art, recently delivered before the University of Oxford, and read passage number seventy. Let us read it together, as we sit here in the presence of the sensitive poet.

"I want you to think over the relation of expression to character in two great masters of the absolute art of language, Virgil and Pope. You are perhaps surprised at the last named; and indeed you have in English much higher grasp and melody of language from more passionate minds, but you have nothing else, in its range, so perfect. I name, therefore, these two men, because they are the two most accomplished *artists*, merely as such, whom I know, in literature; and because I think you will be afterwards interested in investigating how the infinite grace in the words of the one, the severity in those of the other, and the precision in those of both, arise wholly out of the moral elements of their minds, — out of the deep tenderness in Virgil which enabled him to write the stories of Nisus and Lausus, and the serene and just benevolence which placed Pope, in his theology, two centuries in advance of his time, and enabled him to sum the law of noble life in two lines which, so far as I know, are the most complete, the most concise, and the most lofty expression of moral temper existing in English words: —

'Never elated, while one man's oppressed;
Never dejected, while another's blessed.'

I wish you also to remember these lines of Pope, and to make yourselves entirely masters of his system of ethics; because, putting Shakespeare aside as rather the world's than ours, I hold Pope to be the most perfect representative we have, since Chaucer, of the true English mind; and I think the Dunciad is the most absolutely chiselled and monumental work 'exacted' in our country. You will find, as you study Pope, that he has expressed for you, in the strictest language and within the briefest limits, every law of art, of criticism, of economy, of policy, and, finally, of a benevolence, humble, rational, and resigned, contented with its allotted share of life, and trusting the problem of its salvation to Him in whose hands lies that of the universe."

Glance up at the tender eyes of the poet, who seems to have been eagerly listening while we have been reading Ruskin's beautiful tribute. As he is so intent upon us, let me gratify still further the honest pride of "the little nightingale," as they used to call him when he was a child, and read to you from the "Causeries du Lundi" what that wise French critic, Sainte-Beuve, has written of his favorite English poet: —

"The natural history of Pope is very simple: delicate persons, it has been said, are unhappy, and he was doubly delicate, delicate of mind, delicate and infirm of body; he was doubly irritable. But what grace, what taste, what swiftness to feel, what justness and perfection in expressing his feeling! . . . . His first masters were insignificant; he educated himself: at twelve years old he learned Latin and Greek together, and almost without a master; at fifteen he resolved to go to London, in order to learn French and Italian there, by reading the authors. His family, retired from trade, and Catholic, lived at this time upon an estate in the forest of Windsor. This desire of his was considered as an odd caprice, for his health from that time hardly permitted him to move about. He persisted, and accomplished his project; he learned nearly everything thus by himself, making his own choice among authors, getting the grammar quite alone, and his pleasure was to translate into verse the finest passages he met with among the Latin and Greek poets. When he was about sixteen years old, he said, his taste was formed as much as it was later. . . . . If such a thing as literary temperament exist, it never discovered itself in a manner more clearly defined and more decided than with Pope. Men ordinarily become classic by means of the fact and discipline of education; he was so by vocation, so to speak, and by a natural originality. At the same time with the poets, he read the best among the critics, and prepared himself to speak after them.

. . . .

"Pope had the characteristic sign of literary natures, the faithful worship of genius. . . . . He said one day to a friend: 'I have always been particularly struck with this passage of Homer where he represents to us Priam transported with grief for the loss of Hector, on the point of breaking out into reproaches and invectives against the servants who surrounded him and against his sons. It would be impossible for me to read this passage without weeping over the disasters of the unfortunate old king.' And then he took the book, and tried to read aloud the passage, 'Go, wretches, curse of my life,' but he was interrupted by tears.

. . . .

"No example could prove to us better than his to what degree the faculty of tender, sensitive criticism is an active faculty. We

Dear Dr Clingson

The first mS goes to New York on Friday. Therefore every Saturday, my letter to you is put off till each Thursday. Every Thursday, till Friday morning, till Friday morning, it is too late for the post.

The main real reason of my postponing has been first much fatigue of eyes, diff. which obliges I been in many matters — what I left till after the New Year — second, a great puzzlement about your Thomas commission. I cannot [?] myself to [?] in any way, too [?] leaving England — a long post on board a ship — and did not know well how true is however it bulky, beautiful white marble & Enid's superbia — lighted by a glare, lives Turner under a green curtain — on a certain number I hope admitted for they & now to see more than 10, I however . ! ! . There a plan for Ym.

I sent one of my drawings to Black (Campbell) a study of three plein-air young ash — wild geranium, meets baselwood, tris — by Walker & you have four weeks ago. If I am half finished or but will draw to this there who are interested in the matter & my news of drawing. you will know it was you that beat it & heads send it back to me rather clumsily

I am too generous to see spare bunch a Xmas card but

you know — as for your having it all your own way
in the West there — I won't have it —
— You must have a civil war — and a feudal system
— or there you may be good for something —
Perhaps even this living a new funeral.
For it is 12th December. & Friday is near.

Most truly yours
J Ruskin

The Rev'd L. L. Magnon. M.S.

neither feel nor perceive in this way when there is nothing to give in return. This taste, this sensibility, so swift and alert, justly supposes imagination behind it. It is said that Shelley, the first time he heard the poem of 'Christabel' recited, at a certain magnificent and terrible passage, took fright and suddenly fainted. The whole poem of 'Alastor' was to be foreseen in that fainting. Pope, not less sensitive in his way, could not read through that passage of the Iliad without bursting into tears. To be a critic to that degree, is to be a poet."

Thanks, eloquent and judicious scholar, so lately gone from the world of letters! A love of what is best in art was the habit of Sainte-Beuve's life, and so he too will be remembered as one who has kept the best company in literature, — a man who cheerfully did homage to genius, wherever and whenever it might be found.

I intend to leave as a legacy to a dear friend of mine an old faded book, which I hope he will always prize as it deserves. It is a well-worn, well-read volume, of no value whatever as an *edition*, — but *it belonged to Abraham Lincoln*. It is his copy of "The Poetical Works of Alexander Pope, Esq., to which is prefixed the life of the author by Dr. Johnson." It bears the imprint on the title-page of J. J. Woodward, Philadelphia, and was published in 1839. Our President wrote his own name in it, and chronicles the fact that it was presented to him "by his friend N. W. Edwards." In January, 1861, Mr. Lincoln gave the book to a very dear friend of his, who honored me with it in January, 1867, as a New-Year's present. As long as I live it will remain among my books, specially treasured as having been owned and read by one of the noblest and most sorely tried of men, a hero comparable with any of Plutarch's, —

"The kindly-earnest, brave, foreseeing man,
  Sagacious, patient, dreading praise, not blame,
New birth of our new soil, the first American."

THACKERAY.

What Emerson has said in his fine subtle way of Shakespeare may well be applied to the author of "Vanity Fair."

"One can discern in his ample pictures what forms and humanities pleased him; his delight in troops of friends, in large hospitality, in cheerful giving.

. . . . .

"He read the hearts of men and women, their probity, and their second thought, and wiles; the wiles of innocence, and the transitions by which virtues and vices slide into their contraries."

II.

THACKERAY.

DEAR old Thackeray! — as everybody who knew him intimately calls him, now he is gone. That is his face, looking out upon us, next to Pope's. What a contrast in bodily appearance those two English men of genius present! Thackeray's great burly figure, broad-chested, and ample as the day, seems to overshadow and quite blot out of existence the author of "The Essay on Man." But what friends they would have been had they lived as contemporaries under Queen Anne or Queen Victoria! One can imagine the author of "Pendennis" gently lifting poor little Alexander out of his "chariot" into the club, and revelling in talk with him all night long. Pope's high-bred and gentlemanly manner, combined with his extraordinary sensibility and dread of ridicule, would have modified Thackeray's usual gigantic fun and sometimes boisterous sarcasm into a rich and strange adaptability to his little guest. We can imagine them talking together now, with even a nobler wisdom and ampler charity than were ever vouchsafed to them when they were busy amid the turmoils of their crowded literary lives.

As a reader and lover of all that Thackeray has written and published, as well as a personal friend, I will relate briefly something of his literary habits as I can recall them. It is now nearly twenty years since I first saw him and came to know him familiarly in London. I was very much in earnest to have him come to America, and read his series of lectures on "The English Humorists of the Eighteenth Century," and when I talked the matter over with some of his friends at the little Garrick Club, they all said he could never be induced to leave London long enough for such an expedition. Next morning, after this talk at the Garrick, the elderly damsel of all work announced to me, as I was taking breakfast at my lodgings, that Mr. *Sackville* had called to see me, and was then waiting below. Very soon I heard a heavy tread on the stairs, and then entered a tall, white-haired stranger, who held out his hand, bowed profoundly, and with a most comical expression announced himself as Mr. Sackville. Recognizing at once the face from published portraits, I knew that my visitor was none other than Thackeray himself, who, having heard the servant give the wrong name, determined to assume it on this occasion. For years afterwards, when he would drop in unexpectedly, both at home and abroad, he delighted to call himself Mr. Sackville, until a certain Milesian waiter at the Tremont House addressed him as Mr. Thack*uary*, when he adopted that name in preference to the other.

Questions are frequently asked as to the habits of thought and composition of authors one has happened to know, as if an author's friends were commonly invited to observe the growth of works he was by and by to launch from the press. It is not customary for the doors of the writer's work-shop to be thrown open, and for this reason it is all the more interesting to notice, when it is possible, how an essay, a history, a novel, or a poem is conceived, grows up, and is corrected for publication. One would like very much to be informed how Shakespeare put together the scenes of Hamlet or Macbeth, whether the subtile thought accumulated easily on the page before him, or whether he struggled for it with anxiety and distrust. We know that Milton troubled himself about little matters of punctuation, and obliged the printer to take special note of his requirements, scolding him roundly when he neglected his instructions. We also know that Melanchthon was in his library hard at work by two or three o'clock in the morning both in summer and winter, and that Sir William Jones began his studies with the dawn.

The most popular female writer of America, whose great novel struck a chord of universal sympathy throughout the civilized world, has habits of composition peculiarly her own, and unlike those belonging to any author of whom we have record. She *croons*, so to speak, over her writings, and it makes very little difference to her whether there is a crowd of people about her or whether she is alone during the composition of her books. "Uncle Tom's Cabin" was wholly prepared for the press in a little wooden house in Maine, from week to week, while the story was coming out in a Washington newspaper. Most of it was written by the evening lamp, on a pine table, about which the children of the family were gathered together conning their various lessons for the next day. Amid the busy hum of earnest voices, constantly asking questions of the mother, intent on her world-renowned task, Mrs. Stowe wove together those thrilling chapters which were destined to find readers in so many languages throughout the globe. No work of similar importance, so far as we know, was ever written amid so much that seemed hostile to literary composition.

I had the opportunity, both in England and America, of observing the literary habits of Thackeray, and it always seemed to me that he did his work with comparative ease, but was somewhat influenced by a custom of procrastination. Nearly all his stories were written in monthly instalments for magazines, with the press at his heels. He told me that when he began a novel he rarely knew how many people were to figure in it, and, to use his own words, he was always very shaky about their moral conduct. He said that sometimes, especially if he had been dining late and did not feel in remarkably good-humor next morning, he was inclined to make his characters villanously wicked; but if he rose serene with an unclouded brain, there was no end to the lovely actions he was willing to make his men and women perform. When he had written a passage that pleased him very much he could not resist clapping on his hat and rushing forth to find an acquaintance to whom he might instantly read his successful composition. Gilbert Wakefield, universally acknowledged to have been the best Greek scholar of his time, said he would have turned out a much better one, if he had begun earlier to study that language; but unfortunately he did not begin till he was fifteen years of age. Thackeray, in quoting to me this saying of Wakefield, remarked: "My English would have been very much better if I had read Fielding before I was ten." This observation was a valuable hint, on the part of Thackeray, as to whom he considered his master in art.

James Hannay paid Thackeray a beautiful compliment when he said: "If he had had his choice he would rather have been famous as an artist than as a writer; but it was destined that he should paint in colors which will never crack and never need restoration." Thackeray's characters are, indeed, not so much *inventions* as *existences*, and we know them as we know our best friends or our most intimate enemies.

When I was asked, the other day, which of his books I like best, I gave the old answer to a similar question, "*The last one I read.*" If I could possess only *one* of his works, I think I should choose "Henry Esmond." To my thinking, it is a marvel in literature, and I have read it oftener than any of the other works. Perhaps the reason of my partiality lies somewhat in this little incident. One day, in the snowy winter of 1852, I met Thackeray sturdily ploughing his way down Beacon Street with a copy of "Henry Esmond"' (the English edition, then just issued) under his arm. Seeing me some way off, he held aloft the volumes and began to shout in great glee. When I came up to him he cried out, " Here is the *very* best I can do, and I am carrying it to Prescott as a reward of merit for having given me my first dinner in America. I stand by this book, and am willing to leave it, when I go, as my card."

As he wrote from month to month, and liked to put off the inevitable chapters till the last moment, he was often in great tribulation. I happened to be one of a large company whom he had invited to a six-o'clock dinner at Greenwich one summer afternoon, several years ago. We were all to go down from London, assemble in a particular room at the hotel, where he was to meet us at six o'clock, *sharp*. Accordingly we took steamer and gathered ourselves together in the reception-room at the appointed time. When the clock struck six, our host had not fulfilled his part of the contract. His burly figure was yet wanting among the company assembled. As the guests were nearly all strangers to each other, and as there was no one present to introduce us, a profound silence fell upon the room, and we anxiously looked out of the windows, hoping every moment that Thackeray would arrive. This untoward state of things went on for one hour, still no Thackeray and no dinner. English reticence would not allow any remark as to the absence of our host. Everybody felt serious and a gloom fell upon the assembled party. Still no Thackeray. The landlord, the butler, and the waiters rushed in and out the room, shrieking for the master of the feast, who as yet had not arrived. It was confidentially whispered by a fat gentleman, with a hungry look, that the dinner was utterly spoiled twenty minutes ago, when we heard a merry shout in the entry and Thackeray bounced into the room. He had not changed his morning dress, and ink was still visible upon his fingers. Clapping his hands and pirouetting briskly on one leg, he cried out, "Thank Heaven, the last sheet of The Virginians has just gone to the printer." He made no apology for his late appearance, introduced nobody, shook hands heartily with everybody, and begged us all to be seated as quickly as possible. His exquisite delight at completing his book swept away every other feeling, and we all shared his pleasure, albeit the dinner was overdone throughout.

The most finished and elegant of all *lecturers*, Thackeray often made a very poor appearance when he attempted to deliver a set speech to a public assembly. He frequently broke down after the first two or three sentences. He prepared what he intended to say with great exactness, and his favorite delusion was that he was about to astonish everybody with a remarkable effort. It never disturbed him that he commonly made a woful failure when he attempted speech-making, but he sat down with such cool serenity if he found that he could not recall what he wished to say, that his audience could not help joining in and smiling with him when he came to a stand-still. Once he asked me to travel with him from London to Manchester to hear a great speech he was going to make at the founding of the Free Library Institution in that city. All the way down he was discoursing of certain effects he intended to produce on the Manchester dons by his eloquent appeals to their pockets. This passage was to have great influence with the rich merchants, this one with the clergy, and so on. He said that although Dickens and Bulwer and Sir James Stephen, all eloquent speakers, were to precede him, he intended to beat each of them on this special occasion. He insisted that I should be seated directly in front of him, so that I should have the full force of his magic eloquence. The occasion was a most brilliant one; tickets had been in demand at unheard-of prices several weeks before the day appointed; the great hall, then opened for the first time to the public, was filled by an audience such as is seldom convened, even in England. The three speeches which came before Thackeray was called upon were admirably suited to the occasion, and most eloquently spoken. Sir John Potter, who presided, then rose, and after some complimentary allusions to the author of "Vanity Fair," introduced him to the crowd, who welcomed him with ringing plaudits. As he rose, he gave me a half-wink from under his spectacles, as if to say: "Now for it; the others have done very well, but I will show 'em a grace beyond the reach of their art." He began in a clear and charming manner, and was absolutely perfect for three minutes. In the middle of a most earnest and elaborate sentence he suddenly stopped, gave a look of comic despair at the ceiling, crammed both hands into his trousers' pockets, and deliberately sat down. Everybody seemed to understand that it was one of Thackeray's unfinished speeches and there were no signs of surprise or discontent among his audience. He continued to sit on the platform in a perfectly composed manner; and when the meeting was over he said to me, without a sign of discomfiture, "My boy, you have my profoundest sympathy; this day you have accidentally missed hearing one of the finest speeches ever composed for delivery by a great British orator." And I never heard him mention the subject again.

Thackeray rarely took any exercise, thus living in striking contrast to the other celebrated novelist of our time, who was remarkable for the number of hours he daily spent in the open air. It seems to be almost certain now, from concurrent testimony, gathered from physicians and those who knew him best in England, that Thackeray's premature death was hastened by an utter disregard of the natural laws. His vigorous frame gave ample promise of longevity, but he drew too largely on his brain and not enough on his legs. *High* living and high *thinking*, he used to say, was the correct reading of the proverb.

He was a man of the tenderest feelings, very apt to be cajoled into doing what the world calls foolish things, and constantly performing feats of unwisdom, which performances he was immoderately laughing at all the while in his books. No man has impaled snobbery with such a stinging rapier, but he always accused himself of being a snob, past all cure. This I make no doubt was one of his exaggerations, but there was a grain of truth in the remark, which so sharp an observer as himself could not fail to notice, even though the victim was so near home.

Thackeray announced to me by letter in the early autumn of 1852 that he had determined to visit America, and would sail for Boston by the Canada on the 30th of October. All the necessary arrangements for his lecturing tour had been made without troubling him with any of the details. He arrived on a frosty November evening, and went directly to the Tremont House, where rooms had been engaged for him. I remember his delight in getting off the sea, and the enthusiasm with which he hailed the announcement that dinner would be ready shortly. A few friends were ready to sit down with him, and he seemed greatly to enjoy the novelty of an American repast. In London he had been very curious in his inquiries about American oysters, as marvellous stories, which he did not believe, had been told him of their great size. We apologized — although we had taken care that the largest specimens to be procured should startle his unwonted vision when he came to the table — for what we called the extreme *smallness* of the oysters, promising that we would do better next time. Six bloated Falstaffian bivalves lay before him in their shells. I noticed that he gazed at them anxiously with fork upraised; then he whispered to me, with a look of anguish, "How shall I do it?" I described to him the simple process by which the free-born citizens of America were accustomed to accomplish such a task. He seemed satisfied that the thing was feasible, selected the smallest one in the half-dozen (rejecting a large one, "because," he said, "it resembled the High Priest's servant's ear that Peter cut off"), and then bowed his head as if he were saying grace. All eyes were upon him to watch the effect of a new sensation in the person of a great British author. Opening his mouth very wide, he struggled for a moment, and then all was over. I shall never forget the comic look of despair he cast upon the other five over-occupied shells. I broke the perfect stillness by asking him how he felt. "Profoundly grateful," he gasped, "and as if I had swallowed a little baby." It was many years ago since we gathered about him on that occasion, but, if my memory serves me, we had what might be called *a pleasant evening*. Indeed, I remember much hilarity, and sounds as of men laughing and singing far into midnight. I could not deny, if called upon to testify in court, that we had a *good time* on that frosty November evening.

We had many happy days and nights together both in England and America, but I remember none happier than that evening we passed with him when the Punch people came to dine at his own table with the silver statuette of Mr. Punch in full dress looking down upon the hospitable board from the head of the table. This silver figure always stood in a conspicuous place when Tom **Taylor,** **Mark** Lemon, Shirley Brooks, and the rest of his jolly companions and life-long cronies were gathered together. If I were to say here that there were any dull moments on *that* occasion, I should not expect to be strictly believed.

Thackeray's playfulness was a marked peculiarity; a great deal of the time he seemed like a school-boy, just released from his task. In the midst of the most serious topic under discussion he was fond of asking permission to sing a comic song, or he would beg to be allowed to enliven the occasion by the instant introduction of a brief double-shuffle. Barry Cornwall told me that when he and Charles Lamb were once making up a dinner-party together, Charles asked him not to invite a certain lugubrious friend of theirs. "Because," said Lamb, "he would cast a damper even over a funeral." I have often contrasted the habitual qualities of that gloomy friend of theirs with the astounding spirits of both Thackeray and Dickens. They always seemed to me to be standing in the sunshine, and to be constantly warning other people out of cloudland. During Thackeray's first visit to America his jollity knew no bounds, and it became necessary often to repress him when he was walking in the street. I well remember his uproarious shouting and dancing when he was told that the tickets to his first course of readings were all sold, and when we rode together from his hotel to the lecture-hall he insisted on thrusting both his long legs out of the carriage window, in deference, as he said, to his magnanimous ticket-holders. An instance of his procrastination occurred the evening of his first public appearance in America. His lecture was advertised to take place at half past seven, and when he was informed of the hour, he said he would try and be ready at eight o'clock, but thought it very doubtful. Horrified at this assertion, I tried to impress upon him the importance of punctuality on this, the night of his first bow to an American audience. At a quarter past seven I called for him, and found him not only unshaved and undressed for the evening, but rapturously absorbed in making a pen-and-ink drawing to illustrate a passage in Goethe's Sorrows of Werther, for a lady, which illustration, — a charming one, by the way, for he was greatly skilled in drawing, — he vowed he would finish before he would budge an inch in the direction of the (I omit the adjective) Melodeon. A comical incident occurred just as he was about leaving the hall, after his first lecture in Boston. A shabby, ungainly looking man stepped briskly up to him in the anteroom, seized his hand and announced himself as "proprietor of the Mammoth Rat," and proposed to exchange season tickets. Thackeray, with the utmost gravity, exchanged cards and promised to call on the wonderful quadruped next day.

Thackeray's motto was 'Avoid performing to-day, if possible, what can be postponed till to-morrow.' Although he received large sums for his writings, he managed without much difficulty to keep his expenditures fully abreast, and often in advance of, his receipts. His pecuniary object in visiting America the second time was to lay up, as he said, a "pot of money" for his two daughters, and he left the country with more than half his lecture engagements unfulfilled. He was to have visited various cities in the Middle and Western States; but he took up a newspaper one night, in his hotel in New York, before retiring, saw a steamer advertised to sail the next morning for England, was seized with a sudden fit of homesickness, rang the bell for his servant, who packed up his luggage that night, and the next day he sailed. The first intimation I had of his departure was a card which he sent by the pilot of the steamer, with these words upon it: "Good by, Fields; good by, Mrs. Fields; God bless everybody, says W. M. T." Of course he did not avail himself of the opportunity afforded him for receiving a very large sum in America, and he afterwards told me in London, that if Mr. Astor had offered him half his fortune if he would allow that particular steamer to sail without him, he should have declined the well-intentioned but impossible favor, and gone on board.

No man has left behind him a tenderer regard for his genius and foibles among his friends than Thackeray. He had a natural love of good which nothing could wholly blur or destroy. He was a most generous critic of the writings of his contemporaries, and no one has printed or spoken warmer praise of Dickens, in one sense his great rival, than he.

Thackeray was not a voluminous correspondent, but what exquisite letters he has left in the hands of many of his friends! "Should any letters arrive," he says in a little missive from Philadelphia, "addressed to the care of J. T. F. for the ridiculous author of this, that, and the other, F. is requested to send them to Mercantile Library, Baltimore. My ghostly enemy will be delighted (or will gnash his teeth with rage) to hear that the lectures in the capital of Pa. have been very well attended. No less than 750 people paid at the door on Friday night, and though last night there was a storm of snow so furious that no reasonable mortal could face it, 500 (at least) amiable maniacs were in the lecture-room, and wept over the fate of the last king of these colonies."

Almost every day, while he was lecturing in America, he would send off little notes exquisitely written in point of penmanship, and sometimes embellished with characteristic pen-drawings. Having attended an extemporaneous supper festival at "Porter's," he was never tired of

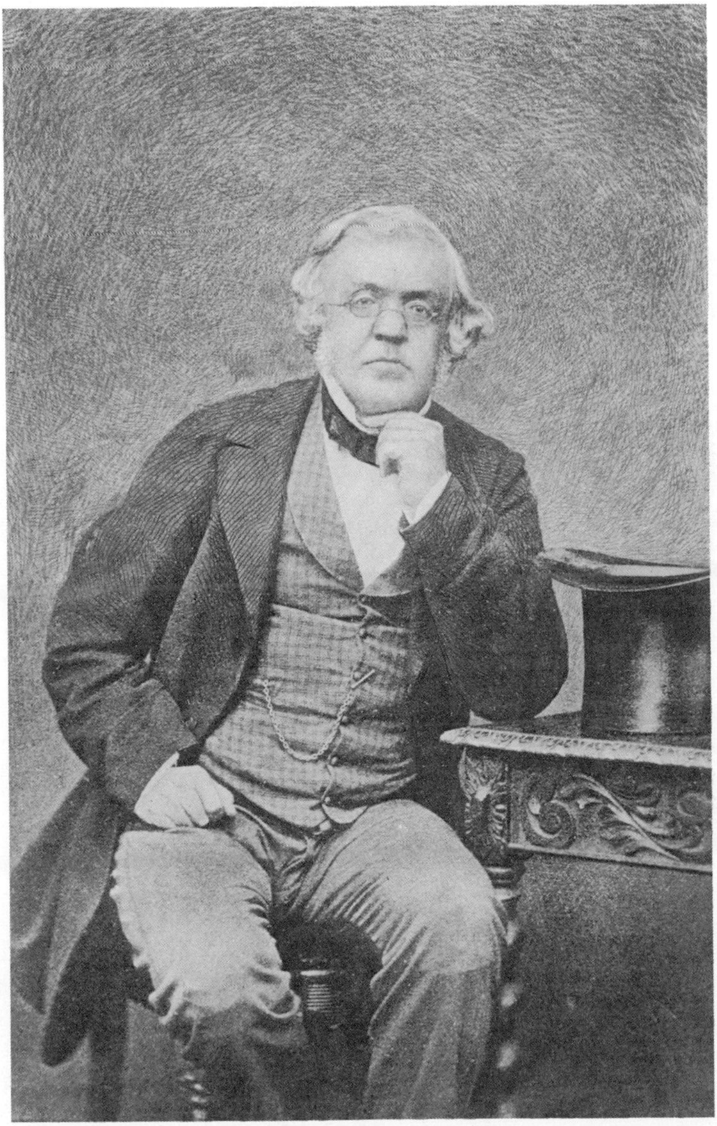

W M Thackeray

"going again." Here is a scrap of paper holding these few words, written in 1852.

"Nine o'clock, P. M. Tremont.

"Arrangements have just been concluded for a meeting *somewhere* to-night, which we much desire you should attend. Are you equal to two nights running of good time?"

Then follows a pen portrait of a friend of his with a cloven foot and a devil's tail just visible under his cloak. Sometimes, to puzzle his correspondent, he would write in so small a hand that the note could not be read without the aid of a magnifying-glass. Calligraphy was to him one of the fine arts, and he once told Dr. John Brown of Edinburgh, that if all trades failed, he would earn sixpences by writing the Lord's Prayer and the Creed (not the Athanasian) in the size of that coin. He greatly delighted in rhyming and lisping notes and billets. Here is one of them, dated from Baltimore without signature:—

"Dear F——th! The thanguinary fateth (I don't know what their anger meanth) brought me your letter of the eighth, yethterday, only the fifteenth! What blunder cauthed by chill delay (thee Doctor Johnthon'th noble verthe) Thuth kept my longing thoul away, from all that motht I love on earth? Thankth for the happy contenth!—thothe Dithpatched to J. G. K. and Thonth, and that thmall letter you inclothe from Parith, from my dearetht oneth! I pray each month may tho increathe my thmall account with J. G. King, that all the thipth which croth the theath, good tidingth of my girlth may bring!—that every blething fortune yieldth, I altho pray, may come to path on Mithter and Mrth. J. T. F——th, and all good friendth in Bothton, Math.!"

While he was staying at the Clarendon Hotel, in New York, every morning's mail brought a few lines, sometimes only one line, sometimes only two words, from him, reporting progress. One day he tells me: "Immense hawdience last night." Another day he says: "Our shares look very much up this morning." On the 29th of

November, 1852, he writes: "I find I have a much bigger voice than I knew of, and am not afraid of anybody." At another time he writes: "I make no doubt you have seen that admirable paper, the New York Herald, and are aware of the excellent reception my lectures are having in this city. It was a lucky Friday when first I set foot in this country. I have nearly saved the fifty dollars you lent me in Boston." In a letter from Savannah, dated the 19th of March, 1853, in answer to one I had written to him, telling him that a charming epistle, which accompanied the gift of a silver mug he had sent to me some time before, had been stolen from me, he says: —

"My dear fellow, I remember I asked you in that letter to accept a silver mug in token of our pleasant days together, and to drink a health sometimes in it to a sincere friend. . . . . Smith and Elder write me word they have sent by a Cunard to Boston a packet of paper, stamped etc. in London. I want it to be taken from the Custom-House, dooties paid etc., and dispatched to Miss ——, New York. Hold your tongue, and don't laugh, you rogue. Why should n't she have her paper, and I my pleasure, without your wicked, wicked sneers and imperence? I 'm only a cipher in the young lady's estimation, and why should n't I sigh for her if I like. I hope I shall see you all at Boston before very long. I always consider Boston as my native place, you know."

I wish I could recall half the incidents connected with the dear, dear old Thackeray days, when I saw him so constantly and enjoyed him so hugely; but, alas! many of them are gone, with much more that is lovely and would have been of *good report*, could they be now remembered; — they are dead as — (Holmes always puts your simile quite right for you), —

"Dead as the bulrushes round little Moses,
On the old banks of the Nile."

But while I sit here quietly, and have no fear of any bad, unsympathizing listeners who might, if some other subject were up, frown upon my levity, let me walk through the dusky chambers of my memory and report what I find there, just as the records turn up, without regard to method.

I once made a pilgrimage with Thackeray (at my request, of course, the visits were planned) to the various houses where his books had been written; and I remember when we came to Young Street, Kensington, he said, with mock gravity, "Down on your knees, you rogue, for here 'Vanity Fair' was penned! And I will go down with you, for I have a high opinion of that little production myself." He was always perfectly honest in his expressions about his own writings, and it was delightful to hear him praise them when he could depend on his listeners. A friend congratulated him once on that touch in "Vanity Fair" in which Becky "*admires*" her husband when he is giving Steyne the punishment which ruins *her* for life. "Well," he said, "when I wrote the sentence, I slapped my fist on the table and said, '*That* is a touch of genius!'"

He told me he was nearly forty years old before he was recognized in literature as belonging to a class of writers at all above the ordinary magazinists of his day. "I turned off far better things then than I do now," said he, "and I wanted money sadly, (my parents were rich but respectable, and I had spent my guineas in my youth,) but how little I got for my work! It makes me laugh," he continued, "at what The Times pays me now, when I think of the old days, and how much better I wrote for them then, and got a shilling where I now get ten."

One day he wanted a little service done for a friend, and I remember his very quizzical expression, as he said, "Please say the favor asked will greatly oblige a man of the name of Thackeray, whose only recommendation is, that he has seen Napoleon and Goethe, and is the owner of Schiller's sword."

I think he told me he and Tennyson were at one time intimate; but I distinctly remember a description he gave me of having heard the poet, when a young man, storming about in the first rapture of composing his poem of "Ulysses." One line of it Tennyson greatly revelled in,—

"And see the great Achilles, whom we knew."

"He went through the streets," said Thackeray, "screaming about his great Achilles, whom we knew," as if we had all made the acquaintance of that gentleman, and were very proud of it.

One of the most comical and interesting occasions I remember, in connection with Thackeray, was going with him to a grand concert given fifteen or twenty years ago by Madame Sontag. We sat near an entrance door in the hall, and every one who came in, male and female, Thackeray pretended to know, and gave each one a name and brief chronicle, as the presence flitted by. It was in Boston, and as he had been in town only a day or two, and knew only half a dozen people in it, the biographies were most amusing. As I happened to know several people who passed, it was droll enough to hear this great master of character give them their dues. Mr. Choate moved along in his regal, affluent manner. The large style of the man, so magnificent and yet so modest, at once arrested Thackeray's attention, and he forbore to place him in his extemporaneous catalogue. I remember a pallid, sharp-faced girl fluttering past, and how Thackeray exulted in the history of this "frail little bit of porcelain," as he called her. There was something in her manner that made him hate her, and he insisted she had murdered somebody on her way to the hall. Altogether this marvellous prelude to the concert made a deep impression on Thackeray's one listener, into whose ear he whispered his fatal insinuations. There is one man still living and moving about the streets I walk in occasionally, whom I never encounter without almost a shudder, remembering as I do the unerring shaft which Thackeray sent that night into the unknown man's character.

One day, many years ago, I saw him chaffing on the sidewalk in London, in front of the Athenæum Club, with a monstrous-sized, "copiously ebriose" cabman, and I judged from the driver's ludicrously careful way of landing the coin deep down in his breeches-pocket, that Thackeray had given him a very unusual fare. "Who is your fat friend?" I asked, crossing over to shake hands with him. "O, that indomitable youth is an old crony of mine," he replied; and then, quoting Falstaff, "a goodly, portly man, i' faith, and a corpulent, of a cheerful look, a pleasing eye, and a most noble *carriage*." It was the *manner* of saying this, then, and there in the London street, the cabman moving slowly off on his sorry vehicle, with one eye (an eye dewy with gin and water, and a tear of gratitude, perhaps) on Thackeray, and the great man himself so jovial and so full of kindness!

It was a treat to hear him, as I once did, discourse of Shakespeare's probable life in Stratford among his neighbors. He painted, as he alone could paint, the great poet sauntering about the lanes without the slightest show of greatness, having a crack with the farmers, and in very earnest talk about the crops. "I don't believe," said Thackeray, "that these village cronies of his ever looked upon him as the mighty poet,

> 'Sailing with supreme dominion
> Through the azure deep of air,'

but simply as a wholesome, good-natured citizen, with whom it was always pleasant to have a chat. I can see him now," continued Thackeray, "leaning over a cottage gate, and tasting good Master Such-a-one's home-brewed, and inquiring with a real interest after the mistress and her children." Long before he put it into his lecture, I heard him say in words to the same effect: "I should like to have been Shakespeare's shoe-black, just to have lived in his house, just to have worshipped him, to have run on his errands, and seen that sweet, serene face." To have heard Thackeray depict, in his own charming manner, and at considerable length, the imaginary walks and talks of Shakespeare, when he would return to his home from occasional visits to London, pouring into the ready ears of his unsophisticated friends and neighbors the gossip from town which he thought would be likely to interest them, is something to remember all one's days.

The enormous circulation achieved by the Cornhill Magazine, when it was first started with Thackeray for its editor in chief, is a matter of literary history. The announcement by his publishers that a sale of a hundred and ten thousand of the first number had been reached made the editor half delirious with joy, and he ran away to Paris to be rid of the excitement for a few days. I met him by appointment at his hotel in the Rue de la Paix, and found him wild with exultation and full of enthusiasm for excellent George Smith, his publisher. "London," he exclaimed, "is not big enough to contain me now, and I am obliged to add Paris to my residence! Great heavens," said he, throwing up his long arms, "where will this tremendous circulation stop! Who knows but that I shall have to add Vienna and Rome to my whereabouts? If the worst comes to the worst, New York, also, may fall into my clutches, and only the Rocky Mountains may be able to stop my progress!" Those days in Paris with him were simply tremendous. We dined at all possible and impossible places together. We walked round and round the glittering court of the Palais Royal, gazing in at the windows of the jewellers' shops, and all my efforts were necessary to restrain him from rushing in and ordering a pocketful of diamonds and "other trifles," as he called them; "for," said he, "how can I spend the princely income which Smith allows me for editing the Cornhill, unless I begin instantly somewhere?" If he saw a group of three or four persons talking together in an excited way, after the manner of that then riant Parisian people, he would whisper to me with immense gesticulation: "There, there, you see the news has reached Paris, and perhaps the number has gone up since my last accounts from London." His spirits during those few days were colossal, and he told me that he found it impossible to sleep, "for counting up his subscribers."

I happened to know personally (and let me modestly add, with some degree of sympathy) what he suffered editorially, when he had the charge and responsibility of a magazine. With first-class contributors he got on very well, he said, but the extortioners and revilers bothered the very life out of him. He gave me some amusing accounts of his misunderstandings with the "fair" (as he loved to call them), some of whom followed him up so closely with their poetical compositions, that his house (he was then living in Onslow Square) was never free of interruption. "The darlings demanded," said he, "that I should re-write, if I could not understand their —— nonsense and put their halting lines into proper form." "I was so appalled," said he, "when they set upon me with their 'ipics and their ipecacs,' that you might have knocked me down with a feather, sir. It was insupportable, and I fled away into France." As he went on, waxing drolly furious at the recollection of various editorial scenes, I could not help remembering Mr. Yellowplush's recommendation, thus characteristically expressed: "Take my advice, honrabble sir,—listen to a humble footmin: it's genrally best in poatry to understand puffickly what you mean yourself, and to igspress your meaning clearly afterwoods, — in the simpler words the better, p'r'aps."

He took very great delight in his young daughter's first contributions to the Cornhill, and I shall always remember how he made me get into a cab, one day in London, that I might hear, as we rode along, the joyful news he had to impart, that he had just been reading his daughter's first paper, which was entitled "Little Scholars." "When I read it," said he, "I blubbered like a child, it is so good so simple, and so honest; and my little girl wrote it, every word of it."

During his second visit to Boston I was asked to invite him to attend an evening meeting of a scientific club, which was to be held at the house of a distinguished member. I was very reluctant to ask him to be present, for I knew he could be easily bored, and I was fearful that a prosy essay or geological speech might ensue, and I knew he would be exasperated with me, even although I were the *innocent* cause of his affliction. My worst fears were realized. We had hardly got seated, before a dull, bilious-looking old gentleman rose, and applied his auger with such pertinacity that we were all bored nearly to distraction. I dared not look at Thackeray, but I felt that his eye was upon me. My distress may be imagined, when he got up quite deliberately from the prominent place where a chair had been set for him, and made his exit very noiselessly into a small anteroom leading into the larger room, and in which no one was sitting. The small apartment was dimly lighted, but he knew that I knew *he* was there. Then commenced a series of pantomimic feats impossible to describe adequately. He threw an imaginary person (myself, of course) upon the floor, and proceeded to stab him several times with a paper-folder, which he caught up for the purpose. After disposing of his victim in this way, he was not satisfied, for the dull lecture still went on in the other room, and he fired an imaginary revolver several times at an imaginary head. Still, the droning speaker proceeded with his frozen subject (it was something about the Arctic regions, if I remember rightly), and now began the greatest pantomimic scene of all, namely, murder by poison, after the manner in which the player king is disposed of in Hamlet. Thackeray had found a small vial on the mantel-shelf, and out of that he proceeded to pour the imaginary "juice of cursed hebenon" into the imaginary porches of somebody's ears. The whole thing was inimitably done, and I hoped nobody saw it but myself; but years afterwards, a ponderous, fat-witted young man put the question squarely to me: "What *was* the matter with Mr. Thackeray, that night the club met at Mr. ——'s house?"

Overhearing me say one morning something about the vast attractions of London to a greenhorn like myself, he broke in with, "Yes, but you have not seen the grandest one yet! Go with me to-day to St. Paul's and hear the charity children sing." So we went, and I saw the "head cynic of literature," the "hater of humanity," as a critical dunce in the Times once called him, hiding his bowed face, wet with tears, while his whole frame shook with emotion, as the children of poverty rose to pour out their anthems of praise. Afterwards he wrote in one of his books this passage, which seems to me perfect in its feeling and tone: —

"And yet there is one day in the year when I think St. Paul's presents the noblest sight in the whole world; when five thousand charity children, with cheeks like nosegays, and sweet, fresh voices, sing the hymn which makes every heart thrill with praise and happiness. I have seen a hundred grand sights in the world, — coronations, Parisian splendors, Crystal Palace openings, Pope's chapels with their processions of long-tailed cardinals and quavering choirs of fat soprani, — but think in all Christendom there is no such sight as Charity Children's day. *Non Anglei, sed angeli.* As one looks at that beautiful multitude of innocents: as the first note strikes: indeed one may almost fancy that cherubs are singing."

I parted with Thackeray for the last time in the street, at midnight, in London, a few months before his death. The Cornhill Magazine, under his editorship, having proved a very great success, grand dinners were given every month in honor of the new venture. We had been sitting late at one of these festivals, and, as it was getting toward morning, I thought it wise, as far as I was concerned, to be moving homeward before the sun rose. Seeing my intention to withdraw, he insisted on driving me in his brougham to my lodgings. When we reached the outside door of our host, Thackeray's servant, seeing a stranger with his master, touched his hat and asked where he should drive us. It was then between one and two o'clock, — time certainly for all decent diners-out to be at rest. Thackeray put on one of his most quizzical expressions, and said to John, in answer to his question, "I think we will make a morning call on the Lord Bishop of London." John knew his master's quips and cranks too well to suppose he was in earnest, so I gave him my address, and we went on. When we reached my lodgings the clocks were striking two, and the early morning air was raw and piercing. Opposing all my entreaties for leave-taking in the carriage, he insisted upon getting out on the sidewalk and escorting me up to my door, saying, with a mock heroic protest to the heavens above us, "That it would be shameful for a full-blooded Britisher to leave an unprotected Yankee friend exposed to ruffians, who prowl about the streets with an eye to plunder." Then giving me a gigantic embrace, he sang a verse of which he knew me to be very fond; and so vanished out of my sight the great-hearted author of "Pendennis" and "Vanity Fair." But I think of him still as moving, in

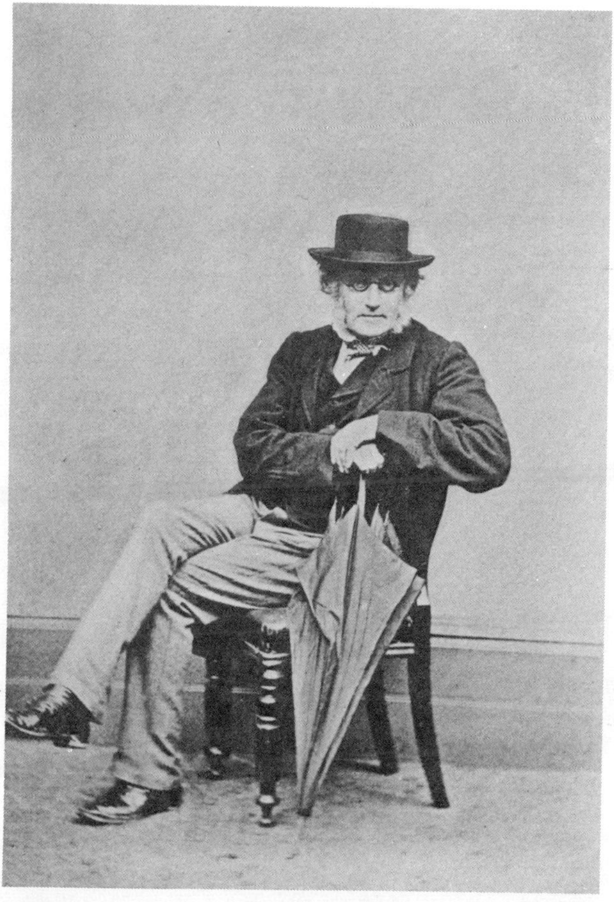

his own stately way, up and down the crowded thoroughfares of London, dropping in at the Garrick, or sitting at the window of the Athenæum Club, and watching the stupendous tide of life that is ever moving past in that wonderful city.

Thackeray was a *master* in every sense, having as it were, in himself, a double quantity of being. Robust humor and lofty sentiment alternated so strangely in him, that sometimes he seemed like the natural son of Rabelais, and at others he rose up a very twin brother of the Stratford Seer. There was nothing in him amorphous and unconsidered. Whatever he chose to do was always perfectly done. There was a genuine Thackeray flavor in everything he was willing to say or to write. He detected with unfailing skill the good or the vile wherever it existed. He had an unerring eye, a firm understanding, and abounding truth. "Two of his great master powers," said the chairman at a dinner given to him many years ago in Edinburgh, "are *satire* and *sympathy*." George Brimley remarked, "That he could not have painted Vanity Fair as he has, unless Eden had been shining in his inner eye." He had, indeed, an awful insight, with a world of solemn tenderness and simplicity, in his composition. Those who heard the same voice that withered the memory of King George the Fourth repeat "The spacious firmament on high" have a recollection not easily to be blotted from the mind, and I have a kind of pity for all who were born so recently as not to have heard and understood Thackeray's Lectures. But they can read him, and I beg of them to try and appreciate the tenderer phase of his genius, as well as the sarcastic one. He teaches many lessons to young men, and here is one of them, which I quote *memoriter* from "Barry Lyndon" : "Do you not, as a boy, remember waking of bright summer mornings and finding your mother looking over you? had not the gaze of her tender eyes stolen into your senses long before you woke, and cast over your slumbering spirit a sweet spell of peace, and love, and fresh-springing joy?" My dear friend, John Brown, of Edinburgh (whom may God long preserve to both countries where he is so loved and honored), chronicles this touching incident. "We cannot resist here recalling one Sunday evening in December, when Thackeray was walking with two friends along the Dean Road, to the west of Edinburgh, — one of the noblest outlets to any city. It was a lovely evening; such a sunset as one never forgets; a rich dark bar of cloud hovered over the sun, going down behind the Highland hills, lying bathed in amethystine bloom; between this cloud and the hills there was a narrow slip of the pure ether, of a tender cowslip color, lucid, and as if it were the very body of heaven in its clearness; every object standing out as if etched upon the sky. The northwest end of Corstorphine Hill, with its trees and rocks, lay in the heart of this pure radiance; and there a wooden crane, used in the granary below, was so placed as to assume the figure of a cross; there it was, unmistakable, lifted up against the crystalline sky. All three gazed at it silently. As they gazed, Thackeray gave utterance in a tremulous, gentle, and rapid voice to what all were feeling, in the word, 'CALVARY!' The friends walked on in silence, and then turned to other things. All that evening he was very gentle and serious, speaking, as he seldom did, of divine things, — of death, of sin, of eternity, of salvation, expressing his simple faith in God and in his Saviour."

Thackeray was found dead in his bed on Christmas morning, and he probably died without pain. His mother and his daughters were sleeping under the same roof when he passed away alone. Dickens told me that, looking on him as he lay in his coffin, he wondered that the figure he had known in life as one of such noble presence could seem so shrunken and wasted; but there had been years of sorrow, years of labor, years of pain, in that now exhausted life. It was his happiest Christmas morning when he heard the Voice calling him homeward to unbroken rest.

HAWTHORNE.

A hundred years ago Henry Vaughan seems almost to have anticipated Hawthorne's appearance when he wrote that beautiful line,

"*Feed on the vocal silence of his eye.*"

III.

HAWTHORNE.

I AM sitting to-day opposite the likeness of the rarest genius America has given to literature, — a man who lately sojourned in this busy world of ours, but during many years of his life

"Wandered lonely as a cloud," —

a man who had, so to speak, a physical affinity with solitude. The writings of this author have never soiled the public mind with one unlovely image. His men and women have a magic of their own, and we shall wait a long time before another arises among us to take his place. Indeed, it seems probable no one will ever walk precisely the same round of fiction which he traversed with so free and firm a step.

The portrait I am looking at was made by Rowse (an exquisite drawing), and is a very truthful representation of the head of Nathaniel Hawthorne. He was several times painted and photographed, but it was impossible for art to give the light and beauty of his wonderful eyes. I remember to have heard, in the literary circles of Great Britain, that, since Burns, no author had appeared there with a finer face than Hawthorne's. Old Mrs. Basil Montagu told me, many years ago, that she sat next to Burns at dinner, when he appeared in society in the first flush of his fame, after the Edinburgh edition of his poems had been published. She said, among other things, that, although the company consisted of some of the best bred men of England, Burns seemed to her the most perfect gentleman among them. She noticed, particularly, his genuine grace and deferential manner toward women, and I was interested to hear Mrs. Montagu's brilliant daughter, when speaking of Hawthorne's advent in English society, describe him in almost the same terms as I had heard her mother, years before, describe the Scottish poet. I happened to be in London with Hawthorne during his consular residence in England, and was always greatly delighted at the rustle of admiration his personal appearance excited when he entered a room. His bearing was modestly grand, and his voice touched the ear like a melody.

Here is a golden curl which adorned the head of Nathaniel Hawthorne when he lay a little child in his cradle. It was given to me many years ago by one near and dear to him. I have two other similar "blossoms," which I keep pressed in the same book of remembrance. One is from the head of John Keats, and was given to me by Charles Cowden Clarke, and the other graced the head of Mary Mitford, and was sent to me after her death by her friendly physician, who watched over her last hours. Leigh Hunt says with a fine poetic emphasis,

> "There seems a love in hair, though it be dead.
> It is the gentlest, yet the strongest thread
> Of our frail plant, — a blossom from the tree
> Surviving the proud trunk; — as though it said,
> Patience and Gentleness is Power. In me
> Behold affectionate eternity."

There is a charming old lady, now living two doors from me, who dwelt in Salem when Hawthorne was born, and, being his mother's neighbor at that time (Mrs. Hawthorne then lived in Union Street), there came a message to her intimating that the baby could be seen by calling. So my friend tells me she went in, and saw the little

Robert Burns

winking thing in its mother's arms. She is very clear as to the beauty of the infant, even when only a week old, and remembers that "he was a pleasant child, quite handsome, with golden curls." She also tells me that Hawthorne's mother was a beautiful woman, with remarkable eyes, full of sensibility and expression, and that she was a person of singular purity of mind. Hawthorne's father, whom my friend knew well, she describes as a warm-hearted and kindly man, very fond of children. He was somewhat inclined to melancholy, and of a reticent disposition. He was a great reader, employing all his leisure time at sea over books.

Hawthorne's father died when Nathaniel was four years old, and from that time his uncle Robert Manning took charge of his education, sending him to the best schools and afterwards to college. When the lad was about nine years old, while playing bat and ball at school, he lamed his foot so badly that he used two crutches for more than a year. His foot ceased to grow like the other, and the doctors of the town were called in to examine the little lame boy. He was not perfectly restored till he was twelve years old. His kind-hearted schoolmaster, Joseph Worcester, the author of the Dictionary, came every day to the house to hear the boy's lessons, so that he did not fall behind in his studies. [There is a tradition in the Manning family that Mr. Worcester was very much interested in Maria Manning (a sister of Mrs. Hawthorne), who died in 1814, and that this was one reason of his attention to Nathaniel.] The boy used to lie flat upon the carpet, and read and study the long days through. Some time after he had recovered from this lameness he had an illness causing him to lose the use of his limbs, and he was obliged to seek again the aid of his old crutches, which were then pieced out at the ends to make them longer. While a little child, and as soon almost as he began to read, the authors he most delighted in were Shakespeare, Milton, Pope, and Thomson. The "Castle of Indolence" was an especial favorite with him during boyhood. The first book he bought with his own money was a copy of Spenser's "Faery Queen."

One who watched him during his childhood tells me, that "when he was six years old his favorite book was Bunyan's 'Pilgrim's Progress': and that whenever he went to visit his Grandmother Hawthorne, he used to take the old family copy to a large chair in a corner of the room near a window, and read it by the hour, without once speaking. No one ever thought of asking how much of it he understood. I think it one of the happiest circumstances of his training, that nothing was ever explained to him, and that there was no professedly intellectual person in the family to usurp the place of Providence and supplement its shortcomings, in order to make him what he was never intended to be. His mind developed itself; intentional cultivation might have spoiled it. . . . . He used to invent long stories, wild and fanciful, and tell where he was going when he grew up, and of the wonderful adventures he was to meet with, always ending with, 'And I'm never coming back again,' in quite a solemn tone, that enjoined upon us the advice to value him the more while he stayed with us."

When he could scarcely speak plain, it is recalled by members of the family that the little fellow would go about the house, repeating with vehement emphasis and gestures certain stagy lines from Shakespeare's Richard III., which he had overheard from older persons about him. One line, in particular, made a great impression upon him, and he would start up on the most unexpected occasions and fire off in his loudest tone,

"Stand back, my Lord, and let the coffin pass."

On the 21st of August, 1820, No. 1 of "The Spectator,

edited by N. Hathorne," neatly written in printed letters by the editor's own hand, appeared. A prospectus was issued the week before, setting forth that the paper would be published on Wednesdays, " price 12 cents per annum, payment to be made at the end of the year." Among the advertisements is the following : —

"Nathaniel Hathorne proposes to publish by subscription a NEW EDITION of the MISERIES OF AUTHORS, to which will be added a SEQUEL, containing FACTS and REMARKS drawn from his own experience."

Six numbers only were published. The following subjects were discussed by young " Hathorne " in the Spectator, — " On Solitude," " The End of the Year," " On Industry," " On Benevolence," " On Autumn," " On Wealth," " On Hope," " On Courage." The poetry on the last page of each number was evidently written by the editor, except in one instance, when an Address to the Sun is signed by one of his sisters. In one of the numbers he apologizes that no deaths of any importance have taken place in the town. Under the head of Births, he gives the following news, " The lady of Dr. Winthrop Brown, a son and heir. Mrs. Hathorne's cat, seven kittens. We hear that both of the above ladies are in a state of convalescence." One of the literary advertisements reads : —

"Blank Books made and for sale by N. Hathorne."

While Hawthorne was yet a little fellow the family moved to Raymond in the State of Maine; here his out-of-door life did him great service, for he grew tall and strong, and became a good shot and an excellent fisherman. Here also his imagination was first stimulated, the wild scenery and the primitive manners of the people contributing greatly to awaken his thought. At seventeen he entered Bowdoin College, and after his graduation returned again to live in Salem. During his youth he had an impression that he would die before the age of twenty-five; but the Mannings, his ever-watchful and kind relations, did everything possible for the care of his health, and he was tided safely over the period when he was most delicate. Professor Packard told me that when Hawthorne was a student at Bowdoin in his freshman year, his Latin compositions showed such facility that they attracted the special attention of those who examined them. The Professor also remembers that Hawthorne's English compositions elicited from Professor Newman (author of the work on Rhetoric) high commendations.

When a youth Hawthorne made a journey into New Hampshire with his uncle, Samuel Manning. They travelled in a two-wheeled chaise, and met with many adventures which the young man chronicled in his home letters. Some of the touches in these epistles were very characteristic and amusing, and showed in those early years his quick observation and descriptive power. The travellers "put up" at Farmington, in order to rest over Sunday. Hawthorne writes to a member of the family in Salem: "As we were wearied with rapid travelling, we found it impossible to attend divine service, which was, of course, very grievous to us both. In the evening, however, I went to a Bible class, with a very polite and agreeable gentleman, whom I afterwards discovered to be a strolling tailor, of very questionable habits."

When the travellers arrived in the Shaker village of Canterbury, Hawthorne at once made the acquaintance of the Community there, and the account which he sent home was to the effect that the brothers and sisters led a good and comfortable life, and he wrote: "If it were not for the ridiculous ceremonies, a man might do a worse thing than to join them." Indeed, he spoke to them about becoming a member of the Society, and was evidently much impressed with the thrift and peace of the establishment.

This visit in early life to the Shakers is interesting as suggesting to Hawthorne his beautiful story of "The Canterbury Pilgrims," which is in his volume of "The Snow-Image, and other Twice-Told Tales."

A lady of my acquaintance (the identical "Little Annie" of the "Ramble" in "Twice-Told Tales") recalls the young man "when he returned home after his collegiate studies." "He was even then," she says, "a most noticeable person, never going into society, and deeply engaged in reading everything he could lay his hands on. It was said in those days that he had read every book in the Athenæum Library in Salem." This lady remembers that when she was a child, and before Hawthorne had printed any of his stories, she used to sit on his knee and lean her head on his shoulder, while by the hour he would fascinate her with delightful legends, much more wonderful and beautiful than any she has ever read since in printed books.

The traits of the Hawthorne character were stern probity and truthfulness. Hawthorne's mother had many characteristics in common with her distinguished son, she also being a reserved and thoughtful person. Those who knew the family describe the son's affection for her as of the deepest and tenderest nature, and they remember that when she died his grief was almost insupportable. The anguish he suffered from her loss is distinctly recalled by many persons still living, who visited the family at that time in Salem.

I first saw Hawthorne when he was about thirty-five years old. He had then published a collection of his sketches, the now famous "Twice-Told Tales." Longfellow, ever alert for what is excellent, and eager to do a brother author opportune and substantial service, at once came before the public with a generous estimate of the work in the North American Review; but the choice little volume, the most promising addition to American literature that had appeared for many years, made little impression on the public mind. Discerning readers, however, recognized the supreme beauty in this new writer, and they never afterwards lost sight of him.

In 1828 Hawthorne published a short anonymous romance called Fanshawe. I once asked him about this disowned publication, and he spoke of it with great disgust, and afterwards he thus referred to the subject in a letter written to me in 1851: "You make an inquiry about some supposed former publication of mine. I cannot be sworn to make correct answers as to all the literary or other follies of my nonage; and I earnestly recommend you not to brush away the dust that may have gathered over them. Whatever might do me credit you may be pretty sure I should be ready enough to bring forward. Anything else it is our mutual interest to conceal; and so far from assisting your researches in that direction, I especially enjoin it on you, my dear friend, not to read any unacknowledged page that you may suppose to be mine."

When Mr. George Bancroft, then Collector of the Port of Boston, appointed Hawthorne weigher and gauger in the custom-house, he did a wise thing, for no public officer ever performed his disagreeable duties better than our romancer. Here is a tattered little official document signed by Hawthorne when he was watching over the interests of the country: it certifies his attendance at the unlading of a brig, then lying at Long Wharf in Boston. I keep this precious relic side by side with one of a similar custom-house character, signed *Robert Burns*.

I came to know Hawthorne very intimately after the

Whigs displaced the Democratic romancer from office. In my ardent desire to have him retained in the public service, his salary at that time being his sole dependence, — not foreseeing that his withdrawal from that sort of employment would be the best thing for American letters that could possibly happen, — I called, in his behalf, on several influential politicians of the day, and well remember the rebuffs I received in my enthusiasm for the author of the "Twice-Told Tales." One pompous little gentleman in authority, after hearing my appeal, quite astounded me by his ignorance of the claims of a literary man on his country. "Yes, yes," he sarcastically croaked down his public turtle-fed throat, "I see through it all, I see through it; this Hawthorne is one of them 'ere visionists, and we don't want no such a man as him round." So the "visionist" was not allowed to remain in office, and the country was better served by him in another way. In the winter of 1849, after he had been ejected from the custom-house, I went down to Salem to see him and inquire after his health, for we heard he had been suffering from illness. He was then living in a modest wooden house in Mall Street, if I remember rightly the location. I found him alone in a chamber over the sitting-room of the dwelling; and as the day was cold, he was hovering near a stove. We fell into talk about his future prospects, and he was, as I feared I should find him, in a very desponding mood. "Now," said I, "is the time for you to publish, for I know during these years in Salem you must have got something ready for the press." "Nonsense," said he; "what heart had I to write anything, when my publishers (M. and Company) have been so many years trying to sell a small edition of the 'Twice-Told Tales'?" I still pressed upon him the good chances he would have now with something new. "Who would risk publishing a book for *me*, the most unpopular writer in America?" "I would," said I, "and would start with an edition of two thousand copies of anything you write." "What madness!" he exclaimed; "your friendship for me gets the better of your judgment. No, no," he continued; "I have no money to indemnify a publisher's losses on my account." I looked at my watch and found that the train would soon be starting for Boston, and I knew there was not much time to lose in trying to discover what had been his literary work during these last few years in Salem. I remember that I pressed him to reveal to me what he had been writing. He shook his head and gave me to understand he had produced nothing. At that moment I caught sight of a bureau or set of drawers near where we were sitting; and immediately it occurred to me that hidden away somewhere in that article of furniture was a story or stories by the author of the "Twice-Told Tales," and I became so positive of it that I charged him vehemently with the fact. He seemed surprised, I thought, but shook his head again; and I rose to take my leave, begging him not to come into the cold entry, saying I would come back and see him again in a few days. I was hurrying down the stairs when he called after me from the chamber, asking me to stop a moment. Then quickly stepping into the entry with a roll of manuscript in his hands, he said: "How in Heaven's name did you know this thing was there? As you have found me out, take what I have written, and tell me, after you get home and have time to read it, if it is good for anything. It is either very good or very bad, — I don't know which." On my way up to Boston I read the germ of "The Scarlet Letter"; before I slept that night I wrote him a note all aglow with admiration of the marvellous story he had put into my hands, and told him that I would come again to Salem the next day and arrange for its publication. I went on in such an amazing state of excitement when we met again in the little house, that he would not believe I was really in earnest. He seemed to think I was beside myself, and laughed sadly at my enthusiasm. However, we soon arranged for his appearance again before the public with a book.

This quarto volume before me contains numerous letters, written by him from 1850 down to the month of his death. The first one refers to "The Scarlet Letter," and is dated in January, 1850. At my suggestion he had altered the plan of that story. It was his intention to make "The Scarlet Letter" one of several short stories, all to be included in one volume, and to be called

OLD-TIME LEGENDS:
TOGETHER WITH SKETCHES,
EXPERIMENTAL AND IDEAL.

His first design was to make "The Scarlet Letter" occupy about two hundred pages in his new book; but I persuaded him, after reading the first chapters of the story, to elaborate it, and publish it as a separate work. After it was settled that "The Scarlet Letter" should be enlarged and printed by itself in a volume he wrote to me: —

"I am truly glad that you like the Introduction, for I was rather afraid that it might appear absurd and impertinent to be talking about myself, when nobody, that I know of, has requested any information on that subject.

"As regards the size of the book, I have been thinking a good deal about it. Considered merely as a matter of taste and beauty, the form of publication which you recommend seems to me much preferable to that of the 'Mosses.'

"In the present case, however, I have some doubts of the expediency, because, if the book is made up entirely of 'The Scarlet Letter,' it will be too sombre. I found it impossible to relieve the shadows of the story with so much light as I would gladly have thrown in. Keeping so close to its point as the tale does, and diversified no otherwise than by turning different sides of the same dark idea to the reader's eye, it will weary very many people and disgust some. Is it safe, then, to stake the fate of the book entirely on this one chance? A hunter loads his gun with a bullet and several buckshot; and, following his sagacious example, it was my purpose to conjoin the one long story with half a dozen shorter ones, so that, failing to kill the public outright with my biggest and heaviest lump of lead, I might have other chances with the smaller bits, individually and in the aggregate. However, I am willing to leave these considerations to your judgment, and should not be sorry to have you decide for the separate publication.

"In this latter event it appears to me that the only proper title for the book would be 'The Scarlet Letter,' for 'The Custom-House' is merely introductory, — an entrance-hall to the magnificent edifice which I throw open to my guests. It would be funny if, seeing the further passages so dark and dismal, they should all choose to stop there! If 'The Scarlet Letter' is to be the title, would it not be well to print it on the title-page in red ink? I am not quite sure about the good taste of so doing, but it would certainly be piquant and appropriate, and, I think, attractive to the great gull whom we are endeavoring to circumvent."

One beautiful summer day, twenty years ago, I found Hawthorne in his little red cottage at Lenox, surrounded by his happy young family. He had the look, as somebody said, of a banished lord, and his grand figure among the hills of Berkshire seemed finer than ever. His boy and girl were swinging on the gate as we drove up to his door, and with their sunny curls formed an attractive feature in the landscape. As the afternoon was cool and delightful, we proposed a drive over to Pittsfield to see Holmes, who was then living on his ancestral farm. Hawthorne was in a cheerful condition, and seemed to enjoy the beauty of the day to the utmost. Next morning we were all invited by Mr. Dudley Field, then living at Stockbridge, to ascend Monument Mountain. Holmes, Hawthorne, Duyckinck, Herman Melville, Headley, Sedgwick, Matthews, and several ladies, were of the party. We scrambled to the top with great spirit, and when we arrived, Melville, I remember, bestrode a peaked rock, which ran

Salem. January 2nd. 1850.

My dear Fields

I am truly glad that you like the introduction; for I was rather afraid that it might appear absurd and injudicious to be thing about myself, when nobody that I know of, has requested any information on that subject.

As regards the size of the book, I have been thinking a good deal about it. On mature consideration, I am of a taste and beauty, the form of publication which you recommend seems to me unexceptionable together with the advantage of being preferable in the present case, however, I have some doubts of the expediency, because, if the book is made up entirely of "the Scarlet Letter", it will be too sombre. I found it impossible to relieve the shadows of the story with so much light as I would gladly have thrown in. Keeping so close to its point as a tale naturally does, and diffusing itself through so if the worst is merely to reveal luck that; and following you with a bullet it was my purpose to confess the on his deserving example, a dozen shoter ones; so that, facing boys story will help a dozen shoter ones; so that, facing heaviest to talk the public outright with my biggest and heaviest climb of least, I might have other chances with the smaller bits, individually and in the aggregate. I am willing to leave there are ideas here to However, by an evidently to come to have you decide.

Your Judgment are thanks out be sorry

Your Judgment are thanked for publication. It appears to me that the only hope for the separate event, be the "carlet letter"; for the in the latter event. be the "carlet letter"; for the title for the book would introductory an extra a - hate to Carpter Crowns, is wearily self is not or I thrown you to my facts. the way of "intrical adj is not or I thrown you to my facts. It would be showing. Seeing the further perhaps to death and absurd, they attended all closer to stop there. If "The Scarlet Letter" is to be the title it would not to inte to permit it in the title page a send up? of am not quite sine about the found taste of so doing; but if it would certainly be highest and most "priete" and I think, attractive to the finest feels whom we are endeavoring to evidence cent.

very truly yours
Nath Hawthorne

P. S. Fields, Esq.

out like a bowsprit, and pulled and hauled imaginary ropes for our delectation. Then we all assembled in a shady spot, and one of the party read to us Bryant's beautiful poem commemorating Monument Mountain. Then we lunched among the rocks, and somebody proposed Bryant's health, and "long life to the dear old poet." This was the most popular toast of the day, and it took, I remember, a considerable quantity of Heidsieck to do it justice. In the afternoon, pioneered by Headley, we made our way, with merry shouts and laughter, through the Ice-Glen. Hawthorne was among the most enterprising of the merry-makers; and being in the dark much of the time, he ventured to call out lustily and pretend that certain destruction was inevitable to all of us. After this extemporaneous jollity, we dined together at Mr. Dudley Field's in Stockbridge, and Hawthorne rayed out in a sparkling and unwonted manner. I remember the conversation at table chiefly ran on the physical differences between the present American and English men, Hawthorne stoutly taking part in favor of the American. This 5th of August was a happy day throughout, and I never saw Hawthorne in better spirits.

Often and often I have seen him sitting in the chair I am now occupying by the window, looking out into the twilight. He liked to watch the vessels dropping down the stream, and nothing pleased him more than to go on board a newly arrived bark from Down East, as she was just moored at the wharf. One night we made the acquaintance of a cabin-boy on board a brig, whom we found off duty and reading a large subscription volume, which proved, on inquiry, to be a Commentary on the Bible. When Hawthorne questioned him why he was reading, then and there, that particular book, he replied with a knowing wink at both of us, "There's consider-'ble her'sy in our place, and I'm a studying up for 'em."

He liked on Sunday to mouse about among the books, and there are few volumes in this room that he has not handled or read. He knew he could have unmolested habitation here, whenever he chose to come, and he was never allowed to be annoyed by intrusion of any kind. He always slept in the same room, — the one looking on the water; and many a night I have heard his solemn footsteps over my head, long after the rest of the house had gone to sleep. Like many other nervous men of genius, he was a light sleeper, and he liked to be up and about early; but it was only for a ramble among the books again. One summer morning I found him as early as four o'clock reading a favorite poem, on Solitude, a piece he very much admired. That morning I shall not soon forget, for he was in the vein for autobiographical talk, and he gave me a most interesting account of his father, the sea-captain, who died of the yellow-fever in Surinam in 1808, and of his beautiful mother, who dwelt a secluded mourner ever after the death of her husband. Then he told stories of his college life, and of his one sole intimate, Franklin Pierce, whom he loved devotedly his life long.

In the early period of our acquaintance he much affected the old Boston Exchange Coffee-House in Devonshire Street, and once I remember to have found him shut up there before a blazing coal-fire, in the "tumultuous privacy" of a great snow-storm, reading with apparent interest an obsolete copy of the "Old Farmer's Almanac," which he had picked up about the house. He also delighted in the Old Province House, at that time an inn, kept by one Thomas Waite, whom he has immortalized. After he was chosen a member of the Saturday Club he came frequently to dinner with Felton, Longfellow, Holmes, and the rest of his friends, who assembled once a month to dine together. At the table, on these occasions, he was rather reticent than conversational, but when he chose to talk it was observed that the best things said that day came from him.

As I turn over his letters, the old days, delightful to recall, come back again with added interest.

"I sha'n't have the new story," he says in one of them, dated from Lenox on the 1st of October, 1850, "ready by November, for I am never good for anything in the literary way till after the first autumnal frost, which has somewhat such an effect on my imagination that it does on the foliage here about me, — multiplying and brightening its hues; though they are likely to be sober and shabby enough after all.

"I am beginning to puzzle myself about a title for the book. The scene of it is in one of those old projecting-storied houses, familiar to my eye in Salem; and the story, horrible to say, is a little less than two hundred years long; though all but thirty or forty pages of it refer to the present time. I think of such titles as 'The House of the Seven Gables,' there being that number of gable-ends to the old shanty; or 'The Seven-Gabled House'; or simply 'The Seven Gables.' Tell me how these strike you. It appears to me that the latter is rather the best, and has the great advantage that it would puzzle the Devil to tell what it means."

A month afterwards he writes further with regard to "The House of the Seven Gables," concerning the title to which he was still in a quandary: —

"'The Old Pyncheon House: A Romance'; 'The Old Pyncheon Family; or the House of the Seven Gables: A Romance'; — choose between them. I have rather a distaste to a double title? otherwise, I think I should prefer the second. Is it any matter under which title it is announced? If a better should occur hereafter, we can substitute. Of these two, on the whole, I judge the first to be the better.

"I write diligently, but not so rapidly as I had hoped. I find the book requires more care and thought than 'The Scarlet Letter'; also I have to wait oftener for a mood. 'The Scarlet Letter' being all in one tone, I had only to get my pitch, and could then go on interminably. Many passages of this book ought to be finished with the minuteness of a Dutch picture, in order to give them their proper effect. Sometimes, when tired of it, it strikes me that the whole is an absurdity, from beginning to end; but the fact is, in writing a romance, a man is always, or always ought to be, careering on the utmost verge of a precipitous absurdity, and the skill lies in coming as close as possible, without actually tumbling over. My prevailing idea is, that the book ought to succeed better than 'The Scarlet Letter,' though I have no idea that it will."

On the 9th of December he was still at work on the new romance, and writes : —

"My desire and prayer is to get through with the business in hand. I have been in a Slough of Despond for some days past, having written so fiercely that I came to a stand-still. There are points where a writer gets bewildered and cannot form any judgment of what he has done, or tell what to do next. In these cases it is best to keep quiet."

On the 12th of January, 1851, he is still busy over his new book, and writes: "My 'House of the Seven Gables' is, so to speak, finished; only I am hammering away a little on the roof, and doing up a few odd jobs, that were left incomplete.' At the end of the month the manuscript of his second great romance was put into the hands of the expressman at Lenox, by Hawthorne himself, to be delivered to me. On the 27th he writes : —

"If you do not soon receive it, you may conclude that it has miscarried; in which case, I shall not consent to the universe existing a moment longer. I have no copy of it, except the wildest scribble of a first draught, so that it could never be restored.

"It has met with extraordinary success from that portion of the public to whose judgment it has been submitted, viz. from my wife. I likewise prefer it to 'The Scarlet Letter'; but an author's opinion of his book just after completing it is worth little or nothing, he being then in the hot or cold fit of a fever, and certain to rate it too high or too low.

"It has undoubtedly one disadvantage in being brought so close to the present time; whereby its romantic improbabilities become more glaring.

"I deem it indispensable that the proof-sheets should be sent me for correction. It will cause some delay, no doubt, but probably not much more than if I lived in Salem. At all events, I don't see how it can be helped. My autography is sometimes villanously blind;

and it is odd enough that whenever the printers do mistake a word, it is just the very jewel of a word, worth all the rest of the dictionary."

I well remember with what anxiety I awaited the arrival of the expressman with the precious parcel, and with what keen delight I read every word of the new story before I slept. Here is the original manuscript, just as it came that day, twenty years ago, fresh from the author's hand. The printers carefully preserved it for me; and Hawthorne once made a formal presentation of it, with great mock solemnity, in this very room where I am now sitting.

After the book came out he wrote:—

"I have by no means an inconvenient multitude of friends; but if they ever do appear a little too numerous, it is when I am making a list of those to whom presentation copies are to be sent. Please send one to General Pierce, Horatio Bridge, R. W. Emerson, W. E. Channing, Longfellow, Hillard, Sumner, Holmes, Lowell, and Thompson the artist. You will yourself give one to Whipple, whereby I shall make a saving. I presume you won't put the portrait into the book. It appears to me an improper accompaniment to a new work. Nevertheless, if it be ready, I should be glad to have each of these presentation copies accompanied by a copy of the engraving put loosely between the leaves. Good by. I must now trudge two miles to the village, through rain and mud knee-deep, after that accursed proof-sheet. The book reads very well in proofs, but I don't believe it will take like the former one. The preliminary chapter was what gave 'The Scarlet Letter' its vogue."

The engraving he refers to in this letter was made from a portrait by Mr. C. G. Thompson, and at that time, 1851, was an admirable likeness. On the 6th of March he writes:—

"The package, with my five heads, arrived yesterday afternoon, and we are truly obliged to you for putting so many at our disposal. They are admirably done. The children recognized their venerable sire with great delight. My wife complains somewhat of a want of cheerfulness in the face; and, to say the truth, it does appear to be afflicted with a bedevilled melancholy; but it will do all the better for the author of 'The Scarlet Letter.' In the expression there is a singular resemblance (which I do not remember in Thompson's picture) to a miniature of my father."

His letters to me, during the summer of 1851, were frequent and sometimes quite long. "The House of the Seven Gables" was warmly welcomed, both at home and abroad. On the 23d of May he writes: —

"Whipple's notices have done more than pleased me, for they have helped me to see my book. Much of the censure I recognize as just; I wish I could feel the praise to be so fully deserved. Being better (which I insist it is) than 'The Scarlet Letter,' I have never expected it to be so popular (this steel pen makes me write awfully). —— —— Esq., of Boston, has written to me, complaining that I have made his grandfather infamous! It seems there was actually a Pyncheon (or Pynchon, as he spells it) family resident in Salem, and that their representative, at the period of the Revolution, was a certain Judge Pynchon, a Tory and a refugee. This was Mr. ——'s grandfather, and (at least, so he dutifully describes him) the most exemplary old gentleman in the world. There are several touches in my account of the Pyncheons which, he says, make it probable that I had this actual family in my eye, and he considers himself infinitely wronged and aggrieved, and thinks it monstrous that the 'virtuous dead' cannot be suffered to rest quietly in their graves. He further complains that I speak disrespectfully of the ——'s in Grandfather's Chair. He writes more in sorrow than in anger, though there is quite enough of the latter quality to give piquancy to his epistle. The joke of the matter is, that I never heard of his grandfather, nor knew that any Pyncheons had ever lived in Salem, but took the name because it suited the tone of my book, and was as much my property, for fictitious purposes, as that of Smith. I have pacified him by a very polite and gentlemanly letter, and if ever you publish any more of the Seven Gables, I should like to write a brief preface, expressive of my anguish for this unintentional wrong, and making the best reparation possible; else these wretched old Pyncheons will have no peace in the other world, nor in this. Furthermore, there is a Rev. Mr. ——, resident within four miles of me, and a cousin of Mr. ——, who states that he likewise is highly indignant. Who would have dreamed of claimants starting up for such an inheritance as the House of the Seven Gables!

"I mean to write, within six weeks or two months next ensuing, a book of stories made up of classical myths. The subjects are: The Story of Midas, with his Golden Touch, Pandora's Box, The Adventure of Hercules in quest of the Golden Apples, Bellerophon and the Chimera, Baucis and Philemon, Perseus and Medusa; these, I think, will be enough to make up a volume. As a framework, I shall have a young college student telling these stories to his cousins and brothers and sisters, during his vacations, sometimes at the fireside, sometimes in the woods and dells. Unless I greatly mistake, these old fictions will work up admirably for the purpose; and I shall aim at substituting a tone in some degree Gothic or romantic, or any such tone as may best please myself, instead of the classic coldness, which is as repellant as the touch of marble.

"I give you these hints of my plan, because you will perhaps think it advisable to employ Billings to prepare some illustrations. There is a good scope in the above subjects for fanciful designs. Bellerophon and the Chimera, for instance: the Chimera a fantastic monster with three heads, and Bellerophon fighting him, mounted on Pegasus; Pandora opening the box; Hercules talking with Atlas, an enormous giant who holds the sky on his shoulders, or sailing across the sea in an immense bowl; Perseus transforming a king and all his subjects to stone, by exhibiting the Gorgon's head. No particular accuracy in costume need be aimed at. My stories will bear out the artist in any liberties he may be inclined to take. Billings would do these things well enough, though his characteristics are grace and delicacy rather than wildness of fancy. The book, if it comes out of my mind as I see it now, ought to have pretty wide success amongst young people; and, of course, I shall purge out all the old heathen wickedness, and put in a moral wherever practicable. For a title how would this do: 'A Wonder-Book for Girls and Boys'; or, 'The Wonder-Book of Old Stories'? I prefer the former. Or 'Myths Modernized for my Children'; that won't do.

"I need a little change of scene, and meant to have come to Boston and elsewhere before writing this book; but I cannot leave home at present."

Throughout the summer Hawthorne was constantly worried by people who insisted that they, or their families in the present or past generations, had been deeply wronged in "The House of the Seven Gables." In a note, received from him on the 5th of June, he says:—

"I have just received a letter from still another claimant of the Pyncheon estate. I wonder if ever, and how soon, I shall get a just estimate of how many jackasses there are in this ridiculous world. My correspondent, by the way, estimates the number of these Pyncheon jackasses at about twenty; I am doubtless to be remonstrated with by each individual. After exchanging shots with all of them, I shall get you to publish the whole correspondence, in a style to match that of my other works, and I anticipate a great run for the volume.

"P. S. My last correspondent demands that another name be substituted, instead of that of the family; to which I assent, in case the publishers can be prevailed on to cancel the stereotype plates. Of course you will consent! Pray do!"

Praise now poured in upon him from all quarters. Hosts of critics, both in England and America, gallantly came forward to do him service, and his fame was assured. On the 15th of July he sends me a jubilant letter from Lenox, from which I will copy several passages: —

"Mrs. Kemble writes very good accounts from London of the reception my two romances have met with there. She says they have made a greater sensation than any book since 'Jane Eyre'; but probably she is a little or a good deal too emphatic in her representation of the matter. At any rate, she advises that the sheets of any future book be sent to Moxon, and such an arrangement made that a copyright may be secured in England as well as here. Could this be done with the Wonder-Book? And do you think it would be worth while? I must see the proof-sheets of this book. It is a cursed bore; for I want to be done with it from this moment. Can't you arrange it so that two or three or more sheets may be sent at once, on stated days, and so my journeys to the village be fewer?

"That review which you sent me is a remarkable production. There is praise enough to satisfy a greedier author than myself. I set it aside, as not being able to estimate how far it is deserved. I can better judge of the censure, much of which is undoubtedly just; and I shall profit by it if I can. But, after all, there would be no great use in attempting it. There are weeds enough in my mind, to be sure, and I might pluck them up by the handful; but in so doing I should root up the few flowers along with them. It is also to be considered, that what one man calls weeds another classifies among the choicest flowers in the garden. But this reviewer is certainly a man of sense, and sometimes tickles me under the fifth rib. I beg you to observe, however, that I do not acknowledge his justice in cutting and slashing among the characters of the two books at the rate he does; sparing nobody, I think, except Pearl and Phœbe. Yet I think he is right as to my tendency as respects individual character.

"I am going to begin to enjoy the summer now, and to read foolish novels, if I can get any, and smoke cigars, and think of nothing at all; which is equivalent to thinking of all manner of things."

The composition of the "Tanglewood Tales" gave him pleasant employment, and all his letters, during the period he was writing them, overflow with evidences of his felicitous mood. He requests that Billings should pay especial attention to the drawings, and is anxious that the porch of Tanglewood should be "well supplied with shrubbery." He seemed greatly pleased that Mary Russell Mitford had fallen in with his books and had written to me about them. "Her sketches," he said, "long ago as I read them, are as sweet in my memory as the scent of new hay." On the 18th of August he writes:—

"You are going to publish another thousand of the Seven Gables. I promised those Pyncheons a preface. What if you insert the following?

"(The author is pained to learn that, in selecting a name for the fictitious inhabitants of a castle in the air, he has wounded the feelings of more than one respectable descendant of an old Pyncheon family. He begs leave to say that he intended no reference to any individual of the name, now or heretofore extant; and further, that, at the time of writing his book, he was wholly unaware of the existence of such a family in New England for two hundred years back, and that whatever he may have since learned of them is altogether to their credit.)

"Insert it or not, as you like. I have done with the matter."

I advised him to let the Pyncheons rest as they were, and omit any addition, either as note or preface, to the romance.

Near the close of 1851 his health seemed unsettled, and he asked me to look over certain proofs "carefully," for he did not feel well enough to manage them himself. In one of his notes, written from Lenox at that time, he says : —

"Please God, I mean to look you in the face towards the end of next week; at all events, within ten days. I have stayed here too long and too constantly. To tell you a secret, I am sick to death of Berkshire, and hate to think of spending another winter here. But I must. The air and climate do not agree with my health at all; and, for the first time since I was a boy, I have felt languid and dispirited during almost my whole residence here. O that Providence would build me the merest little shanty, and mark me out a rood or two of garden-ground, near the sea-coast. I thank you for the two volumes of De Quincey. If it were not for your kindness in supplying me with books now and then, I should quite forget how to read."

Hawthorne was a hearty devourer of books, and in certain moods of mind it made very little difference what the volume before him happened to be. An old play or an old newspaper sometimes gave him wondrous great content, and he would ponder the sleepy, uninteresting sentences as if they contained immortal mental aliment. He once told me he found such delight in old advertisements in the newspaper files at the Boston Athenæum, that he had passed delicious hours among them. At other times he was very fastidious, and threw aside book after book until he found the right one. De Quincey was a special favorite with him, and the Sermons of Laurence Sterne he once commended to me as the best sermons ever written. In his library was an early copy of Sir Philip Sidney's "Arcadia," which had floated down to him from a remote ancestry, and which he had read so industriously for forty years that it was nearly worn out of its thick leathern cover. Hearing him say once that the old English State Trials were enchanting reading, and knowing that he did not possess a copy of those heavy folios, I picked up a set one day in a bookshop and sent them to him. He often told me that he spent more hours over them and got more delectation out of them than tongue could tell, and he said, if five lives were vouchsafed to him, he could employ them all in writing stories out of those books. He had sketched, in his mind, several romances founded on the remarkable trials reported in the ancient volumes; and one day, I remember, he made my blood tingle by relating some of the situations he intended, if his life was spared, to weave into future romances. Sir Walter Scott's novels he continued almost to worship, and was accustomed to read them aloud in his family. The novels of G. P. R. James, both the early and the later ones, he insisted were admirable stories, admirably told, and he had high praise to bestow on the works of Anthony Trollope. "Have you ever read these novels?" he wrote to me in a letter from England, some time before Trollope began to be much known in America. "They precisely suit my taste; solid and substantial, written on the strength of beef and through the inspiration of ale, and just as real as if some giant had hewn a great lump out of the earth and put it under a glass case, with all its inhabitants going about their daily business and not suspecting that they were made a show of. And these books are as English as a beefsteak. Have they ever been tried in America? It needs an English residence to make them thoroughly comprehensible; but still I should think that the human nature in them would give them success anywhere."

I have often been asked if all his moods were sombre, and if he was never jolly sometimes like other people. Indeed he was; and although the humorous side of Hawthorne was not easily or often discoverable, yet have I seen him marvellously moved to fun, and no man laughed more heartily in his way over a good story. Wise and witty H——, in whom wisdom and wit are so ingrained that age only increases his subtile spirit, and greatly enhances the power of his cheerful temperament, always had the talismanic faculty of breaking up that thoughtfully sad face into mirthful waves; and I remember how Hawthorne writhed with hilarious delight over Professor L——'s account of a butcher who remarked that "Idees had got afloat in the public mind with respect to sassingers." I once told him of a young woman who brought in a manuscript, and said, as she placed it in my hands, "I don't know what to do with myself sometimes, I'm so filled with *mammoth thoughts.*" A series of convulsive efforts to suppress explosive laughter followed, which I remember to this day.

He had an inexhaustible store of amusing anecdotes to relate of people and things he had observed on the road. One day he described to me, in his inimitable and quietly ludicrous manner, being *watched*, while on a visit to a distant city, by a friend who called, and thought he needed a protector, his health being at that time not so good as usual. "He stuck by me," said Hawthorne, "as if he were afraid to leave me alone; he stayed past the dinner hour, and when I began to wonder if he never took meals himself, he departed and set another man to *watch* me till he should return. That man *watched* me so, in his unwearying kindness, that when I left the house I forgot half my luggage, and left behind, among other things, a beautiful pair of slippers. They *watched* me so, among them, I swear to you I forgot nearly everything I owned."

Hawthorne is still looking at me in his far-seeing way, as if he were pondering what was next to be said about him. It would not displease him, I know, if I were to begin my discursive talk to-day by telling a little incident connected with a famous American poem.

Hawthorne dined one day with Longfellow, and brought

with him a friend from Salem. After dinner the friend said: "I have been trying to persuade Hawthorne to write a story, based upon a legend of Acadie, and still current there; a legend of a girl who, in the dispersion of the Acadians, was separated from her lover, and passed her life in waiting and seeking for him, and only found him dying in a hospital, when both were old." Longfellow wondered that this legend did not strike the fancy of Hawthorne, and said to him: "If you have really made up your mind not to use it for a story, will you give it to me for a poem?" To this Hawthorne assented, and moreover promised not to treat the subject in prose till Longfellow had seen what he could do with it in verse. And so we have "Evangeline" in beautiful hexameters, — a poem that will hold its place in literature while true affection lasts. Hawthorne rejoiced in this great success of Longfellow, and loved to count up the editions, both foreign and American, of this now world-renowned poem.

I have lately met an early friend of Hawthorne's, older than himself, who knew him intimately all his life long, and I have learned some additional facts about his youthful days. Soon after he left college he wrote some stories which he called "Seven Tales of my Native Land." The motto which he chose for the title-page was "We are Seven," from Wordsworth. My informant read the tales in manuscript, and says some of them were very striking, particularly one or two Witch Stories. As soon as the little book was well prepared for the press he deliberately threw it into the fire, and sat by to see its destruction.

When about fourteen he wrote out for a member of his family a list of the books he had at that time been reading. The catalogue was a long one, but my informant remembers that The Waverley Novels, Rousseau's Works, and The Newgate Calender were among them. Serious remonstrances were made by the family touching the perusal of this last work, but he persisted in going through it to the end. He had an objection in his boyhood to reading much that was called "true and useful." Of history in general he was not very fond, but he read Froissart with interest, and Clarendon's History of the Rebellion. He is remembered to have said at that time "he cared very little for the history of the world before the fourteenth century." After he left college he read a great deal of French literature, especially the works of Voltaire and his contemporaries. He rarely went into the streets during the daytime, unless there was to be a gathering of the people for some public purpose, such as a political meeting, a military muster, or a fire. A great conflagration attracted him in a peculiar manner, and he is remembered, while a young man in Salem, to have been often seen looking on, from some dark corner, while the fire was raging. When General Jackson, of whom he professed himself a partisan, visited Salem in 1833, he walked out to the boundary of the town to meet him, — not to speak to him, but only to look at him. When he came home at night he said he found only a few men and boys collected, not enough people, without the assistance he rendered, to welcome the General with a good cheer. It is said that Susan, in the "Village Uncle," one of the "Twice-Told Tales," is not altogether a creation of his fancy. Her father was a fisherman living in Salem, and Hawthorne was constantly telling the members of his family how charming she was, and he always spoke of her as his "mermaid." He said she had a great deal of what the French call *espièglerie*. There was another young beauty, living at that time in his native town, quite captivating to him, though in a different style from the mermaid. But if his head and heart were turned in his youth by these two nymphs in his native town, there was soon a transfer of his affections to quite another direction. His new passion was a much more permanent one, for now there dawned upon him so perfect a creature that he fell in love irrevocably; all his thoughts and all his delights centred in her, who suddenly became indeed the mistress of his soul. She filled the measure of his being, and became a part and parcel of his life. Who was this mysterious young person that had crossed his boyhood's path and made him hers forever? Whose daughter was she that could thus enthrall the ardent young man in Salem, who knew as yet so little of the world and its sirens? She is described by one who met her long before Hawthorne made her acquaintance as "the prettiest low-born lass that ever ran on the greensward," and she must have been a radiant child of beauty, indeed, that girl! She danced like a fairy, she sang exquisitely, so that every one who knew her seemed amazed at her perfect way of doing everything she attempted. Who was it that thus summoned all this witchery, making such a tumult in young Hawthorne's bosom? She was "daughter to Leontes and Hermione," king and queen of Sicilia, and her name was Perdita! It was Shakespeare who introduced Hawthorne to his first real love, and the lover never forgot his mistress. He was constant ever, and worshipped her through life. Beauty always captivated him. Where there was beauty he fancied other good gifts must naturally be in possession. During his childhood homeliness was always repulsive to him. When a little boy he is remembered to have said to a woman who wished to be kind to him, "Take her away! She is ugly and fat, and has a loud voice."

When quite a young man he applied for a situation under Commodore Wilkes on the Exploring Expedition, but did not succeed in obtaining an appointment. He thought this a great misfortune, as he was fond of travel, and he promised to do all sorts of wonderful things, should he be allowed to join the voyagers.

One very odd but characteristic notion of his, when a youth, was, that he should like a competent income which should neither increase nor diminish, for then, he said, it would not engross too much of his attention. Surrey's little poem, "The Means to obtain a Happy Life," expressed exactly what his idea of happiness was when a lad. When a school-boy he wrote verses for the newspapers, but he ignored their existence in after years with a smile of droll disgust. One of his quatrains lives in the memory of a friend, who repeated it to me recently: —

> "The ocean hath its silent caves,
> Deep, quiet, and alone;
> Above them there are troubled waves,
> Beneath them there are none."

When the Atlantic Cable was first laid, somebody, not knowing the author of the lines, quoted them to Hawthorne as applicable to the calmness said to exist in the depths of the ocean. He listened to the verse, and then laughingly observed, "I know something of the deep sea myself."

In 1836 he went to Boston, I am told, to edit the "American Magazine of Useful Knowledge," for which he was to be paid a salary of six hundred dollars a year. The proprietors soon became insolvent, so that he received nothing, but he kept on just the same as if he had been paid regularly. The plan of the work proposed by the publishers of the magazine admitted no fiction into its pages. The magazine was printed on coarse paper and was illustrated by engravings painful to look at. There were no contributors except the editor, and he wrote the whole of every number. Short biographical sketches of eminent men and historical narratives filled up its pages. I have examined the columns of this deceased magazine, and read Hawthorne's narrative of Mrs. Dustan's captivity. Mrs. Dustan was carried off by the Indians from Haverhill, and Hawthorne does not much commiserate the hardships she endured, but reserves his sympathy for her husband, who was *not* carried into captivity, and suffered nothing from the Indians, but who, he says, was a tender-hearted man, and took care of the children during Mrs. D.'s absence from home, and probably knew that his wife would be more than a match for a whole tribe of savages.

When the Rev. Mr. Cheever was knocked down and flogged in the streets of Salem and then imprisoned, Hawthorne came out of his retreat and visited him regularly in jail, showing strong sympathy for the man and great indignation for those who had maltreated him.

Those early days in Salem, — how interesting the memory of them must be to the friends who knew and followed the gentle dreamer in his budding career! When the whisper first came to the timid boy, in that "dismal chamber in Union Street," that he too possessed the soul of an artist, there were not many about him to share the divine rapture that must have filled his proud young heart. Outside of his own little family circle, doubting and desponding eyes looked upon him, and many a stupid head wagged in derision as he passed by. But there was always waiting for him a sweet and honest welcome by the pleasant hearth where his mother and sisters sat and listened to the beautiful creations of his fresh and glowing fancy. We can imagine the happy group gathered around the evening lamp! "Well, my son," says the fond mother, looking up from her knitting-work, "what have you got for us to-night? It is some time since you read us a story, and your sisters are as impatient as I am to have a new one." And then we can hear, or think we hear, the young man begin in a low and modest tone the story of "Edward Fane's Rosebud," or "The Seven Vagabonds," or perchance (O tearful, happy evening!) that tender idyl of "The Gentle Boy!" What a privilege to hear for the first time a "Twice-Told Tale," before it was even *once* told to the public! And I know with what rapture the delighted little audience must have hailed the advent of every fresh indication that genius, so seldom a visitant at any fireside, had come down so noiselessly to bless their quiet hearthstone in the sombre old town. In striking contrast to Hawthorne's audience nightly convened to listen while he read his charming tales and essays, I think of poor Bernardin de Saint-Pierre, facing those hard-eyed critics at the house of Madame Neckar, when as a young man and entirely unknown he essayed to read his then unpublished story of "Paul and Virginia." The story was simple and the voice of the poor and nameless reader trembled. Everybody was unsympathetic and gaped, and at the end of a quarter of an hour Monsieur de Buffon, who always had a loud way with him, cried out to Madame Neckar's servant, "Let the horses be put to my carriage!"

Hawthorne seems never to have known that raw period in authorship which is common to most growing writers, when the style is "overlanguaged," and when it plunges wildly through the "sandy deserts of rhetoric," or struggles as if it were having a personal difficulty with Ignorance and his brother Platitude. It was capitally said of Chateaubriand that "he lived on the summits of syllables," and of another young author that he was so dully good, that he made even virtue disreputable." Hawthorne had no such literary vices to contend with. His looks seemed from the start to be

"Commercing with the skies,"

and he marching upward to the goal without impediment. I was struck a few days ago with the untruth, so far as

Hawthorne is concerned, of a passage in the Preface to Endymion. Keats says: "The imagination of a boy is healthy, and the mature imagination of a man is healthy; but there is a space of life between, in which the soul is in a ferment, the character undecided, the way of life uncertain, the ambition thick-sighted." Hawthorne's imagination had no middle period of decadence or doubt, but continued, as it began, in full vigor to the end.

In 1852 I went to Europe, and while absent had frequent most welcome letters from the delightful dreamer. He had finished the "Blithedale Romance" during my wanderings, and I was fortunate enough to arrange for its publication in London simultaneously with its appearance in Boston. One of his letters (dated from his new residence in Concord, June 17, 1852) runs thus:—

"You have succeeded admirably in regard to the 'Blithedale Romance,' and have got £150 more than I expected to receive. It will come in good time, too; for my drafts have been pretty heavy of late, in consequence of buying an estate!!! and fitting up my house. What a truant you are from the Corner! I wish, before leaving London, you would obtain for me copies of any English editions of my writings not already in my possession. I have Routledge's edition of 'The Scarlet Letter,' the 'Mosses,' and 'Twice-Told Tales'; Bohn's editions of 'The House of the Seven Gables,' the 'Snow-Image' and the 'Wonder-Book,' and Bogue's edition of 'The Scarlet Letter';— these are all, and I should be glad of the rest. I meant to have written another 'Wonder-Book' this summer, but another task has unexpectedly intervened. General Pierce of New Hampshire, the Democratic nominee for the Presidency, was a college friend of mine, as you know, and we have been intimate through life. He wishes me to write his biography, and I have consented to do so; somewhat reluctantly, however, for Pierce has now reached that altitude when a man, careful of his personal dignity, will begin to think of cutting his acquaintance. But I seek nothing from him, and therefore need not be ashamed to tell the truth of an old friend. . . . . I have written to Barry Cornwall, and shall probably enclose the letter along with this. I don't more than half believe what you tell me of my reputation in England, and am only so far credulous on the strength of the £ 200, and shall have a somewhat stronger sense of this latter reality when I finger the cash. Do come home in season to preside over the publication of the Romance."

He had christened his estate The Wayside, and in a postscript to the above letter he begs me to consider the name and tell him how I like it.

Another letter, evidently foreshadowing a foreign appointment from the newly elected President, contains this passage: —

"Do make some inquiries about Portugal; as, for instance, in what part of the world it lies, and whether it is an empire, a kingdom, or a republic. Also, and more particularly, the expenses of living there, and whether the Minister would be likely to be much pestered with his own countrymen. Also, any other information about foreign countries would be acceptable to an inquiring mind."

When I returned from abroad I found him getting matters in readiness to leave the country for a consulship in Liverpool. He seemed happy at the thought of flitting, but I wondered if he could possibly be as contented across the water as he was in Concord. I remember walking with him to the Old Manse, a mile or so distant from The Wayside, his new residence, and talking over England and his proposed absence of several years. We strolled round the house, where he spent the first years of his married life, and he pointed from the outside to the windows, out of which he had looked and seen supernatural and other visions. We walked up and down the avenue, the memory of which he has embalmed in the "Mosses," and he discoursed most pleasantly of all that had befallen him since he led a lonely, secluded life in Salem. It was a sleepy, warm afternoon, and he proposed that we should wander up the banks of the river and lie down and watch the clouds float above and in the quiet stream. I recall his lounging, easy air as he tolled me along until we came to a spot secluded, and ofttimes sacred to his wayward thoughts. He bade me lie down on the grass and hear the birds sing. As we steeped ourselves in the delicious idleness, he began to murmur some half-forgotten lines from Thomson's "Seasons," which he said had been favorites of his from boyhood. While we lay there, hidden in the grass, we heard approaching footsteps, and Hawthorne hurriedly whispered, "Duck! or we shall be interrupted by somebody." The solemnity of his manner, and the thought of the down-flat position in which we had both placed ourselves to avoid being seen, threw me into a foolish, semi-hysterical fit of laughter, and when he nudged me, and again whispered more lugubriously than ever, "Heaven help me, Mr. —— is close upon us!" I felt convinced that if the thing went further, suffocation, in my case at least, must ensue.

He kept me constantly informed, after he went to Liverpool, of how he was passing his time; and his charming "English Note-Books" reveal the fact that he was never idle. There were touches, however, in his private letters which escaped daily record in his journal, and I remember how delightful it was, after he landed in Europe, to get his frequent missives. In one of the first he gives me an account of a dinner where he was obliged to make a speech. He says: —

"I tickled up John Bull's self-conceit (which is very easily done) with a few sentences of most outrageous flattery, and sat down in a general puddle of good feeling." In another he says: "I have taken a house in Rock Park, on the Cheshire side of the Mersey, and am as snug as a bug in a rug. Next year you must come and see how I live. Give my regards to everybody, and my love to half a dozen. . . . . I wish you would call on Mr. Savage, the antiquarian, if you know him, and ask whether he can inform me what part of England the original William Hawthorne came from. He came over, I think, in 1634. . . . . It would really be a great obligation if he could answer the above query. Or, if the fact is not within his own knowledge, he might perhaps indicate some place where such information might be obtained here in England. I presume there are records still extant somewhere of all the passengers by those early ships, with their English localities annexed to their names. Of all things, I should like to find a gravestone in one of these old churchyards with my own name upon it, although, for myself, I should wish to be buried in America. The graves are too horribly damp here."

The hedgerows of England, the grassy meadows, and the picturesque old cottages delighted him, and he was never tired of writing to me about them. While wandering over the country, he was often deeply touched by meeting among the wild-flowers many of his old New England favorites, — bluebells, crocuses, primroses, foxglove, and other flowers which are cultivated in our gardens, and which had long been familiar to him in America.

I can imagine him, in his quiet, musing way, strolling through the daisied fields on a Sunday morning and hearing the distant church-bells chiming to service. His religion was deep and broad, but it was irksome for him to be fastened in by a pew-door, and I doubt if he often heard an English sermon. He very rarely described himself as *inside* a church, but he liked to wander among the graves in the churchyards and read the epitaphs on the moss-grown slabs. He liked better to meet and have a talk with the *sexton* than with the *rector*.

He was constantly demanding longer letters from home; and nothing gave him more pleasure than monthly news from "The Saturday Club," and detailed accounts of what was going forward in literature. One of his letters dated in January, 1854, starts off thus: —

"I wish your epistolary propensities were stronger than they are. All your letters to me since I left America might be squeezed into one. . . . . I send Ticknor a big cheese, which I long ago promised

him, and my advice is, that he keep it in the shop, and daily, between eleven and one o'clock, distribute slices of it to your half-starved authors, together with crackers and something to drink. . . . .
I thank you for the books you send me, and more especially for Mrs. Mowatt's Autobiography, which seems to me an admirable book. Of all things I delight in autobiographies; and I hardly ever read one that interested me so much. She must be a remarkable woman, and I cannot but lament my ill fortune in never having seen her on the stage or elsewhere. . . . . I count strongly upon your promise to be with us in May. Can't you bring Whipple with you?"

One of his favorite resorts in Liverpool was the boarding-house of good Mrs. Blodgett, in Duke Street, a house where many Americans have found delectable quarters, after being tossed on the stormy Atlantic. "I have never known a better woman," Hawthorne used to say, "and her motherly kindness to me and mine I can never forget." Hundreds of American travellers will bear witness to the excellence of that beautiful old lady, who presided with such dignity and sweetness over her hospitable mansion.

On the 13th of April, 1854, Hawthorne wrote to me this characteristic letter from the consular office in Liverpool: —

"I am very glad that the 'Mosses' have come into the hands of our firm; and I return the copy sent me, after a careful revision. When I wrote those dreamy sketches, I little thought that I should ever preface an edition for the press amidst the bustling life of a Liverpool consulate. Upon my honor, I am not quite sure that I entirely comprehend my own meaning, in some of these blasted allegories; but I remember that I always had a meaning, or at least thought I had. I am a good deal changed since those times; and, to tell you the truth, my past self is not very much to my taste, as I see myself in this book. Yet certainly there is more in it than the public generally gave me credit for at the time it was written.

"But I don't think myself worthy of very much more credit than I got. It has been a very disagreeable task to read the book. The story of 'Rappacini's Daughter' was published in the Democratic Review, about the year 1844; and it was prefaced by some remarks on the celebrated French author (a certain M. de l'Aubépine), from whose works it was translated. I left out this preface when the story was republished; but I wish you would turn to it in the Democratic, and see whether it is worth while to insert it in the new edition. I leave it altogether to your judgment.

"A young poet named —— has called on me, and has sent me some copies of his works to be transmitted to America. It seems to me there is good in him; and he is recognized by Tennyson, by Carlyle, by Kingsley, and others of the best people here. He writes me that this edition of his poems is nearly exhausted, and that Routledge is going to publish another, enlarged and in better style.

"Perhaps it might be well for you to take him up in America. At all events, try to bring him into notice; and some day or other you may be glad to have helped a famous poet in his obscurity. The poor fellow has left a good post in the customs to cultivate literature in London!

"We shall begin to look for you now by every steamer from Boston. You must make up your mind to spend a good while with us before going to see your London friends.

"Did you read the article on your friend De Quincey in the last Westminster? It was written by Mr. —— of this city, who was in America a year or two ago. The article is pretty well, but does nothing like adequate justice to De Quincey; and in fact no Englishman cares a pin for him. We are ten times as good readers and critics as they.

"Is not Whipple coming here soon?"

Hawthorne's first visit to London afforded him great pleasure, but he kept out of the way of literary people as much as possible. He introduced himself to nobody, except Mr. ——, whose assistance he needed, in order to be identified at the bank. He wrote to me from 24 George Street, Hanover Square, and told me he delighted in London, and wished he could spend a year there. He enjoyed floating about, in a sort of unknown way, among the rotund and rubicund figures made jolly with ale and port-wine. He was greatly amused at being told (his informants meaning to be complimentary) "that he would never be taken for anything but an Englishman." He called Tennyson's "Charge of the Light Brigade," just

Thomas de Quincey.

printed at that time, "a broken-kneed gallop of a poem." He writes:—

"John Bull is in high spirits just now at the taking of Sebastopol. What an absurd personage John is! I find that my liking for him grows stronger the more I see of him, but that my admiration and respect have constantly decreased."

One of his most intimate friends (a man unlike that individual of whom it was said that he was the friend of everybody that did not need a friend) was Francis Bennoch, a merchant of Wood Street, Cheapside, London, the gentleman to whom Mrs. Hawthorne dedicated the English Note-Books. Hawthorne's letters abounded in warm expressions of affection for the man whose noble hospitality and deep interest made his residence in England full of happiness. Bennoch was indeed like a brother to him, sympathizing warmly in all his literary projects, and giving him the benefit of his excellent judgment while he was sojourning among strangers. Bennoch's record may be found in Tom Taylor's admirable life of poor Haydon, the artist. All literary and artistic people who have had the good fortune to enjoy his friendship have loved him. I happen to know of his bountiful kindness to Miss Mitford and Hawthorne and poor old Jerdan, for these hospitalities happened in my time; but he began to befriend all who needed friendship long before I knew him. His name ought never to be omitted from the literary annals of England; nor that of his wife either, for she has always made her delightful fireside warm and comforting to her husband's friends.

Many and many a happy time Bennoch, Hawthorne, and myself have had together on British soil. I remember we went once to dine at a great house in the country, years ago, where it was understood there would be no dinner speeches. The banquet was in honor of some society, — I have quite forgotten what, — but it was a jocose and not a serious club. The gentleman who gave it, Sir ———, was a most kind and genial person, and gathered about him on this occasion some of the brightest and best from London. All the way down in the train Hawthorne was rejoicing that this was to be a dinner without speech-making; "for," said he, "nothing would tempt me to go if toasts and such confounded deviltry were to be the order of the day." So we rattled along, without a fear of any impending cloud of oratory. The entertainment was a most exquisite one, about twenty gentlemen sitting down at the beautifully ornamented table. Hawthorne was in uncommonly good spirits, and, having the seat of honor at the right of his host, was pretty keenly scrutinized by his British brethren of the quill. He had, of course, banished all thought of speech-making, and his knees never smote together once, as he told me afterwards. But it became evident to my mind that Hawthorne's health was to be proposed with all the honors. I glanced at him across the table, and saw that he was unsuspicious of any movement against his quiet serenity. Suddenly and without warning our host rapped the mahogany, and began a set speech of welcome to the "distinguished American romancer." It was a very honest and a very hearty speech, but I dared not look at Hawthorne. I expected every moment to see him glide out of the room, or sink down out of sight from his chair. The tortures I suffered on Hawthorne's account, on that occasion, I will not attempt to describe now. I knew nothing would have induced the shy man of letters to go down to Brighton, if he had known he was to be spoken at in that manner. I imagined his face a deep crimson, and his hands trembling with nervous horror; but judge of my surprise, when he rose to reply with so calm a voice and so composed a manner, that, in all my experience of dinner-speaking, I never witnessed such a case of apparent ease. (Easy-Chair C—— himself, one of the best makers of after-dinner or any other speeches of our day, according to Charles Dickens, — no inadequate judge, all will allow, — never surpassed in eloquent effect this speech by Hawthorne.) There was no hesitation, no sign of lack of preparation, but he went on for about ten minutes in such a masterly manner, that I declare it was one of the most successful efforts of the kind ever made. Everybody was delighted, and, when he sat down, a wild and unanimous shout of applause rattled the glasses on the table. The meaning of his singular composure on that occasion I could never get him satisfactorily to explain, and the only remark I ever heard him make, in any way connected with this marvellous exhibition of coolness, was simply, "What a confounded fool I was to go down to that speech-making dinner!"

During all those long years, while Hawthorne was absent in Europe, he was anything but an idle man. On the contrary, he was an eminently busy one, in the best sense of that term; and if his life had been prolonged, the public would have been a rich gainer for his residence abroad. His brain teemed with romances, and once I remember he told me he had no less than five stories, well thought out, any one of which he could finish and publish whenever he chose to. There was one subject for a work of imagination that seems to have haunted him for years, and he has mentioned it twice in his journal. This was the subsequent life of the young man whom Jesus, looking on, "loved," and whom he bade to sell all that he had and give to the poor, and take up his cross and follow him. "Something very deep and beautiful might be made out of this," Hawthorne said, "for the young man went away sorrowful, and is not recorded to have done what he was bidden to do."

One of the most difficult matters he had to manage

while in England was the publication of Miss Bacon's singular book on Shakespeare. The poor lady, after he had agreed to see the work through the press, broke off all correspondence with him in a storm of wrath, accusing him of pusillanimity in not avowing full faith in her theory; so that, as he told me, so far as her good-will was concerned, he had not gained much by taking the responsibility of her book upon his shoulders. It was a heavy weight for him to bear in more senses than one, for he paid out of his own pocket the expenses of publication.

I find in his letters constant references to the kindness with which he was treated in London. He spoke of Mrs. S. C. Hall as "one of the best and warmest-hearted women in the world." Leigh Hunt, in his way, pleased and satisfied him more than almost any man he had seen in England. "As for other literary men," he says in one of his letters, "I doubt whether London can muster so good a dinner-party as that which assembles every month at the marble palace in School Street."

All sorts of adventures befell him during his stay in Europe, even to that of having his house robbed, and his causing the thieves to be tried and sentenced to transportation. In the summer-time he travelled about the country in England and pitched his tent wherever fancy prompted. One autumn afternoon in September he writes to me from Leamington:—

"I received your letter only this morning, at this cleanest and prettiest of English towns, where we are going to spend a week or two before taking our departure for Paris. We are acquainted with Leamington already, having resided here two summers ago; and the country round about is unadulterated England, rich in old castles, manor-houses, churches, and thatched cottages, and as green as Paradise itself. I only wish I had a house here, and that you could come and be my guest in it; but I am a poor wayside vagabond, and only find shelter for a night or so, and then trudge onward again. My wife and children and myself are familiar with all

Leigh Hunt

kinds of lodgement and modes of living, but we have forgotten what home is, — at least the children have, poor things! I doubt whether they will ever feel inclined to live long in one place. The worst of it is, I have outgrown my house in Concord, and feel no inclination to return to it.

"We spent seven weeks in Manchester, and went most diligently to the Art Exhibition; and I really begin to be sensible of the rudiments of a taste in pictures."

It was during one of his rambles with Alexander Ireland through the Manchester Exhibition rooms that Hawthorne saw Tennyson wandering about. I have always thought it unfortunate that these two men of genius could not have been introduced on that occasion. Hawthorne was too shy to seek an introduction, and Tennyson was not aware that the American author was present. Hawthorne records in his journal that he gazed at Tennyson with all his eyes, "and rejoiced more in him than in all the other wonders of the Exhibition." When I afterwards told Tennyson that the author whose "Twice-Told Tales" he happened to be then reading at Farringford had met him at Manchester, but did not make himself known, the Laureate said in his frank and hearty manner: "Why did n't he come up and let me shake hands with him? I am sure I should have been glad to meet a man like Hawthorne anywhere."

At the close of 1857 Hawthorne writes to me that he hears nothing of the appointment of his successor in the consulate, since he had sent in his resignation. "Somebody may turn up any day," he says, "with a new commission in his pocket." He was meanwhile getting ready for Italy, and he writes, "I expect shortly to be released from durance."

In his last letter before leaving England for the Continent he says: —

"I made up a huge package the other day, consisting of seven closely written volumes of journal, kept by me since my arrival in

England, and filled with sketches of places and men and manners, many of which would doubtless be very delightful to the public. I think I shall seal them up, with directions in my will to have them opened and published a century hence; and your firm shall have the refusal of them then.

"Remember me to everybody, for I love all my friends at least as well as ever."

Released from the cares of office, and having nothing to distract his attention, his life on the Continent opened full of delightful excitement. His pecuniary situation was such as to enable him to live very comfortably in a country where, at that time, prices were moderate.

In a letter dated from a villa near Florence on the 3d of September, 1858, he thus describes in a charming manner his way of life in Italy: —

"I am afraid I have stayed away too long, and am forgotten by everybody. You have piled up the dusty remnants of my editions, I suppose, in that chamber over the shop, where you once took me to smoke a cigar, and have crossed my name out of your list of authors, without so much as asking whether I am dead or alive. But I like it well enough, nevertheless. It is pleasant to feel at last that I am really away from America, — a satisfaction that I never enjoyed as long as I stayed in Liverpool, where it seemed to me that the quintessence of nasal and hand-shaking Yankeedom was continually filtered and sublimated through my consulate, on the way outward and homeward. I first got acquainted with my own countrymen there. At Rome, too, it was not much better. But here in Florence, and in the summer-time, and in this secluded villa, I have escaped out of all my old tracks, and am really remote.

"I like my present residence immensely. The house stands on a hill, overlooking Florence, and is big enough to quarter a regiment; insomuch that each member of the family, including servants, has a separate suite of apartments, and there are vast wildernesses of upper rooms into which we have never yet sent exploring expeditions.

"At one end of the house there is a moss-grown tower, haunted by owls and by the ghost of a monk, who was confined there in the thirteenth century, previous to being burned at the stake in the principal square of Florence. I hire this villa, tower and all, at twenty-eight dollars a month; but I mean to take it away bodily and clap it into a romance, which I have in my head ready to be written out.

"Speaking of romances, I have planned two, one or both of which I could have ready for the press in a few months if I were either in England or America. But I find this Italian atmosphere not favorable to the close toil of composition, although it is a very good air to dream in. I must breathe the fogs of old England or the east-winds of Massachusetts, in order to put me into working trim. Nevertheless, I shall endeavor to be busy during the coming winter at Rome, but there will be so much to distract my thoughts that I have little hope of seriously accomplishing anything. It is a pity; for I have really a plethora of ideas, and should feel relieved by discharging some of them upon the public.

"We shall continue here till the end of this month, and shall then return to Rome, where I have already taken a house for six months. In the middle of April we intend to start for home by the way of Geneva and Paris; and, after spending a few weeks in England, shall embark for Boston in July or the beginning of August. After so long an absence (more than five years already, which will be six before you see me at the old Corner), it is not altogether delightful to think of returning. Everybody will be changed, and I myself, no doubt, as much as anybody. Ticknor and you, I suppose, were both upset in the late religious earthquake, and when I inquire for you the clerks will direct me to the 'Business Men's Conference.' It won't do. I shall be forced to come back again and take refuge in a London lodging. London is like the grave in one respect, — any man can make himself at home there; and whenever a man finds himself homeless elsewhere, he had better either die or go to London.

"Speaking of the grave reminds me of old age and other disagreeable matters; and I would remark that one grows old in Italy twice or three times as fast as in other countries. I have three gray hairs now for one that I brought from England, and I shall look venerable indeed by next summer, when I return.

"Remember me affectionately to all my friends. Whoever has a kindness for me may be assured that I have twice as much for him."

Hawthorne's second visit to Rome, in the winter of 1859, was not a fortunate one. His own health was excellent during his sojourn there, but several members of his family fell ill, and he became very nervous and longed to get away. In one of his letters he says: —

"I bitterly detest Rome, and shall rejoice to bid it farewell forever; and I fully acquiesce in all the mischief and ruin that has happened to it, from Nero's conflagration downward. In fact, I wish the very site had been obliterated before I ever saw it."

He found solace, however, during the series of domestic troubles (continued illness in his family) that befell, in writing memoranda for "The Marble Faun." He thus announces to me the beginning of the new romance: —

"I take some credit to myself for having sternly shut myself up for an hour or two almost every day, and come to close grips with a romance which I have been trying to tear out of my mind. As for my success, I can't say much; indeed, I don't know what to say at all. I only know that I have produced what seems to be a larger amount of scribble than either of my former romances, and that portions of it interested me a good deal while I was writing them; but I have had so many interruptions, from things to see and things to suffer, that the story has developed itself in a very imperfect way, and will have to be revised hereafter. I could finish it for the press in the time that I am to remain here (till the 15th of April), but my brain is tired of it just now; and, besides, there are many objects that I shall regret not seeing hereafter, though I care very little about seeing them now; so I shall throw aside the romance, and take it up again next August at The Wayside."

He decided to be back in England early in the summer, and to sail for home in July. He writes to me from Rome: —

"I shall go home, I fear, with a heavy heart, not expecting to be very well contented there. . . . . If I were but a hundred times richer than I am, how very comfortable I could be! I consider it a great piece of good fortune that I have had experience of the discomforts and miseries of Italy, and did not go directly home from England. Anything will seem like Paradise after a Roman winter.

"If I had but a house fit to live in, I should be greatly more reconciled to coming home; but I am really at a loss to imagine how we are to squeeze ourselves into that little old cottage of mine. We had outgrown it before we came away, and most of us are twice as big now as we were then.

"I have an attachment to the place, and should be sorry to give it up; but I shall half ruin myself if I try to enlarge the house, and quite if I build another. So what is to be done? Pray have some plan for me before I get back; not that I think you can possibly hit on anything that will suit me...... I shall return by way of Venice and Geneva, spend two or three weeks or more in Paris, and sail for home, as I said, in July. It would be an exceeding delight to me to meet you or Ticknor in England, or anywhere else. At any rate, it will cheer my heart to see you all and the old Corner itself, when I touch my dear native soil again."

I went abroad again in 1859, and found Hawthorne back in England, working away diligently at "The Marble Faun." While travelling on the Continent, during the autumn I had constant letters from him, giving accounts of his progress on the new romance. He says: "I get along more slowly than I expected..... If I mistake not, it will have some good chapters." Writing on the 10th of October he tells me: —

"The romance is almost finished, a great heap of manuscript being already accumulated, and only a few concluding chapters remaining behind. If hard pushed, I could have it ready for the press in a fortnight; but unless the publishers [Smith and Elder were to bring out the work in England] are in a hurry, I shall be somewhat longer about it. I have found far more work to do upon it than I anticipated. To confess the truth, I admire it exceedingly at intervals, but am liable to cold fits, during which I think it the most infernal nonsense. You ask for the title. I have not yet fixed upon one, but here are some that have occurred to me; neither of them exactly meets my idea: 'Monte Beni; or, The Faun. A Romance.' 'The Romance of a Faun.' 'The Faun of Monte Beni.' 'Monte Beni: a Romance.' 'Miriam: a Romance.' 'Hilda: a Romance.' 'Donatello: a Romance.' 'The Faun: a Romance.' 'Marble and Man: a Romance.' When you have read the work (which I especially wish you to do before it goes to press), you will be able to select one of them, or imagine something better. There is an objection in my mind to an Italian name, though perhaps Monte Beni might do. Neither do I wish, if I can help it, to make the fantastic aspect of the book too prominent by putting the Faun into the title-page."

Hawthorne wrote so intensely on his new story, that he was quite worn down before he finished it. To recruit his strength he went to Redcar, where the bracing air of the German Ocean soon counteracted the ill effect of overwork. "The Marble Faun" was in the London printing-office in November, and he seemed very glad to have it off his hands. His letters to me at this time (I was still on the Continent) were jubilant with hope. He was living in Leamington, and was constantly writing to me that I should find the next two months more comfortable in England than anywhere else. On the 17th he writes: —

"The Italian spring commences in February, which is certainly an advantage, especially as from February to May is the most disagreeable portion of the English year. But it is always summer by a bright coal-fire. We find nothing to complain of in the climate of Leamington. To be sure, we cannot always see our hands before us for fog; but I like fog, and do not care about seeing my hand before me. We have thought of staying here till after Christmas and then going somewhere else, — perhaps to Bath, perhaps to Devonshire. But all this is uncertain. Leamington is not so desirable a residence in winter as in summer; its great charm consisting in the many delightful walks and drives, and in its neighborhood to interesting places. I have quite finished the book (some time ago) and have sent it to Smith and Elder, who tell me it is in the printer's hands, but I have received no proof-sheets. They wrote to request another title instead of the 'Romance of Monte Beni,' and I sent them their choice of a dozen. I don't know what they have chosen; neither do I understand their objection to the above. Perhaps they don't like the book at all; but I shall not trouble myself about that, as long as they publish it and pay me my £600. For my part, I think it much my best romance; but I can see some points where it is open to assault. If it could have appeared first in America, it would have been a safe thing. . . .

"I mean to spend the rest of my abode in England in blessed idleness: and as for my journal, in the first place I have not got it here; secondly, there is nothing in it that will do to publish."

Hawthorne was, indeed, a consummate artist, and I do not remember a single slovenly passage in all his acknowledged writings. It was a privilege, and one that

I can never sufficiently estimate, to have known him personally through so many years. He was unlike any other author I have met, and there were qualities in his nature so sweet and commendable, that, through all his shy reserve, they sometimes asserted themselves in a marked and conspicuous manner. I have known rude people, who were jostling him in a crowd, give way at the sound of his low and almost irresolute voice, so potent was the gentle spell of command that seemed born of his genius.

Although he was apt to keep aloof from his kind, and did not hesitate frequently to announce by his manner that

> "Solitude to him
> Was blithe society, who filled the air
> With gladness and involuntary songs,"

I ever found him, like Milton's Raphael, an "affable" angel, and inclined to converse on whatever was human and good in life.

Here are some more extracts from the letters he wrote to me while he was engaged on "The Marble Faun." On the 11th of February, 1860, he writes from Leamington in England (I was then in Italy) : —

"I received your letter from Florence, and conclude that you are now in Rome, and probably enjoying the Carnival, — a tame description of which, by the by, I have introduced into my Romance.

"I thank you most heartily for your kind wishes in favor of the forthcoming work, and sincerely join my own prayers to yours in its behalf, but without much confidence of a good result. My own opinion is, that I am not really a popular writer, and that what popularity I have gained is chiefly accidental, and owing to other causes than my own kind or degree of merit. Possibly I may (or may not) deserve something better than popularity; but looking at all my productions, and especially this latter one, with a cold or critical eye, I can see that they do not make their appeal to the popular mind. It is odd enough, moreover, that my own individual taste is for quite another class of works than those which I myself am able to write. If I were to meet with such books as mine, by another writer, I don't believe I should be able to get through them.

. . . . .

"To return to my own moonshiny Romance; its fate will soon be settled, for Smith and Elder mean to publish on the 28th of this month. Poor Ticknor will have a tight scratch to get his edition out contemporaneously; they having sent him the third volume only a week ago. I think, however, there will be no danger of piracy in America. Perhaps nobody will think it worth stealing. Give my best regards to William Story, and look well at his Cleopatra, for you will meet her again in one of the chapters which I wrote with most pleasure. If he does not find himself famous henceforth, the fault will be none of mine. I, at least, have done my duty by him, whatever delinquency there may be on the part of other critics.

"Smith and Elder persist in calling the book 'Transformation,' which gives one the idea of Harlequin in a pantomime; but I have strictly enjoined upon Ticknor to call it 'The Marble Faun; a Romance of Monte Beni.'"

In one of his letters written at this period, referring to his design of going home, he says: —

"I shall not have been absent seven years till the 5th of July next, and I scorn to touch Yankee soil sooner than that. . . . . As regards going home I alternate between a longing and a dread."

Returning to London from the Continent, in April, I found this letter, written from Bath, awaiting my arrival: —

"You are welcome back. I really began to fear that you had been assassinated among the Apennines or killed in that outbreak at Rome. I have taken passages for all of us in the steamer which sails the 16th of June. Your berths are Nos. 19 and 20. I engaged them with the understanding that you might go earlier or later, if you chose; but I would advise you to go on the 16th; in the first place, because the state-rooms for our party are the most eligible in the ship; secondly, because we shall otherwise mutually lose the pleasure of each other's company. Besides, I consider it my duty, towards Ticknor and towards Boston, and America at large, to take you into custody and bring you home; for I know you will never come except upon compulsion. Let me know at once whether I am to use force.

"The book (The Marble Faun) has done better than I thought it would; for you will have discovered, by this time, that it is an audacious attempt to impose a tissue of absurdities upon the public by the mere art of style of narrative. I hardly hoped that it would go down with John Bull; but then it is always my best point of writing, to undertake such a task, and I really put what strength I have into many parts of this book.

"The English critics generally (with two or three unimportant exceptions) have been sufficiently favorable, and the review in the Times awarded the highest praise of all. At home, too, the notices have been very kind, so far as they have come under my eye. Lowell had a good one in the Atlantic Monthly, and Hillard an excellent one in the Courier; and yesterday I received a sheet of the May number of the Atlantic containing a really keen and profound article by Whipple, in which he goes over all my works, and recognizes that element of unpopularity which (as nobody knows better than myself) pervades them all. I agree with almost all he says, except that I am conscious of not deserving nearly so much praise. When I get home, I will try to write a more genial book; but the Devil himself always seems to get into my inkstand, and I can only exorcise him by pensful at a time.

"I am coming to London very soon, and mean to spend a fortnight of next month there. I have been quite homesick through this past dreary winter. Did you ever spend a winter in England? If not, reserve your ultimate conclusion about the country until you have done so."

We met in London early in May, and, as our lodgings were not far apart, we were frequently together. I recall many pleasant dinners with him and mutual friends in various charming seaside and country-side places. We used to take a run down to Greenwich or Blackwall once or twice a week, and a trip to Richmond was always grateful to him. Bennoch was constantly planning a day's happiness for his friend, and the hours at that pleasant season of the year were not long enough for our delights. In London we strolled along the Strand, day after day, now diving into Bolt Court, in pursuit of Johnson's whereabouts, and now stumbling around the Temple, where Goldsmith at one time had his quarters. Hawthorne was never weary of standing on London Bridge, and watching the steamers plying up and down the Thames. I was much amused by his manner towards importunate and sometimes impudent beggars, scores of whom would attack us even in the shortest walk. He had a mild way of making a severe and cutting remark, which used to remind me of a little incident which Charlotte Cushman once related to me. She said a man in the gallery of a theatre (I think she was on the stage at the time) made such a disturbance that the play could not proceed. Cries of "Throw him over" arose from all parts of the house, and the noise became furious. All was tumultuous chaos until a sweet and gentle female voice was heard in the pit, exclaiming, "No! I pray you don't throw him over! I beg of you, dear friends, don't throw him over, but — *kill him where he is.*"

One of our most royal times was at a parting dinner at the house of Barry Cornwall. Among the notables present were Kinglake and Leigh Hunt. Our kind-hearted host and his admirable wife greatly delighted in Hawthorne, and they made this occasion a most grateful one to him. I remember when we went up to the drawing room to join the ladies after dinner, the two dear old poets, Leigh Hunt and Barry Cornwall, mounted the stairs with their arms round each other in a very tender and loving way. Hawthorne often referred to this scene as one he would not have missed for a great deal.

His renewed intercourse with Motley in England gave him peculiar pleasure, and his genius found an ardent admirer in the eminent historian. He did not go much into society at that time, but there were a few houses in London where he always seemed happy.

I met him one night at a great evening-party, looking on from a nook a little removed from the full glare of the *soirée*. Soon, however, it was whispered about that the famous American romance-writer was in the room, and an enthusiastic English lady, a genuine admirer and intelligent reader of his books, ran for her album and attacked him for " a few words and his name at the end." He looked dismally perplexed, and turning to me said imploringly in a whisper, "For pity's sake, what shall I write? I can't think of a word to add to my name. Help me to something." Thinking him partly in fun, I said, "Write an original couplet, — this one, for instance, —

> 'When this you see,
> Remember me,'"

and to my amazement he stepped forward at once to the table, wrote the foolish lines I had suggested, and, shutting the book, handed it very contentedly to the happy lady.

We sailed from England together in the month of June, as we had previously arranged, and our voyage home was, to say the least, an unusual one. We had calm summer, moonlight weather, with no storms. Mrs. Stowe was on board, and in her own cheery and delightful way she enlivened the passage with some capital stories of her early life.

When we arrived at Queenstown, the captain announced to us that, as the ship would wait there six hours, we might go ashore and see something of our Irish friends. So we chartered several jaunting-cars, after much tribulation and delay in arranging terms with the drivers thereof, and started off on a merry exploring expedition. I remember there was a good deal of racing up and down the hills of Queenstown, much shouting and laughing, and crowds of beggars howling after us for pence and beer. The Irish jaunting-car is a peculiar institution, and we all sat with our legs dangling over the road in a "dim and perilous way." Occasionally a horse would give out, for the animals were sad specimens, poorly fed and wofully driven. We were almost devoured by the ragamuffins that ran beside our wheels, and I remember the "sad civility" with which Hawthorne regarded their clamors. We had provided ourselves before starting with much small coin, which, however, gave out during our first mile. Hawthorne attempted to explain our inability further to supply their demands, having, as he said to them, nothing less than a sovereign in his pocket, when a voice from the crowd shouted, "Bedad, your honor, I can change that for ye"; and the knave actually did it on the spot.

Hawthorne's love for the sea amounted to a passionate worship; and while I (the worst sailor probably on this planet) was longing, spite of the good company on board, to reach land as soon as possible, Hawthorne was constantly saying in his quiet, earnest way, "I should like to sail on and on forever, and never touch the shore again." He liked to stand alone in the bows of the ship and see the sun go down, and he was never tired of walking the deck at midnight. I used to watch his dark, solitary figure under the stars, pacing up and down some unfrequented part of the vessel, musing and half melancholy. Sometimes he would lie down beside me and commiserate my unquiet condition. Seasickness, he declared, he could not understand, and was constantly recommending most extraordinary dishes and drinks, "all made out of the *artist's* brain," which he said were sovereign remedies for nautical illness. I remember to this day some of the preparations which, in his revelry of fancy, he would advise me to take, a farrago of good things almost rivalling "Oberon's Feast," spread out so daintily in Herrick's "Hesperides." He thought, at first, if I could bear a few roc's eggs beaten up by a mermaid on a dolphin's back, I might be benefited. He decided that a gruel made from a sheaf of Robin Hood's arrows would be strengthening. When suffering pain, "a right gude willie-waught," or a stiff cup of hemlock of the Socrates brand, before retiring, he considered very good. He said he had heard recommended a dose of salts distilled from the tears of Niobe, but he did n't approve of that remedy. He observed that he had a high opinion of hearty food, such as potted owl with Minerva sauce, airy tongues of sirens, stewed ibis, livers of Roman Capitol geese, the wings of a Phœnix not too much done, love-lorn nightingales cooked briskly over Aladdin's lamp, chicken-pies made of fowls raised by Mrs. Carey, Nautilus chowder, and the like. Fruit, by all means, should always be taken by an uneasy victim at sea, especially Atalanta pippins and purple grapes raised by Bacchus & Co. Examining my garments one day as I lay on deck, he thought I was not warmly enough clad, and he recommended, before I took another voyage, that I should fit myself out in Liverpool with a good warm shirt from the shop of Nessus & Co. in Bold Street, where I could also find stout seven-league boots to keep out the damp. He knew another shop, he said, where I could buy raven-down stockings, and sable clouds with a silver lining, most warm and comfortable for a sea voyage.

His own appetite was excellent, and day after day he used to come on deck after dinner and describe to me what he had eaten. Of course his accounts were always exaggerations, for my amusement. I remember one night he gave me a running catalogue of what food he had partaken during the day, and the sum total was convulsing from its absurdity. Among the viands he had consumed, I remember he stated there were "several yards of steak," and a "whole warrenful of Welsh rabbits." The "divine spirit of Humor" was upon him during many of those days at sea, and he revelled in it like a careless child.

That was a voyage, indeed, long to be remembered, and I shall ever look back upon it as the most satisfactory "sea turn" I ever happened to experience. I have sailed many a weary, watery mile since then, but *Hawthorne* was not on board!

The summer after his arrival home he spent quietly in Concord, at the Wayside, and illness in his family made him at times unusually sad. In one of his notes to me he says: —

"I am continually reminded nowadays of a response which I once heard a drunken sailor make to a pious gentleman, who asked him how he felt, 'Pretty d—d miserable, thank God!' It very well expresses my thorough discomfort and forced acquiescence."

Occasionally he wrote requesting me to make a change, here and there, in the new edition of his works then passing through the press. On the 23d of September, 1860, he writes: —

"Please to append the following note to the foot of the page, at the commencement of the story called 'Dr. Heidegger's Experiment, in the 'Twice-Told Tales': 'In an English Review, not long since, I have been accused of plagiarizing the idea of this story from a chapter in one of the novels of Alexandre Dumas. There has undoubtedly been a plagiarism, on one side or the other; but as my story was written a good deal more than twenty years ago, and as the novel is of considerably more recent date, I take pleasure in thinking that M. Dumas has done me the honor to appropriate one of the fanciful conceptions of my earlier days. He is heartily welcome to it; nor is it the only instance, by many, in which the great French romancer has exercised the privilege of commanding genius by confiscating the intellectual property of less famous people to his own use and behoof.'"

Hawthorne was a diligent reader of the Bible, and when sometimes, in my ignorant way, I would question, in a proof-sheet, his use of a word, he would almost always refer me to the Bible as his authority. It was a great pleasure to hear him talk about the Book of Job, and his voice would be tremulous with feeling, as he sometimes quoted a touching passage from the New Testament. In one of his letters he says to me: —

"Did not I suggest to you, last summer, the publication of the Bible in ten or twelve 12mo volumes? I think it would have great success, and, at least (but, as a publisher, I suppose this is the very smallest of your cares), it would result in the salvation of a great many souls, who will never find their way to heaven, if left to learn it from the inconvenient editions of the Scriptures now in use. It is very singular that this form of publishing the Bible in a single bulky or closely printed volume should be so long continued. It was first adopted, I suppose, as being the universal mode of publication at the time when the Bible was translated. Shakespeare, and the other old dramatists and poets, were first published in the same form; but all of them have long since been broken into dozens and scores of portable and readable volumes; and why not the Bible?"

During this period, after his return from Europe, I saw him frequently at the Wayside, in Concord. He now seemed happy in the dwelling he had put in order for the calm and comfort of his middle and later life. He had added a tower to his house, in which he could be safe from intrusion, and where he could muse and write. Never was poet or romancer more fitly shrined. Drummond at Hawthornden, Scott at Abbotsford, Dickens at Gad's Hill, Irving at Sunnyside, were not more appropriately sheltered. Shut up in his tower, he could escape from the tumult of life, and be alone with only the birds and the bees in concert outside his casement. The view from this apartment, on every side, was lovely, and Hawthorne enjoyed the charming prospect as I have known few men to enjoy nature.

His favorite walk lay near his house, — indeed it was part of his own grounds, — a little hillside, where he had worn a foot-path, and where he might be found in good weather, when not employed in the tower. While walking to and fro on this bit of rising ground he meditated and composed innumerable romances that were never written, as well as some that were. Here he first announced to me his plan of "The Dolliver Romance," and, from what he told me of his design of the story as it existed in his mind, I thought it would have been the greatest of his books. An enchanting memory is left of that morning when he laid out the whole story before me as he intended to write it. The plot was a grand one, and I tried to tell him how much I was impressed by it. Very soon after our interview, he wrote to me: —

"In compliance with your exhortations, I have begun to think seriously of that story, not, as yet, with a pen in my hand, but trudging to and fro on my hilltop. . . . . I don't mean to let you see the first chapters till I have written the final sentence of the story. Indeed, the first chapters of a story ought always to be the last written. . . . . If you want me to write a good book, send me a good pen; not a gold one, for they seldom suit me; but a pen flexible and capacious of ink, and that will not grow stiff and rheumatic the moment I get attached to it. I never met with a good pen in my life."

Time went on, the war broke out, and he had not the heart to go on with his new Romance. During the month of April, 1862, he made a visit to Washington with his friend Ticknor, to whom he was greatly attached. While on this visit to the capital he sat to Leutze for a portrait. He took a special fancy to the artist, and, while he was sitting to him, wrote a long letter to me. Here is an extract from it: —

"I stay here only while Leutze finishes a portrait, which I think will be the best ever painted of the same unworthy subject. One charm it must needs have, — an aspect of immortal jollity and well-to-doness; for Leutze, when the sitting begins, gives me a first-rate cigar, and when he sees me getting tired, he brings out a bottle of splendid champagne; and we quaffed and smoked yesterday, in a blessed state of mutual good-will, for three hours and a half, during which the picture made a really miraculous progress. Leutze is the best of fellows."

TICKNOR, FIELDS, AND HAWTHORNE

In the same letter he thus describes the sinking of the Cumberland, and I know of nothing finer in its way: —

"I see in a newspaper that Holmes is going to write a song on the sinking of the Cumberland; and feeling it to be a subject of national importance, it occurs to me that he might like to know her present condition. She lies with her three masts sticking up out of the water, and careened over, the water being nearly on a level with her maintop, — I mean that first landing-place from the deck of the vessel, after climbing the shrouds. The rigging does not appear at all damaged. There is a tattered bit of a pennant, about a foot and a half long, fluttering from the tip-top of one of the masts; but the flag, the ensign of the ship (which never was struck, thank God), is under water, so as to be quite invisible, being attached to the gaff, I think they call it, of the mizzen-mast; and though this bald description makes nothing of it, I never saw anything so gloriously forlorn as those three masts. I did not think it was in me to be so moved by any spectacle of the kind. Bodies still occasionally float up from it. The Secretary of the Navy says she shall lie there till she goes to pieces, but I suppose by and by they will sell her to some Yankee for the value of her old iron.

"P. S. My hair really is not so white as this photograph, which I enclose, makes me. The sun seems to take an infernal pleasure in making me venerable, — as if I were as old as himself."

Hawthorne has rested so long in the twilight of impersonality, that I hesitate sometimes to reveal the man even to his warmest admirers. This very day Sainte-Beuve has made me feel a fresh reluctance in unveiling my friend, and there seems almost a reproof in these words, from the eloquent French author: —

"We know nothing or nearly nothing of the life of La Bruyère, and this obscurity adds, it has been remarked, to the effect of his work, and, it may be said, to the piquant happiness of his destiny. If there was not a single line of his unique book, which from the first instant of its publication did not appear and remain in the clear light, so, on the other hand, there was not one individual detail regarding the author which was well known. Every ray of the century fell upon each page of the book and the face of the man who held it open in his hand was veiled from our sight."

Beautifully said, as usual with Sainte-Beuve, but venture, notwithstanding such eloquent warning, to proceed.

After his return home from Washington Hawthorne sent to me, during the month of May, an article for the Atlantic Monthly, which he entitled "Chiefly about War-Matters." The paper, excellently well done throughout, of course, contained a personal description of President Lincoln, which I thought, considered as a portrait of a living man, and drawn by Hawthorne, it would not be wise or tasteful to print. The office of an editor is a disagreeable one sometimes, and the case of Hawthorne on Lincoln disturbed me not a little. After reading the manuscript, I wrote to the author, and asked his permission to omit his description of the President's personal appearance. As usual — for he was the kindest and sweetest of contributors, the most good-natured and the most amenable man to advise I ever knew, — he consented to my proposal, and allowed me to print the article with the alterations. If any one will turn to the paper in the Atlantic Monthly (it is in the number for July, 1862), it will be observed there are several notes; all of these were written by Hawthorne himself. He complied with my request without a murmur, but he always thought I was wrong in my decision. He said the whole description of the interview and the President's personal appearance were, to his mind, the only parts of the article worth publishing. "What a terrible thing," he complained, "it is to try to let off a little bit of truth into this miserable humbug of a world!" President Lincoln is dead, and as Hawthorne once wrote to me, "Upon my honor, it seems to me the passage omitted has an historical value," I will copy here verbatim what I advised my friend, both on his own account and the President's, not to print nine years ago. Hawthorne and his party had gone into the President's room, annexed, as he says, as supernumeraries to a deputation from a Massachusetts whip-factory, with a present of a splendid whip to the Chief Magistrate:—

"By and by there was a little stir on the staircase and in the passage-way, and in lounged a tall, loose-jointed figure, of an exaggerated Yankee port and demeanor, whom (as being about the homeliest man I ever saw, yet by no means repulsive or disagreeable) it was impossible not to recognize as Uncle Abe.

"Unquestionably, Western man though he be, and Kentuckian by birth, President Lincoln is the essential representative of all Yankees, and the veritable specimen, physically, of what the world seems determined to regard as our characteristic qualities. It is the strangest and yet the fittest thing in the jumble of human vicissitudes, that he, out of so many millions, unlooked for, unselected by any intelligible process that could be based upon his genuine qualities, unknown to those who chose him, and unsuspected of what endowments may adapt him for his tremendous responsibility, should have found the way open for him to fling his lank personality into the chair of state,—where, I presume, it was his first impulse to throw his legs on the council-table, and tell the Cabinet Ministers a story. There is no describing his lengthy awkwardness, nor the uncouthness of his movement; and yet it seemed as if I had been in the habit of seeing him daily, and had shaken hands with him a thousand times in some village street; so true was he to the aspect of the pattern American, though with a certain extravagance which, possibly, I exaggerated still further by the delighted eagerness with which I took it in. If put to guess his calling and livelihood, I should have taken him for a country schoolmaster as soon as anything else. He was dressed in a rusty black frock-coat and pantaloons, unbrushed, and worn so faithfully that the suit had adapted itself to the curves and angularities of his figure, and had grown to be an outer skin of the man. He had shabby slippers on his feet. His hair was black, still unmixed with gray, stiff, somewhat bushy, and had apparently been acquainted with neither brush nor comb that morning, after the disarrangement of the pillow; and as to a nightcap, Uncle Abe probably knows nothing of such effeminacies. His complexion is dark and sallow, betokening, I fear, an insalubrious atmosphere around the White House; he has thick black eyebrows and an impending brow; his nose is large, and the lines about his mouth are very strongly defined.

"The whole physiognomy is as coarse a one as you would meet anywhere in the length and breadth of the States; but, withal, it is redeemed, illuminated, softened, and brightened by a kindly though serious look out of his eyes, and an expression of homely sagacity, that seems weighted with rich results of village experience. A great deal of native sense; no bookish cultivation, no refinement; honest at heart, and thoroughly so, and yet, in some sort, sly,— at least, endowed with a sort of tact and wisdom that are akin to craft, and would impel him, I think, to take an antagonist in flank, rather than to make a bull-run at him right in front. But, on the whole, I liked this sallow, queer, sagacious visage, with the homely human sympathies that warmed it; and, for my small share in the matter, would as lief have Uncle Abe for a ruler as any man whom it would have been practicable to put in his place.

"Immediately on his entrance the President accosted our member of Congress, who had us in charge, and, with a comical twist of his face, made some jocular remark about the length of his breakfast. He then greeted us all round, not waiting for an introduction, but shaking and squeezing everybody's hand with the utmost cordiality, whether the individual's name was announced to him or not. His manner towards us was wholly without pretence, but yet had a kind of natural dignity, quite sufficient to keep the forwardest of us from clapping him on the shoulder and asking for a story. A mutual acquaintance being established, our leader took the whip out of its case, and began to read the address of presentation. The whip was an exceedingly long one, its handle wrought in ivory (by some artist in the Massachusetts State Prison, I believe), and ornamented with a medallion of the President, and other equally beautiful devices; and along its whole length there was a succession of golden bands and ferrules. The address was shorter than the whip, but equally well made, consisting chiefly of an explanatory description of these artistic designs, and closing with a hint that the gift was a suggestive and emblematic one, and that the President would recognize the use to which such an instrument should be put.

"This suggestion gave Uncle Abe rather a delicate task in his reply, because, slight as the matter seemed, it apparently called for some declaration, or intimation, or faint foreshadowing of policy in reference to the conduct of the war, and the final treatment of the Rebels. But the President's Yankee aptness and not-to-be-caughtness stood him in good stead, and he jerked or wiggled himself out of the dilemma with an uncouth dexterity that was entirely in character; although, without his gesticulation of eye and mouth, — and especially the flourish of the whip, with which he imagined himself touching up a pair of fat horses, — I doubt whether his words would be worth recording, even if I could remember them. The gist of the reply was, that he accepted the whip as an emblem of peace, not punishment; and, this great affair over, we retired out of the presence in high good-humor, only regretting that we could not have seen the President sit down and fold up his legs (which is said to be a most extraordinary spectacle), or have heard him tell one of those delectable stories for which he is so celebrated. A good many of them are afloat upon the common talk of Washington, and are certainly the aptest, pithiest, and funniest little things imaginable; though, to be sure, they smack of the frontier freedom, and would not always bear repetition in a drawing-room, or on the immaculate page of the Atlantic."

So runs the passage which caused some good-natured discussion nine years ago, between the contributor and the editor. Perhaps I was squeamish not to have been willing to print this matter at that time. Some persons, no doubt, will adopt that opinion, but as both President and author have long ago met on the other side of criticism and magazines, we will leave the subject to their decision, they being most interested in the transaction. I did what seemed best in 1862. In 1871 "circumstances have changed" with both parties, and I venture to-day what I hardly dared then.

Whenever I look at Hawthorne's portrait, and that is pretty often, some new trait or anecdote or reminiscence comes up and clamors to be made known to those who feel an interest in it. But time and eternity call loudly for mortal gossip to be brief, and I must hasten to my last session over that child of genius, who first saw the light on the 4th of July, 1804.

One of his favorite books was Lockhart's Life of Sir

Walter Scott, and in 1862 I dedicated to him the Household Edition of that work. When he received the first volume, he wrote to me a letter of which I am so proud that I keep it among my best treasures.

"I am exceedingly gratified by the dedication. I do not deserve so high an honor; but if you think me worthy, it is enough to make the compliment in the highest degree acceptable, no matter who may dispute my title to it. I care more for your good opinion than for that of a host of critics, and have an excellent reason for so doing; inasmuch as my literary success, whatever it has been or may be, is the result of my connection with you. Somehow or other you smote the rock of public sympathy on my behalf, and a stream gushed forth in sufficient quantity to quench my thirst though not to drown me. I think no author can ever have had publisher that he valued so much as I do mine."

He began in 1862 to send me some articles from his English Journal for the Atlantic magazine, which he afterwards collected into a volume and called "Our Old Home." On forwarding one for December of that year he says: —

"I hope you will like it, for the subject seemed interesting to me when I was on the spot, but I always feel a singular despondency and heaviness of heart in reopening those old journals now. However, if I can make readable sketches out of them, it is no matter."

In the same letter he tells me he has been re-reading Scott's Life, and he suggests some additions to the concluding volume. He says: —

"If the last volume is not already printed and stereotyped, I think you ought to insert in it an explanation of all that is left mysterious in the former volumes, — the name and family of the lady he was in love with, etc. It is desirable, too, to know what have been the fortunes and final catastrophes of his family and intimate friends since his death, down to as recent a period as the death of Lockhart. All such matter would make your edition more valuable; and I see no reason why you should be bound by the deference to living connections of the family that may prevent the English publishers from inserting these particulars. We stand in the light of posterity to them, and have the privileges of posterity. . . . . I should be glad to know something of the personal character and life of his eldest son, and whether (as I have heard) he was ashamed of his father for being a literary man. In short, fifty pages devoted to such elucidation would make the edition unique. Do come and see us before the leaves fall."

While he was engaged in copying out and rewriting his papers on England for the magazine he was despondent about their reception by the public. Speaking of them, one day, to me, he said: "We must remember that there is a good deal of intellectual ice mingled with this wine of memory." He was sometimes so dispirited during the war that he was obliged to postpone his contributions for sheer lack of spirit to go on. Near the close of the year 1862 he writes: —

"I am delighted at what you tell me about the kind appreciation of my articles, for I feel rather gloomy about them myself. I am really much encouraged by what you say; not but what I am sensible that you mollify me with a good deal of soft soap, but it is skilfully applied and effects all you intend it should. . . . . I cannot come to Boston to spend more than a day, just at present. It would suit me better to come for a visit when the spring of next year is a little advanced, and if you renew your hospitable proposition then, I shall probably be glad to accept it; though I have now been a hermit so long, that the thought affects me somewhat as it would to invite a lobster or a crab to step out of his shell."

He continued, during the early months of 1863, to send now and then an article for the magazine from his English Note-Books. On the 22d of February he writes: —

"Here is another article. I wish it would not be so wretchedly long, but there are many things which I shall find no opportunity to say unless I say them now; so the article grows under my hand, and one part of it seems just about as well worth printing as another. Heaven sees fit to visit me with an unshakable conviction that all this series of articles is good for nothing; but that is none of my business, provided the public and you are of a different opinion. If you think any part of it can be left out with advantage, you are quite at liberty to do so. Probably I have not put Leigh Hunt quite high enough for your sentiments respecting him; but no more genuine characterization and criticism (so far as the writer's purpose to be true goes) was ever done. It is very slight. I might have made more of it, but should not have improved it.

"I mean to write two more of these articles, and then hold my hand. I intend to come to Boston before the end of this week, if the weather is good. It must be nearly or quite six months since I was there! I wonder how many people there are in the world who would keep their nerves in tolerably good order through such a length of nearly solitary imprisonment?"

I advised him to begin to put the series in order for a volume, and to preface the book with his "Consular Experiences." On the 18th of April he writes:—

"I don't think the public will bear any more of this sort of thing. .... I had a letter from ——, the other day, in which he sends me the enclosed verses, and I think he would like to have them published in the Atlantic. Do it if you like, I pretend to no judgment in poetry. He also sent this epithalamium by Mrs. ——, and I doubt not the good lady will be pleased to see it copied into one of our American newspapers with a few laudatory remarks. Can't you do it in the Transcript, and send her a copy? You cannot imagine how a little praise jollifies us poor authors to the marrow of our bones. Consider, if you had not been a publisher, you would certainly have been one of our wretched tribe, and therefore ought to have a fellow-feeling for us. Let Michael Angelo write the remarks, if you have not the time."

("Michael Angelo" was a clever little Irish-boy who had the care of my room. Hawthorne conceived a fancy for the lad, and liked to hear stories of his smart replies to persistent authors who called during my absence with unpromising-looking manuscripts.) On the 30th of April he writes:—

"I send the article with which the volume is to commence, and you can begin printing it whenever you like. I can think of no better title than this, 'Our Old Home; a Series of English Sketches, by,' etc. I submit to your judgment whether it would not be well to print these 'Consular Experiences' in the volume without depriving them of any freshness they may have by previous publication in the magazine?

"The article has some of the features that attract the curiosity of the foolish public, being made up of personal narrative and gossip, with a few pungencies of personal satire, which will not be the less effective because the reader can scarcely find out who was the individual meant. I am not without hope of drawing down upon myself a good deal of critical severity on this score, and would gladly incur more of it if I could do so without seriously deserving censure.

"The story of the Doctor of Divinity, I think, will prove a good card in this way. It is every bit true (like the other anecdotes), only not told so darkly as it might have been for the reverend gentleman. I do not believe there is any danger of his identity being ascertained, and do not care whether it is or no, as it could only be done by the impertinent researches of other people. It seems to me quite essential to have some novelty in the collected volume, and, if possible, something that may excite a little discussion and remark. But decide for yourself and me; and if you conclude not to publish it in the magazine, I think I can concoct another article in season for the August number, if you wish. After the publication of the volume, it seems to me the public had better have no more of them.

"J—— has been telling us a mythical story of your intending to walk with him from Cambridge to Concord. We should be delighted to see you, though more for our own sakes than yours, for our aspect here is still a little winterish. When you come, let it be on Saturday, and stay till Monday. I am hungry to talk with you."

I was enchanted, of course, with the "Consular Experiences," and find from his letters, written at that time, that he was made specially happy by the encomiums I could not help sending upon that inimitable sketch. When the "Old Home" was nearly all in type, he began to think about a dedication to the book. On the 3d of May he writes: —

"I am of three minds about dedicating the volume. First, it seems due to Frank Pierce (as he put me into the position where I made all those profound observations of English scenery, life, and character) to inscribe it to him with a few pages of friendly and explanatory talk, which also would be very gratifying to my own lifelong affection for him.

"Secondly, I want to say something to Bennoch to show him that I am thoroughly mindful of all his hospitality and kindness; and I suppose he might be pleased to see his name at the head of a book of mine.

"Thirdly, I am not convinced that it is worth while to inscribe it to anybody. We will see hereafter."

The book moved on slowly through the press, and he seemed more than commonly nervous about the proof-sheets. On the 28th of May he says in a note to me: —

"In a proof-sheet of 'Our Old Home' which I sent you to-day (page 43, or 4, or 5 or thereabout) I corrected a line thus, 'possessing a happy faculty of seeing my own interest.' Now as the public interest was my sole and individual object while I held office, I think that as a matter of scanty justice to myself, the line ought to stand thus, 'possessing a happy faculty of seeing my own interest and the public's.' Even then, you see, I only give myself credit for half the disinterestedness I really felt. Pray, by all means, have it altered as above, even if the page is stereotyped; which it can't have been, as the proof is now in the Concord post-office, and you will have it at the same time with this.

"We are getting into full leaf here, and your walk with J—— might come off any time."

An arrangement was made with the liberal house of Smith and Elder, of London, to bring out "Our Old Home" on the same day of its publication in Boston. On the 1st of July Hawthorne wrote to me from the Wayside as follows: —

"I am delighted with Smith and Elder, or rather with you; for it is you that squeeze the English sovereigns out of the poor devils. On my own behalf I never could have thought of asking more than £50, and should hardly have expected to get £10; I look upon the £180 as the only trustworthy funds I have, our own money being of such a gaseous consistency. By the time I can draw for it, I expect it will be worth at least fifteen hundred dollars.

"I shall think over the prefatory matter for 'Our Old Home' to-day, and will write it to-morrow. It requires some little thought and policy in order to say nothing amiss at this time; for I intend to dedicate the book to Frank Pierce, come what may. It shall reach you on Friday morning.

"We find —— a comfortable and desirable guest to have in the house. My wife likes her hugely, and for my part, I had no idea that there was such a sensible woman of letters in the world. She is just as healthy-minded as if she had never touched a pen. I am glad she had a pleasant time, and hope she will come back.

"I mean to come to Boston whenever I can be sure of a cool day.

"What a prodigious length of time you stayed among the mountains!

"You ought not to assume such liberties of absence without the consent of your friends, which I hardly think you would get. I, at least, want you always within attainable distance, even though I never see you. Why can't you come and stay a day or two with us, and drink some spruce beer?"

Those were troublous days, full of war gloom and general despondency. The North was naturally suspicious of all public men, who did not bear a conspicuous part in helping to put down the Rebellion. General Pierce had been President of the United States, and was not identified, to say the least, with the great party which favored the vigorous prosecution of the war. Hawthorne proposed to dedicate his new book to a very dear friend, indeed, but in doing so he would draw public attention in a marked way to an unpopular name. Several of Hawthorne's friends, on learning that he intended to inscribe his book to Franklin Pierce, came to me and begged that I would, if possible, help Hawthorne to see that he ought not to do anything to jeopardize the currency of his new volume. Accordingly I wrote to him, just what many of his friends had said to me, and this is his reply to my letter, which bears date the 18th of July, 1863: —

"I thank you for your note of the 15th instant, and have delayed my reply thus long in order to ponder deeply on your advice, smoke cigars over it, and see what it might be possible for me to do towards taking it. I find that it would be a piece of poltroonery in me to withdraw either the dedication or the dedicatory letter. My long and intimate personal relations with Pierce render the dedication altogether proper, especially as regards this book, which would have had no existence without his kindness; and if he is so exceedingly unpopular that his name is enough to sink the volume, there is so much the more need that an old friend should stand by him. I cannot, merely on account of pecuniary profit or literary reputation, go back from what I have deliberately felt and thought it right to do; and if I were to tear out the dedication, I should never look at the volume again without remorse and shame. As for the literary public, it must accept my book precisely as I think fit to give it, or let it alone.

"Nevertheless, I have no fancy for making myself a martyr when it is honorably and conscientiously possible to avoid it; and I always measure out my heroism very accurately according to the exigencies of the occasion, and should be the last man in the world to throw away a bit of it needlessly. So I have looked over the concluding paragraph and have amended it in such a way that, while doing what I know to be justice to my friend, it contains not a word that ought to be objectionable to any set of readers. If the public of the North see fit to ostracize me for this, I can only say that I would gladly sacrifice a thousand or two of dollars rather than retain the good-will of such a herd of dolts and mean-spirited scoundrels. I enclose the rewritten paragraph, and shall wish to see a proof of that and the whole dedication.

"I had a call from an Englishman yesterday, and kept him to dinner; not the threatened ——, but a Mr. ——, introduced by ——. He says he knows you, and he seems to be a very good fellow. I have strong hopes that he will never come back here again, for J—— took him on a walk of several miles, whereby they both caught a most tremendous ducking, and the poor Englishman was frightened half to death by the thunder. . . . . On the other page is the list of presentation people, and it amounts to twenty-four, which your liberality and kindness allow me. As likely as not I have forgotten two or three, and I held my pen suspended over one or two of the names, doubting whether they deserved of me so especial a favor as a portion of my heart and brain. I have few friends. Some authors, I should think, would require half the edition for private distribution."

"Our Old Home" was published in the autumn of 1863, and although it was everywhere welcomed, in England the strictures were applied with a liberal hand. On the 18th of October he writes to me: —

"You sent me the 'Reader' with a notice of the book, and I have received one or two others, one of them from Bennoch. The English critics seem to think me very bitter against their countrymen, and it is, perhaps, natural that they should, because their self-conceit can accept nothing short of indiscriminate adulation; but I really think that Americans have more cause than they to complain of me. Looking over the volume, I am rather surprised to find that whenever I draw a comparison between the two people, I almost invariably cast the balance against ourselves. It is not a good nor a weighty book, nor does it deserve any great amount either of praise or censure. I don't care about seeing any more notices of it."

Meantime the "Dolliver Romance," which had been laid aside on account of the exciting scenes through which we were then passing, and which unfitted him for the composition of a work of the imagination, made little progress. In a note written to me at this time he says:—

"I can't tell you when to expect an instalment of the Romance, if ever. There is something preternatural in my reluctance to begin. I linger at the threshold, and have a perception of very disagreeable phantasms to be encountered if I enter. I wish God had given me the faculty of writing a sunshiny book."

I invited him to come to Boston and have a cheerful week among his old friends, and threw in as an inducement a hint that he should hear the great organ in the Music Hall. I also suggested that we could talk over the new Romance together, if he would gladden us all by coming to the city. Instead of coming, he sent this reply:—

"I thank you for your kind invitation to hear the grand instrument; but it offers me no inducement additional to what I should always have for a visit to your abode. I have no ear for an organ or a jewsharp, nor for any instrument between the two; so you had better invite a worthier guest, and I will come another time.

"I don't see much probability of my having the first chapter of the Romance ready so soon as you want it. There are two or three chapters ready to be written, but I am not yet robust enough to begin, and I feel as if I should never carry it through.

"Besides, I want to prefix a little sketch of Thoreau to it, because, from a tradition which he told me about this house of mine, I got the idea of a deathless man, which is now taking a shape very different from the original one. It seems the duty of a live literary man to perpetuate the memory of a dead one, when there is such fair opportunity as in this case: but how Thoreau would scorn me for thinking that *I* could perpetuate him! And I don't think so.

"I can think of no title for the unborn Romance. Always heretofore I have waited till it was quite complete before attempting to name it, and I fear I shall have to do so now. I wish you or Mrs. Fields would suggest one. Perhaps you may snatch a title out of the infinite void that will miraculously suit the book, and give me a needful impetus to write it.

"I want a great deal of money. . . . . I wonder how people manage to live economically. I seem to spend little or nothing, and yet it will get very far beyond the second thousand, for the present year. . . . . If it were not for these troublesome necessities, I doubt whether you would ever see so much as the first chapter of the new Romance.

"Those verses entitled 'Weariness,' in the last magazine, seem to me profoundly touching. I too am weary, and begin to look ahead for the Wayside Inn."

I had frequent accounts of his ill health and changed appearance, but I supposed he would rally again soon, and become hale and strong before the winter fairly set in. But the shadows even then were about his pathway, and Allan Cunningham's lines, which he once quoted to me, must often have occurred to him, —

> "Cauld 's the snaw at my head,
> And cauld at my feet,
> And the finger o' death 's at my een,
> Closing them to sleep."

We had arranged together that the "Dolliver Romance" should be first published in the magazine, in monthly instalments, and we decided to begin in the January number of 1864. On the 8th of November came a long letter from him : —

Concord Oct 5th 1841

Dear French,

I send you Williams' letter as the best remembrancer to one of those "whose acquaintance he had the pleasure to form while in Concord." It came quite unexpectedly to me, but I was very glad to receive it — though I hardly know whether my utmost sincerity and interest can inspire a sufficient answer — but I should like to have you send it back by some convenient opportunity.

Pray let me know what you are thinking about any day,— what most nearly concerns you.— Last winter, you know, you did more than your share of the talking, and I did not complain for want of an opportunity.— Imagine your stove-door out of order, at least, and that while I am fixing it, you will think of enough things to say.

What makes the value of your life at present? What dreams have you? and what realizations? You know there is a

high table-land which
not even the east wind
reaches,— Now, can't
we walk and chat upon
its plane still, as if there
were no lower latitudes?
Surely our two destinies
are topics interesting and
grand enough for any
occasion. I hope you have
many gleams of serenity
and health, or if your
body will grant you
no positive respite — that you
may, at any rate, enjoy
your sickness occasionally,
as much as I used to
tell you— But here is
the bungle going to

be done up, so accept
a "good-night" from
		Henry D. Thoreau

Mrs. Lucy G. Brown
		Plymouth

"I foresee that there is little probability of my getting the first chapter ready by the 15th, although I have a resolute purpose to write it by the end of the month. It will be in time for the February number, if it turns out fit for publication at all. As to the title, we must defer settling that till the book is fully written, and meanwhile I see nothing better than to call the series of articles 'Fragments of a Romance.' This will leave me to exercise greater freedom as to the mechanism of the story than I otherwise can, and without which I shall probably get entangled in my own plot. When the work is completed in the magazine, I can fill up the gaps and make straight the crookednesses, and christen it with a fresh title. In this untried experiment of a serial work I desire not to pledge myself, or promise the public more than I may confidently expect to achieve. As regards the sketch of Thoreau, I am not ready to write it yet, but will mix him up with the life of The Wayside, and produce an autobiographical preface for the finished Romance. If the public like that sort of stuff, I too find it pleasant and easy writing, and can supply a new chapter of it for every new volume, and that, moreover, without infringing upon my proper privacy. An old Quaker wrote me, the other day, that he had been reading my Introduction to the 'Mosses' and the 'Scarlet Letter,' and felt as if he knew me better than his best friend; but I think he considerably overestimates the extent of his intimacy with me.

"I received several private letters and printed notices of 'Our Old Home' from England. It is laughable to see the innocent wonder with which they regard my criticisms, accounting for them by jaundice, insanity, jealousy, hatred, on my part, and never admitting the least suspicion that there may be a particle of truth in them. The monstrosity of their self-conceit is such that anything short of unlimited admiration impresses them as malicious caricature. But they do me great injustice in supposing that I hate them. I would as soon hate my own people.

"Tell Ticknor that I want a hundred dollars more, and I suppose I shall keep on wanting more and more till the end of my days. If I subside into the almshouse before my intellectual faculties are quite extinguished, it strikes me that I would make a very pretty book out of it; and, seriously, if I alone were concerned, I should not have any great objection to winding up there."

On the 14th of November came a pleasant little note from him, which seemed to have been written in better spirits than he had shown of late. Photographs of himself always amused him greatly, and in the little note I refer to there is this pleasant passage: —

"Here is the photograph, — a grandfatherly old figure enough; and I suppose that is the reason why you select it.

"I am much in want of *cartes de visite* to distribute on my own account, and am tired and disgusted with all the undesirable likenesses as yet presented of me. Don't you think I might sell my head to some photographer who would be willing to return me the value in small change; that is to say, in a dozen or two of cards?"

The first part of Chapter I. of "The Dolliver Romance" came to me from the Wayside on the 1st of December. Hawthorne was very anxious to see it in type as soon as possible, in order that he might compose the rest in a similar strain, and so conclude the preliminary phase of Dr. Dolliver. He was constantly imploring me to send him a good pen, complaining all the while that everything had failed him in that line. In one of his notes begging me to hunt him up something that he could write with, he says: —

"Nobody ever suffered more from pens than I have, and I am glad that my labor with the abominable little tool is drawing to a close."

In the month of December Hawthorne attended the funeral of Mrs. Franklin Pierce, and, after the ceremony, came to stay with us. He seemed ill and more nervous than usual. He said he found General Pierce greatly needing his companionship, for he was overwhelmed with grief at the loss of his wife. I well remember the sadness of Hawthorne's face when he told us he felt obliged to look on the dead. "It was," said he, "like a carven image laid in its richly embossed enclosure, and there was a remote expression about it as if the whole had nothing to do with things present." He told us, as an instance of the ever-constant courtesy of his friend General Pierce, that while they were standing at the grave, the General, though completely overcome with his own sorrow, turned and drew up the collar of Hawthorne's coat to shield him from the bitter cold.

The same day, as the sunset deepened and we sat together, Hawthorne began to talk in an autobiographical vein, and gave us the story of his early life, of which I have already written somewhat. He said at an early age he accompanied his mother and sister to the township in Maine, which his grandfather had purchased. That, he continued, was the happiest period of his life, and it lasted through several years, when he was sent to school in Salem. "I lived in Maine," he said, "like a bird of the air, so perfect was the freedom I enjoyed. But it was there I first got my cursed habits of solitude." During the moonlight nights of winter he would skate until midnight all alone upon Sebago Lake, with the deep shadows of the icy hills on either hand. When he found himself far away from his home and weary with the exertion of skating, he would sometimes take refuge in a log-cabin, where half a tree would be burning on the broad hearth. He would sit in the ample chimney and look at the stars through the great aperture through which the flames went roaring up. "Ah," he said, "how well I recall the summer days also, when, with my gun, I roamed at will through the woods of Maine. How sad middle life looks to people of erratic temperaments. Everything is beautiful in youth, for all things are allowed to it then."

The early home of the Hawthornes in Maine must have been a lonely dwelling-place indeed. A year ago (May 12, 1870) the old place was visited by one who had a true feeling for Hawthorne's genius, and who thus graphically described the spot.

"A little way off the main-travelled road in the town of Raymond there stood an old house which has much in common with houses of its day, but which is distinguished from them by the more evident marks of neglect and decay. Its unpainted walls are deeply stained by time. Cornice and window-ledge and threshold are fast falling with the weight of years. The fences were long since removed from all the enclosures, the garden-wall is broken down, and the garden itself is now grown up to pines whose shadows fall dark and heavy upon the old and mossy roof; fitting roof-trees for such a mansion, planted there by the hands of Nature herself, as if she could not realize that her darling child was ever to go out from his early home. The highway once passed its door, but the location of the road has been changed; and now the old house stands solitarily apart from the busy world. Longer than I can remember, and I have never learned how long, this house has stood untenanted and wholly unused, except, for a few years, as a place of public worship; but, for myself, and for all who know its earlier history, it will ever have the deepest interest, for it was *the early home of Nathaniel Hawthorne.*

"Often have I, when passing through that town, turned aside to study the features of that landscape, and to reflect upon the influence which his surroundings had upon the development of this author's genius. A few rods to the north runs a little mill-stream, its sloping bank once covered with grass, now so worn and washed by the rains as to show but little except yellow sand. Less than half a mile to the west, this stream empties into an arm of Sebago Lake. Doubtless, at the time the house was built, the forest was so much cut away in that direction as to bring into view the waters of the lake, for a mill was built upon the brook about half-way down the valley, and it is reasonable to suppose that a clearing was made from the mill to the landing upon the shore of the pond; but the pines have so far regained their old dominion as completely to shut out the whole prospect in that direction. Indeed, the site affords but a limited survey, except to the northwest. Across a narrow valley in that direction lie open fields and dark pine-covered slopes. Beyond these rise long ranges of forest-crowned hills, while in the far distance every hue of rock and tree, of field and grove, melts into the soft blue of Mount Washington. The spot must ever have had the utter loneliness of the pine forests upon the borders of our northern lakes. The deep silence and dark shadows of the old woods must have filled the imagination of a youth possessing Hawthorne's sensibility with images which later years could not dispel.

"To this place came the widowed mother of Hawthorne in company with her brother, an original proprietor and one of the early settlers of the town of Raymond. This house was built for her, and here she lived with her son for several years in the most complete seclusion. Perhaps she strove to conceal here a grief which she could not forget. In what way, and to what extent, the surroundings of his boyhood operated in moulding the character and developing the genius of that gifted author, I leave to the reader to determine. I have tried simply to draw a faithful picture of his early home."

On the 15th of December Hawthorne wrote to me: —

"I have not yet had courage to read the Dolliver proof-sheet, but will set about it soon, though with terrible reluctance, such as I never felt before. . . . . I am most grateful to you for protecting me from that visitation of the elephant and his cub. If you happen to see Mr. —— of L——, a young man who was here last summer, pray tell him anything that your conscience will let you, to induce him to spare me another visit, which I know he intended. I really am not well and cannot be disturbed by strangers without more suffering than it is worth while to endure. I thank Mrs. F—— and yourself for your kind hospitality, past and prospective. I never come to see you without feeling the better for it, but I must not test so precious a remedy too often."

The new year found him incapacitated from writing much on the Romance. On the 17th of January, 1864, he says: —

"I am not quite up to writing yet, but shall make an effort as soon as I see any hope of success. You ought to be thankful that (like most other broken-down authors) I do not pester you with decrepit pages, and insist upon your accepting them as full of the old spirit and vigor. That trouble, perhaps, still awaits you, after I shall have reached a further stage of decay. Seriously, my mind has, for the present, lost its temper and its fine edge, and I have an instinct that I had better keep quiet. Perhaps I shall have a new spirit of vigor, if I wait quietly for it; perhaps not."

The end of February found him in a mood which is best indicated in this letter, which he addressed to me on the 25th of the month: —

"I hardly know what to say to the public about this abortive

Romance, though I know pretty well what the case will be. I shall never finish it. Yet it is not quite pleasant for an author to announce himself, or to be announced, as finally broken down as to his literary faculty. It is a pity that I let you put this work in your programme for the year, for I had always a presentiment that it would fail us at the pinch. Say to the public what you think best, and as little as possible; for example: 'We regret that Mr. Hawthorne's Romance, announced for this magazine some months ago, still lies upon the author's writing-table, he having been interrupted in his labor upon it by an impaired state of health'; or, 'We are sorry to hear (but know not whether the public will share our grief) that Mr. Hawthorne is out of health and is thereby prevented, for the present, from proceeding with another of his promised (or threatened) Romances, intended for this magazine'; or, 'Mr. Hawthorne's brain is addled at last, and, much to our satisfaction, he tells us that he cannot possibly go on with the Romance announced on the cover of the January magazine. We consider him finally shelved, and shall take early occasion to bury him under a heavy article, carefully summing up his merits (such as they were) and his demerits, what few of them can be touched upon in our limited space'; or, 'We shall commence the publication of Mr. Hawthorne's Romance as soon as that gentleman chooses to forward it. We are quite at a loss how to account for this delay in the fulfilment of his contract; especially as he has already been most liberally paid for the first number.' Say anything you like, in short, though I really don't believe that the public will care what you say or whether you say anything. If you choose, you may publish the first chapter as an insulated fragment, and charge me with the overpayment. I cannot finish it unless a great change comes over me; and if I make too great an effort to do so, it will be my death; not that I should care much for that, if I could fight the battle through and win it, thus ending a life of much smoulder and scanty fire in a blaze of glory. But I should smother myself in mud of my own making. I mean to come to Boston soon, not for a week but for a single day, and then I can talk about my sanitary prospects more freely than I choose to write. I am not low-spirited, nor fanciful, nor freakish, but look what seem to be realities in the face, and am ready to take whatever may come. If I could but go to England now, I think that the sea voyage and the 'Old Home' might set me all right.

"This letter is for your own eye, and I wish especially that no echo of it may come back in your notes to me.

"P. S. Give my kindest regards to Mrs. F——, and tell her that one of my choicest ideal places is her drawing-room and therefore I seldom visit it."

On Monday, the 28th of March, Hawthorne came to town and made my house his first station on a journey to the South for health. I was greatly shocked at his invalid appearance, and he seemed quite deaf. The light in his eye was beautiful as ever, but his limbs seemed shrunken and his usual stalwart vigor utterly gone. He said to me with a pathetic voice, "Why does Nature treat us like little children! I think we could bear it all if we knew our fate; at least it would not make much difference to me now what became of me." Toward night he brightened up a little, and his delicious wit flashed out, at intervals, as of old; but he was evidently broken and dispirited about his health. Looking out on the bay that was sparkling in the moonlight, he said he thought the moon rather lost something of its charm for him as he grew older. He spoke with great delight of a little story, called "Pet Marjorie," and said he had read it carefully through twice, every word of it. He had much to say about England, and observed, among other things, that "the extent over which her dominions are spread leads her to fancy herself stronger than she really is; but she is not to-day a powerful empire; she is much like a squash-vine, which runs over a whole garden, but, if you cut it at the root, it is at once destroyed." At breakfast, next morning, he spoke of his kind neighbors in Concord, and said Alcott was one of the most excellent men he had ever known. "It is impossible to quarrel with him, for he would take all your harsh words like a saint."

He left us shortly after this for a journey to Washington, with his friend Mr. Ticknor. The travellers spent several days in New York, and then proceeded to Philadelphia. Hawthorne wrote to me from the Continental

Hotel, dating his letter "Saturday evening," announcing the severe illness of his companion. He did not seem to anticipate a fatal result, but on Sunday morning the news came that Mr. Ticknor was dead. Hawthorne returned at once to Boston, and stayed here over night. He was in a very excited and nervous state, and talked incessantly of the sad scenes he had just been passing through. We sat late together, conversing of the friend we had lost, and I am sure he hardly closed his eyes that night. In the morning he went back to his own home in Concord.

His health, from that time, seemed to give way rapidly, and in the middle of May his friend, General Pierce, proposed that they should go among the New Hampshire hills together and meet the spring there.

The first letter we received from Mrs. Hawthorne[*] after her husband's return to Concord in April gave us great anxiety. It was dated "Monday eve," and here are some extracts from it: —

"I have just sent Mr. Hawthorne to bed, and so have a moment to speak to you. Generally it has been late and I have not liked to disturb him by sitting up after him, and so I could not write since he returned, though I wished very much to tell you about him, ever since he came home. He came back unlooked for that day; and when I heard a step on the piazza, I was lying on a couch and feeling quite indisposed. But as soon as I saw him I was frightened out of all knowledge of myself, — so haggard, so white, so deeply

---

[*] As I write this paragraph, my friend, the Reverend James Freeman Clarke, puts into my hand the following note, which Hawthorne sent to him nearly thirty years ago: —

54 Pinckney Street, Friday, July 8, 1842.

My dear Sir, — Though personally a stranger to you, I am about to request of you the greatest favor which I can receive from any man. I am to be married to Miss Sophia Peabody; and it is our mutual desire that you should perform the ceremony. Unless it should be decidedly a rainy day, a carriage will call for you at half past eleven o'clock in the forenoon.

Very respectfully yours,
Nath. Hawthorne.

Rev. James F. Clarke, Chestnut Street.

scored with pain and fatigue was the face, so much more ill he looked than I ever saw him before. He had walked from the station because he saw no carriage there, and his brow was streaming with a perfect rain, so great had been the effort to walk so far. .... He needed much to get home to me, where he could fling off all care of himself and give way to his feelings, pent up and kept back for so long, especially since his watch and ward of most excellent, kind Mr. Ticknor. It relieved him somewhat to break down as he spoke of that scene. .... But he was so weak and weary he could not sit up much, and lay on the couch nearly all the time in a kind of uneasy somnolency, not wishing to be read to even, not able to attend or fix his thoughts at all. On Saturday he unfortunately took cold, and, after a most restless night, was seized early in the morning with a very bad stiff neck, which was acutely painful all Sunday. Sunday night, however, a compress of linen wrung in cold water cured him, with belladonna. But he slept also most of this morning. .... He could as easily build London as go to the Shakespeare dinner. It tires him so much to get entirely through his toilet in the morning, that he has to lie down a long time after it. To-day he walked out on the grounds, and could not stay ten minutes, because I would not let him sit down in the wind, and he could not bear any longer exercise. He has more than lost all he gained by the journey, by the sad event. From being the nursed and cared for, — early to bed and late to rise, — led, as it were, by the ever-ready hand of kind Mr. Ticknor, to become the nurse and night-watcher with all the responsibilities, with his mighty power of sympathy and his vast apprehension of suffering in others, and to see death for the first time in a state so weak as his, — the death also of so valued a friend, — as Mr. Hawthorne says himself, 'it told upon him' fearfully. There are lines ploughed on his brow which never were there before. .... I have been up and alert ever since his return, but one day I was obliged, when he was busy, to run off and lie down for fear I should drop before his eyes. My head was in such an agony I could not endure it another moment. But I am well now. I have wrestled and won, and now I think I shall not fail again. Your most generous kindness of hospitality I heartily thank you for, but Mr. Hawthorne says he cannot leave home. He wants rest, and he says when the wind is *warm* he shall feel well. This cold wind ruins him. I wish he were in Cuba or on some isle in the Gulf Stream. But I must say I could not think him able to go anywhere, unless I could go with him. He is too weak to take care of himself. I do not like to have him go up and down stairs alone. I have read to him all the afternoon and evening and after he walked in the morning to-day. I do nothing but sit with him, ready to do or not to do, just as he wishes. The wheels of my small *ménage* are all stopped. He is my world and all the business of it. He has not smiled since he came home till to-day, and I made him laugh with Thackeray's humor in reading to him; but a smile looks strange on a face that once shone like a thousand suns with smiles. The light for the time has gone out of his eyes, entirely. An infinite weariness films them quite. I thank Heaven that summer and not winter approaches."

On Friday evening of the same week Mrs. Hawthorne sent off another despatch to us: —

"Mr. Hawthorne has been miserably ill for two or three days, so that I could not find a moment to speak to you. I am most anxious to have him leave Concord again, and General Pierce's plan is admirable, now that the General is well himself. I think the serene jog-trot in a private carriage into country places, by trout-streams and to old farm-houses, away from care and news, will be very restorative. The boy associations with the General will refresh him. They will fish, and muse, and rest, and saunter upon horses' feet, and be in the air all the time in fine weather. I am quite content, though I wish I could go for a few *petits soins*. But General Pierce has been a most tender, constant nurse for many years, and knows how to take care of the sick. And his love for Mr. Hawthorne is the strongest passion of his soul, now his wife is departed. They will go to the Isles of Shoals together probably, before their return.

"Mr. Hawthorne cannot walk ten minutes now without wishing to sit down, as I think I told you, so that he cannot take sufficient air except in a carriage. And his horror of hotels and rail-cars is immense, and human beings beset him in cities. He is indeed *very* weak. I hardly know what takes away his strength. I now am obliged to superintend my workman, who is arranging the grounds. Whenever my husband lies down (which is sadly often) I rush out of doors to see what the gardener is about.

"I cannot feel rested till Mr. Hawthorne is better, but I get along. I shall go to town when he is safe in the care of General Pierce."

On Saturday this communication from Mrs. Hawthorne reached us: —

Nathaniel Hawthorne.

"General Pierce wrote yesterday to say he wished to meet Mr. Hawthorne in Boston on Wednesday, and go from thence on their way.

"Mr. Hawthorne is much weaker, I find, than he has been before at any time, and I shall go down with him, having a great many things to do in Boston; but I am sure he is not fit to be left by himself, for his steps are so uncertain, and his eyes are very uncertain too. Dear Mr. Fields, I am very anxious about him, and I write now to say that he absolutely refuses to see a physician officially, and so I wish to know whether Dr. Holmes could not see him in some ingenious way on Wednesday as a friend; but with his experienced, acute observation, to look at him also as a physician, to note how he is and what he judges of him comparatively since he last saw him. It almost deprives me of my wits to see him growing weaker with no aid. He seems quite bilious, and has a restlessness that is infinite. His look is more distressed and harassed than before; and he has so little rest, that he is getting worn out. I hope immensely in regard of this sauntering journey with General Pierce.

"I feel as if I ought not to speak to you of anything when you are so busy and weary and bereaved. But yet in such a sad emergency as this, I am sure your generous, kind heart will not refuse me any help you can render. .... I wish Dr. Holmes would feel his pulse; I do not know how to judge of it, but it seems to me irregular."

His friend, Dr. O. W. Holmes, in compliance with Mrs. Hawthorne's desire, expressed in this letter to me, saw the invalid, and thus describes his appearance in an article full of tenderness and feeling which was published in the "Atlantic Monthly" for July, 1864: —

"Late in the afternoon of the day before he left Boston on his last journey I called upon him at the hotel where he was staying. He had gone out but a moment before. Looking along the street, I saw a form at some distance in advance which could only be his, — but how changed from his former port and figure! There was no mistaking the long iron-gray locks, the carriage of the head, and the general look of the natural outlines and movement; but he seemed to have shrunken in all his dimensions, and faltered along with an uncertain, feeble step, as if every movement were an effort. I joined him, and we walked together half an hour, during which time I learned so much of his state of mind and body as could be got at without worrying him with suggestive questions, — my object being to form an opinion of his condition, as I had been requested to do, and to give him some hints that might be useful to him on his journey.

"His aspect, medically considered, was very unfavorable. There were persistent local symptoms, referred especially to the stomach, — 'boring pain,' distension, difficult digestion, with great wasting of flesh and strength. He was very gentle, very willing to answer questions, very docile to such counsel as I offered him, but evidently had no hope of recovering his health. He spoke as if his work were done, and he should write no more.

"With all his obvious depression, there was no failing noticeable in his conversational powers. There was the same backwardness and hesitancy which in his best days it was hard for him to overcome, so that talking with him was almost like love-making, and his shy, beautiful soul had to be wooed from its bashful prudency like an unschooled maiden. The calm despondency with which he spoke about himself confirmed the unfavorable opinion suggested by his look and history."

I saw Hawthorne alive, for the last time, the day he started on this his last mortal journey. His speech and his gait indicated severe illness, and I had great misgivings about the jaunt he was proposing to take so early in the season. His tones were more subdued than ever, and he scarcely spoke above a whisper. He was very affectionate in parting, and I followed him to the door, looking after him as he went up School Street. I noticed that he faltered from weakness, and I should have taken my hat and joined him to offer my arm, but I knew he did not wish to *seem* ill, and I feared he might be troubled at my anxiety. Fearing to disturb him, I followed him with my eyes only, and watched him till he turned the corner and passed out of sight.

On the morning of the 19th of May, 1864, a telegram, signed by Franklin Pierce, stunned us all. It announced the death of Hawthorne. In the afternoon of the same day came this letter to me : —

"PEMIGEWASSET HOUSE, PLYMOUTH, N. H.,
Thursday morning, 5 o'clock.

"MY DEAR SIR, — The telegraph has communicated to you the fact of our dear friend Hawthorne's death. My friend Colonel Hibbard, who bears this note, was a friend of H——, and will tell you more than I am able to write.

"I enclose herewith a note which I commenced last evening to dear Mrs. Hawthorne. O, how will she bear this shock! Dear mother — dear children —

"When I met Hawthorne in Boston a week ago, it was apparent that he was much more feeble and more seriously diseased than I had supposed him to be. We came from Centre Harbor yesterday afternoon, and I thought he was on the whole brighter than he was the day before. Through the week he had been inclined to somnolency during the day, but restless at night. He retired last night soon after nine o'clock, and soon fell into a quiet slumber. In less than half an hour changed his position, but continued to sleep. I left the door open between his bedroom and mine, — our beds being opposite to each other, — and was asleep myself before eleven o'clock. The light continued to burn in my room. At two o'clock, I went to H——'s bedside; he was apparently in a sound sleep, and I did not place my hand upon him. At four o'clock I went into his room again, and, as his position was unchanged, I placed my hand upon him and found that life was extinct. I sent, however, immediately for a physician, and called Judge Bell and Colonel Hibbard, who occupied rooms upon the same floor and near me. He lies upon his side, his position so perfectly natural and easy, his eyes closed, that it is difficult to realize, while looking upon his noble face, that this is death. He must have passed from natural slumber to that from which there is no waking without the slightest movement.

"I cannot write to dear Mrs. Hawthorne, and you must exercise your judgment with regard to sending this and the unfinished note, enclosed, to her.

"Your friend,

"FRANKLIN PIERCE."

Hawthorne's lifelong desire that the end might be a sudden one was gratified. Often and often he has said to me, "What a blessing to go quickly!" So the same swift angel that came as a messenger to Allston, Irving,

Prescott, Macaulay, Thackeray, and Dickens was commissioned to touch his forehead, also, and beckon him away.

The room in which death fell upon him,

> "Like a shadow thrown
> Softly and lightly from a passing cloud,"

looks toward the east; and standing in it, as I have frequently done, since he passed out silently into the skies, it is easy to imagine the scene on that spring morning which President Pierce so feelingly describes in his letter.

On the 24th of May we carried Hawthorne through the blossoming orchards of Concord, and laid him down under a group of pines, on a hillside, overlooking historic fields. All the way from the village church to the grave the birds kept up a perpetual melody. The sun shone brightly, and the air was sweet and pleasant, as if death had never entered the world. Longfellow and Emerson, Channing and Hoar, Agassiz and Lowell, Greene and Whipple, Alcott and Clarke, Holmes and Hillard, and other friends whom he loved, walked slowly by his side that beautiful spring morning. The companion of his youth and his manhood, for whom he would willingly, at any time, have given up his own life, Franklin Pierce, was there among the rest, and scattered flowers into the grave. The unfinished Romance, which had cost him so much anxiety, the last literary work on which he had ever been engaged, was laid on his coffin.

> "Ah! who shall lift that wand of magic power,
> And the lost clew regain?
> The unfinished window in Aladdin's tower
> Unfinished must remain."

Longfellow's beautiful poem will always be associated with the memory of Hawthorne, and most fitting was it that his fellow-student, whom he so loved and honored, should sing his requiem.

DICKENS.

*"O friend with heart as gentle for distress,
As resolute with wise true thoughts to bind
The happiest with the unhappiest of our kind."*

JOHN FORSTER.

" All men are to an unspeakable degree brothers, each man's life a strange emblem of every man's; and Human Portraits, faithfully drawn, are of all pictures the welcomest on human walls." — CARLYLE.

IV.

DICKENS.

I OBSERVE my favorite chair is placed to-day where the portraits of Charles Dickens are easiest seen, and I take the hint accordingly. Those are likenesses of him from the age of twenty-eight down to the year when he passed through "the golden gate," as that wise mystic William Blake calls death. One would hardly believe these pictures represented the same man! See what a beautiful young person Maclise represents in this early likeness of the great author, and then contrast the face with that worn one in the photograph of 1869. The same man, but how different in aspect! I sometimes think, while looking at those two portraits, I must have known two individuals bearing the same name, at various periods of my own life. Let me speak to-day of the younger Dickens. How well I recall the bleak winter evening in 1842 when I first saw the handsome, glowing face of the young man who was even then famous over half the globe! He came bounding into the Tremont House, fresh from the steamer that had brought him to our shores, and his cheery voice rang through the hall, as he gave a quick glance at the new scenes opening upon him in a strange land on first arriving at a Transatlantic hotel. "Here we are!" he shouted, as the lights burst upon the merry party just entering the house, and several gentlemen came forward to greet him. Ah, how happy and buoyant he was then! Young, handsome, almost worshipped for his genius, belted round by such troops of friends as rarely ever man had, coming to a new country to make new conquests of fame and honor, — surely it was a sight long to be remembered and never wholly to be forgotten. The splendor of his endowments and the personal interest he had won to himself called forth all the enthusiasm of old and young America, and I am glad to have been among the first to witness his arrival. You ask me what was his appearance as he ran, or rather flew, up the steps of the hotel, and sprang into the hall. He seemed all on fire with curiosity, and alive as I never saw mortal before. From top to toe every fibre of his body was unrestrained and alert. What vigor, what keenness, what freshness of spirit, possessed him! He laughed all over, and did not care who heard him! He seemed like the Emperor of Cheerfulness on a cruise of pleasure, determined to conquer a realm or two of fun every hour of his overflowing existence. That night impressed itself on my memory for all time, so far as I am concerned with things sublunary. It was Dickens, the true "Boz," in flesh and blood, who stood before us at last, and with my companions, three or four lads of my own age, I determined to sit up late that night. None of us then, of course, had the honor of an acquaintance with the delightful stranger, and I little thought that I should afterwards come to know him in the beaten way of friendship, and live with him day after day in years far distant; that I should ever be so near to him that he would reveal to me his joys and his sorrows, and thus that I should learn the story of his life from his own lips.

About midnight on that eventful landing, "Boz," — everybody called him "Boz" in those days, — having finished his supper, came down into the office of the hotel, and, joining the young Earl of M——, his fellow-voyager, sallied out for a first look at Boston streets. It was a stinging night, and the moon was at the full. Every object stood out sharp and glittering, and "Boz," muffled up in a shaggy fur coat, ran over the shining frozen snow, wisely keeping the middle of the street for the most part. We boys followed cautiously behind, but near enough not to lose any of the fun. Of course the two gentlemen soon lost their way on emerging into Washington from Tremont Street. Dickens kept up one continual shout of uproarious laughter as he went rapidly forward, reading the signs on the shops, and observing the "architecture" of the new country into which he had dropped as if from the clouds. When the two arrived opposite the "Old South Church" Dickens screamed. To this day I could never tell why. Was it because of its fancied resemblance to St. Paul's or the Abbey? I declare firmly, the mystery of that shout is still a mystery to me!

The great event of Boz's first visit to Boston was the dinner of welcome tendered to him by the young men of the city. It is idle to attempt much talk about the banquet given on that Monday night in February, twenty-nine years ago. Papanti's Hall (where many of us learned to dance, under the guidance of that master of legs, now happily still among us and pursuing the same highly useful calling which he practised in 1842) was the scene of that festivity. It was a glorious episode in all our lives, and whoever was not there has suffered a loss not easy to estimate. We younger members of that dinner-party sat in the seventh heaven of happiness, and were translated into other spheres. Accidentally, of course, I had a seat just in front of the honored guest; saw him take a pinch of snuff out of Washington Allston's box, and heard him joke with old President Quincy. Was there ever such a night before in our staid city? Did ever mortal preside with such felicitous success as did Mr. Quincy? How he went on with his delicious compliments to our guest! How he revelled in quotations from "Pickwick" and "Oliver Twist" and "The Curiosity Shop"! And how admirably he closed his speech of welcome, calling up the young author amid a perfect volley of applause! "Health, Happiness, and a Hearty Welcome to Charles Dickens." I can see and hear Mr. Quincy now, as he spoke the words. Were ever heard such cheers before? And when Dickens stood up at last to answer for himself, so fresh and so handsome, with his beautiful eyes moist with feeling, and his whole frame aglow with excitement, how we did hurrah, we young fellows! Trust me, it *was* a great night; and we must have made a mighty noise at our end of the table, for I remember frequent messages came down to us from the "Chair," begging that we would hold up a little and moderate if possible the rapture of our applause.

After Dickens left Boston he went on his American travels, gathering up materials, as he journeyed, for his "American Notes." He was accompanied as far as New York by a very dear friend, to whom he afterwards addressed several most interesting letters. For that friend he always had the warmest enthusiasm; and when he came the second time to America, there was no one of his old companions whom he missed more. Let us read some of these letters written by Dickens nearly thirty years ago. The friend to whom they were addressed was also an intimate and dear associate of mine, and his children have kindly placed at my disposal the whole correspondence. Here is the first letter, time-stained, but preserved with religious care.

FULLER'S HOTEL, WASHINGTON, Monday, March 14, 1842.

MY DEAR FELTON: I was more delighted than I can possibly tell you to receive (last Saturday night) your welcome letter. We and the oysters missed you terribly in New York. You carried

C. C. Felton.

away with you more than half the delight and pleasure of my New World; and I heartily wish you could bring it back again.

There are very interesting men in this place, — highly interesting, of course, — but it's not a comfortable place; is it? If spittle could wait at table we should be nobly attended, but as that property has not been imparted to it in the present state of mechanical science, we are rather lonely and orphan-like, in respect of "being looked arter." A blithe black was introduced on our arrival, as our peculiar and especial attendant. He is the only gentleman in the town who has a peculiar delicacy in intruding upon my valuable time. It usually takes seven rings and a threatening message from —— to produce him; and when he comes he goes to fetch something, and, forgetting it by the way, comes back no more.

We have been in great distress, really in distress, at the non-arrival of the Caledonia. You may conceive what our joy was, when, while we were dining out yesterday, H. arrived with the joyful intelligence of her safety. The very news of her having really arrived seemed to diminish the distance between ourselves and home, by one half at least.

And this morning (though we have not yet received our heap of despatches, for which we are looking eagerly forward to this night's mail), — this morning there reached us unexpectedly, through the government bag (Heaven knows how they came there), two of our many and long-looked-for letters, wherein was a circumstantial account of the whole conduct and behavior of our pets; with marvellous narrations of Charley's precocity at a Twelfth Night juvenile party at Macready's; and tremendous predictions of the governess, dimly suggesting his having got out of pot-hooks and hangers, and darkly insinuating the possibility of his writing us a letter before long; and many other workings of the same prophetic spirit, in reference to him and his sisters, very gladdening to their mother's heart, and not at all depressing to their father's. There was, also, the doctor's report, which was a clean bill; and the nurse's report, which was perfectly electrifying; showing as it did how Master Walter had been weaned, and had cut a double tooth, and done many other extraordinary things, quite worthy of his high descent. In short, we were made very happy and grateful; and felt as if the prodigal father and mother had got home again.

What do you think of this incendiary card being left at my door last night? "General G. sends compliments to Mr. Dickens, and called with two literary ladies. As the two L. L.'s are ambitious of the honor of a personal introduction to Mr. D., General G.

requests the honor of an appointment for to-morrow." I draw a veil over my sufferings. They are sacred.

We have altered our route, and don't mean to go to Charleston, for I want to see the West, and have taken it into my head that as I am not obliged to go to Charleston, and don't exactly know why I should go there, I need do no violence to my own inclinations. My route is of Mr. Clay's designing, and I think it a very good one. We go on Wednesday night to Richmond in Virginia. On Monday we return to Baltimore for two days. On Thursday morning we start for Pittsburg, and so go by the Ohio to Cincinnati, Louisville, Kentucky, Lexington, St. Louis; and either down the Lakes to Buffalo, or back to Philadelphia, and by New York to that place, where we shall stay a week, and then make a hasty trip into Canada. We shall be in Buffalo, please Heaven, on the 30th of April. If I don't find a letter from you in the care of the postmaster at that place, I 'll never write to you from England.

But if I *do* find one, my right hand shall forget its cunning, before I forget to be your truthful and constant correspondent; not, dear Felton, because I promised it, nor because I have a natural tendency to correspond (which is far from being the case), nor because I am truly grateful to you for, and have been made truly proud by, that affectionate and elegant tribute which —— sent me, but because you are a man after my own heart, and I love you *well*. And for the love I bear you, and the pleasure with which I shall always think of you, and the glow I shall feel when I see your handwriting in my own home, I hereby enter into a solemn league and covenant to write as many letters to you as you write to me, at least. Amen.

Come to England! Come to England! Our oysters are small I know; they are said by Americans to be coppery, but our hearts are of the largest size. We are thought to excel in shrimps, to be far from despicable in point of lobsters, and in periwinkles are considered to challenge the universe. Our oysters, small though they be, are not devoid of the refreshing influence which that species of fish is supposed to exercise in these latitudes. Try them and compare.

Affectionately yours,

CHARLES DICKENS.

His next letter is dated from Niagara, and I know every one will relish his allusion to oysters with wet feet, and his reference to the squeezing of a Quaker.

CLIFTON HOUSE, NIAGARA FALLS, 29th April, 1842.

MY DEAR FELTON: Before I go any farther, let me explain to you what these great enclosures portend, lest — supposing them part and parcel of my letter, and asking to be read — you shall fall into fits, from which recovery might be doubtful.

They are, as you will see, four copies of the same thing. The nature of the document you will discover at a glance. As I hoped and believed, the best of the British brotherhood took fire at my being attacked because I spoke my mind and theirs on the subject of an international copyright; and with all good speed, and hearty private letters, transmitted to me this small parcel of gauntlets for immediate casting down.

Now my first idea was, publicity being the object, to send one copy to you for a Boston newspaper, another to Bryant for his paper, a third to the New York Herald (because of its large circulation), and a fourth to a highly respectable journal at Washington (the property of a gentleman, and a fine fellow named Seaton, whom I knew there), which I think is called the Intelligencer. Then the Knickerbocker stepped into my mind, and then it occurred to me that possibly the North American Review might be the best organ after all, because indisputably the most respectable and honorable, and the most concerned in the rights of literature.

Whether to limit its publication to one journal, or to extend it to several, is a question so very difficult of decision to a stranger, that I have finally resolved to send these papers to you, and ask you (mindful of the conversation we had on this head one day, in that renowned oyster-cellar) to resolve the point for me. You need feel no weighty sense of responsibility, my dear Felton, for whatever you do is *sure* to please me. If you see Sumner, take him into our councils. The only two things to be borne in mind are, first, that if they be published in several quarters, they must be published in all *simultaneously;* secondly, that I hold them in trust, to put them before the people.

I fear this is imposing a heavy tax upon your friendship; and I don't fear it the less, by reason of being well assured that it is one you will most readily pay. I shall be in Montreal about the 11th of May. Will you write to me there, to the care of the Earl of Mulgrave, and tell me what you have done?

So much for that. Bisness first, pleasure artervards, as King Richard the Third said ven he stabbed the tother king in the Tower, afore he murdered the babbies.

I have long suspected that oysters have a rheumatic tendency

Their feet are always wet; and so much damp company in a man's inside cannot contribute to his peace. But whatever the cause of your indisposition, we are truly grieved and pained to hear of it, and should be more so, but that we hope from your account of that farewell dinner, that you are all right again. I *did* receive Longfellow's note. Sumner I have not yet heard from; for which reason I am constantly bringing telescopes to bear on the ferry-boat, in hopes to see him coming over, accompanied by a modest portmanteau.

To say anything about this wonderful place would be sheer nonsense. It far exceeds my most sanguine expectations, though the impression on my mind has been, from the first, nothing but beauty and peace. I have n't drunk the water. Bearing in mind your caution, I have devoted myself to beer, whereof there is an exceedingly pretty fall in this house.

One of the noble hearts who sat for the Cheeryble brothers is dead. If I had been in England, I would certainly have gone into mourning for the loss of such a glorious life. His brother is not expected to survive him. I am told that it appears from a memorandum found among the papers of the deceased, that in his lifetime he gave away in charity £600,000, or three millions of dollars!

What do you say to my *acting* at the Montreal Theatre? I am an old hand at such matters, and am going to join the officers of the garrison in a public representation for the benefit of a local charity. We shall have a good house, they say. I am going to enact one Mr. Snobbington in a funny farce called A Good Night's Rest. I shall want a flaxen wig and eyebrows; and my nightly rest is broken by visions of there being no such commodities in Canada. I wake in the dead of night in a cold perspiration, surrounded by imaginary barbers, all denying the existence or possibility of obtaining such articles. If —— had a flaxen head, I would certainly have it shaved and get a wig and eyebrows out of him, for a small pecuniary compensation.

By the by, if you could only have seen the man at Harrisburg, crushing a friendly Quaker in the parlor door! It was the greatest sight I ever saw. I had told him not to admit anybody whatever, forgetting that I had previously given this honest Quaker a special invitation to come. The Quaker would not be denied, and H. was stanch. When I came upon them, the Quaker was black in the face, and H. was administering the final squeeze. The Quaker was still rubbing his waistcoat with an expression of acute inward suffering, when I left the town. I have been looking for his death in the newspapers almost daily.

Do you know one General G.? He is a weazen-faced warrior, and in his dotage. I had him for a fellow-passenger on board a steamboat. I had also a statistical colonel with me, outside the coach from Cincinnati to Columbus. A New England poet buzzed about me on the Ohio, like a gigantic bee. A mesmeric doctor, of an impossibly great age, gave me pamphlets at Louisville. I have suffered much, very much.

If I could get beyond New York to see anybody, it would be (as you know) to see *you*. But I do not expect to reach the " Carlton " until the last day of May, and then we are going with the Coldens somewhere on the banks of the North River for a couple of days. So you see we shall not have much leisure for our voyaging preparations.

You and Dr. Howe (to whom my love) MUST come to New York. On the 6th of June, you must engage yourselves to dine with us at the " Carlton "; and if we don't make a merry evening of it, the fault shall not be in us.

Mrs. Dickens unites with me in best regards to Mrs. Felton and your little daughter, and I am always, my dear Felton,

Affectionately your friend,

CHARLES DICKENS.

P. S. I saw a good deal of Walker at Cincinnati. I like him very much. We took to him mightily at first, because he resembled you in face and figure, we thought. You will be glad to hear that our news from home is cheering from first to last, all well, happy, and loving. My friend Forster says in his last letter that he " wants to know you," and looks forward to Longfellow.

When Dickens arrived in Montreal he had, it seems, a busy time of it, and I have often heard of his capital acting in private theatricals while in that city.

MONTREAL, Saturday, 21st May, 1842.

MY DEAR FELTON: I was delighted to receive your letter yesterday, and was well pleased with its contents. I anticipated objection to Carlyle's letter. I called particular attention to it for three reasons. Firstly, because he boldly *said* what all the others *think*, and therefore deserved to be manfully supported. Secondly, because it is my deliberate opinion that I have been assailed on this subject in a manner in which no man with any pretensions to public respect or with the remotest right to express an opinion on a subject of universal literary interest would be assailed in any other country. . . . .

I really cannot sufficiently thank you, dear Felton, for your warm and hearty interest in these proceedings. But it would be idle to pursue that theme, so let it pass.

The wig and whiskers are in a state of the highest preservation. The play comes off next Wednesday night, the 25th. What would I give to see you in the front row of the centre box, your spectacles gleaming not unlike those of my dear friend Pickwick, your face radiant with as broad a grin as a staid professor may indulge in, and your very coat, waistcoat, and shoulders expressive of what we should take together when the performance was over! I would give something (not so much, but still a good round sum) if you could only stumble into that very dark and dusty theatre in the daytime (at any minute between twelve and three), and see me with my coat off, the stage manager and universal director, urging impracticable ladies and impossible gentlemen on to the very confines of insanity, shouting and driving about, in my own person, to an extent which would justify any philanthropic stranger in clapping me into a strait-waistcoat without further inquiry, endeavoring to goad H. into some dim and faint understanding of a prompter's duties, and struggling in such a vortex of noise, dirt, bustle, confusion, and inextricable entanglement of speech and action as you would grow giddy in contemplating. We perform A Roland for an Oliver, A good Night's Rest, and Deaf as a Post. This kind of voluntary hard labor used to be my great delight. The *furor* has come strong upon me again, and I begin to be once more of opinion that nature intended me for the lessee of a national theatre, and that pen, ink, and paper have spoiled a manager.

O, how I look forward across that rolling water to home and its small tenantry! How I busy myself in thinking how my books look, and where the tables are, and in what positions the chairs stand relatively to the other furniture; and whether we shall get there in the night, or in the morning, or in the afternoon; and whether we shall be able to surprise them, or whether they will be too sharply looking out for us; and what our pets will say; and how they 'll look, and who will be the first to come and shake hands, and so forth! If I could but tell you how I have set my heart on rushing into Forster's study (he is my great friend, and writes at the bottom of all his letters, "My love to Felton"), and into Maclise's painting-room, and into Macready's managerial ditto, without a moment's warning, and how I picture every little trait and circumstance of our arrival to myself, down to the very color of the bow on the cook's cap, you would almost think I had changed places with my eldest son, and was still in pantaloons of the thinnest texture. I left all these things — God only knows what a love I have for them — as coolly and calmly as any animated cucumber; but when I come upon them again I shall have lost all power of self-restraint, and shall as certainly make a fool of myself (in the popular meaning of that expression) as ever Grimaldi did in his way, or George III. in his.

And not the less so, dear Felton, for having found some warm hearts, and left some instalments of earnest and sincere affection, behind me on this continent. And whenever I turn my mental telescope hitherward, trust me that one of the first figures it will descry will wear spectacles so like yours that the maker could n't tell the difference, and shall address a Greek class in such an exact imitation of your voice, that the very students hearing it should cry, " That 's he! Three cheers. Hoo-ray-ay-ay-ay-ay!"

About those joints of yours, I think you are mistaken. They *can't* be stiff. At the worst they merely want the air of New York, which, being impregnated with the flavor of last year's oysters, has a surprising effect in rendering the human frame supple and flexible in all cases of rust.

A terrible idea occurred to me as I wrote those words. The oyster-cellars, — what do they do when oysters are not in season? Is pickled salmon vended there? Do they sell crabs, shrimps, winkles, herrings? The oyster-openers, — what do *they* do? Do they commit suicide in despair, or wrench open tight drawers and cupboards and hermetically sealed bottles for practice? Perhaps they are dentists out of the oyster season. Who knows?

Affectionately yours,
CHARLES DICKENS.

Dickens always greatly rejoiced in the theatre; and, having seen him act with the Amateur Company of the Guild of Literature and Art, I can well imagine the delight his impersonations in Montreal must have occasioned. I have seen him play Sir Charles Coldstream, in the comedy of Used Up, with such perfection that all other performers in the same part have seemed dull by comparison. Even Matthews, superb artist as he is, could not rival Dickens in the character of Sir Charles. Once I saw Dickens, Mark Lemon, and Wilkie Collins on the stage together. The play was called Mrs. Nightingale's Diary (a farce in one act, the joint production of Dickens and Mark Lemon), and Dickens played six characters in the piece. Never have I seen such wonderful changes of face and form as he gave us that night. He was alternately a rattling lawyer of the Middle Temple, a boots, an eccentric pedestrian and cold-water drinker, a deaf sexton, an invalid captain, and an old woman. What fun it was, to be sure, and how we roared over the performance! Here is the playbill which I held in my hand nineteen years ago, while the great writer was proving himself to be as pre-eminent an actor as he was an author. One can see by reading the bill that Dickens was manager of the company, and that it was under his direction that the plays were produced. Observe the clear evidence of his hand in the very wording of the bill:—

"On Wednesday evening, September 1, 1852.

"THE AMATEUR COMPANY
OF THE
GUILD OF LITERATURE AND ART;

To encourage Life Assurance and other provident habits among Authors and Artists; to render such assistance to both as shall never compromise their independence; and to found a new Institution where honorable rest from arduous labors shall still be associated with the discharge of congenial duties;

"Will have the honor of presenting," etc., etc.,

But let us go on with the letters. Here is the first one to his friend after Dickens arrived home again in England. It is delightful, through and through.

LONDON, 1 DEVONSHIRE TERRACE, YORK GATE, REGENT'S PARK,
Sunday, July 31, 1842.

MY DEAR FELTON: Of all the monstrous and incalculable amount of occupation that ever beset one unfortunate man, mine has been the most stupendous since I came home. The dinners I have had to eat, the places I have had to go to, the letters I have had to answer, the sea of business and of pleasure in which I have been plunged, not even the genius of an —— or the pen of a —— could describe.

Wherefore I indite a monstrously short and wildly uninteresting epistle to the American Dando; but perhaps you don't know who Dando was. He was an oyster-eater, my dear Felton. He used to go into oyster-shops, without a farthing of money, and stand at the counter eating natives, until the man who opened them grew pale, cast down his knife, staggered backward, struck his white forehead with his open hand, and cried, "You are Dando!!!" He has been known to eat twenty dozen at one sitting, and would have eaten forty, if the truth had not flashed upon the shopkeeper. For these offences he was constantly committed to the House of Correction. During his last imprisonment he was taken ill, got worse and worse, and at last began knocking violent double-knocks at Death's door. The doctor stood beside his bed, with his fingers on his pulse. "He is going," says the doctor. "I see it in his eye. There is only one thing that would keep life in him for another hour, and that is — oysters." They were immediately brought. Dando swallowed eight, and feebly took a ninth. He held it in his mouth and looked round the bed strangely. "Not a bad one, is it?" says the doctor. The patient shook his head, rubbed his trembling hand upon his stomach, bolted the oyster, and fell back — dead. They buried him in the prison yard, and paved his grave with oyster-shells.

We are all well and hearty, and have already begun to wonder what time next year you and Mrs. Felton and Dr. Howe will come across the briny sea together. To-morrow we go to the seaside for two months. I am looking out for news of Longfellow, and shall be delighted when I know that he is on his way to London and this house.

I am bent upon striking at the piratical newspapers with the sharpest edge I can put upon my small axe, and hope in the next session of Parliament to stop their entrance into Canada. For the first time within the memory of man, the professors of English literature seem disposed to act together on this question. It is a good thing to aggravate a scoundrel, if one can do nothing else, and I think we *can* make them smart a little in this way. . . . .

I wish you had been at Greenwich the other day, where a party of friends gave me a private dinner; public ones I have refused. C. was perfectly wild at the reunion, and, after singing all manner of marine songs, wound up the entertainment by coming home (six miles) in a little open phaeton of mine, *on his head*, to the mingled delight and indignation of the metropolitan police. We were very jovial indeed; and I assure you that I drank your health with fearful vigor and energy.

On board that ship coming home I established a club, called the United Vagabonds, to the large amusement of the rest of the passengers. This holy brotherhood committed all kinds of absurdities, and dined always, with a variety of solemn forms, at one end of the table, below the mast, away from all the rest. The captain being ill when we were three or four days out, I produced my medicine-chest and recovered him. We had a few more sick men after that, and I went round "the wards" every day in great state, accompanied by two Vagabonds, habited as Ben Allen and Bob Sawyer, bearing enormous rolls of plaster and huge pairs of scissors. We were really very merry all the way, breakfasted in one party at Liverpool, shook hands, and parted most cordially. . . . .

                Affectionately
                          Your faithful friend,
                                        C. D.

P. S. I have looked over my journal, and have decided to produce my American trip in two volumes. I have written about half the first since I came home, and hope to be out in October. This is "exclusive news," to be communicated to any friends to whom you may like to intrust it, my dear F.

What a capital epistolary pen Dickens held! He seems never to have written the shortest note without something piquant in it; and when he attempted a *letter*, he always made it entertaining from sheer force of habit.

When I think of this man, and all the lasting good and abounding pleasure he has brought into the world, I wonder at the superstition that dares to arraign him. A sound philosopher once said: "He that thinks any innocent pastime foolish has either to grow wiser, or is past the ability to do so"; and I have always counted it an impudent fiction that playfulness is inconsistent with greatness. Many men and women have died of Dignity, but the disease which sent them to the tomb was not contracted from Charles Dickens. Not long ago, I met in the street a bleak old character, full of dogmatism, egotism, and rheumatism, who complained that Dickens had "too much exuberant sociality" in his books for *him*, and he wondered how any one could get through Pickwick. My solemn friend evidently preferred the dropping-down-deadness of manner, which he had been accustomed to find in Hervey's "Meditations," and other kindred authors, where it always seems to be urged that life would be endurable but for its pleasures. A person once commended to my acquaintance an individual whom he described as "a fine, pompous, gentlemanly man," and I thought it prudent, under the circumstances, to decline the proffered introduction.

But I will proceed with those outbursts of bright-heartedness vouchsafed to us in Dickens's letters. To me these epistles are good as fresh "Uncommercials," or unpublished "Sketches by Boz."

1 DEVONSHIRE TERRACE, YORK GATE, REGENT'S PARK, LONDON,
1st September, 1842.

MY DEAR FELTON: OF COURSE that letter in the papers was as foul a forgery as ever felon swung for. . . . . I have not contradicted it publicly, nor shall I. When I tilt at such wringings out of the dirtiest mortality, I shall be another man — indeed, almost the creature they would make me.

I gave your message to Forster, who sends a despatch-box full of kind remembrances in return. He is in a great state of delight with the first volume of my American book (which I have just finished), and swears loudly by it. It is *True*, and Honorable I know, and I shall hope to send it you, complete, by the first steamer in November.

Your description of the porter and the carpet-bags prepares me for a first-rate facetious novel, brimful of the richest humor, on which I have no doubt you are engaged. What is it called? Sometimes I imagine the title-page thus: —

OYSTERS
IN
EVERY STYLE
OR
OPENINGS
OF
LIFE
BY
YOUNG DANDO.

As to the man putting the luggage on his head, as a sort of sign, adopt it from this hour.

I date this from London, where I have come, as a good, profligate, graceless bachelor, for a day or two; leaving my wife and babbies at the seaside. . . . . Heavens! if you were but here at this minute! A piece of salmon and a steak are cooking in the kitchen; it's a very wet day, and I have had a fire lighted; the wine sparkles on a side-table; the room looks the more snug from being the only *un*dismantled one in the house; plates are warming for Forster and Maclise, whose knock I am momentarily expecting; that groom I told you of, who never comes into the house, except when we are all out of town, is walking about in his shirt-sleeves without the smallest consciousness of impropriety; a great mound of proofs are waiting to be read aloud, after dinner. With what a shout I would clap you down into the easiest chair, my genial Felton, if you could but appear, and order you a pair of slippers instantly!

Since I have written this, the aforesaid groom — a very small man (as the fashion is) with fiery-red hair (as the fashion is *not*) — has looked very hard at me and fluttered about me at the same time, like a giant butterfly. After a pause, he says, in a Sam Wellerish kind of way: "I vent to the club this mornin', sir. There vorn't no letters, sir." "Very good, Topping." "How's missis, sir?" "Pretty well, Topping." "Glad to hear it, sir. *My* missis ain't wery well, sir." "No!" "No, sir, she's a goin', sir, to have a hincrease wery soon, and it makes her rather nervous, sir; and ven a young voman gets at all down at sich a time, sir, she goes down wery deep, sir." To this sentiment I reply affirmatively, and then he adds, as he stirs the fire (as if he were thinking out loud), "Wot a mystery it is! Wot a go is natur'!" With which scrap of philosophy, he gradually gets nearer to the door, and so fades out of the room.

This same man asked me one day, soon after I came home, what Sir John Wilson was. This is a friend of mine, who took our house and servants, and everything as it stood, during our absence in America. I told him an officer. "A wot, sir?" "An officer." And then, for fear he should think I meant a police-officer, I added, "An officer in the army." "I beg your pardon, sir," he said, touching his hat, "but the club as I always drove him to wos the United Servants."

The real name of this club is the United Service, but I have no doubt he thought it was a high-life-below-stairs kind of resort, and that this gentleman was a retired butler or superannuated footman.

There's the knock, and the Great Western sails, or steams rather, to-morrow. Write soon again, dear Felton, and ever believe me, ...

Your affectionate friend,

CHARLES DICKENS.

P. S. All good angels prosper Dr. Howe. He, at least, will not like me the less, I hope, for what I shall say of Laura.

LONDON, 1 DEVONSHIRE TERRACE, YORK GATE, REGENT'S PARK,
31st December, 1842.

MY DEAR FELTON: Many and many happy New Years to you and yours! As many happy children as may be quite convenient (no more)! and as many happy meetings between them and our children, and between you and us, as the kind fates in their utmost kindness shall favorably decree!

The American book (to begin with that) has been a most complete and thorough-going success. Four large editions have now been sold *and paid for*, and it has won golden opinions from all sorts of men, except our friend in F——, who is a miserable creature; a disappointed man in great poverty, to whom I have ever been most kind and considerate (I need scarcely say that); and another friend in B——, no less a person than an illustrious gentleman named ——, who wrote a story called ——. They have done no harm, and have fallen short of their mark, which, of course, was to annoy me. Now I am perfectly free from any diseased curiosity in such respects, and whenever I hear of a notice of this kind, I never read it; whereby I always conceive (don't you?) that I get the victory. With regard to your slave-owners, they may cry, till they are as black in the face as their own slaves, that Dickens lies. Dickens does not write for their satisfaction, and Dickens will not explain for their comfort. Dickens has the name and date of every newspaper in which every one of those advertisements appeared, as they know perfectly well; but Dickens does not choose to give them, and will not at any time between this and the day of judgment. . . . .

I have been hard at work on my new book, of which the first number has just appeared. The Paul Joneses who pursue happiness and profit at other men's cost will no doubt enable you to read it, almost as soon as you receive this. I hope you will like it. And I particularly commend, my dear Felton, one Mr. Pecksniff and his daughters to your tender regards. I have a kind of liking for them myself.

Blessed star of morning, such a trip as we had into Cornwall, just after Longfellow went away! The "we" means Forster, Maclise, Stanfield (the renowned marine painter), and the Inimitable Boz. We went down into Devonshire by the railroad, and there we hired an open carriage from an innkeeper, patriotic in all Pickwick matters, and went on with post horses. Sometimes we travelled all night, sometimes all day, sometimes both. I kept the joint-stock purse, ordered all the dinners, paid all the turnpikes, conducted facetious conversations with the post-boys, and regulated the pace at which we travelled. Stanfield (an old sailor) consulted an enormous map on all disputed points of wayfaring; and referred, moreover, to a pocket-compass and other scientific instruments. The luggage was in Forster's department; and Maclise, having nothing particular to do, sang songs. Heavens! If you could have seen the necks of bottles — distracting in their immense varieties of shape — peering out of the carriage pockets! If you could have witnessed the deep devotion of the post-boys, the wild attachment of the hostlers, the maniac glee of the waiters. If you could have followed us into the earthy old churches we visited, and into the strange caverns on the gloomy sea-shore, and down into the depths of mines, and up to the tops of giddy heights where the unspeakably green water was roaring, I don't know how many hundred feet below! If you could have seen but one gleam of the bright fires by which we sat in the big rooms of ancient inns at night, until long after the small hours had come and gone, or smelt but one steam of the HOT punch (not white, dear Felton, like that amazing compound I sent you a taste of, but a rich, genial, glowing brown) which came in every evening in a huge broad china bowl! I never laughed in my life as I did on this journey. It would have done you good to hear me. I was choking and gasping and bursting the buckle off the back of my stock, all the way. And Stanfield (who is very much of your figure and temperament, but fifteen years older) got into such apoplectic entanglements that we were often obliged to beat him on the back with portmanteaus before we could recover him. Seriously, I do believe there never was such a trip. And they made such sketches, those two men, in the most romantic of our halting-places, that you would have sworn we had the Spirit of Beauty with us, as well as the Spirit of Fun. But stop till you come to England, — I say no more.

The actuary of the national debt could n't calculate the number of children who are coming here on Twelfth Night, in honor of Charley's birthday, for which occasion I have provided a magic lantern and divers other tremendous engines of that nature. But the best of it is that Forster and I have purchased between us the entire stock in trade of a conjurer, the practice and display whereof is intrusted to me. And O my dear eyes, Felton, if you could see me conjuring the company's watches into impossible tea-caddies, and causing pieces of money to fly, and burning pocket-handkerchiefs without hurting 'em, and practising in my own room, without anybody to admire, you would never forget it as long as you live. In those tricks which require a confederate, I am assisted (by reason of his imperturbable good-humor) by Stanfield, who always does his part exactly the wrong way, to the unspeakable delight of all beholders. We come out on a small scale, to-night, at Forster's, where we see the old year out and the new one in. Particulars of shall be forwarded in my next.

I have quite made up my mind that F—— really believes he *does* know you personally, and has all his life. He talks to me about you with such gravity that I am afraid to grin, and feel it necessary to look quite serious. Sometimes he *tells* me things about you, does n't ask me, you know, so that I am occasionally perplexed beyond all telling, and begin to think it was he, and not I, who went to America. It's the queerest thing in the world.

The book I was to have given Longfellow for you is not worth sending by itself, being only a Barnaby. But I will look up some manuscript for you (I think I have that of the American Notes complete), and will try to make the parcel better worth its long conveyance. With regard to Maclise's pictures, you certainly are quite right in your impression of them; but he is "such a discursive devil" (as he says about himself), and flies off at such odd tangents, that I feel it difficult to convey to you any general notion of his purpose. I will try to do so when I write again. I want very much to know about —— and that charming girl. . . . . Give me full particulars. Will you remember me cordially to Sumner,

and say I thank him for his welcome letter? The like to Hillard, with many regards to himself and his wife, with whom I had one night a little conversation which I shall not readily forget. The like to Washington Allston, and all friends who care for me and have outlived my book. . . . . Always, my dear Felton,
With true regard and affection, yours,
CHARLES DICKENS.

Here is a letter that seems to me something tremendous in its fun and pathos: —

1 DEVONSHIRE TERRACE, YORK GATE, REGENT'S PARK, LONDON,
2d March, 1843.

MY DEAR FELTON: I don't know where to begin, but plunge headlong with a terrible splash into this letter, on the chance of turning up somewhere.

Hurrah! Up like a cork again, with the "North American Review" in my hand. Like you, my dear ——, and I can say no more in praise of it, though I go on to the end of the sheet. You cannot think how much notice it has attracted here. Brougham called the other day, with the number (thinking I might not have seen it), and I being out at the time, he left a note, speaking of it, and of the writer, in terms that warmed my heart. Lord Ashburton (one of whose people wrote a notice in the "Edinburgh," which they have since publicly contradicted) also wrote to me about it in just the same strain. And many others have done the like.

I am in great health and spirits and powdering away at Chuzzlewit, with all manner of facetiousness rising up before me as I go on. As to news, I have really none, saving that —— (who never took any exercise in his life) has been laid up with rheumatism for weeks past, but is now, I hope, getting better. My little captain, as I call him, — he who took me out, I mean, and with whom I had that adventure of the cork soles, — has been in London too, and seeing all the lions under my escort. Good heavens! I wish you could have seen certain other mahogany-faced men (also captains) who used to call here for him in the morning, and bear him off to docks and rivers and all sorts of queer places, whence he always returned late at night, with rum-and-water tear-drops in his eyes, and a complication of punchy smells in his mouth! He was better than a comedy to us, having marvellous ways of tying his pocket-handkerchief round his neck at dinner-time in a kind of jolly embarrassment, and then forgetting what he had done with it; also of singing songs to wrong tunes, and calling land objects by

Cambridgeport, 19 April, 1842.

Dear Sir,

I am sorry that I am unable to inform you whether any part of the Ghost Story, you refer to in your letter, was ever in print before it appeared in Coleridge's Table Talk. I related it to Mr C. as I had it from Mr J. F. B. Morse (now President of the New York Institute of Design) ....

both as to the Actors and the Location. The actors were two Russian Officers, and the place was in America — though where I do not remember; in other respects the story is given as I heard it. The mistake however by originating it in Mr Coleridge's conforming it, after the lapse of several years, with some other circumstance I might have mentioned in connexion with the College at which I was educated.

Respectfully,
Yr obdt servt
Wm. Allston.

James T. Fields Esqr.

sea names, and never knowing what o'clock it was, but taking midnight for seven in the evening; with many other sailor oddities, all full of honesty, manliness, and good temper. We took him to Drury Lane Theatre to see Much Ado About Nothing. But I never could find out what he meant by turning round, after he had watched the first two scenes with great attention, and inquiring "whether it was a Polish piece.". . . .

On the 4th of April I am going to preside at a public dinner for the benefit of the printers; and if you were a guest at that table, would n't I smite you on the shoulder, harder than ever I rapped the well-beloved back of Washington Irving at the City Hotel in New York!

You were asking me — I love to say asking, as if we could talk together — about Maclise. He is such a discursive fellow, and so eccentric in his might, that on a mental review of his pictures I can hardly tell you of them as leading to any one strong purpose. But the annual Exhibition of the Royal Academy comes off in May, and then I will endeavor to give you some notion of him. He is a tremendous creature, and might do anything. But, like all tremendous creatures, he takes his own way, and flies off at unexpected breaches in the conventional wall.

You know H——'s Book, I daresay. Ah! I saw a scene of mingled comicality and seriousness at his funeral some weeks ago, which has choked me at dinner-time ever since. C—— and I went as mourners; and as he lived, poor fellow, five miles out of town, I drove C—— down. It was such a day as I hope, for the credit of nature, is seldom seen in any parts but these, — muddy, foggy, wet, dark, cold, and unutterably wretched in every possible respect. Now, C—— has enormous whiskers, which straggle all down his throat in such weather, and stick out in front of him, like a partially unravelled bird's-nest; so that he looks queer enough at the best, but when he is very wet, and in a state between jollity (he is always very jolly with me) and the deepest gravity (going to a funeral, you know), it is utterly impossible to resist him; especially as he makes the strangest remarks the mind of man can conceive, without any intention of being funny, but rather meaning to be philosophical. I really cried with an irresistible sense of his comicality all the way; but when he was dressed out in a black cloak and a very long black hat-band by an undertaker (who, as he whispered me with tears in his eyes — for he had known H—— many years — was "a character, and he would like to sketch him"), I thought I should have been obliged to go away. However, we went into a little parlor where the funeral party was, and God knows it was miserable enough, for the widow and children were crying bitterly in one corner, and the other mourners — mere people of ceremony, who cared no more for the dead man than the hearse did — were talking quite coolly and carelessly together in another; and the contrast was as painful and distressing as anything I ever saw. There was an independent clergyman present, with his bands on and a Bible under his arm, who, as soon as we were seated, addressed —— thus, in a loud, emphatic voice: "Mr. C——, have you seen a paragraph respecting our departed friend, which has gone the round of the morning papers?" "Yes, sir," says C——, "I have," looking very hard at me the while, for he had told me with some pride coming down that it was his composition. "Oh!" said the clergyman. "Then you will agree with me, Mr. C——, that it is not only an insult to me, who am the servant of the Almighty, but an insult to the Almighty, whose servant I am." "How is that, sir?" said C——. "It is stated, Mr. C——, in that paragraph," says the minister, "that when Mr. H—— failed in business as a bookseller, he was persuaded by *me* to try the pulpit, which is false, incorrect, unchristian, in a manner blasphemous, and in all respects contemptible. Let us pray." With which, my dear Felton, and in the same breath, I give you my word, he knelt down, as we all did, and began a very miserable jumble of an extemporary prayer. I was really penetrated with sorrow for the family, but when C—— (upon his knees, and sobbing for the loss of an old friend) whispered me, "that if that was n't a clergyman, and it was n't a funeral, he 'd have punched his head," I felt as if nothing but convulsions could possibly relieve me. . . . .

Faithfully always, my dear Felton,

C. D.

Was there ever such a genial, jovial creature as this master of humor! When we read his friendly epistles, we cannot help wishing he had written letters only, as when we read his novels we grudge the time he employed on anything else.

BROADSTAIRS, KENT, 1st September, 1843.

MY DEAR FELTON: If I thought it in the nature of things that you and I could ever agree on paper, touching a certain Chuzzlewitian question whereupon F—— tells me you have remarks to make, I should immediately walk into the same, tooth and nail. But as I don't, I won't. Contenting myself with this prediction, that one of these years and days, you will write or say to me, "My dear Dickens, you were right, though rough, and did a world of good, though you got most thoroughly hated for it." To which I shall reply, "My dear Felton, I looked a long way off and not immediately under my nose." . . . At which sentiment you will laugh, and I shall laugh; and then (for I foresee this will all happen in my land) we shall call for another pot of porter and two or three dozen of oysters.

Now don't you in your own heart and soul quarrel with me for this long silence? Not half so much as I quarrel with myself, I know; but if you could read half the letters I write to you in imagination, you would swear by me for the best of correspondents. The truth is, that when I have done my morning's work, down goes my pen, and from that minute I feel it a positive impossibility to take it up again, until imaginary butchers and bakers wave me to my desk. I walk about brimful of letters, facetious descriptions, touching morsels, and pathetic friendships, but can't for the soul of me uncork myself. The post-office is my rock ahead. My average number of letters that *must* be written every day is, at the least, a dozen. And you could no more know what I was writing to you spiritually, from the perusal of the bodily thirteenth, than you could tell from my hat what was going on in my head, or could read my heart on the surface of my flannel waistcoat.

This is a little fishing-place; intensely quiet; built on a cliff whereon — in the centre of a tiny semicircular bay — our house stands; the sea rolling and dashing under the windows. Seven miles out are the Goodwin Sands, (you've heard of the Goodwin Sands?) whence floating lights perpetually wink after dark, as if they were carrying on intrigues with the servants. Also there is a big lighthouse called the North Foreland on a hill behind the village, a severe parsonic light, which reproves the young and giddy floaters, and stares grimly out upon the sea. Under the cliff are rare good sands, where all the children assemble every morning and throw up impossible fortifications, which the sea throws down again at high water. Old gentlemen and ancient ladies flirt after their own manner in two reading-rooms and on a great many scattered seats in the open air. Other old gentlemen look all day through telescopes and never see anything. In a bay-window in a one pair sits from nine o'clock to one a gentleman with rather long hair and no neckcloth, who writes and grins as if he thought he were very funny indeed. His name is Boz. At one he disappears, and presently emerges from a bathing-machine, and may be seen — a kind of salmon-colored porpoise

— splashing about in the ocean. After that he may be seen in another bay-window on the ground-floor, eating a strong lunch; after that, walking a dozen miles or so, or lying on his back in the sand reading a book. Nobody bothers him unless they know he is disposed to be talked to; and I am told he is very comfortable indeed. He's as brown as a berry, and they *do* say is a small fortune to the innkeeper who sells beer and cold punch. But this is mere rumor. Sometimes he goes up to London (eighty miles, or so, away), and then I'm told there is a sound in Lincoln Inn Fields at night, as of men laughing, together with a clinking of knives and forks and wine-glasses.

I never shall have been so near you since we parted aboard the George Washington as next Tuesday. Forster, Maclise, and I, and perhaps Stanfield, are then going aboard the Cunard steamer at Liverpool, to bid Macready good by, and bring his wife away. It will be a very hard parting. You will see and know him of course. We gave him a splendid dinner last Saturday at Richmond, whereat I presided with my accustomed grace. He is one of the noblest fellows in the world, and I would give a great deal that you and I should sit beside each other to see him play Virginius, Lear, or Werner, which I take to be, every way, the greatest piece of exquisite perfection that his lofty art is capable of attaining. His Macbeth, especially the last act, is a tremendous reality; but so indeed is almost everything he does. You recollect, perhaps, that he was the guardian of our children while we were away. I love him dearly. . . . .

You asked me, long ago, about Maclise. He is such a wayward fellow in his subjects, that it would be next to impossible to write such an article as you were thinking of about him. I wish you could form an idea of his genius. One of these days a book will come out, " Moore's Irish Melodies," entirely illustrated by him, on every page. *When* it comes, I'll send it to you. You will have some notion of him then. He is in great favor with the queen, and paints secret pictures for her to put upon her husband's table on the morning of his birthday, and the like. But if he has a care, he will leave his mark on more enduring things than palace walls.

And so L—— is married. I remember *her* well, and could draw her portrait, in words, to the life. A very beautiful and gentle creature, and a proper love for a poet. My cordial remembrances and congratulations. Do they live in the house where we breakfasted? . . . .

I very often dream I am in America again; but, strange to say, I never dream of you. I am always endeavoring to get home in disguise, and have a dreary sense of the distance. *Apropos* of dreams, is it not a strange thing if writers of fiction never dream of their own creations; recollecting, I suppose, even in their dreams, that they have no real existence? *I* never dreamed of any of my own characters, and I feel it so impossible that I would wager Scott never did of his, real as they are. I had a good piece of absurdity in my head a night or two ago. I dreamed that somebody was dead. I don't know who, but it's not to the purpose. It was a private gentleman, and a particular friend; and I was greatly overcome when the news was broken to me (very delicately) by a gentleman in a cocked hat, top boots, and a sheet. Nothing else. "Good God!" I said, "is he dead?" "He is as dead, sir," rejoined the gentleman, "as a door-nail. But we must all die, Mr. Dickens; sooner or later, my dear sir." "Ah!" I said. "Yes, to be sure. Very true. But what did he die of?" The gentleman burst into a flood of tears, and said, in a voice broken by emotion: "He christened his youngest child, sir, with a toasting-fork." I never in my life was so affected as at his having fallen a victim to this complaint. It carried a conviction to my mind that he never could have recovered. I knew that it was the most interesting and fatal malady in the world; and I wrung the gentleman's hand in a convulsion of respectful admiration, for I felt that this explanation did equal honor to his head and heart!

What do you think of Mrs. Gamp? And how do you like the undertaker? I have a fancy that they are in your way. O heaven! such green woods as I was rambling among down in Yorkshire, when I was getting that done last July! For days and weeks we never saw the sky but through green boughs; and all day long I cantered over such soft moss and turf, that the horse's feet scarcely made a sound upon it. We have some friends in that part of the country (close to Castle Howard, where Lord Morpeth's father dwells in state, *in* his park indeed), who are the jolliest of the jolly, keeping a big old country house, with an ale cellar something larger than a reasonable church, and everything like Goldsmith's bear dances, "in a concatenation accordingly." Just the place for you, Felton! We performed some madnesses there in the way of forfeits, picnics, rustic games, inspections of ancient monasteries at midnight, when the moon was shining, that would have gone to your heart, and, as Mr. Weller says, "come out on the other side.". . . .

Write soon, my dear Felton; and if I write to you less often than I would, believe that my affectionate heart is with you always Loves and regards to all friends, from yours ever and ever,

CHARLES DICKENS.

These letters grow better and better as we get on. Ah me! and to think we shall have no more from that delightful pen!

DEVONSHIRE TERRACE, LONDON, January 2, 1844.

MY VERY DEAR FELTON: You are a prophet, and had best retire from business straightway. Yesterday morning, New Year's day, when I walked into my little workroom after breakfast, and was looking out of window at the snow in the garden, — not seeing it particularly well in consequence of some staggering suggestions of last night, whereby I was beset, — the postman came to the door with a knock, for which I denounced him from my heart. Seeing your hand upon the cover of a letter which he brought, I immediately blessed him, presented him with a glass of whiskey, inquired after his family (they are all well), and opened the despatch with a moist and oystery twinkle in my eye. And on the very day from which the new year dates, I read your New Year congratulations as punctually as if you lived in the next house. Why don't you?

Now, if instantly on the receipt of this you will send a free and independent citizen down to the Cunard wharf at Boston, you will find that Captain Hewett, of the Britannia steamship (my ship), has a small parcel for Professor Felton of Cambridge; and in that parcel you will find a Christmas Carol in prose; being a short story of Christmas by Charles Dickens. Over which Christmas Carol Charles Dickens wept and laughed and wept again, and excited himself in a most extraordinary manner in the composition; and thinking whereof he walked about the black streets of London, fifteen and twenty miles, many a night when all the sober folks had gone to bed..... Its success is most prodigious. And by every post all manner of strangers write all manner of letters to him about their homes and hearths, and how this same Carol is read aloud there, and kept on a little shelf by itself. Indeed, it is the greatest success, as I am told, that this ruffian and rascal has ever achieved.

Forster is out again; and if he don't go in again, after the manner in which we have been keeping Christmas, he must be very strong indeed. Such dinings, such dancings, such conjurings, such blindman's-buffings, such theatre-goings, such kissings-out of old years and kissings-in of new ones, never took place in these parts before. To keep the Chuzzlewit going, and do this little book, the Carol, in the odd times between two parts of it, was, as you may suppose, pretty tight work. But when it was done I broke out like a madman. And if you could have seen me at a children's party at Macready's the other night, going down a country dance with Mrs. M., you would have thought I was a country gentleman of independent property, residing on a tiptop farm, with the wind blowing straight in my face every day. . . . .

Your friend, Mr. P——, dined with us one day (I don't know whether I told you this before), and pleased us very much. Mr. C—— has dined here once, and spent an evening here. I have not seen him lately, though he has called twice or thrice; for K—— being unwell and I busy, we have not been visible at our accustomed seasons. I wonder whether H—— has fallen in your way. Poor H——! He was a good fellow, and has the most grateful heart I ever met with. Our journeyings seem to be a dream now. Talking of dreams, strange thoughts of Italy and France, and maybe Germany, are springing up within me as the Chuzzlewit clears off. It's a secret I have hardly breathed to any one, but I "think" of leaving England for a year, next midsummer, bag and baggage, little ones and all, — then coming out with *such* a story, Felton, all at once, no parts, sledge-hammer blow.

I send you a Manchester paper, as you desire. The report is not exactly done, but very well done, notwithstanding. It was a very splendid sight, I assure you, and an awful-looking audience. I am going to preside at a similar meeting at Liverpool on the 26th of next month, and on my way home I may be obliged to preside at another at Birmingham. I will send you papers, if the reports be at all like the real thing.

I wrote to Prescott about his book, with which I was perfectly charmed. I think his descriptions masterly, his style brilliant, his purpose manly and gallant always. The introductory account of Aztec civilization impressed me exactly as it impressed you. From beginning to end, the whole history is enchanting and full of genius. I only wonder that, having such an opportunity of illustrating the doctrine of visible judgments, he never remarks, when Cortes and his men tumble the idols down the temple steps and call upon the people to take notice that their gods are powerless to help themselves, that possibly if some intelligent native had tumbled down the image of the Virgin or patron saint after them nothing very remarkable might have ensued in consequence.

Of course you like Macready. Your name's Felton. I wish you could see him play Lear. It is stupendously terrible. But I suppose he would be slow to act it with the Boston company.

Hearty remembrances to Sumner, Longfellow, Prescott, and all whom you know I love to remember. Countless happy years to

you and yours, my dear Felton, and some instalment of them, however slight, in England, in the loving company of
THE PROSCRIBED ONE.
O, breathe not his name.

Here is a portfolio of Dickens's letters, written to me from time to time during the past ten years. As long ago as the spring of 1858 I began to press him very hard to come to America and give us a course of readings from his works. At that time I had never heard him read in public, but the fame of his wonderful performances rendered me eager to have my own country share in the enjoyment of them. Being in London in the summer of 1859, and dining with him one day in his town residence, Tavistock House, Tavistock Square, we had much talk in a corner of his library about coming to America. I thought him over-sensitive with regard to his reception here, and I tried to remove any obstructions that might exist in his mind at that time against a second visit across the Atlantic. I followed up our conversation with a note setting forth the certainty of his success among his Transatlantic friends, and urging him to decide on a visit during the year. He replied to me, dating from "Gad's Hill Place, Higham by Rochester, Kent."

"I write to you from my little Kentish country house, on the very spot where Falstaff ran away.

"I cannot tell you how very much obliged to you I feel for your kind suggestion, and for the perfectly frank and unaffected manner in which it is conveyed to me.

"It touches, I will admit to you frankly, a chord that has several times sounded in my breast, since I began my readings. I should very much like to read in America. But the idea is a mere dream as yet. Several strong reasons would make the journey difficult to me, and — even were they overcome — I would never make it, unless I had great general reason to believe that the American people really wanted to hear me.

"Through the whole of this autumn I shall be reading in various parts of England, Ireland, and Scotland. I mention this, in reference to the closing paragraph of your esteemed favor.

"Allow me once again to thank you most heartily, and to remain,
"Gratefully and faithfully yours,
"CHARLES DICKENS."

Early in the month of July, 1859, I spent a day with him in his beautiful country retreat in Kent. He drove me about the leafy lanes in his basket wagon, pointing out the lovely spots belonging to his friends, and ending with a visit to the ruins of Rochester Castle. We climbed up the time-worn walls and leaned out of the ivied windows, looking into the various apartments below. I remember how vividly he reproduced a probable scene in the great old banqueting-room, and how graphically he imagined the life of *ennui* and every-day tediousness that went on in those lazy old times. I recall his fancy picture of the dogs stretched out before the fire, sleeping and snoring with their masters. That day he seemed to revel in the past, and I stood by, listening almost with awe to his impressive voice, as he spoke out whole chapters of a romance destined never to be written. On our way back to Gad's Hill Place, he stopped in the road, I remember, to have a crack with a gentleman who he told me was a son of Sydney Smith. The only other guest at his table that day was Wilkie Collins; and after dinner we three went out and lay down on the grass, while Dickens showed off a raven that was hopping about, and told anecdotes of the bird and of his many predecessors. We also talked about his visiting America, I putting as many spokes as possible into that favorite wheel of mine. A day or two after I returned to London I received this note from him: —

". . . . Only to say that I heartily enjoyed our day, and shall long remember it. Also that I have been perpetually repeating the —— experience (of a more tremendous sort in the way of ghastly comicality, experience there is none) on the grass, on my back. Also, that I have not forgotten Cobbett. Also, that I shall trouble you at greater length when the mysterious oracle, of New York, pronounces.

"Wilkie Collins begs me to report that he declines pale horse, and all other horse exercise — and all exercise, except eating, drinking, smoking, and sleeping — in the dog days.

"With united kind regards, believe me always cordially yours,
"CHARLES DICKENS."

An agent had come out from New York with offers to induce him to arrange for a speedy visit to America, and Dickens was then waiting to see the man who had been announced as on his way to him. He was evidently giving the subject serious consideration, for on the 20th of July he sends me this note: —

"As I have not yet heard from Mr. —— of New York, I begin to think it likely (or, rather, I begin to think it more likely than I thought it before) that he has not backers good and sufficient, and that his 'mission' will go off. It is possible that I may hear from him before the month is out, and I shall not make any reading arrangements until it has come to a close; but I do not regard it as being very probable that the said —— will appear satisfactorily, either in the flesh or the spirit.

"Now, considering that it would be August before I could move in the matter, that it would be indispensably necessary to choose some business connection and have some business arrangements made in America, and that I am inclined to think it would not be easy to originate and complete all the necessary preparations for beginning in October, I want your kind advice on the following points: —

"1. Suppose I postponed the idea for a year.

"2. Suppose I postponed it until after Christmas.

"3. Suppose I sent some trusty person out to America *now*, to negotiate with some sound, responsible, trustworthy man of business in New York, accustomed to public undertakings of such a nature; my negotiator being fully empowered to conclude any arrangements with him that might appear, on consultation, best.

"Have you any idea of any such person to whom you could recommend me? Or of any such agent here? I only want to see my way distinctly, and to have it prepared before me, out in the

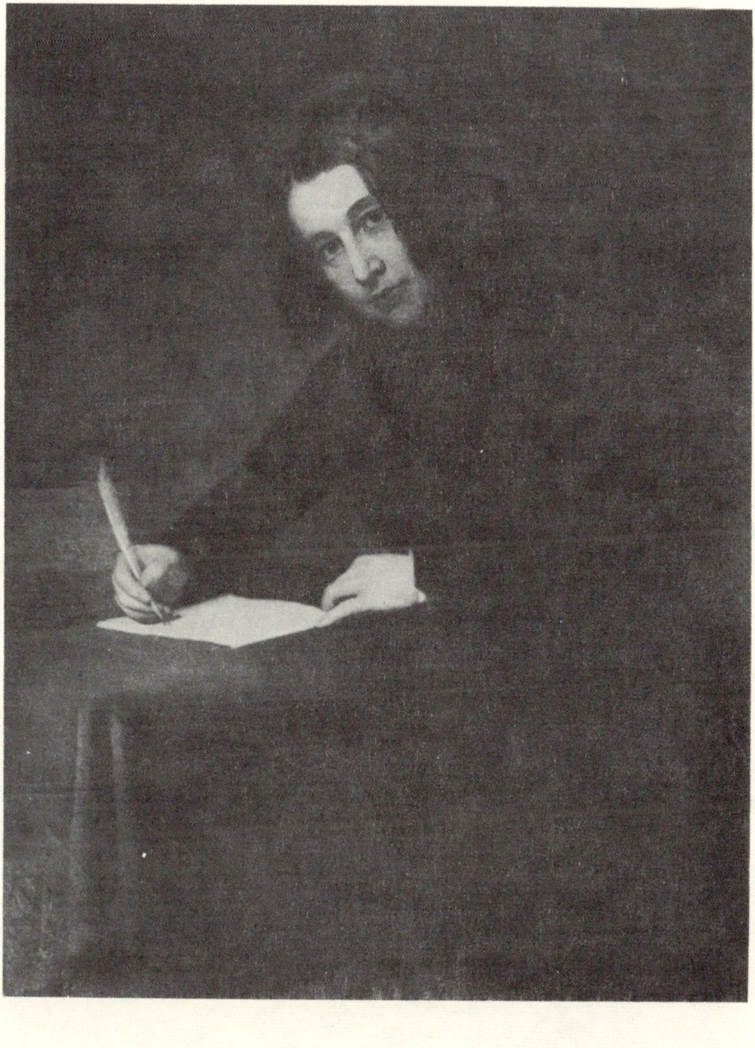

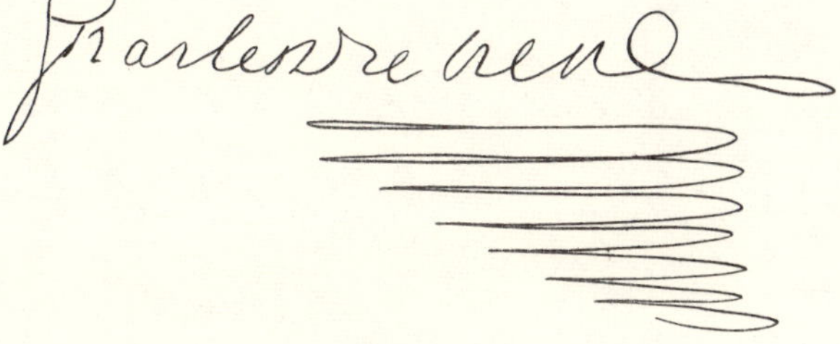

States. Now, I will make no apology for troubling you, because I thoroughly rely on your interest and kindness.

"I am at Gad's Hill, except on Tuesdays and the greater part of Wednesdays.

"With kind regards, very faithfully yours,
"CHARLES DICKENS."

Various notes passed between us after this, during my stay in London in 1859. On the 6th of August he writes:—

"I have considered the subject in every way, and have consulted with the few friends to whom I ever refer my doubts, and whose judgment is in the main excellent. I have (this is between ourselves) come to the conclusion *that I will not go now.*

"A year hence I may revive the matter, and your presence in America will then be a great encouragement and assistance to me. I shall see you (at least I count upon doing so) at my house in town before you turn your face towards the locked-up house; and we will then, reversing Macbeth, 'proceed further in this business.' . . . .

"Believe me always (and here I forever renounce 'Mr.,' as having anything whatever to do with our communication, and as being a mere preposterous interloper),
"Faithfully yours,
"CHARLES DICKENS."

When I arrived in Rome, early in 1860, one of the first letters I received from London was from him. The project of coming to America was constantly before him, and he wrote to me that he should have a great deal to say when I came back to England in the spring; but the plan fell through, and he gave up all hope of crossing the water again. However, I did not let the matter rest; and when I returned home I did not cease, year after year, to keep the subject open in my communications with him. He kept a watchful eye on what was going forward in America, both in literature and politics. During the war, of course, both of us gave up our correspondence about the readings. He was actively engaged all over Great Britain in giving his marvellous entertainments, and there certainly was no occasion for his travelling elsewhere. In October, 1862, I sent him the proof-sheets of an article, that was soon to appear in the Atlantic Monthly, on "Blind Tom," and on receipt of it he sent me a letter, from which this is an extract: —

"I have read that affecting paper you have had the kindness to send me, with strong interest and emotion. You may readily suppose that I have been most glad and ready to avail myself of your permission to print it. I have placed it in our Number made up to-day, which will be published on the 18th of this month, — well before you, — as you desire.

"Think of reading in America? Lord bless you, I think of reading in the deepest depth of the lowest crater in the Moon, on my way there!

"There is no sun-picture of my Falstaff House as yet; but it shall be done, and you shall have it. It has been much improved internally since you saw it. . . . .

"I expect Macready at Gad's Hill on Saturday. You know that his second wife (an excellent one) presented him lately with a little boy? I was staying with him for a day or two last winter, and, seizing an umbrella when he had the audacity to tell me he was growing old, made at him with Macduff's defiance. Upon which he fell into the old fierce guard, with the desperation of thirty years ago.

"Kind remembrances to all friends who kindly remember me.
"Ever heartily yours,
"CHARLES DICKENS."

Every time I had occasion to write to him after the war, I stirred up the subject of the readings. On the 2d of May, 1866, he says: —

"Your letter is an excessively difficult one to answer, because I really do not know that any sum of money that could be laid down would induce me to cross the Atlantic to read. Nor do I think it likely that any one on your side of the great water can be prepared to understand the state of the case. For example, I am now just finishing a series of thirty readings. The crowds attending them have been so astounding, and the relish for them has so far outgone all previous experience, that if I were to set myself the task, 'I will make such or such a sum of money by devoting myself to readings for a certain time,' I should have to go no further than Bond Street or Regent Street, to have it secured to me in a day. Therefore, if a specific offer, and a very large one indeed, were made to me from America, I should naturally ask myself, 'Why go through this wear and tear, merely to pluck fruit that grows on every bough at home?' It is a delightful sensation to move a new people; but I have but to go to Paris, and I find the brightest people in the world quite ready for me. I say thus much in a sort of desperate endeavor to explain myself to you. I can put no price upon fifty readings in America, because I do not know that any possible price could pay me for them. And I really cannot say to any one disposed towards the enterprise, 'Tempt me,' because I have too strong a misgiving that he cannot in the nature of things do it.

" This is the plain truth. If any distinct proposal be submitted to me, I will give it a distinct answer. But the chances are a round thousand to one that the answer will be no, and therefore I feel bound to make the declaration beforehand.

" . . . . This place has been greatly improved since you were here, and we should be heartily glad if you and she could see it.
" Faithfully yours ever,
" CHARLES DICKENS."

On the 16th of October he writes: —

" Although I perpetually see in the papers that I am coming out with a new serial, I assure you I know no more of it at present. I am *not* writing (except for Christmas number of 'All the Year Round'), and am going to begin, in the middle of January, a series of forty-two readings. Those will probably occupy me until Easter. Early in the summer I hope to get to work upon a story that I have in my mind. But in what form it will appear I do not yet know, because when the time comes I shall have to take many circumstances into consideration. . . . .

"A faint outline of a castle in the air always dimly hovers between me and Rochester, in the great hall of which I see myself reading to American audiences. But my domestic surroundings must change before the castle takes tangible form. And perhaps *I* may change first, and establish a castle in the other world. So no more at present.
" Believe me ever faithfully yours,
" CHARLES DICKENS."

In June, 1867, things begin to look more promising,

and I find in one of his letters, dated the 3d of that month, some good news, as follows : —

"I cannot receive your pleasantest of notes, without assuring you of the interest and gratification that *I* feel on *my* side in our alliance. And now I am going to add a piece of intelligence that I hope may not be disagreeable.

"I am trying hard so to free myself, as to be able to come over to read this next winter! Whether I may succeed in this endeavor or no I cannot yet say, but I am trying HARD. So in the mean time don't contradict the rumor. In the course of a few mails I hope to be able to give you positive and definite information on the subject.

"My daughter (whom I shall not bring if I come) will answer for herself by and by. Understand that I am really endeavoring tooth and nail to make my way personally to the American public, and that no light obstacles will turn me aside, now that my hand is in.

"My dear Fields, faithfully yours always,
"CHARLES DICKENS."

This was followed up by another letter, dated the 13th, in which he says : —

"I have this morning resolved to send out to Boston, in the first week in August, Mr. Dolby, the secretary and manager of my readings. He is profoundly versed in the business of those delightful intellectual feasts (!), and will come straight to Ticknor and Fields, and will hold solemn council with them, and will then go to New York, Philadelphia, Hartford, Washington, etc., etc., and see the rooms for himself, and make his estimates. He will then telegraph to me: 'I see my way to such and such results. Shall I go on?' If I reply, 'Yes,' I shall stand committed to begin reading in America with the month of December. If I reply, 'No,' it will be because I do not clearly see the game to be worth so large a candle. In either case he will come back to me.

"He is the brother of Madame Sainton Dolby, the celebrated singer. I have absolute trust in him and a great regard for him. He goes with me everywhere when I read, and manages for me to perfection.

"We mean to keep all this STRICTLY SECRET, as I beg of you to do, until I finally decide for or against. I am beleaguered by every kind of speculator in such things on your side of the water; and it is very likely that they would take the rooms over our heads, — to

charge me heavily for them, — or would set on foot unheard-of devices for buying up the tickets, etc., etc., if the probabilities oozed out. This is exactly how the case stands now, and I confide it to you within a couple of hours after having so far resolved. Dolby quite understands that *he* is to confide in you, similarly, without a particle of reserve.
"Ever faithfully yours,
"CHARLES DICKENS."

On the 12th of July he says: —

"Our letters will be crossing one another rarely! I have received your cordial answer to my first notion of coming out; but there has not yet been time for me to hear again. ....

"With kindest regard to 'both your houses,' public and private,
"Ever faithfully yours,
"CHARLES DICKENS."

He had engaged to write for "Our Young Folks" "A Holiday Romance," and the following note, dated the 25th of July, refers to the story: —

"Your note of the 12th is like a cordial of the best sort. I have taken it accordingly.

"Dolby sails in the Java on Saturday, the 3d of next month, and will come direct to you. You will find him a frank and capital fellow. He is perfectly acquainted with his business and with his chief, and may be trusted without a grain of reserve.

"I hope the Americans will see the joke of 'Holiday Romance.' The writing seems to me so like children's, that dull folks (on *any* side of *any* water) might perhaps rate it accordingly! I should like to be beside you when you read it, and particularly when you read the Pirate's story. It made me laugh to that extent that my people here thought I was out of my wits, until I gave it to them to read, when they did likewise.
"Ever cordially yours,
"CHARLES DICKENS."

On the 3d of September he breaks out in this wise, Dolby having arrived out and made all arrangements for the readings: —

"Your cheering letter of the 21st of August arrived here this morning. A thousand thanks for it. I begin to think (nautically) that I 'head west'ard.' You shall hear from me fully and finally as soon as Dolby shall have reported personally.

"The other day I received a letter from Mr. —— of New York (who came over in the winning yacht, and described the voyage in the Times), saying he would much like to see me. I made an appointment in London, and observed that when he *did* see me he was obviously astonished. While I was sensible that the magnificence of my appearance would fully account for his being overcome, I nevertheless angled for the cause of his surprise. He then told me that there was a paragraph going round the papers, to the effect that I was 'in a critical state of health.' I asked him if he was sure it was n't 'cricketing' state of health? To which he replied, Quite. I then asked him down here to dinner, and he was again staggered by finding me in sporting training; also much amused.

"Yesterday's and to-day's post bring me this unaccountable paragraph from hosts of uneasy friends, with the enormous and wonderful addition that 'eminent surgeons' are sending me to America for 'cessation from literary labor'!!! So I have written a quiet line to the Times, certifying to my own state of health, and have also begged Dixon to do the like in the Athenæum. I mention the matter to you, in order that you may contradict, from me, if the nonsense should reach America unaccompanied by the truth. But I suppose that the New York Herald will probably have got the latter from Mr. —— aforesaid. . . . .

"Charles Reade and Wilkie Collins are here; and the joke of the time is to feel my pulse when I appear at table, and also to inveigle innocent messengers to come over to the summer-house, where I write (the place is quite changed since you were here, and a tunnel under the high road connects this shrubbery with the front garden), to ask, with their compliments, how I find myself *now*.

"If I come to America this next November, even you can hardly imagine with what interest I shall try Copperfield on an American audience, or, if they give me their heart, how freely and fully I shall give them mine. We will ask Dolby then whether he ever heard it before.

"I cannot thank you enough for your invaluable help to Dolby. He writes that at every turn and moment the sense and knowledge and tact of Mr. Osgood are inestimable to him.

"Ever, my dear Fields, faithfully yours,
"CHARLES DICKENS."

Here is a little note dated the 3d of October: —

"I cannot tell you how much I thank you for your kind little letter, which is like a pleasant voice coming across the Atlantic, with that domestic welcome in it which has no substitute on earth. If you knew how strongly I am inclined to allow myself the pleasure of staying at your house, you would look upon me as a kind of ancient Roman (which, I trust in Heaven, I am not) for having the courage to say no. But if I gave myself that gratification in the beginning, I could scarcely hope to get on in the hard 'reading' life, without offending some kindly disposed and hospitable American friend afterwards; whereas if I observe my English principle on such occasions, of having no abiding-place but an hotel, and stick to it from the first, I may perhaps count on being consistently uncomfortable.

"The nightly exertion necessitates meals at odd hours, silence and rest at impossible times of the day, a general Spartan behavior so utterly inconsistent with my nature, that if you were to give me a happy inch, I should take an ell, and frightfully disappoint you in public. I don't want to do that, if I can help it, and so I will be good in spite of myself.

"Ever your affectionate friend,
"CHARLES DICKENS."

A ridiculous paragraph in the papers following close on the public announcement that Dickens was coming to America in November, drew from him this letter to me, dated also early in October: —

"I hope the telegraph clerks did not mutilate out of recognition or reasonable guess the words I added to Dolby's last telegram to Boston. 'Tribune London correspondent totally false.' Not only is there not a word of truth in the pretended conversation, but it is so absurdly unlike me that I cannot suppose it to be even invented by any one who ever heard me exchange a word with mortal creature. For twenty years I am perfectly certain that I have never made any other allusion to the republication of my books in America than the good-humored remark, 'that if there had been international copyright between England and the States, I should have been a man of very large fortune, instead of a man of moderate savings, always supporting a very expensive public position.' Nor have I ever been such a fool as to charge the absence of international copyright upon individuals. Nor have I ever been so ungenerous as to disguise or suppress the fact that I have received handsome sums for advance sheets. When I was in the States, I said what I had to say on the question, and there an end. I am absolutely certain that I have never since expressed myself, even with soreness, on the subject. Reverting to the preposterous fabrication of the London correspondent, the statement that I ever talked about 'these fellows' who republished my books, or pretended to know (what I don't know at this instant) who made how much out of them, or ever talked of their sending me 'conscience money,' is as grossly and completely false as the statement that I ever said anything to the effect that I could not be expected to have an interest in the American people. And nothing can by any possibility be falser than that. Again and again in these pages (All the Year Round) I have expressed my interest in them. You will see it in the 'Child's History of England.' You will see it in the last Preface to 'American Notes.' Every American who has ever spoken with me in London, Paris, or where not, knows whether I have frankly said, 'You could have no better introduction to me than your country.' And for years and years when I have been asked about reading in America, my invariable reply has been, 'I have so many friends there, and constantly receive so many earnest letters from personally unknown readers there, that, but for domestic reasons, I would go to-morrow.' I think I must, in the confidential intercourse between you and me, have written you to this effect more than once.

"The statement of the London correspondent from beginning to end is false. It is false in the letter and false in the spirit. He may have been misinformed, and the statement may not have originated with him. With whomsoever it originated, it never originated with me, and consequently is false. More than enough about it.

"As I hope to see you so soon, my dear Fields, and as I am busily at work on the Christmas number, I will not make this a longer letter than I can help. I thank you most heartily for your proffered hospitality, and need not tell you that if I went to any friend's house in America, I would go to yours. But the readings are very hard work, and I think I cannot do better than observe the rule on that side of the Atlantic which I observe on this, — of never, under such circumstances, going to a friend's house, but always staying at a hotel. I am able to observe it here, by being consistent and never breaking it. If I am equally consistent there, I can (I hope) offend no one.

"Dolby sends his love to you and all his friends (as I do), and is girding up his loins vigorously.

"Ever, my dear Fields, heartily and affectionately yours,
"CHARLES DICKENS.'

Before sailing in November he sent off this note to me from the office of All the Year Round: —

"I received your more than acceptable letter yesterday morning, and consequently am able to send you this line of acknowledgment by the next mail. Please God we will have that walk among the autumn leaves, before the readings set in.

"You may have heard from Dolby that a gorgeous repast is to be given to me to-morrow, and that it is expected to be a notable demonstration. I shall try, in what I say, to state my American case exactly. I have a strong hope and belief that within the compass of a couple of minutes or so I can put it, with perfect truthfulness, in the light that my American friends would be best pleased to see me place it in. Either so, or my instinct is at fault.

"My daughters and their aunt unite with me in kindest loves. As I write, a shrill prolongation of the message comes in from the next room, 'Tell them to take care of you-u-u!'

"Tell Longfellow, with my love, that I am charged by Forster (who has been very ill of diffused gout and bronchitis) with a copy of his Sir John Eliot.

"I will bring you out the early proof of the Christmas number. We publish it here on the 12th of December. I am planning it (No Thoroughfare) out into a play for Wilkie Collins to manipulate after I sail, and have arranged for Fechter to go to the Adelphi Theatre and play a Swiss in it. It will be brought out the day after Christmas day.

"Here, at Boston Wharf, and everywhere else,
"Yours heartily and affectionately,
"C. D."

On a blustering evening in November, 1867, Dickens arrived in Boston Harbor, on his second visit to America. A few of his friends, under the guidance of the Collector of the port, steamed down in the custom-house boat to welcome him. It was pitch dark before we sighted the Cuba and ran alongside. The great steamer stopped for a few minutes to take us on board, and Dickens's cheery voice greeted me before I had time to distinguish him on the deck of the vessel. The news of the excitement the sale of the tickets to his readings had occasioned had been carried to him by the pilot, twenty miles out. He was in capital spirits over the cheerful account that all was going on so well, and I thought he never looked in better health. The voyage had been a good one, and the ten days' rest on shipboard had strengthened him amazingly he said. As we were told that a crowd had assembled in East Boston, we took him in our little tug and landed him safely at Long Wharf in Boston, where carriages were in waiting. Rooms had been taken for him at the Parker House, and in half an hour after he had reached the hotel he was sitting down to dinner with half a dozen friends, quite prepared, he said, to give the first reading in America that very night, if desirable. Assurances that the kindest feelings towards him existed everywhere put him in great spirits, and he seemed happy to be among us. On Sunday he visited the School Ship and said a few words of encouragement and counsel to the boys. He began his long walks at once, and girded himself up for the hard winter's work before him. Steadily refusing all invitations to go out during the weeks he was reading, he only went into one other house besides the Parker, habitually, during his stay in Boston. Every one who was present remembers the delighted crowds that assembled nightly in the Tremont Temple, and no one who heard Dickens, during that eventful month of December, will forget the sensation produced by the great author, actor, and reader. Hazlitt says of Kean's Othello, "The tone of voice in which he delivered the beautiful apostrophe 'Then, O, farewell,' struck on the heart like the swelling notes of some divine music, like the sound of years of departed happiness." There were thrills of pathos in Dickens's readings (of David Copperfield, for instance) which Kean himself never surpassed in dramatic effect.

He went from Boston to New York, carrying with him a severe catarrh contracted in our climate. In reality much of the time during his reading in Boston he was quite ill from the effects of the disease, but he fought courageously against its effects, and always came up, on the night of the reading, all right. Several times I feared he would be obliged to postpone the readings, and I am sure almost any one else would have felt compelled to do so; but he declared no man had a right to break an engagement with the public, if he were able to be out of bed. His spirit was wonderful, and, although he lost all appetite and could partake of very little food, he was always cheerful and ready for his work when the evening came round. Every morning his table was covered with invitations to dinners and all sorts of entertainments, but he said, "I came for hard work, and I must try to fulfil the expectations of the American public." He did accept a dinner which was tendered to him by some of his literary friends in Boston; but the day before it was to come off he was so ill he felt obliged to ask that the banquet might be given up. The strain upon his strength and nerves was very great during all the months he remained in the country, and only a man of iron will could have accomplished all he did. And here let me say, that although he was accustomed to talk and write a great deal about eating and drinking, I have rarely seen a man eat and drink less. He liked to dilate in imagination over the brewing of a bowl of punch, but I always noticed that when the punch was ready, he drank less of it than any one who might be present. It was the sentiment of the thing and not the thing itself that engaged his attention. He liked to have a little supper every night after a reading, and have three or four friends round the table with him, but he only pecked at the viands as a bird might do, and I scarcely saw him eat a hearty meal during his whole stay in the country. Both at Parker's Hotel in Boston, and at the Westminster in New York, everything was arranged by the proprietors for his comfort and happiness, and tempting dishes to pique his invalid appetite were sent up at different hours of the day, with the hope that he might be induced to try unwonted things and get up again the habit of eating more; but the influenza, that seized him with such masterful power, held the strong man down till he left the country.

One of the first letters I had from him, after he had begun his reading tour, was dated from the Westminster Hotel in New York, on the 15th of January, 1868.

MY DEAR FIELDS: On coming back from Philadelphia just now (three o'clock) I was welcomed by your cordial letter. It was a delightful welcome and did me a world of good.

The cold remains just as it was (beastly), and where it was (in my head). We have left off referring to the hateful subject, except in emphatic sniffs on my part, convulsive wheezes, and resounding sneezes.

The Philadelphia audience ready and bright. I think they understood the Carol better than Copperfield, but they were bright and responsive as to both. They also highly appreciated your friend Mr. Jack Hopkins. A most excellent hotel there, and everything satisfactory. While on the subject of satisfaction, I know you will be pleased to hear that a long run is confidently expected for the No Thoroughfare drama. Although the piece is well cast and well played, my letters tell me that Fechter is so remarkably fine as to play down the whole company. The Times, in its account of it, said that "Mr. Fechter" (in the Swiss mountain scene, and in the Swiss Hotel) "was practically alone upon the stage." It is splendidly got up, and the Mountain Pass (I planned it with the scene-painter) was loudly cheered by the whole house. Of course I knew that Fechter would tear himself to pieces rather than fall short, but I was not prepared for his contriving to get the pity and sympathy of the audience out of his passionate love for Marguerite.

My dear fellow, you cannot miss me more than I miss you and yours. And Heaven knows how gladly I would substitute Boston for Chicago, Detroit, and Co.! But the tour is fast shaping itself out into its last details, and we must remember that there is a clear fortnight in Boston, not counting the four Farewells. I look forward to that fortnight as a radiant landing-place in the series.....

Rash youth! No presumptuous hand should try to make the

punch, except in the presence of the hoary sage who pens these lines. With *him* on the spot to perceive and avert impending failure, with timely words of wisdom to arrest the erring hand and curb the straying judgment, and, with such gentle expressions of encouragement as his stern experience may justify, to cheer the aspirant with faint hopes of future excellence, — with these conditions observed, the daring mind may scale the heights of sugar and contemplate the depths of lemon. Otherwise not.

Dolby is at Washington, and will return in the night. ——— is on guard. He made a most brilliant appearance before the Philadelphia public, and looked hard at them. The mastery of his eye diverted their attention from his boots: charming in themselves, but (unfortunately) two left ones.

I send my hearty and enduring love. Your kindness to the British Wanderer is deeply inscribed in his heart.

When I think of L———'s story about Dr. Webster, I feel like the lady in Nickleby who " has had a sensation of alternate cold and biling water running down her back ever since."

Ever, my dear Fields, your affectionate friend,

C. D.

His birthday, 7th of February, was spent in Washington, and on the 9th of the month he sent this little note from Baltimore: —

BALTIMORE, Sunday, February 9, 1868.

MY DEAR FIELDS: I thank you heartily for your pleasant note (I can scarcely tell you *how* pleasant it was to receive the same) and for the beautiful flowers that you sent me on my birthday. For which — and much more — my loving thanks to both.

In consequence of the Washington papers having referred to the august 7th of this month, my room was on that day a blooming garden. Nor were flowers alone represented there. The silversmith, the goldsmith, the landscape-painter, all sent in their contributions. After the reading was done at night, the whole audience rose; and it was spontaneous, hearty, and affecting.

I was very much surprised by the President's face and manner. It is, in its way, one of the most remarkable faces I have ever seen. Not imaginative, but very powerful in its firmness (or perhaps obstinacy), strength of will, and steadiness of purpose. There is a reticence in it too, curiously at variance with that first unfortunate speech of his. A man not to be turned or trifled with. A man (I should say) who must be killed to be got out of the way. His manners, perfectly composed. We looked at one another pretty hard. There was an air of chronic anxiety upon him. But not a crease or a ruffle in his dress, and his papers were as composed as himself. (Mr. Thornton was going in to deliver his credentials, immediately afterwards.)

This day fortnight will find me, please God, in my "native Boston." I wish I were there to-day.

Ever, my dear Fields, your affectionate friend,

CHARLES DICKENS,
Chairman Missionary Society.

When he returned to Boston in the latter part of the month, after his fatiguing campaign in New York, Philadelphia, Baltimore, and Washington, he seemed far from well, and one afternoon sent round from the Parker House to me this little note, explaining why he could not go out on our accustomed walk.

"I have been terrifying Dolby out of his wits, by setting in for a paroxysm of sneezing, and it would be madness in me, with such a cold, and on such a night, and with to-morrow's reading before me, to go out. I need not add that I shall be heartily glad to see you if you have time. Many thanks for the Life and Letters of Wilder Dwight. I shall "save up" that book, to read on the passage home. After turning over the leaves, I have shut it up and put it away; for I am a great reader at sea, and wish to reserve the interest that I find awaiting me in the personal following of the sad war. Good God, when one stands among the hearths that war has broken, what an awful consideration it is that such a tremendous evil *must* be sometimes!

"Ever affectionately yours,
"CHARLES DICKENS."

I will dispose here of the question often asked me by correspondents, and lately renewed in many epistles, "*Was Charles Dickens a believer in our Saviour's life and teachings?*" Persons addressing to me such inquiries must be profoundly ignorant of the works of the great author, whom they endeavor by implication to place among the "Unbelievers." If anywhere, out of the Bible, God's goodness and mercy are solemnly commended to the world's attention, it is in the pages of Dickens. I had supposed that these written words of his, which have been so extensively copied both in Europe and America, from his last will and testament, dated the 12th of May, 1869, would forever remain an emphatic testimony to his Christian faith: —

"I commit my soul to the mercy of God, through our Lord and Saviour Jesus Christ, and I exhort my dear children humbly to try to guide themselves by the teachings of the New Testament."

I wish it were in my power to bring to the knowledge of all who doubt the Christian character of Charles Dickens certain other memorable words of his, written years ago, with reference to Christmas. They are not as familiar as many beautiful things from the same pen on the same subject, for the paper which enshrines them has not as yet been collected among his authorized works. Listen to these loving words in which the Christian writer has embodied the life of his Saviour: —

"Hark! the Waits are playing, and they break my childish sleep! What images do I associate with the Christmas music as I see them set forth on the Christmas tree? Known before all others, keeping far apart from all the others, they gather round my little bed. An angel, speaking to a group of shepherds in a field; some travellers, with eyes uplifted, following a star; a baby in a manger; a child in a spacious temple, talking with grave men; a solemn figure with a mild and beautiful face, raising a dead girl by the hand; again, near a city gate, calling back the son of a widow, on his bier, to life; a crowd of people looking through the opened roof of a chamber where he sits, and letting down a sick person on a bed, with ropes; the same in a tempest, walking on the water to a ship; again, on a sea-shore, teaching a great multitude; again, with a child upon his knee, and other children round; again, restoring sight to the blind, speech to the dumb, hearing to the deaf, health to the sick, strength to the lame, knowledge to the ignorant; again, dying upon a cross, watched by armed soldiers, a thick darkness coming on, the earth beginning to shake, and only one voice heard, — 'Forgive them, for they know not what they do!'"

The writer of these pages begs to say here, most respectfully and emphatically, that he will not feel himself bound, in future, to reply to any inquiries, from however well-meaning correspondents, as to whether Charles Dickens was an "Unbeliever," or a "Unitarian," or an "Episcopalian," or whether "he ever went to church in his life," or "used improper language," or "drank enough to hurt him." He was human, very human, but he was no scoffer or doubter. His religion was of the heart, and his faith beyond questioning. He taught the world, said Dean Stanley over his new-made grave in Westminster Abbey, great lessons of "the eternal value of generosity, of purity, of kindness, and of unselfishness," and by his fruits he shall be known of all men.

Let me commend to the attention of my numerous nameless correspondents, who have attempted to soil the moral character of Dickens, the following little incident, related to me by himself, during a summer-evening walk among the Kentish meadows, a few months before he died. I will try to tell the story, if possible, as simply and naturally as he told it to me.

"I chanced to be travelling some years ago," he said, "in a railroad carriage between Liverpool and London. Beside myself there were two ladies and a gentleman occupying the carriage. We happened to be all strangers to each other, but I noticed at once that a clergyman was of the party. I was occupied with a ponderous article in the 'Times,' when the sound of my own name drew my attention to the fact that a conversation was going forward among the three other persons in the carriage with reference to myself and my books. One of the ladies was perusing 'Bleak House,' then lately published, and the clergyman had commenced a conversation with the ladies by asking what book they were reading. On being told the author's name and the title of the book, he expressed himself greatly grieved that any lady in England should be willing to take up the writings of so vile a character as Charles Dickens. Both the ladies showed great surprise at the low estimate the clergyman put upon an author whom they had been accustomed to read, to say the least, with a certain degree of pleasure. They were evidently much shocked at what the man said of the immoral tendency of these books, which they seemed never before to have suspected; but when he attacked the author's private character, and told monstrous stories of his immoralities in every direction, the volume was shut up and consigned to the dark pockets of a travelling bag. I listened in wonder and astonishment, behind my newspaper, to stories of myself, which if they had been true would have consigned any man to a prison for life. After my fictitious biographer had occupied himself for nearly an hour with the eloquent recital of my delinquencies and crimes, I very quietly joined in the conversation. Of course I began by modestly doubting some statements which I had just heard, touching the author of 'Bleak House,' and other unimportant works of a similar character. The man stared at me, and evidently considered my appearance on the conversational stage an intrusion and an impertinence. 'You seem to speak,' I said, 'from personal knowledge of Mr. Dickens. Are you acquainted with him?' He rather evaded the question, but, following him up closely, I compelled him to say that he had been talking, not from his own knowledge of the author in question; but he said he knew for a certainty that every statement he had made was a true one. I then became more earnest in my inquiries for proofs, which he arrogantly declined giving. The ladies sat by in silence, listening intently to what was going forward. An author they had been accustomed to read for amusement had been traduced for the first time in their hearing, and they were waiting to learn what I had to say in refutation of the clergyman's charges. I was taking up his vile stories, one by one, and stamping them as false in every particular, when the man grew furious, and asked me if I knew Dickens personally. I replied, 'Perfectly well; no man knows him better than I do; and all your stories about him from beginning to end, to these ladies, are unmitigated lies.' The man became livid with rage, and asked for my card. 'You shall have it,' I said, and, coolly taking out one, I presented it to him without bowing. We were just then nearing the station in London, so that I was spared a longer interview with my *truthful* companion; but, if I were to live a hundred years, I should not forget the abject condition into which the narrator of my crimes was instantly plunged. His face turned white as his cravat, and his lips refused to utter words. He seemed like a wilted vegetable, and as if his legs belonged to somebody else. The ladies became aware of the situation at once, and, bidding them 'good day,' I stepped smilingly out of the carriage. Before I could get away from the station the man had mustered up strength sufficient to follow me, and his apologies were so nauseous and craven, that I pitied him from my soul. I left him with this caution, 'Before you make charges against the character of any man again, about whom you know nothing, and of whose works you are utterly ignorant, study to be a seeker after Truth, and avoid Lying as you would eternal perdition.'"

I never ceased to wonder at Dickens's indomitable cheerfulness, even when he was suffering from ill health, and could not sleep more than two or three hours out of the twenty-four. He made it a point never to inflict on another what he might be painfully enduring himself, and I have seen him, with what must have been a great effort, arrange a merry meeting for some friends, when I knew that almost any one else under similar circumstances would have sought relief in bed.

One evening at a little dinner given by himself to half a dozen friends in Boston, he came out very strong. His influenza lifted a little, as he said afterwards, and he took advantage of the lull. Only his own pen could possibly give an idea of that hilarious night, and I will merely attempt a brief reference to it. As soon as we were seated at the table, I read in his lustrous eye, and heard in his jovial voice, that all solemn forms were to be dispensed with on that occasion, and that merriment might be confidently expected. To the end of the feast there was no let up to his magnificent cheerfulness and humor. J—— B——, ex-minister plenipotentiary as he was, went in for nonsense, and he, I am sure, will not soon forget how undignified we all were, and what screams of laughter went up from his own uncontrollable throat. Among other tomfooleries, we had an imitation of scenes at an English hustings, Dickens bringing on his candidate (his friend D——), and I opposing him with mine (the ex-minister). Of course there was nothing spoken in the speeches worth remembering, but it was Dickens's *manner* that carried off the whole thing. D—— necessarily now wears his hair so widely parted in the middle that only two little capillary scraps are left, just over his ears, to show what kind of thatch once covered his jolly cranium. Dickens pretended that *his* candidate was superior to the other, *because* he had no hair; and that mine, being profusely supplied with that commodity was in consequence disqualified in a marked degree for an election. His speech, for volubility and nonsense, was nearly fatal to us all. We roared and writhed in agonies of laughter, and the candidates themselves were literally choking and crying with the humor of the thing. But the fun culminated when I tried to get a hearing in behalf of my man, and

Dickens drowned all my attempts to be heard with imitative jeers of a boisterous election mob. He seemed to have as many voices that night as the human throat is capable of, and the repeated interrupting shouts, among others, of a pretended husky old man bawling out at intervals, "Three cheers for the bald 'un!" "Down vith the hairy aristocracy!" "Up vith the little shiny chap on top!" and other similar outbursts, I can never forget. At last, in sheer exhaustion, we all gave in, and agreed to break up and thus save our lives, if it were not already too late to make the attempt.

The extent and variety of Dickens's tones were wonderful. Once he described to me in an inimitable way a scene he witnessed many years ago at a London theatre, and I am certain no professional ventriloquist could have reproduced it better. I could never persuade him to repeat the description in presence of others; but he did it for me several times during our walks into the country, where he was, of course, unobserved. His recital of the incident was irresistibly droll, and no words of mine can give the *situation* even, as he gave it. He said he was once sitting in the pit of a London theatre, when two men came in and took places directly in front of him. Both were evidently strangers from the country, and not very familiar with the stage. One of them was stone deaf, and relied entirely upon his friend to keep him informed of the dialogue and story of the play as it went on, by having bawled into his ear, word for word, as near as possible what the actors and actresses were saying. The man who could hear became intensely interested in the play, and kept close watch of the stage. The deaf man also shared in the progressive action of the drama, and rated his friend soundly, in a loud voice, if a stitch in the story of the play were inadvertently dropped. Dickens gave the two voices of these two spectators with

CHARLES DICKENS: HIS WIFE, AND HER SISTER
GEORGINA HOGARTH

his best comic and dramatic power. Notwithstanding the roars of the audience, for the scene in the pit grew immensely funny to them as it went on, the deaf man and his friend were too much interested in the main business of the evening to observe that they were noticed. One bawled louder, and the other, with his elevated ear-trumpet, listened more intently than ever. At length the scene culminated in a most unexpected manner. "Now," screamed the hearing man to the deaf one, "they are going to elope!" "*Who* is going to elope?" asked the deaf man, in a loud, vehement tone. "Why, them two, the young man in the red coat and the girl in a white gown, that's a talking together now, and just going off the stage!" "Well, then, you must have missed telling me something they've said before," roared the other in an enraged and stentorian voice; "for there was nothing in their conduct all the evening, as you have been representing it to me, that would warrant them in such a proceeding!" At which the audience could not bear it any longer, and screamed their delight till the curtain fell.

Dickens was always planning something to interest and amuse his friends, and when in America he taught us several games arranged by himself, which we played again and again, he taking part as our instructor. While he was travelling from point to point, he was cogitating fresh charades to be acted when we should again meet. It was at Baltimore that he first conceived the idea of a walking-match, which should take place on his return to Boston, and he drew up a set of humorous "articles," which he sent to me with this injunction, "Keep them in a place of profound safety, for attested execution, until my arrival in Boston." He went into this matter of the walking-match with as much earnest directness as if he were planning a new novel. The articles, as prepared by himself, are thus drawn up: —

"Articles of agreement entered into at Baltimore, in the United States of America, this third day of February in the year of our Lord one thousand eight hundred and sixty-eight, between —— ——, British subject, *alias* the Man of Ross, and —— —— ——, American citizen, *alias* the Boston Bantam.

"Whereas, some Bounce having arisen between the above men in reference to feats of pedestrianism and agility, they have agreed to settle their differences and prove who is the better man, by means of a walking-match for two hats a side and the glory of their respective countries; and whereas they agree that the said match shall come off, whatsoever the weather, on the Mill Dam Road outside Boston, on Saturday, the 29th day of this present month; and whereas they agree that the personal attendants on themselves during the whole walk, and also the umpires and starters and declarers of victory in the match shall be —— —— of Boston, known in sporting circles as Massachusetts Jemmy, and Charles Dickens of Falstaff's Gad's Hill, whose surprising performances (without the least variation) on that truly national instrument, the American catarrh, have won for him the well-merited title of the Gad's Hill Gasper: —

"1. The men are to be started, on the day appointed, by Massachusetts Jemmy and The Gasper.

"2. Jemmy and The Gasper are, on some previous day, to walk out at the rate of not less than four miles an hour by the Gasper's watch, for one hour and a half. At the expiration of that one hour and a half they are to carefully note the place at which they halt. On the match's coming off they are to station themselves in the middle of the road, at that precise point, and the men (keeping clear of them and of each other) are to turn round them, right shoulder inward, and walk back to the starting-point. The man declared by them to pass the starting-point first is to be the victor and the winner of the match.

"3. No jostling or fouling allowed.

"4. All cautions or orders issued to the men by the umpires, starters, and declarers of victory to be considered final and admitting of no appeal.

"5. A sporting narrative of the match to be written by The Gasper within one week after its coming off, and the same to be duly printed (at the expense of the subscribers to these articles) on a broadside. The said broadside to be framed and glazed, and one copy of the same to be carefully preserved by each of the subscribers to these articles.

"6. The men to show on the evening of the day of walking, at six o'clock precisely, at the Parker House, Boston, when and where a dinner will be given them by The Gasper. The Gasper to occupy the chair, faced by Massachusetts Jemmy. The latter promptly and formally to invite, as soon as may be after the date of these presents, the following guests to honor the said dinner with their presence; that is to say [here follow the names of a few of his friends, whom he wished to be invited].

"Now, lastly. In token of their accepting the trusts and offices by these articles conferred upon them, these articles are solemnly and formally signed by Massachusetts Jemmy and by the Gad's Hill Gasper, as well as by the men themselves.

"Signed by the Man of Ross, otherwise —— ——.
"Signed by the Boston Bantam, otherwise —— —— ——.
"Signed by Massachusetts Jemmy, otherwise —— —— ——.
"Signed by the Gad's Hill Gasper, otherwise Charles Dickens.
"Witness to the signatures, —— ——."

When he returned to Boston from Baltimore, he proposed that I should accompany him over the walking-ground "at the rate of not less than four miles an hour, for one hour and a half." I shall not soon forget the tremendous pace at which he travelled that day. I have seen a great many walkers, but never one with whom I found it such hard work to keep up. Of course his object was to stretch out the space as far as possible for our friends to travel on the appointed day. With watch in hand, Dickens strode on over the Mill Dam toward Newton Centre. When we reached the turning-point, and had established the extreme limit, we both felt that we had given the men who were to walk in the match excellent good measure. All along the road people had stared at us, wondering, I suppose, why two men on such a blustering day should be pegging away in the middle of the road as if life depended on the speed they were getting over the ground. We had walked together many a mile before this, but never at such a rate as on this day. I had never seen his full power tested before, and I could not but feel great admiration for his walking pluck. We were both greatly heated, and, seeing a little shop by the roadside, we went in for refreshments. A few sickly-looking oranges were all we could obtain to quench our thirst, and we seized those and sat down on the shop door-steps, tired and panting. After a few minutes' rest we started again and walked back to town. Thirteen miles' stretch on a brisk winter day did neither of us any harm, and Dickens was in great spirits over the match that was so soon to come off. We agreed to walk over the ground again on the appointed day, keeping company with our respective men. Here is the account that Dickens himself drew up, of that day's achievement, for the broadside.

"THE SPORTING NARRATIVE.

"THE MEN.

"The Boston Bantam (*alias* Bright Chanticleer) is a young bird, though too old to be caught with chaff. He comes of a thorough game breed, and has a clear though modest crow. He pulls down the scale at ten stone and a half and add a pound or two. His previous performances in the pedestrian line have not been numerous. He once achieved a neat little match against time in two left boots at Philadelphia; but this must be considered as a pedestrian eccentricity, and cannot be accepted by the rigid chronicler as high art. The old mower with the scythe and hour-glass has not yet laid his mauley heavily on the Bantam's frontispiece, but he has had a grip at the Bantam's top feathers, and in plucking out a handful was very near making him like the great Napoleon Bonaparte (with the exception of the victualling department), when the ancient one found himself too much occupied to carry out the idea, and gave it up. The Man of Ross (*alias* old Alick Pope, *alias* Allourpraiseswhyshouldlords, etc.) is a thought and a half too fleshy, and, if he accidentally sat down upon his baby, would do it to the tune of fourteen stone. This popular codger is of the rubicund and jovial sort, and has long been known as a piscatorial pedestrian on the banks of the Wye. But Izaak Walton had n't pace, — look at his book and you 'll find it slow, — and when that article comes in question, the fishing-rod may prove to some of his disciples a rod in pickle. Howbeit, the Man of Ross is a lively ambler, and has a smart stride of his own.

"The Training.

"If vigorous attention to diet could have brought both men up to the post in tip-top feather, their condition would have left nothing to be desired. But both might have had more daily practice in the poetry of motion. Their breathings were confined to an occasional Baltimore burst under the guidance of The Gasper, and to an amicable toddle between themselves at Washington.

"The Course.

"Six miles and a half, good measure, from the first tree on the Mill Dam Road, lies the little village (with no refreshments in it but five oranges and a bottle of blacking) of Newton Centre. Here Massachusetts Jemmy and The Gasper had established the turning-point. The road comprehended every variety of inconvenience to test the mettle of the men, and nearly the whole of it was covered with snow.

"The Start

was effected beautifully. The men taking their stand in exact line at the starting-post, the first tree aforesaid, received from The Gasper the warning, "Are you ready?" and then the signal, "One, two, three. Go!" They got away exactly together, and at a spinning speed, waited on by Massachusetts Jemmy and the Gasper.

"The Race.

"In the teeth of an intensely cold and bitter wind, before which the snow flew fast and furious across the road from right to left, the Bantam slightly led. But the Man responded to the challenge, and soon breasted him. For the first three miles each led by a yard or so alternately; but the walking was very even. On four miles being called by The Gasper the men were side by side; and then ensued one of the best periods of the race, the same splitting pace being held by both through a heavy snow-wreath and up a dragging hill. At this point it was anybody's game, a dollar on Rossius and two half-dollars on the member of the feathery tribe. When five miles were called, the men were still shoulder to shoulder. At about six miles The Gasper put on a tremendous spirt to leave the men behind and establish himself at the turning-point at the entrance of the village. He afterwards declared that he received a mental knock-downer on taking his station and facing about, to find Bright Chanticleer close in upon him, and Rossius steaming up like a locomotive. The Bantam rounded first; Rossius rounded wide; and from that moment the Bantam steadily shot ahead. Though both were breathed at the town, the Bantam quickly got his bellows into obedient condition, and blew away like an orderly blacksmith in full work. The forcing-pumps of Rossius likewise proved themselves tough and true, and warranted first-rate, but he fell off in pace; whereas the Bantam pegged away with his little drumsticks, as if he saw his wives and a peck of barley waiting for him at the family perch. Continually gaining upon him of Ross, Chanticleer gradually drew ahead within a very few yards of half a mile, finally doing the whole distance in two hours and forty-eight minutes. Ross had ceased to compete three miles short of the winning-post, but bravely walked it out and came in seven minutes later.

"REMARKS.

"The difficulties under which this plucky match was walked can only be appreciated by those who were on the ground. To the excessive rigor of the icy blast and the depth and state of the snow must be added the constant scattering of the latter into the air and into the eyes of the men, while heads of hair, beards, eyelashes, and eyebrows were frozen into icicles. To breathe at all, in such a rarefied and disturbed atmosphere, was not easy; but to breathe up to the required mark was genuine, slogging, ding-dong, hard labor. That both competitors were game to the backbone, doing what they did under such conditions, was evident to all; but to his gameness the courageous Bantam added unexpected endurance and (like the sailor's watch that did three hours to the cathedral clock's one) unexpected powers of going when wound up. The knowing eye could not fail to detect considerable disparity between the lads; Chanticleer being, as Mrs. Cratchit said of Tiny Tim, "very light to carry," and Rossius promising fair to attain the rotundity of the Anonymous Cove in the Epigram: —

'And when he walks the streets the paviors cry,
"God bless you, sir!" — and lay their rammers by.'"

The dinner at the Parker House, after the fatigues of the day, was a brilliant success. The Great International Walking-Match was over; America had won, and England was nowhere. The victor and the vanquished were the heroes of the occasion, for both had shown great powers of endurance and done their work in capital time. We had no set speeches at the table, for we had voted eloquence a bore before we sat down. David Copperfield, Hyperion, Hosea Biglow, the Autocrat, and the Bad Boy were present, and there was no need of set speeches. The ladies present, being all daughters of America, smiled upon the champion, and we had a great, good time. The banquet provided by Dickens was profusely decorated with flowers, arranged by himself. The master of the feast was in his best mood, albeit his country had lost; and we all declared, when we bade him good night, that none of us had ever enjoyed a festival more.

Soon after this Dickens started on his reading travels again, and I received from him frequent letters from various parts of the country. On the 8th of March, 1868, he writes from a Western city: —

Sunday, 8th March, 1868.

MY DEAR FIELDS: We came here yesterday most comfortably in a "drawing-room car," of which (Rule Britannia!) we bought exclusive possession. —— is rather a depressing feather in the eagle's wing, when considered on a Sunday and in a thaw. Its hotel is likewise a dreary institution. But I have an impression that we must be in the wrong one, and buoy myself up with a devout belief in the other, over the way. The awakening to consciousness this morning on a lop-sided bedstead facing nowhere, in a room holding nothing but sour dust, was more terrible than the being afraid to go to bed last night. To keep ourselves up we played whist (double dummy) until neither of us could bear to speak to the other any more. We had previously supped on a tough old nightmare named buffalo.

What do you think of a "Fowl de poulet"? or a "Paettie de Shay"? or "Celary"? or "Murange with cream"? Because all these delicacies are in the printed bill of fare! If Mrs. Fields would like the recipe, how to make a "Paettie de Shay," telegraph instantly, and the recipe shall be purchased. We asked the Irish waiter what this dish was, and he said it was "the Frinch name the steward giv' to oyster pattie." It is usually washed down, I believe, with "Movseaux," or "Table Madeira," or "Abasinthe," or "Curraco," all of which drinks are on the wine list. I mean to drink my love to —— after dinner in Movseaux. Your ruggeder nature shall be pledged in Abasinthe.

Ever affectionately,
CHARLES DICKENS.

On the 19th of March he writes from Albany: —

ALBANY, 19th March, 1868.

MY DEAR ——: I should have answered your kind and welcome note before now, but that we have been in difficulties. After creeping through water for miles upon miles, our train gave it up as a bad job between Rochester and this place, and stranded us, early on Tuesday afternoon, at Utica. There we remained all night, and at six o'clock yesterday morning were ordered up to get ready for starting again. Then we were countermanded. Then we were once more told to get ready. Then we were told to stay where we were. At last we got off at eight o'clock, and after paddling through the flood until half past three, got landed here, — to the great relief of our minds as well as bodies, for the tickets were all sold out for last night. We had all sorts of adventures by the way, among which two of the most notable were: —

1. Picking up two trains out of the water, in which the passengers had been composedly sitting all night, until relief should arrive.

2. Unpacking and releasing into the open country a great train of cattle and sheep that had been in the water I don't know how long, and that had begun in their imprisonment to eat each other. I never could have realized the strong and dismal expressions of which the faces of sheep are capable, had I not seen the haggard countenances of this unfortunate flock as they were tumbled out of their dens and picked themselves up and made off, leaping wildly (many with broken legs) over a great mound of thawing snow, and over the worried body of a deceased companion. Their misery was so very human that I was sorry to recognize several intimate acquaintances conducting themselves in this forlornly gymnastic manner.

As there is no question that our friendship began in some previous state of existence many years ago, I am now going to make bold to mention a discovery we have made concerning Springfield.

Albany, Nineteenth March 1868.

My Dear Mrs Fields

I should have answered your kind and welcome note before now, but that we have been in difficulties. After creeping through water for miles upon miles, our train gave it up as a bad job, between Rochester and this place, and stranded us — say on Tuesday afternoon — at Utica. There we remained all night, and at 6 o'Clock yesterday morning were ordered up to get ready for starting again. Then, we were countermanded. Then, we were once more told to get ready. Then, we were told to stay where we were. At last we got off at 8 o'Clock, and after paddling through the floods until ½ past 3 yesterday got landed here: — to the great relief of our minds as well as bodies, for the tickets were all sold out for last night. We had all sorts of adventures by the way; among which two of the most notable were —

1. Picking up 2 trains out of the water

in which the passengers had been composed of, sitting all night in 't'il relief should arrive.

2. Unpacking and releasing into the open country, a great train of cattle and sheep that had been in the cars, waiting I don't know how long, and that had begun in their imprisonment to eat each other. I never could have realized the strong and dismal expression of which the faces of sheep are capable, had I not seen the haggard countenances of this unfortunate flock as they were tumbled out of their dens, and picked themselves up, and made off in — leaping wildly (many with broken legs) over a great mound of thawing snow, and over the worried body of a deceased companion. Their misery was so very human, that I was sorry to recognize several intimate acquaintances conducting themselves in this forlorn & gymnastic manner.

As there is no question that our friendship began in some previous state of existence many ages ago, I am now going to make bold to mention a discovery we have made concerning Springfield. We find that by remaining there next Saturday and Sunday, instead of coming on to Boston, we shall save several hours travel, and much wear and tear of our baggage and camp followers. Turned up at the Springfield Hotel. Excellent. Now, will you and Fields come and pass Sunday with us there? It will be delightful if you can. If you cannot, will you defer our Boston dinner until the following Sunday? Send me a hopeful word to Springfield (Massasoit House) in reply, please.

Lowell's delightful note enclosed with thanks. Do make a trial for Springfield. We saw Professor White at Syracuse and went out for a ride with him. Queer quarters at Utica, and nothing particular to eat; but the people so very anxious to please, that it was better than the best cuisine. I made a jug of Punch (in the bedroom pitcher) and we drank our love to you and Fields. Dolby had more than his share, in due practice of devoted enthusiasm.

 Dear Mrs Fields
  ever affectionately yours
   Charles Dickens

We find that by remaining there next Saturday and Sunday, instead of coming on to Boston, we shall save several hours' travel, and much wear and tear of our baggage and camp-followers. Ticknor reports the Springfield hotel excellent. Now will you and Fields come and pass Sunday with us there ? It will be delightful, if you can. If you cannot, will you defer our Boston dinner until the following Sunday ? Send me a hopeful word to Springfield (Massasoit House) in reply, please.

Lowell's delightful note enclosed with thanks. *Do* make a trial for Springfield. We saw Professor White at Syracuse, and went out for a ride with him. Queer quarters at Utica, and nothing particular to eat; but the people so very anxious to please, that it was better than the best cuisine. I made a jug of punch (in the bedroom pitcher), and we drank our love to you and Fields. Dolby had more than his share, under pretence of devoted enthusiasm.

Ever affectionately yours,
CHARLES DICKENS.

His readings everywhere were crowned with enthusiastic success, and if his strength had been equal to his will, he could have stayed in America another year, and occupied every night of it with his wonderful impersonations. I regretted extremely that he felt obliged to give up visiting the West. Invitations which greatly pleased him came day after day from the principal cities and towns, but his friends soon discovered that his health would not allow him to extend his travels beyond Washington.

He sailed for home on the 19th of April, 1868, and we shook hands with him on the deck of the Russia as the good ship turned her prow toward England. He was in great spirits at the thought of so soon again seeing Gad's Hill, and the prospect of a rest after all his toilsome days and nights in America. While at sea he wrote the following letter to me : —

ABOARD THE RUSSIA, BOUND FOR LIVERPOOL, Sunday, 26th April, 1868.

MY DEAR FIELDS : In order that you may have the earliest intelligence of me, I begin this note to-day in my small cabin, purposing (if it should prove practicable) to post it at Queenstown for the return steamer.

We are already past the Banks of Newfoundland, although our course was seventy miles to the south, with the view of avoiding ice seen by Judkins in the Scotia on his passage out to New York. The Russia is a magnificent ship, and has dashed along bravely. We had made more than thirteen hundred and odd miles at noon to-day. The wind, after being a little capricious, rather threatens at the present time to turn against us, but our run is already eighty miles ahead of the Russia's last run in this direction, — a very fast one.
. . . . To all whom it may concern, report the Russia in the highest terms. She rolls more easily than the other Cunard Screws, is kept in perfect order, and is most carefully looked after in all departments. We have had nothing approaching to heavy weather; still, one can speak to the trim of the ship. Her captain, a gentleman; bright, polite, good-natured, and vigilant. . . . .

As to me, I am greatly better, I hope. I have got on my right boot to-day for the first time; the "true American" seems to be turning faithless at last; and I made a Gad's Hill breakfast this morning, as a further advance on having otherwise eaten and drunk all day ever since Wednesday.

You will see Anthony Trollope, I dare say. What was my amazement to see him with these eyes come aboard in the mail tender just before we started! He had come out in the Scotia just in time to dash off again in said tender to shake hands with me, knowing me to be aboard here. It was most heartily done. He is on a special mission of convention with the United States post-office.

We have been picturing your movements, and have duly checked off your journey home, and have talked about you continually. But I have thought about you both, even much, much more. You will never know how I love you both; or what you have been to me in America, and will always be to me everywhere; or how fervently I thank you.

All the working of the ship seems to be done on my forehead. It is scrubbed and holystoned (my head — not the deck) at three every morning. It is scraped and swabbed all day. Eight pairs of heavy boots are now clattering on it, getting the ship under sail again. Legions of ropes'-ends are flopped upon it as I write, and I must leave off with Dolby's love.

Thursday, 30th.

Soon after I left off as above we had a gale of wind, which blew all night. For a few hours on the evening side of midnight there was no getting from this cabin of mine to the saloon, or *vice versa*, so heavily did the sea break over the decks. The ship, however, made nothing of it, and we were all right again by Monday afternoon. Except for a few hours yesterday (when we had a very light head wind), the weather has been constantly favorable, and we are now bowling away at a great rate, with a fresh breeze filling all our sails. We expect to be at Queenstown between midnight and three in the morning.

I hope, my dear Fields, you may find this legible, but I rather doubt it; for there is motion enough on the ship to render writing to a landsman, however accustomed to pen and ink, rather a difficult achievement. Besides which, I slide away gracefully from the paper, whenever I want to be particularly expressive. . . . .

——, sitting opposite to me at breakfast, always has the following items: A large dish of porridge, into which he casts slices of butter and a quantity of sugar. Two cups of tea. A steak. Irish stew. Chutnee, and marmalade. Another deputation of two has solicited a reading to-night. Illustrious novelist has unconditionally and absolutely declined.

More love, and more to that, from your ever affectionate friend,
C. D.

His first letter from home gave us all great pleasure, for it announced his complete recovery from the severe influenza that had fastened itself upon him so many months before. Among his earliest notes I find these paragraphs : —

"I have found it so extremely difficult to write about America (though never so briefly) without appearing to blow trumpets on the one hand, or to be inconsistent with my avowed determination *not* to write about it on the other, that I have taken the simple course enclosed. The number will be published on the 6th of June. It appears to me to be the most modest and manly course, and to derive some graceful significance from its title. . . . .

"Thank my dear —— for me for her delightful letter received on the 16th. I will write to her very soon, and tell her about the dogs. I would write by this post, but that Wills's absence (in Sussex, and getting no better there as yet) so overwhelms me with business that I can scarcely get through it.

"Miss me? Ah, my dear fellow, but how do I miss *you!* We talk about you both at Gad's Hill every day of our lives. And I never see the place looking very pretty indeed, or hear the birds sing all day long and the nightingales all night, without restlessly wishing that you were both there.

"With best love, and truest and most enduring regard, ever, my dear Fields,

"Your most affectionate,

"C. D."

". . . . I hope you will receive by Saturday's Cunard a case containing:

"1. A trifling supply of the pen-knibs that suited your hand.

"2. A do. of unfailing medicine for cockroaches.

"3. Mrs. Gamp, for ——.

"The case is addressed to you at Bleecker Street, New York. If it should be delayed for the knibs (or nibs) promised to-morrow, and should be too late for the Cunard packet, it will in that case come by the next following Inman steamer.

"Everything here looks lovely, and I find it (you will be surprised to hear) really a pretty place! I have seen No Thoroughfare twice. Excellent things in it; but it drags, to my thinking. It is, however, a great success in the country, and is now getting up with great force in Paris. Fechter is ill, and was ordered off to Brighton yesterday. Wills is ill too, and banished into Sussex for perfect rest. Otherwise, thank God, I find everything well and thriving. You and my dear Mrs. F—— are constantly in my mind. Procter greatly better. . . . ."

On the 25th of May he sent off the following from Gad's Hill:—

MY DEAR ——: As you ask me about the dogs, I begin with them. When I came down first, I came to Gravesend, five miles off. The two Newfoundland dogs coming to meet me, with the usual carriage and the usual driver, and beholding me coming in my usual dress out at the usual door, it struck me that their recollection of my having been absent for any unusual time was at once cancelled. They behaved (they are both young dogs) exactly in their usual manner; coming behind the basket phaeton as we trotted along, and lifting their heads to have their ears pulled, — a special attention which they receive from no one else. But when I drove into the stable-yard, Linda (the St. Bernard) was greatly excited; weeping profusely, and throwing herself on her back that she might caress my foot with her great fore-paws. M——'s little dog too, Mrs. Bouncer, barked in the greatest agitation on being called down and asked by M——, "Who is this?" and tore round and round me, like the dog in the Faust outlines. You must know that all the farmers turned out on the road in their market-chaises to say, "Welcome home, sir!" that all the houses along the road were dressed with flags; and that our servants, to cut out the rest, had dressed this house so, that every brick of it was hidden. They had asked M——'s permission to "ring the alarm-bell (!) when master drove up"; but M——, having some slight idea that that compliment might awaken master's sense of the ludicrous, had recommended bell abstinence. But on Sunday, the village choir (which includes the bell-ringers) made amends. After some unusually brief pious reflection in the crowns of their hats at the end of the sermon, the ringers bolted out and rang like mad until I got home. (There had been a conspiracy among the villagers to take the horse out, if I had come to our own station, and draw me here. M—— and G—— had got wind of it and warned me.)

Divers birds sing here all day, and the nightingales all night. The place is lovely, and in perfect order. I have put five mirrors in the Swiss Chalet (where I write), and they reflect and refract in all kinds of ways the leaves that are quivering at the windows, and the great fields of waving corn, and the sail-dotted river. My room is up among the branches of the trees; and the birds and the butterflies fly in and out, and the green branches shoot in, at the open windows, and the lights and shadows of the clouds come and go with the rest of the company. The scent of the flowers, and indeed of everything that is growing for miles and miles, is most delicious.

Dolby (who sends a world of messages) found his wife much better than he expected, and the children (wonderful to relate!) perfect. The little girl winds up her prayers every night with a special commendation to Heaven of me and the pony,—as if I must mount him to get there! I dine with Dolby (I was going to write "him," but found it would look as if I were going to dine with the pony) at Greenwich this very day, and if your ears do not burn from six to nine this evening, then the Atlantic is a non-conductor. We are already settling—think of this!—the details of my farewell course of readings. I am brown beyond relief, and cause the greatest disappointment in all quarters by looking so well. It is really wonderful what those fine days at sea did for me! My doctor was quite broken down in spirits when he saw me, for the first time since my return, last Saturday. "Good Lord!" he said, recoiling, "seven years younger!"

It is time I should explain the otherwise inexplicable enclosure. Will you tell Fields, with my love, (I suppose he has n't used *all* the pens yet?) that I think there is in Tremont Street a set of my books, sent out by Chapman, not arrived when I departed. Such set of the immortal works of our illustrious, etc., is designed for the gentleman to whom the enclosure is addressed. If T., F., & Co. will kindly forward the set (carriage paid) with the enclosure to ——'s address, I will invoke new blessings on their heads, and will get Dolby's little daughter to mention them nightly.

"No Thoroughfare" is very shortly coming out in Paris, where it is now in active rehearsal. It is still playing here, but without Fechter, who has been very ill. The doctor's dismissal of him to Paris, however, and his getting better there, enables him to get up the play there. He and Wilkie missed so many pieces of stage effect here, that, unless I am quite satisfied with his report, I shall go over and try my stage-managerial hand at the Vaudeville Theatre. I particularly want the drugging and attempted robbing in the bedroom scene at the Swiss inn to be done to the sound of a waterfall rising and falling with the wind. Although in the very opening of that scene they speak of the waterfall and listen to it, nobody thought of its mysterious music. I could make it, with a good stage carpenter, in an hour. Is it not a curious thing that they want to make me a governor of the Foundling Hospital, because, since the Christmas number, they have had such an amazing access of visitors and money?

My dear love to Fields once again. Same to you and him from M—— and G——. I cannot tell you both how I miss you, or how overjoyed I should be to see you here.

Ever, my dear ——, your most affectionate friend,

C. D.

Excellent accounts of his health and spirits continued to come from Gad's Hill, and his letters were full of plans for the future. On the 7th of July he writes from Gad's Hill as usual: —

GAD'S HILL PLACE, Tuesday, 7th July, 1868.

MY DEAR FIELDS: I have delayed writing to you (and ——, to whom my love) until I should have seen Longfellow. When he was in London the first time he came and went without reporting himself, and left me in a state of unspeakable discomfiture. Indeed, I should not have believed in his having been here at all, if Mrs. Procter had not told me of his calling to see Procter. However, on his return he wrote to me from the Langham Hotel, and I went up to town to see him, and to make an appointment for his coming here. He, the girls, and —— came down last Saturday night, and stayed until Monday forenoon. I showed them all the neighboring country that could be shown in so short a time, and they finished off with a tour of inspection of the kitchens, pantry, wine-cellar, pickles, sauces, servants' sitting-room, general household stores, and even the Cellar Book, of this illustrious establishment. Forster and Kent (the latter wrote certain verses to Longfellow, which have been published in the "Times," and which I sent to D——) came down for a day, and I hope we all had a really "good time." I turned out a couple of postilions in the old red jacket of the old red royal Dover road, for our ride; and it was like a holiday ride in England fifty years ago. Of course we went to look at the old houses in Rochester, and the old cathedral, and the old castle, and the house for the six poor travellers who, "not being rogues or proctors, shall have lodging, entertainment, and four pence each."

Nothing can surpass the respect paid to Longfellow here, from the Queen downward. He is everywhere received and courted, and finds (as I told him he would, when we talked of it in Boston) the workingmen at least as well acquainted with his books as the classes socially above them. . . . .

Last Thursday I attended, as sponsor, the christening of Dolby's son and heir, — a most jolly baby, who held on tight by the rector's left whisker while the service was performed. What time, too, his little sister, connecting me with the pony, trotted up and down the centre isle, noisily driving herself as that celebrated animal, so that it went very hard with the sponsorial dignity.

—— is not yet recovered from that concussion of the brain, and I have all his work to do. This may account for my not being able to devise a Christmas number, but I seem to have left my invention in America. In case you should find it, please send it over. I am going up to town to-day to dine with Longfellow. And now, my dear Fields, you know all about me and mine.

You are enjoying your holiday? and are still thinking sometimes of our Boston days, as I do? and are maturing schemes for coming here next summer? A satisfactory reply to the last question is particularly entreated.

I am delighted to find you both so well pleased with the Blind Book scheme. I said nothing of it to you when we were together, though I had made up my mind, because I wanted to come upon you with that little burst from a distance. It seemed something like meeting again when I remitted the money and thought of your talking of it.

The dryness of the weather is amazing. All the ponds and surface wells about here are waterless, and the poor people suffer greatly. The people of this village have only one spring to resort to, and it is a couple of miles from many cottages. I do not let the great dogs swim in the canal, because the people have to drink of it. But when they get into the Medway, it is hard to get them out again. The other day Bumble (the son, Newfoundland dog) got into difficulties among some floating timber, and became frightened. Don (the father) was standing by me, shaking off the wet and looking on carelessly, when all of a sudden he perceived something amiss, and went in with a bound and brought Bumble out by the ear. The scientific way in which he towed him along was charming.

Ever your loving
C. D.

During the summer of 1868 constant messages and letters came from Dickens across the seas, containing pleasant references to his visit in America, and giving charming accounts of his way of life at home. Here is a letter announcing the fact that he had decided to close forever his appearance in the reading-desk: —

LIVERPOOL, Friday, October 30, 1868.

MY DEAR ——: I ought to have written to you long ago. But I have begun my one hundred and third Farewell Readings, and have been so busy and so fatigued that my hands have been quite full. Here are Dolby and I again leading the kind of life that you know so well. We stop next week (except in London) for the month of November, on account of the elections, and then go on again, with a short holiday at Christmas. We have been doing wonders, and the crowds that pour in upon us in London are beyond all precedent or means of providing for. I have serious thoughts of doing the murder from Oliver Twist; but it is so horrible, that I am going to try it on a dozen people in my London hall one night next month, privately, and see what effect it makes.

My reason for abandoning the Christmas number was, that I became weary of having my own writing swamped by that of other people. This reminds me of the Ghost story. I don't think so well

Henry W. Longfellow

of it, my dear Fields, as you do. It seems to me to be too obviously founded on Bill Jones (in Monk Lewis's Tales of Terror), and there is also a remembrance in it of another Sea-Ghost story entitled, I think, "Stand from Under," and written by I don't know whom. *Stand from under* is the cry from aloft when anything is going to be sent down on deck, and the ghost is aloft on a yard. . . . .

You know all about public affairs, Irish churches, and party squabbles. A vast amount of electioneering is going on about here; but it has not hurt us; though Gladstone has been making speeches, north, east, south, and west of us. I hear that C—— is on his way here in the Russia. Gad's Hill must be thrown open. . . . .

Your most affectionate
CHARLES DICKENS.

We had often talked together of the addition to his *répertoire* of some scenes from "Oliver Twist," and the following letter explains itself: —

GLASGOW, Wednesday, December 16, 1868.

MY DEAR ——: . . . . And first, as you are curious about the Oliver murder, I will tell you about that trial of the same at which you *ought* to have assisted. There were about a hundred people present in all. I have changed my stage. Besides that back screen which you know so well, there are two large screens of the same color, set off, one on either side, like the "wings" at a theatre. And besides those again, we have a quantity of curtains of the same color, with which to close in any width of room from wall to wall. Consequently, the figure is now completely isolated, and the slightest action becomes much more important. This was used for the first time on the occasion. But behind the stage — the orchestra being very large and built for the accommodation of a numerous chorus — there was ready, on the level of the platform, a very long table, beautifully lighted, with a large staff of men ready to open oysters and set champagne corks flying. Directly I had done, the screens being whisked off by my people, there was disclosed one of the prettiest banquets you can imagine; and when all the people came up, and the gay dresses of the ladies were lighted by those powerful lights of mine, the scene was exquisitely pretty; the hall being newly decorated, and very elegantly; and the whole looking like a great bed of flowers and diamonds.

Now, you must know that all this company were, before the

wine went round, unmistakably pale, and had horror-stricken faces. Next morning, Harness (Fields knows — Rev. William — did an edition of Shakespeare — old friend of the Kembles and Mrs. Siddons), writing to me about it, and saying it was " a most amazing and terrific thing," added, " but I am bound to tell you that I had an almost irresistible impulse upon me to *scream*, and that, if any one had cried out, I am certain I should have followed." He had no idea that on the night P——, the great ladies' doctor, had taken me aside and said, "My dear Dickens, you may rely upon it that if only one woman cries out when you murder the girl, there will be a contagion of hysteria all over this place." It is impossible to soften it without spoiling it, and you may suppose that I am rather anxious to discover how it goes on the 5th of January ! ! ! We are afraid to announce it elsewhere, without knowing, except that I have thought it pretty safe to put it up once in Dublin. I asked Mrs. K——, the famous actress, who was at the experiment: " What do *you* say? Do it, or not?" "Why, of course, do it," she replied. "Having got at such an effect as that, it must be done. But," rolling her large black eyes very slowly, and speaking very distinctly, "the public have been looking out for a sensation these last fifty years or so, and by Heaven they have got it!" With which words, and a long breath and a long stare, she became speechless. Again, you may suppose that I am a little anxious! I had previously tried it, merely sitting over the fire in a chair, upon two ladies separately, one of whom was G——. They had both said, "O, good gracious! if you are going to do *that*, it ought to be seen; but it's awful." So once again you may suppose I am a little anxious! . . . .

Not a day passes but Dolby and I talk about you both, and recall where we were at the corresponding time of last year. My old likening of Boston to Edinburgh has been constantly revived within these last ten days. There is a certain remarkable similarity of *tone* between the two places. The audiences are curiously alike, except that the Edinburgh audience has a quicker sense of humor and is a little more genial. No disparagement to Boston in this, because I consider an Edinburgh audience perfect.

I trust, my dear Eugenius, that you have recognized yourself in a certain Uncommercial, and also some small reference to a name rather dear to you? As an instance of how strangely something comic springs up in the midst of the direst misery, look to a succeeding Uncommercial, called "A Small Star in the East," published to-day, by the by. I have described, *with exactness*, the poor places into which I went, and how the people behaved, and what they said. I was wretched, looking on; and yet the boiler-maker and the poor man with the legs filled me with a sense of drollery not to be kept down by any pressure.

The atmosphere of this place, compounded of mists from the highlands and smoke from the town factories, is crushing my eyebrows as I write, and it rains as it never does rain anywhere else, and always does rain here. It is a dreadful place, though much improved and possessing a deal of public spirit. Improvement is beginning to knock the old town of Edinburgh about, here and there; but the Canongate and the most picturesque of the horrible courts and wynds are not to be easily spoiled, or made fit for the poor wretches who people them to live in. Edinburgh is so changed as to its notabilities, that I had the only three men left of the Wilson and Jeffrey time to dine with me there, last Saturday.

I read here to-night and to-morrow, go back to Edinburgh on Friday morning, read there on Saturday morning, and start southward by the mail that same night. After the great experiment of the 5th, — that is to say, on the morning of the 6th, — we are off to Belfast and Dublin. On every alternate Tuesday I am due in London, from wheresoever I may be, to read at St. James's Hall.

I think you will find "Fatal Zero" (by Percy Fitzgerald) a very curious analysis of a mind, as the story advances. A new beginner in A. Y. R. (Hon. Mrs. Clifford, Kinglake's sister), who wrote a story in the series just finished, called "The Abbot's Pool," has just sent me another story. I have a strong impression that, with care, she will step into Mrs. Gaskell's vacant place. W—— is no better, and I have work enough even in that direction.

God bless the woman with the black mittens, for making me laugh so this morning! I take her to be a kind of public-spirited Mrs. Sparsit, and as such take her to my bosom. God bless you both, my dear friends, in this Christmas and New Year time, and in all times, seasons, and places, and send you to Gad's Hill with the next flowers!

Ever your most affectionate
C. D.

All who witnessed the reading of Dickens in the "Oliver Twist" murder scene unite in testifying to the wonderful effect he produced in it. Old theatrical *habitués* have told me that, since the days of Edmund Kean and Cooper, no mimetic representation had been superior to it.

I became so much interested in all I heard about it, that I resolved early in the year 1869 to step across the water (it is only a stride of three thousand miles) and see it done. The following is Dickens's reply to my announcement of the intended voyage: —

A. Y. R. OFFICE, LONDON, Monday, February 15, 1869.

MY DEAR FIELDS: Hurrah, hurrah, hurrah! It is a remarkable instance of magnetic sympathy that before I received your joyfully welcomed announcement of your probable visit to England, I was waiting for the enclosed card to be printed, that I might send you a clear statement of my Readings. I felt almost convinced that you would arrive before the Farewells were over. What do you say to *that*?

The final course of Four Readings in a week, mentioned in the enclosed card, is arranged to come off, on

Monday, June 7th;
Tuesday, June 8th;
Thursday, June 10th; and
Friday, June 11th : last night of all.

We hoped to have finished in May, but cannot clear the country off in sufficient time. I shall probably be about the Lancashire towns in that month. There are to be three morning murders in London not yet announced, but they will be extra the London nights I send you, and will in no wise interfere with them. We are doing most amazingly. In the country the people usually collapse with the murder, and don't fully revive in time for the final piece; in London, where they are much quicker, they are equal to both. It is very hard work; but I have never for a moment lost voice or been unwell; except that my foot occasionally gives me a twinge. We shall have in London on the 2d of March, for the second murder night, probably the greatest assemblage of notabilities of all sorts ever packed together. D—— continues steady in his allegiance to the Stars and Stripes, sends his kindest regard, and is immensely excited by the prospect of seeing you. Gad's Hill is all ablaze on the subject. We are having such wonderfully warm weather that I fear we shall have a backward spring there. You'll excuse east-winds, won't you, if they shake the flowers roughly when you first set foot on the lawn? I have only seen it once since Christmas, and that was from last Saturday to Monday, when I went there for my birthday, and had the Forsters and Wilkie to keep it. I had had ——'s letter four days before, and drank to you both most heartily and lovingly.

I was with M—— a week or two ago. He is quite surprisingly infirm and aged. Could not possibly get on without his second wife to take care of him, which she does to perfection. I went to Cheltenham expressly to do the murder for him, and we put him in the front row, where he sat grimly staring at me. After it was over, he thus delivered himself, on my laughing it off and giving him some wine: "No, Dickens — er — er — I will NOT," with sudden emphasis, — "er — have it — er — put aside. In my — er — best times — er — you remember them, my dear boy — er — gone, gone! — no," — with great emphasis again, — "it comes to this — er — TWO MACBETHS!" with extraordinary energy. After which he stood (with his glass in his hand and his old square jaw of its old fierce form) looking defiantly at Dolby as if Dolby had contradicted him; and then trailed off into a weak pale likeness of himself as if his whole appearance had been some clever optical illusion.

I am away to Scotland on Wednesday next, the 17th, to finish there. Ireland is already disposed of, and Manchester and Liverpool will follow within six weeks. "Like lights in a theatre, they are being snuffed out fast," as Carlyle says of the guillotined in his Revolution. I suppose I shall be glad when they are all snuffed out. Anyhow, I think so *now*.

The N——s have a very pretty house at Kensington. He has quite recovered, and is positively getting fat. I dined with them last Friday at F——'s, having (marvellous to relate!) a spare day in London. The warm weather has greatly spared F——'s bronchitis; but I fear that he is quite unable to bear cold, or even changes of temperature, and that he will suffer exceedingly if east-winds obtain. One would say they must at last, for it has been blowing a tempest from the south and southwest for weeks and weeks.

The safe arrival of my boy's ship in Australia has been telegraphed home, but I have not yet heard from him. His post will be due a week or so hence in London. My next boy is doing very well, I hope, at Trinity Hall, Cambridge. Of my seafaring boy's luck in getting a death-vacancy of First Lieutenant, aboard a new ship-of-war on the South American Station, I heard from a friend, a captain in the Navy, when I was at Bath the other day; though we have not yet heard it from himself. Bath (setting aside remembrances of Roderick Random and Humphrey Clinker) looked, I fancied, just as if a cemetery-full of old people had somehow made a successful rise against death, carried the place by assault, and built a city with their gravestones; in which they were trying to look alive, but with very indifferent success.

C—— is no better, and no worse. M—— and G—— send all manner of loves, and have already represented to me that the red-jacketed post-boys must be turned out for a summer expedition to Canterbury, and that there must be lunches among the cornfields, walks in Cobham Park, and a thousand other expeditions. Pray give our pretty M—— to understand that a great deal will be expected of her, and that she will have to look her very best, to look as I have drawn her. If your Irish people turn up at Gad's at the same time, as they probably will, they shall be entertained in the yard, with muzzled dogs. I foresee that they will come over, haymaking and hopping, and will recognize their beautiful vagabonds at a glance.

I wish Reverdy Johnson would dine in private and hold his tongue. He overdoes the thing. C—— is trying to get the Pope to subscribe, and to run over to take the chair at his next dinner, on which occasion Victor Emmanuel is to propose C——'s health, and may all differences among friends be referred to him. With much love always, and in high rapture at the thought of seeing you both here,

Ever your most affectionate
C. D.

A few weeks later, while on his reading tour, he sent off the following: —

Adelphi Hotel, Liverpool, Friday, April 9, 1869.

My dear Fields: The faithful Russia will bring this out to you, as a sort of warrant to take you into loving custody and bring you back on her return trip.

I have been "reading" here all this week, and finish here for good to-night. To-morrow the Mayor, Corporation, and citizens give me a farewell dinner in St. George's Hall. Six hundred and fifty are to dine, and a mighty show of beauty is to be mustered besides. N—— had a great desire to see the sight, and so I suggested him as a friend to be invited. He is over at Manchester now on a visit, and will come here at midday to-morrow, and go back to London with us on Sunday afternoon. On Tuesday I read in London, and on Wednesday start off again. To-night is No. 68 out of one hundred. I am very tired of it, but I could have no such good fillip as you among the audience, and that will carry me on gayly to the end. So please to look sharp in the matter of landing on the bosom of the used-up, worn-out, and rotten old Parient.

I rather think that when the 12th of June shall have shaken off these shackles, there *will* be borage on the lawn at Gad's. Your heart's desire in that matter, and in the minor particulars of Cobham Park, Rochester Castle, and Canterbury shall be fulfilled, please God! The red jackets shall turn out again upon the turnpike road, and picnics among the cherry-orchards and hop-gardens shall be heard of in Kent. Then, too, shall the Uncommercial resuscitate (being at present nightly murdered by Mr. W. Sikes) and uplift his voice again.

The chief officer of the Russia (a capital fellow) was at the Reading last night, and Dolby specially charged him with the care of you and yours. We shall be on the borders of Wales, and probably about Hereford, when you arrive. Dolby has insane projects of getting over here to meet you; so amiably hopeful and obviously impracticable, that I encourage him to the utmost. The regular little captain of the Russia, Cook, is just now changed into the Cuba, whence arise disputes of seniority, etc. I wish he had been with you, for I liked him very much when I was his passenger. I like to think of your being in *my* ship!

—— and —— have been taking it by turns to be "on the point of death," and have been complimenting one another greatly on the fineness of the point attained. My people got a very good impression of ——, and thought her a sincere and earnest little woman.

The Russia hauls out into the stream to-day, and I fear her people may be too busy to come to us to-night. But if any of them do, they shall have the warmest of welcomes for your sake. (By the by, a very good party of seamen from the Queen's ship Donegal, lying in the Mersey, have been told off to decorate St. George's Hall with the ship's bunting. They were all hanging on aloft upside down, holding to the gigantically high roof by nothing, this morning, in the most wonderfully cheerful manner.)

My son Charley has come for the dinner, and Chappell (my Proprietor, as — is n't it Wemmick? — says) is coming to-day, and Lord Dufferin (Mrs. Norton's nephew) is to come and make *the* speech. I don't envy the feelings of my noble friend when he sees the hall. Seriously, it is less adapted to speaking than Westminster Abbey, and is as large. . . . .

I hope you will see Fechter in a really clever piece by Wilkie. Also you will see the Academy Exhibition, which will be a very good one; and also we will, please God, see everything and more, and everything else after that. I begin to doubt and fear on the subject of your having a horror of me after seeing the murder. I don't think a hand moved while I was doing it last night, or an eye looked away. And there was a fixed expression of horror of me, all over the theatre, which could not have been surpassed if I had been going to be hanged to that red velvet table. It is quite a new sensation to be execrated with that unanimity; and I hope it will remain so!

[Is it lawful — would that woman in the black gaiters, green veil, and spectacles, hold it so — to send my love to the pretty M——?]

Pack up, my dear Fields, and be quick.

Ever your most affectionate

C. D.

It will be remembered that Dickens broke down entirely during the month of April, being completely worn out with hard work in the Readings. He described to me with graphic earnestness, when we met in May, all the incidents connected with the final crisis, and I shall never forget how he imitated himself during that last Reading, when he nearly fell before the audience. It was a terrible blow to his constitution, and only a man of the greatest strength and will could have survived it. When we arrived in Queenstown, this note was sent on board our steamer.

Loving welcome to England. Hurrah!

OFFICE OF ALL THE YEAR ROUND, Wednesday, May 5, 1869.

MY DEAR ——: I fear you will have been uneasy about me, and will have heard distorted accounts of the stoppage of my Readings. It is a measure of precaution, and not of cure. I was too tired and too jarred by the railway fast express, travelling night and day. No half-measure could be taken; and rest being medically considered essential, we stopped. I became, thank God, myself again, almost as soon as I could rest! I am good for all country pleasures with you, and am looking forward to Gad's, Rochester Castle, Cobham Park, red jackets, and Canterbury. When you come to London we shall probably be staying at our hotel. You will learn, *here*, where to find us. I yearn to be with you both again!

Love to M——.

Ever your affectionate C. D.

I hope this will be put into your hands on board, in Queenstown Harbor.

We met in London a few days after this, and I found him in capital spirits, with such a protracted list of things we were to do together, that, had I followed out the prescribed programme, it would have taken many more months of absence from home than I had proposed to myself. We began our long rambles among the thoroughfares that had undergone important changes since I was last in London, taking in the noble Thames embankments, which I had never seen, and the improvements in the city markets. Dickens had moved up to London for the purpose of showing us about, and had taken rooms only a few streets off from our hotel. Here are two specimens of the welcome little notes which I constantly found on my breakfast-table: —

OFFICE OF ALL THE YEAR ROUND, LONDON, Wednesday, May 19, 1869.

MY DEAR FIELDS: Suppose we give the weather a longer chance, and say Monday instead of Friday. I think we must be safer with that precaution. If Monday will suit you, I propose that we meet here that day, — your ladies and you and I, — and cast ourselves on the stony-hearted streets. If it be bright for St. Paul's, good; if not, we can take some other lion that roars in dull weather. We will dine here at six, and meet here at half past two. So IF you should want to go elsewhere after dinner, it can be done, notwithstanding. Let me know in a line what you say.

O the delight of a cold bath this morning, after those lodging-houses! And a mild sniffler of punch, on getting into the hotel last night, I found what my friend Mr. Wegg calls, "Mellering, sir, very mellering."

With kindest regards, ever affectionately,

CHARLES DICKENS.

OFFICE OF ALL THE YEAR ROUND, LONDON, Tuesday, May 25, 1869.

MY DEAR FIELDS: First, you leave Charing Cross Station, by North Kent railway, on Wednesday, June 2d, at 2.10 for Higham Station, the next station beyond Gravesend. Now, bring your lofty mind back to the previous Saturday, next Saturday. There is only one way of combining Windsor and Richmond. That way will leave us but two hours and a half at Windsor. This would not be long enough to enable us to see the inside of the castle, but would admit of our seeing the outside, the Long Walk, etc. I will assume that such a survey will suffice. That taken for granted, meet me at Waterloo Terminus (Loop Line for Windsor) at 10.35, on Saturday morning.

The rendezvous for Monday evening will be *here at half past eight.* As I don't know Mr. Eytinge's number in Guildford Street, will you kindly undertake to let him know that we are going out with the great Detective? And will you also give him the time and place for Gad's?

I shall be here on Friday for a few hours; meantime at Gad's aforesaid.

With love to the ladies, ever faithfully,

C. D.

During my stay in England in that summer of 1869, I made many excursions with Dickens both around the city and into the country. Among the most memorable of these London rambles was a visit to the General Post-Office, by arrangement with the authorities there, a stroll among the cheap theatres and lodging-houses for the poor, a visit to Furnival's Inn and the very room in it where "Pickwick" was written, and a walk through the thieves' quarter. Two of these expeditions were made on two consecutive nights, under the protection of police detailed for the service. On one of these nights we also visited the lock-up houses, watch-houses, and opium-eating establishments. It was in one of the horrid opium-dens that he gathered the incidents which he has related in the opening pages of "Edwin Drood." In a miserable court we found the haggard old woman blowing at a kind of pipe made of an old penny ink-bottle. The identical words which Dickens puts into the mouth of this wretched creature in "Edwin Drood" we heard her croon as we leaned over the tattered bed on which she was lying. There was something hideous in the way this woman kept repeating, "Ye'll pay up according, deary, won't ye?" and the Chinamen and Lascars made never-to-be-forgotten pictures in the scene. I watched Dickens intently as he went among these outcasts of London, and saw with what deep sympathy he encountered the sad and suffering in their horrid abodes. At the door of one of the penny lodging-houses (it was growing toward morning, and the raw air almost cut one to the bone), I saw him snatch a little child out of its poor drunken mother's arms, and bear it in, filthy as it was, that it might be warmed and cared for. I noticed that whenever he entered one of these wretched rooms he had a word of cheer for its inmates, and that when he left the apartment he always had a pleasant "Good night" or "God bless you" to bestow upon them. I do not think his person was ever recognized in any of these haunts, except in one instance. As we entered a low room in the worst alley we had yet visited, in which were huddled together some forty or fifty half-starved-looking wretches, I noticed a man among the crowd whispering to another and pointing out Dickens. Both men regarded him with marked interest all the time he remained in the room, and tried to get as near him, without observation, as possible. As he turned to go out, one of these men pressed forward and said, "Good night, sir," with much feeling, in reply to Dickens's parting word.

Among other places, we went, a little past midnight, into one of the Casual Wards, which were so graphically described, some years ago, in an English magazine, by a gentleman who, as a pretended tramp, went in on a reporting expedition. We walked through an avenue of poor tired sleeping forms, all lying flat on the floor, and not one of them raised a head to look at us as we moved thoughtfully up the aisle of sorrowful humanity. I think we counted sixty or seventy prostrate beings, who had come in for a night's shelter, and had lain down worn out with fatigue and hunger. There was one pale young face to which I whispered Dickens's attention, and he stood over it with a look of sympathizing interest, not to be easily forgotten. There was much ghastly comicality mingled with the horror in several of the places we visited on those two nights. We were standing in a room half filled with people of both sexes, whom the police accompanying us knew to be thieves. Many of these abandoned persons had served out their terms in jail or prison, and would probably be again sentenced under the law. They were all silent and sullen as we entered the room, until an old woman spoke up with a strong, beery voice: "Good evening, gentlemen. We are all wery poor, but strictly honest." At which cheerful apocryphal statement, all the inmates of the room burst into boisterous laughter, and began pelting the imaginative female with epithets uncomplimentary and unsavory. Dickens's quick eye never for a moment ceased to study all these scenes of vice and gloom, and he told me afterwards that, bad as the whole thing was, it had improved infinitely since he first began to study character in those regions of crime and woe.

Between eleven and twelve o'clock on one of the evenings I have mentioned we were taken by Dickens's favorite Detective W—— into a sort of lock-up house, where persons are brought from the streets who have been engaged in brawls, or detected in the act of thieving, or who have, in short, committed any offence against the laws. Here they are examined for commitment by a sort of presiding officer, who sits all night for that purpose. We looked into some of the cells, and found them nearly filled with wretched-looking objects who had been brought in that night. To this establishment are also brought lost children who are picked up in the streets by the police, — children who have wandered away from their homes, and are not old enough to tell the magistrate where they live. It was well on toward morning, and we were sitting in conversation with one of the officers, when the ponderous door opened and one of these small wanderers was brought in. She was the queerest little figure I ever beheld, and she walked in, holding the police officer by the hand as solemnly and as quietly if she were attending her own obsequies. She was between four and five years old, and had on what was evidently her mother's bonnet, — an enormous production, resembling a sort of coal-scuttle, manufactured after the fashion of ten or fifteen years ago. The child had, no doubt, caught up this wonderful head-gear in the absence of her parent, and had gone forth in quest of adventure. The officer reported that he had discovered her in the middle of the street, moving ponderingly along, without any regard to the horses and vehicles all about her. When asked where she lived, she mentioned a street which only existed in her own imagination, and she knew only her Christian name. When she was interrogated by the proper authorities, without the slightest apparent discomposure she replied in a steady voice, as she thought proper, to their questions. The magistrate inadvertently repeated a question as to the number of her brothers and sisters, and the child snapped out, "I told ye wunst; can't ye hear?" When asked if she would like anything, she gayly answered, "Candy, cake and *candy*." A messenger was sent out to procure these commodities, which she instantly seized on their arrival and began to devour. She showed no signs of fear, until one of the officers untied the huge bonnet and took it off, when she tearfully insisted upon being put into it again. I was greatly impressed by the ingenious efforts of the excellent men in the room to learn from the child where she lived, and who her parents were. Dickens sat looking at the little figure with profound interest, and soon came forward and asked permission to speak with the child. Of course his request was granted, and I don't know when I have enjoyed a conversation more. She made some very smart answers, which convulsed us all with laughter as we stood looking on; and the creator of "little Nell" and "Paul Dombey" gave her up in despair. He was so much interested in the little vagrant, that he sent a messenger next morning to learn if the rightful owner of the bonnet had been found. Report came back, on a duly printed form, setting forth that the anxious father and mother had applied for the child at three o'clock in the morning, and had borne her away in triumph to her home.

It was a warm summer afternoon towards the close of the day, when Dickens went with us to visit the London Post-Office. He said: "I know nothing which could give a stranger a better idea of the size of London than that great institution. The hurry and rush of letters! men up to their chin in letters! nothing but letters everywhere! the air full of letters!— suddenly the clock strikes; not a person is to be seen, *nor* a letter: only one man with a lantern peering about and putting one drop-letter into a box." For two hours we went from room to room, with him as our guide, up stairs and down stairs, observing the myriad clerks at their various avocations, with letters for the North Pole, for the South Pole, for Egypt and Alaska, Darien and the next street.

The "Blind Man," as he was called, appeared to afford Dickens as much amusement as if he saw his work then for the first time; but this was one of the qualities of his genius; there was inexhaustibility and freshness in everything to which he turned his attention. The ingenuity and loving care shown by the "Blind Man" in deciphering or guessing at the apparently inexplicable addresses on letters and parcels excited his admiration. "What a lesson to all of us," he could not help saying, "to be careful in preparing our letters for the mail!" His own were always directed with such exquisite care, however, that had he been brother to the "Blind Man," and considered it his special work in life to teach others how to save that officer trouble, he could hardly have done better.

Leaving the hurry and bustle of the Post-Office behind us, we strolled out into the streets of London. It was past eight o'clock, but the beauty of the soft June sunset was only then overspreading the misty heavens. Every sound of traffic had died out of those turbulent thoroughfares; now and then a belated figure would hurry past us and disappear, or perhaps in turning the corner would linger to "take a good look" at Charles Dickens. But even these stragglers soon dispersed, leaving us alone in the light of day and the sweet living air to heighten the sensation of a dream. We came through White Friars to the Temple, and thence into the Temple Garden, where our very voices echoed. Dickens pointed up to Talfourd's room, and recalled with tenderness the merry hours they had passed together in the old place. Of course we hunted out Goldsmith's abode, and Dr. Johnson's, saw the site of the Earl of Essex's palace, and the steps by which he was wont to descend to the river, now so far removed. But most interesting of all to us there was "Pip's" room, to which Dickens led us, and the staircase where the convict stumbled up in the dark, and the chimney nearest the river where, although less exposed than in "Pip's" days, we could well understand how "the wind shook the house that night like discharges of cannon, or breakings of a sea." We looked in at the dark old staircase, so dark on that night when "the lamps were blown out, and the lamps on the bridges and the shore were shuddering," and then went on to take a peep, half shuddering ourselves, at the narrow street where "Pip" by and by found a lodging for the convict. Nothing dark could long survive in our minds on that June night, when the whole scene was so like the airy work of imagination. Past the Temple, past the garden to the river, mistily fair, with a few boats moving upon its surface, the convict's story was forgotten, and we only knew this was Dickens's home, where he had lived and written, lying in the calm light of its fairest mood.

Dickens had timed our visit to his country house in Kent, and arranged that we should appear at Gad's Hill with the nightingales. Arriving at the Higham station on a bright June day in 1869, we found his stout little pony ready to take us up the hill; and before we had proceeded far on the road, the master himself came out to welcome us on the way. He looked brown and hearty, and told us he had passed a breezy morning writing in the châlet. We had parted from him only a few days before in London, but I thought the country air had already begun to exert its strengthening influence, — a process he said which commonly set in the moment he reached his garden gate.

It was ten years since I had seen Gad's Hill Place, and I observed at once what extensive improvements had been made during that period. Dickens had increased his estate by adding quite a large tract of land on the opposite side of the road, and a beautiful meadow at the back of the house. He had connected the front lawn, by a passageway running under the road, with beautifully wooded grounds, on which was erected the Swiss châlet, a present from Fechter. The old house, too, had been greatly improved, and there was an air of assured comfort and ease about the charming establishment. No one could surpass Dickens as a host; and as there were certain household rules (hours for meals, recreation, etc.), he at once announced them, so that visitors never lost any time "wondering" when this or that was to happen.

Lunch over, we were taken round to see the dogs, and Dickens gave us a rapid biographical account of each as we made acquaintance with the whole colony. One old fellow, who had grown superannuated and nearly blind, raised himself up and laid his great black head against Dickens's breast as if he loved him. All were spoken to with pleasant words of greeting, and the whole troop seemed wild with joy over the master's visit. "Linda" put up her shaggy paw to be shaken at parting; and as we left the dog-houses, our host told us some amusing anecdotes of his favorite friends.

Dickens's admiration of Hogarth was unbounded, and he had hung the staircase leading up from the hall of his house with fine old impressions of the great master's best works. Observing our immediate interest in these pictures, he seemed greatly pleased, and proceeded at once to point out in his graphic way what had struck his own fancy most in Hogarth's genius. He had made a study of the painter's *thought* as displayed in these works, and his talk about the artist was delightful. He used to say he never came down the stairs without pausing with new wonder over the fertility of the mind that had conceived and the hand that had executed these powerful pictures of human life; and I cannot forget with what fervid energy and feeling he repeated one day, as we were standing together on the stairs in front of the Hogarth pictures, Dr. Johnson's epitaph, on the painter: —

> "The hand of him here torpid lies,
> That drew the essential form of grace;
> Here closed in death the attentive eyes
> That saw the manners in the face."

Every day we had out-of-door games, such as "Bowls," "Aunt Sally," and the like, Dickens leading off with great spirit and fun. Billiards came after dinner, and during the evening we had charades and dancing. There was no end to the new divertisements our kind host was in the habit of proposing, so that constant cheerfulness reigned at Gad's Hill. He went into his work-room, as he called it, soon after breakfast, and wrote till twelve o'clock; then he came out, ready for a long walk. The country about Gad's Hill is admirably adapted for pedestrian exercise, and we went forth every day, rain or shine, for a stretcher. Twelve, fifteen, even twenty miles were not too much for Dickens, and many a long tramp we have had over the hop-country together. Chatham, Rochester, Cobham Park, Maidstone,— anywhere, out under the open sky and into the free air! Then Dickens was at his best, and talked. Swinging his blackthorn stick, his lithe figure sprang forward over the ground, and it took a practised pair of legs to keep alongside of his voice. In these expeditions I heard from his own lips delightful reminiscences of his early days in the region we were then traversing, and charming narratives of incidents connected with the writing of his books.

Dickens's association with Gad's Hill, the city of Rochester, the road to Canterbury, and the old cathedral town itself, dates back to his earliest years. In "David Copperfield," the most autobiographic of all his books, we find him, a little boy, (so small, that the landlady is called to peer over the counter and catch a glimpse of the tiny lad who possesses such "a spirit,") trudging over the old Kent Road to Dover. "I see myself," he writes, "as evening closes in, coming over the bridge at Rochester, footsore and tired, and eating bread that I had bought for supper. One or two little houses, with the notice, 'Lodgings for Travellers,' hanging out, had tempted me; but I was afraid of spending the few pence I had, and was even more afraid of the vicious looks of the trampers I had met or overtaken. I sought no shelter, therefore, but the sky; and toiling into Chatham,— which in that night's aspect is a mere dream of chalk, and drawbridges, and mastless ships in a muddy river, roofed like Noah's arks,— crept, at last, upon a sort of grass-grown battery overhanging a lane, where a sentry was walking to and fro. Here I lay down near a cannon; and, happy in the society of the sentry's footsteps, though he knew no more of my being above him than the boys at Salem House had known of my lying by the wall, slept soundly until morning." Thus early he noticed "the trampers" which infest the old Dover Road, and observed them in their numberless gypsy-like variety; thus early he looked lovingly on Gad's Hill Place, and wished it might be his own, if he ever grew up to be a man. His earliest memories were filled with pictures of the endless hop-grounds and orchards, and the little child "thought it all extremely beautiful!"

Through the long years of his short life he was always consistent in his love for Kent and the old surroundings. When the after days came and while travelling abroad, how vividly the childish love returned! As he passed rapidly over the road on his way to France he once wrote: "Midway between Gravesend and Rochester the widening river was bearing the ships, white-sailed or black-smoked, out to sea, when I noticed by the wayside a very queer small boy.

"'Halloa!' said I to the very queer small boy, 'where do you live?'

"'At Chatham,' says he.

"'What do you do there?' said I.

"'I go to school,' says he.

"I took him up in a moment, and we went on. Presently the very queer small boy says, 'This is Gad's Hill we are coming to, where Falstaff went out to rob those travellers, and ran away.'

"'You know something about Falstaff, eh?' said I.

"'All about him,' said the very queer small boy. 'I am old (I am nine) and I read all sorts of books. But *do* let us stop at the top of the hill, and look at the house there, if you please!'

"'You admire that house,' said I.

"'Bless you, sir,' said the very queer small boy, 'when I was not more than half as old as nine, it used to be a treat for me to be brought to look at it. And now I am nine, I come by myself to look at it. And ever since I can recollect, my father, seeing me so fond of it, has often said to me, "If you were to be very persevering and were to work hard, you might some day come to live in it." Though that's impossible!' said the very queer small boy, drawing a low breath, and now staring at the house out of window with all his might. I was rather annoyed to be told this by the very queer small boy; for that house happens to be *my* house, and I have reason to believe that what he said was true."

What stay-at-home is there who does not know the Bull Inn at Rochester, from which Mr. Tupman and Mr. Jingle attended the ball, Mr. Jingle wearing Mr. Winkle's coat? or who has not seen in fancy the "gypsy-tramp," the "show-tramp," the "cheap jack," the "tramp-children," and the "Irish hoppers" all passing over "the Kentish Road, bordered" in their favorite resting-place "on either side by a wood, and having on one hand, between the road-dust and the trees, a skirting patch of grass? Wild-flowers grow in abundance on this spot, and it lies high and airy, with the distant river stealing steadily away to the ocean, like a man's life."

Sitting in the beautiful châlet during his later years and

watching this same river stealing away like his own life, he never could find a harsh word for the tramps, and many and many a one has gone over the road rejoicing because of some kindness received from his hands. Every precaution was taken to protect a house exposed as his was to these wild rovers, several dogs being kept in the stable-yard, and the large outer gates locked. But he seldom made an excursion in any direction without finding some opportunity to benefit them. One of these many kindnesses came to the public ear during the last summer of his life. He was dressing in his own bedroom in the morning, when he saw two Savoyards and two bears come up to the Falstaff Inn opposite. While he was watching the odd company, two English bullies joined the little party and insisted upon taking the muzzles off the bears in order to have a dance with them. "At once," said Dickens, "I saw there would be trouble, and I watched the scene with the greatest anxiety. In a moment I saw how things were going, and without delay I found myself at the gate. I called the gardener by the way, but he managed to hold himself at safe distance behind the fence. I put the Savoyards instantly in a secure position, asked the bullies what they were at, forced them to muzzle the bears again, under threat of sending for the police, and ended the whole affair in so short a time that I was not missed from the house. Unfortunately, while I was covered with dust and blood, for the bears had already attacked one of the men when I arrived, I heard a carriage roll by. I thought nothing of it at the time, but the report in the foreign journals which startled and shocked my friends so much came probably from the occupants of that vehicle. Unhappily, in my desire to save the men, I entirely forgot the dogs, and ordered the bears to be carried into the stable-yard until the scuffle should be over, when a tremendous tumult arose between the bears and the dogs. Fortunately we were able to separate them without injury, and the whole was so soon over that it was hard to make the family believe, when I came in to breakfast, that anything of the kind had gone forward." It was the newspaper report, causing anxiety to some absent friends, which led, on inquiry, to this rehearsal of the incident.

Who does not know Cobham Park? Has Dickens not invited us there in the old days to meet Mr. Pickwick, who pronounced it "delightful! — thoroughly delightful," while "the skin of his expressive countenance was rapidly peeling off with exposure to the sun"? Has he not invited the world to enjoy the loveliness of its solitudes with him, and peopled its haunts for us again and again?

Our first *real* visit to Cobham Park was on a summer morning when Dickens walked out with us from his own gate, and, strolling quietly along the road, turned at length into what seemed a rural wooded pathway. At first we did not associate the spot in its spring freshness with that morning after Christmas when he had supped with the "Seven Poor Travellers," and lain awake all night with thinking of them; and after parting in the morning with a kindly shake of the hand all round, started to walk through Cobham woods on his way towards London. Then on his lonely road, "the mists began to rise in the most beautiful manner and the sun to shine; and as I went on," he writes, "through the bracing air, seeing the hoar frost sparkle everywhere, I felt as if all nature shared in the joy of the great Birthday. Going through the woods, the softness of my tread upon the mossy ground and among the brown leaves enhanced the Christmas sacredness by which I felt surrounded. As the whitened stems environed me, I thought how the Founder of the time had never raised his benignant hand, save to bless and heal, except in the case of one unconscious tree."

Now we found ourselves on the same ground, surrounded by the full beauty of the summer-time. The hand of Art conspiring with Nature had planted rhododendrons, as if in their native soil beneath the forest-trees. They were in one universal flame of blossoms, as far as the eye could see. Lord and Lady D——, the kindest and most hospitable of neighbors, were absent; there was not a living figure beside ourselves to break the solitude, and we wandered on and on with the wild birds for companions as in our native wildernesses. By and by we came near Cobham Hall, with its fine lawns and far-sweeping landscape, and workmen and gardeners and a general air of summer luxury. But to-day we were to go past the hall and lunch on a green slope under the trees, (was it *just* the spot where Mr. Pickwick tried the cold punch and found it satisfactory? I never liked to ask!) and after making the old woods ring with the clatter and clink of our noontide meal, mingled with floods of laughter, were to come to the village, and to the very inn from which the disconsolate Mr. Tupman wrote to Mr. Pickwick, after his adventure with Miss Wardle. There is the old sign, and here we are at the Leather Bottle, Cobham, Kent. "There's no doubt whatever about that." Dickens's modesty would not allow him to go in, so we made the most of an outside study of the quaint old place as we strolled by; also of the cottages whose inmates were evidently no strangers to our party, but were cared for by them as English cottagers are so often looked after by the kindly ladies in their neighborhood. And there was the old churchyard, "where the dead had been quietly buried 'in the sure and certain hope' which Christmas-time inspired." There too were the children, whom, seeing at their play, he could not but be loving, remembering who had loved them! One party of urchins swinging on a gate reminded us vividly of Collins, the painter. Here was his composition to the life. Every lover of rural scenery must recall the little fellow on the top of a five-barred gate in the picture Collins painted, known widely by the fine engraving made of it at the time. And there too were the blossoming gardens, which now shone in their new garments of resurrection. The stillness of midsummer noon crept over everything as we lingered in the sun and shadow of the old village. Slowly circling the hall, we came upon an avenue of lime-trees leading up to a stately doorway in the distance. The path was overgrown, birds and squirrels were hopping unconcernedly over the ground, and the gates and chains were rusty with disuse. "This avenue," said Dickens, as we leaned upon the wall and looked into its cool shadows, "is never crossed except to bear the dead body of the lord of the hall to its last resting-place; a remnant of superstition, and one which Lord and Lady D—— would be glad to do away with, but the villagers would never hear of such a thing, and would consider it certain death to any person who should go or come through this entrance. It would be a highly unpopular movement for the present occupants to attempt to uproot this absurd idea, and they have given up all thoughts of it for the time."

It was on a subsequent visit to Cobham village that we explored the "College," an old foundation of the reign of Edward III. for the aged poor of both sexes. Each occupant of the various small apartments was sitting at his or her door, which opened on a grassy enclosure with arches like an abandoned cloister of some old cathedral. Such a motley society, brought together under such unnatural circumstances, would of course interest Dickens. He seemed to take a profound pleasure in wandering about the place, which was evidently filled with the associations of former visits in his own mind. He was usually possessed by a childlike eagerness to go to any spot which he had made up his mind it was best to visit, and quick to come away, but he lingered long about this leafy old haunt on that Sunday afternoon.

Of Cobham Hall itself much might be written without conveying an adequate idea of its peculiar interest to this generation. The terraces, and lawns, and cedar-trees, and deer-park, the names of Edward III. and Elizabeth, the famous old Cobhams and their long line of distinguished descendants, their invaluable pictures and historic chapel, have all been the common property of the past and of the present. But the air of comfort and hospitality diffused about the place by the present owners belongs exclusively to our time, and a little Swiss châlet removed from Gad's Hill, standing not far from the great house, will always connect the name of Charles Dickens with the place he loved so well. The châlet has been transferred thither as a tribute from the Dickens family to the kindness of their friends and former neighbors. We could not fail, during our visit, to think of the connection his name would always have with Cobham Hall, though he was then still by our side, and the little châlet yet remained embowered in its own green trees overlooking the sail-dotted Medway as it flowed towards the Thames.

The old city of Rochester, to which we have already referred as being particularly well known to all Mr. Pickwick's admirers, is within walking distance from Gad's Hill Place, and was the object of daily visits from its occupants. The ancient castle, one of the best ruins in England, as Dickens loved to say, because less has been done to it, rises with rugged walls precipitously from the river. It is wholly unrestored; just enough care has been bestowed to prevent its utter destruction, but otherwise it stands as it has stood and crumbled from year to year

We climbed painfully up to the highest steep of its loftiest tower, and looked down on the wonderful scene spread out in the glory of a summer sunset. Below, a clear trickling stream flowed and tinkled as it has done since the rope was first lowered in the year 800 to bring the bucket up over the worn stones which still remain to attest the fact. How happy Dickens was in the beauty of that scene! What delight he took in rebuilding the old place, with every legend of which he proved himself familiar, and repeopling it out of the storehouse of his fancy. "Here was the kitchen, and there the dining-hall! How frightfully dark they must have been in those days, with such small slits for windows, and the fireplaces without chimneys! There were the galleries; this is one of the four towers; the others, you will understand, corresponded with this; and now, if you're not dizzy, we will come out on the battlements for the view!" Up we went, of course, following our cheery leader until we stood among the topmost wall-flowers, which were waving yellow and sweet in the sunset air. East and west, north and south, our eyes traversed the beautiful garden land of Kent, the land beloved of poets through the centuries. Below lay the city of Rochester on one hand, and in the heart of it an old inn where a carrier was even then getting out, or putting in, horses and wagon for the night. A procession, with banners and music, was moving slowly by the tavern, and the quaint costumes in which the men were dressed suggested days long past, when far other scenes were going forward in this locality. It was almost like a pageant marching out of antiquity for our delectation. Our master of ceremonies revelled that day in repeopling the queer old streets down into which we were looking from our charming elevation. His delightful fancy seemed especially alert on that occasion, and we lived over again with him

KEEP OF ROCHESTER CASTLE

many a chapter in the history of Rochester, full of interest to those of us who had come from a land where all is new and comparatively barren of romance.

Below, on the other side, was the river Medway, from whose depths the castle once rose steeply. Now the *débris* and perhaps also a slight swerving of the river from its old course have left a rough margin, over which it would not be difficult to make an ascent. Rochester Bridge, too, is here, and the "windy hills" in the distance; and again, on the other hand, Chatham, and beyond, the Thames, with the sunset tingeing the many-colored sails. We were not easily persuaded to descend from our picturesque vantage-ground; but the master's hand led us gently on from point to point, until we found ourselves, before we were aware, on the grassy slope outside the castle wall. Besides, there was the cathedral to be visited, and the tomb of Richard Watts, "with the effigy of worthy Master Richard starting out of it like a ship's figure-head."

After seeing the cathedral, we went along the silent High Street, past queer Elizabethan houses with endless gables and fences and lattice-windows, until we came to Watts's Charity, the house of entertainment for six poor travellers. The establishment is so familiar to all lovers of Dickens through his description of it in the article entitled "Seven Poor Travellers" among his "Uncommercial" papers, that little is left to be said on that subject; except perhaps that no autobiographic sketch ever gave a more faithful picture, a closer portrait, than is there conveyed.

Dickens's fancy for Rochester, and his numberless associations with it, have left traces of that city in almost everything he wrote. From the time when Mr. Snodgrass first discovered the castle ruin from Rochester Bridge, to the last chapter of Edwin Drood, we observe hints of the city's quaintness or silence; the unending pavements, which go on and on till the wisest head would be puzzled to know where Rochester ends and where Chatham begins; the disposition of Father Time to have his own unimpeded way therein, and of the gray cathedral towers which loom up in the background of many a sketch and tale. Rochester, too, is on the way to Canterbury, Dickens's best loved cathedral, the home of Agnes Wickfield, the sunny spot in the life and memory of David Copperfield. David was particularly small, as we are told, when he first saw Canterbury, but he was already familiar with Roderick Random, Peregrine Pickle, Humphrey Clinker, Tom Jones, The Vicar of Wakefield, Don Quixote, Gil Blas, and Robinson Crusoe, who came out, as he says, a glorious host, to keep him company. Naturally, the calm old place, the green nooks, the beauty of the cathedral, possessed a better chance with him than with many others, and surely no one could have loved them more. In the later years of his life the crowning-point of the summer holidays was "a pilgrimage to Canterbury."

The sun shone merrily through the day when he chose to carry us thither. Early in the morning the whole house was astir; large hampers were packed, ladies and gentlemen were clad in gay midsummer attire, and, soon after breakfast, huge carriages with four horses, and postilions with red coats and top-boots, after the fashion of the olden time, were drawn up before the door. Presently we were moving lightly over the road, the hop-vines dancing on the poles on either side, the orchards looking invitingly cool, the oast-houses fanning with their wide arms, the river glowing from time to time through the landscape. We made such a clatter passing through Rochester, that all the main street turned out to see the carriages, and, being obliged to stop the horses a moment, a shopkeeper, desirous of discovering Dickens among the party, hit upon the wrong man, and confused an humble individual among the company by calling a crowd, pointing him out as Dickens, and making him the mark of eager eyes. This incident seemed very odd to us in a place he knew so well. On we clattered, leaving the echoing street behind us, on and on for many a mile, until noon, when, finding a green wood and clear stream by the roadside, we encamped under the shadow of the trees in a retired spot for lunch. Again we went on, through quaint towns and lonely roads, until we came to Canterbury, in the yellow afternoon. The bells for service were ringing as we drove under the stone archway into the soundless streets. The whole town seemed to be enjoying a simultaneous nap, from which it was aroused by our horses' hoofs. Out the people ran, at this signal, into the highway, and we were glad to descend at some distance from the centre of the city, thus leaving the excitement behind us. We had been exposed to the hot rays of the sun all day, and the change into the shadow of the cathedral was refreshing. Service was going forward as we entered; we sat down, therefore, and joined our voices with those of the choristers. Dickens, with tireless observation, noted how sleepy and inane were the faces of many of the singers, to whom this beautiful service was but a sickening monotony of repetition. The words, too, were gabbled over in a manner anything but impressive. He was such a downright enemy to form, as substituted for religion, that any dash of untruth or unreality was abhorrent to him. When the last sounds died away in the cathedral we came out again into the cloisters, and sauntered about until the shadows fell over the beautiful enclosure. We were hospitably entreated, and listened to many an historical tale of tomb and stone and grassy nook; but under all we were listening to the heart of our companion, who had so often wandered thither in his solitude, and was now rereading the stories these urns had prepared for him.

During one of his winter visits, he says (in "Copperfield"):—

"Coming into Canterbury, I loitered through the old streets with a sober pleasure that calmed my spirits and eased my heart. There were the old signs, the old names over the shops, the old people serving in them. It appeared so long since I had been a school-boy there, that I wondered the place was so little changed, until I reflected how little I was changed myself. Strange to say, that quiet influence which was inseparable in my mind from Agnes seemed to pervade even the city where she dwelt. The venerable cathedral towers, and the old jackdaws and rooks, whose airy voices made them more retired than perfect silence would have done; the battered gateways, once stuck full with statues, long thrown down and crumbled away, like the reverential pilgrims who had gazed upon them; the still nooks, where the ivied growth of centuries crept over gabled ends and ruined walls; the ancient houses; the pastoral landscape of field, orchard, and garden;— everywhere, in everything, I felt the same serene air, the same calm, thoughtful, softening spirit."

Walking away and leaving Canterbury behind us forever, we came again into the voiceless streets, past a "very old house bulging out over the road, ... quite spotless in its cleanliness, the old-fashioned brass knocker on the low, arched door ornamented with carved garlands of fruit and flowers, twinkling like a star," the very house, perhaps, "with angles and corners and carvings and mouldings," where David Copperfield was sent to school. We were turned off with a laughing reply, when we ventured to accuse this particular house of being *the one*, and were told there were several that "would do"; which was quite true, for nothing could be more quaint, more satisfactory to all, from the lovers of Chaucer to the lovers of Dickens, than this same city of Canterbury. The sun had set as we rattled noisily out of the ancient place that afternoon, and along the high road, which was quite novel in its evening aspect. There was no lingering now; on and on we went, the postilions flying up and down on the backs of their huge horses, their red coats glancing in the occasional gleams of wayside lamps, fireflies making the orchards shine, the sunset lighting up vast clouds that lay across the western sky, and the whole scene filled with evening stillness. When we stopped to change horses, the quiet was almost oppressive. Soon after nine we espied the welcome lantern of Gad's Hill Place and the open gates. And so ended Dickens's last pilgrimage to Canterbury.

There was another interesting spot near Gad's Hill which was one of Dickens's haunts, and this was the "Druid-stone," as it is called, at Maidstone. This is within walking distance of his house, along the breezy hillside road, which we remember blossomy and wavy in the summer season, with open spaces in the hedges where one may look over wide hilly slopes, and at times come upon strange cuts down into the chalk which pervades this district. We turned into a lane from the dusty road, and, following our leader over a barred gate, came into wide grassy fields full of summer's bloom and glory. A short walk farther brought us to the Druidstone, which Dickens thought to be, from the fitness of its position, simply a vantage-ground chosen by priests, — whether Druid or Christian of course it would be impossible to say, — from which to address a multitude. The rock served as a kind of background and sounding-board, while the beautiful sloping of the sward upward from the speaker made it an excellent position for out-of-door discourses. On this day it was only a blooming solitude, where the birds had done all the talking, until we arrived.

It was a fine afternoon haunt, and one worthy of a visit, apart from the associations which make the place dear.

One of the weirdest neighborhoods to Gad's Hill, and one of those most closely associated with Dickens, is the village of Cooling. A cloudy day proved well enough for Cooling; indeed, was undoubtedly chosen by the adroit master of hospitalities as being a fitting sky to show the dark landscape of "Great Expectations." The pony-carriage went thither to accompany the walking party and carry the baskets; the whole way, as we remember, leading on among narrow lanes, where heavy carriages were seldom seen. We are told in the novel, "On every rail and gate, wet lay clammy, and the marsh mist was so thick that the wooden finger on the post directing people to our village — a direction which they never accepted, for they never came there — was invisible to me until I was close under it." The lanes certainly wore that aspect of never being accepted as a way of travel; but this was a delightful recommendation to our walk, for summer kept her own way there, and grass and wild-flowers were abundant. It was already noon, and low clouds and mists were lying about the earth and sky as we approached a forlorn little village on the edge of the wide marshes described in the opening of the novel. This was Cooling, and passing by the few cottages, the decayed rectory, and straggling buildings, we came at length to the churchyard. It took but a short time to make us feel at home there, with the marshes on one hand, the low wall over which Pip saw the convict climb before he dared to run away; "the five little stone lozenges, each about a foot and a half long, ... sacred to the memory of five little brothers, ... to which I had been indebted for a belief that they all had been born on their backs, with their hands in their trousers pockets, and had never taken them out in this state of existence"; — all these points, combined with the general dreariness of the landscape, the far-stretching marshes, and the distant sea-line, soon revealed to us that this was Pip's country, and we might momently expect to see the convict's head, or to hear the clank of his chain, over that low wall.

We were in the churchyard now, having left the pony within eye-shot, and taken the baskets along with us, and were standing on one of those very lozenges, somewhat grass-grown by this time, and deciphering the inscriptions. On tiptoe we could get a wide view of the marsh, with the wind sweeping in a lonely limitless way through the tall grasses. Presently hearing Dickens's cheery call, we turned to see what he was doing. He had chosen a good flat gravestone in one corner (the corner farthest from the marsh and Pip's little brothers and the expected convict), had spread a wide napkin thereupon after the fashion of a domestic dinner-table, and was rapidly transferring the contents of the hampers to that point. The horrible whimsicality of trying to eat and make merry under these deplorable circumstances, the tragic-comic character of the scene, appeared to take him by surprise. He at once threw himself into it (as he says in "Copperfield" he was wont to do with anything to which he had laid his hand) with fantastic eagerness. Having spread the table after the most approved style, he suddenly disappeared behind the wall for a moment, transformed himself by the aid of a towel and napkin into a first-class head-waiter, reappeared, laid a row of plates along the top of the wall, as at a bar-room or eating-house, again retreated to the other side with some provisions, and, making the gentlemen of the party stand up to the wall, went through the whole play with most entire gravity. When we had wound up with a good laugh, and were again seated together on the grass around the table, we espied two wretched figures, not the convicts this time, although we might have easily persuaded ourselves so, but only tramps gazing at us over the wall from the marsh side as they approached, and finally sitting down just outside the churchyard gate. They looked wretchedly hungry and miserable, and Dickens said at once, starting up, "Come, let us offer them a glass of wine and something good for lunch." He was about to carry them himself, when what he considered a happy thought seemed to strike him. "*You* shall carry it to them," he cried, turning to one of the ladies; "it will be less like a charity and more like a kindness if one of you should speak to the poor souls!" This was so much in character for him, who stopped always to choose the most delicate way of doing a kind deed, that the memory of this little incident remains, while much, alas! of his wit and wisdom have vanished beyond the power of reproducing. We feasted on the satisfaction the tramps took in their lunch, long after our own was concluded; and, seeing them well off on their road again, took up our own way to Gad's Hill Place. How comfortable it looked on our return; how beautifully the afternoon gleams of sunshine shone upon the holly-trees by the porch; how we turned away from the door and went into the playground, where we bowled on the green turf, until the tall maid in her spotless cap was seen bringing the five-o'clock tea thitherward; how the dews and the setting sun warned us at last we must prepare for dinner; and how Dickens played longer and harder than any one of the company, scorning the idea of going in to tea at that hour, and beating his ball instead, quite the youngest of the company up to the last moment! — all this returns with vivid distinctness as I write these inadequate words.

Many days and weeks passed over after those June days were ended before we were to see Dickens again. Our meeting then was at the station in London, on our way to Gad's Hill once more. He was always early at a railway station, he said, if only to save himself the unnecessary and wasteful excitement hurry commonly produces; and so he came to meet us with a cheery manner, as if care were shut up in some desk or closet he had left behind, and he were ready to make the day a gay one, whatever the sun might say to it. A small roll of manuscript in his hand led him soon to confess that a new story was already begun; but this communication was made in the utmost confidence, as if to account for any otherwise unexplainable absences, physically or mentally, from our society, which might occur. But there were no gaps during that autumn afternoon of return to Gad's Hill. He told us how summer had brought him no vacation this year, and only two days of recreation. One of those, he said, was spent with his family at "Rosherville Gardens," "the place," as a huge advertisement informed us, "to spend a happy day." His curiosity with regard to all entertainments for the people, he said to us, carried him thither, and he seemed to have been amused and rewarded by his visit. The previous Sunday had found him in London; he was anxious to reach Gad's Hill before the afternoon, but in order to accomplish this he must walk nine miles to a way station, which he did. Coming to the little village, he inquired where the station was, and, being shown in the wrong direction, walked calmly down a narrow road which did not lead there at all. "On I went," he said, "in the perfect sunshine, over yellow leaves, without even a wandering breeze to break the silence, when suddenly I came upon three or four antique wooden houses standing under trees on the borders of a lovely stream, and, a little farther, upon an ancient doorway to a grand hall, perhaps the home of some bishop of the olden time. The road came to an end there, and I was obliged to retrace my steps; but anything more entirely peaceful and beautiful in its aspect on that autumnal day than this retreat, forgotten by the world, I almost never saw." He was eager, too, to describe for our entertainment one of the yearly cricket-matches among the villagers at Gad's Hill which had just come off. Some of the toasts at the supper afterward were as old as the time of Queen Anne. For instance, —

"More pigs,
Fewer parsons";

delivered with all seriousness; a later one was, "May the walls of old England never be covered with French polish!"

Once more we recall a morning at Gad's Hill, a soft white haze over everything, and the yellow sun burning through. The birds were singing, and beauty and calm pervaded the whole scene. We strayed through Cobham Park and saw the lovely vistas through the autumnal haze; once more we reclined in the cool châlet in the afternoon, and watched the vessels going and coming upon the ever-moving river. Suddenly all has vanished; and now, neither spring nor autumn, nor flowers nor birds, nor dawn nor sunset, nor the ever-moving river, can be the same to any of us again. We have all drifted down upon the river of Time, and one has already sailed out into the illimitable ocean.

On a pleasant Sunday morning in October, 1869, as I sat looking out on the beautiful landscape from my chamber window at Gad's Hill, a servant tapped at my door and gave me a summons from Dickens, written in his drollest manner on a sheet of paper, bidding me descend into his study on business of great importance. That day I heard from the author's lips the first chapters

GADSHILL FROM THE REAR: DICKENS'S HOME

of "Edwin Drood" the concluding lines of which initial pages were then scarcely dry from the pen. The story is unfinished, and he who read that autumn morning with such vigor of voice and dramatic power is in his grave. This private reading took place in the little room where the great novelist for many years had been accustomed to write, and in the house where on a pleasant evening in the following June he died. The spot is one of the loveliest in Kent, and must always be remembered as the last residence of Charles Dickens. He used to declare his firm belief that Shakespeare was specially fond of Kent, and that the poet chose Gad's Hill and Rochester for the scenery of his plays from intimate personal knowledge of their localities. He said he had no manner of doubt but that one of Shakespeare's haunts was the old inn at Rochester, and that this conviction came forcibly upon him one night as he was walking that way, and discovered Charles's Wain over the chimney just as Shakespeare has described it, in words put into the mouth of the carrier in King Henry IV. There is no prettier place than Gad's Hill in all England for the earliest and latest flowers, and Dickens chose it, when he had arrived at the fulness of his fame and prosperity, as the home in which he most wished to spend the remainder of his days. When a boy, he would often pass the house with his father, and frequently said to him, "If ever I have a dwelling of my own, Gad's Hill Place is the house I mean to buy." In that beautiful retreat he had for many years been accustomed to welcome his friends, and find relaxation from the crowded life of London. On the lawn playing at bowls, in the Swiss summer-house charmingly shaded by green leaves, he always seemed the best part of summer, beautiful as the season is in the delightful region where he lived.

There he could be most thoroughly enjoyed, for he

never seemed so cheerfully at home anywhere else. At his own table, surrounded by his family, and a few guests, old acquaintances from town, — among them sometimes Forster, Carlyle, Reade, Collins, Layard, Maclise, Stone, Macready, Talfourd, — he was always the choicest and liveliest companion. He was not what is called in society a professed talker, but he was something far better and rarer.

In his own inimitable manner he would frequently relate to me, if prompted, stories of his youthful days, when he was toiling on the London Morning Chronicle, passing sleepless hours as a reporter on the road in a post-chaise, driving day and night from point to point to take down the speeches of Shiel or O'Connell. He liked to describe the post-boys, who were accustomed to hurry him over the road that he might reach London in advance of his rival reporters, while, by the aid of a lantern, he was writing out for the press, as he flew over the ground, the words he had taken down in short-hand. Those were his days of severe training, when in rain and sleet and cold he dashed along, scarcely able to keep the blinding mud out of his tired eyes; and he imputed much of his ability for steady hard work to his practice as a reporter, kept at his grinding business, and determined if possible to earn seven guineas a week. A large sheet was started at this period of his life, in which all the important speeches of Parliament were to be reported *verbatim* for future reference. Dickens was engaged on this gigantic journal. Mr. Stanley (afterwards Lord Derby) had spoken at great length on the condition of Ireland. It was a long and eloquent speech, occupying many hours in the delivery. Eight reporters were sent in to do the work. Each one was required to report three quarters of an hour, then to retire, write out his portion, and to be succeeded by the next. Young Dickens was detailed to lead off with the first part. It also fell to his lot, when the time came round, to report the closing portions of the speech. On Saturday the whole was given to the press, and Dickens ran down to the country for a Sunday's rest. Sunday morning had scarcely dawned, when his father, who was a man of immense energy, made his appearance in his son's sleeping-room. Mr. Stanley was so dissatisfied with what he found in print, except the beginning and ending of his speech (just what Dickens had reported) that he sent immediately to the office and obtained the sheets of those parts of the report. He there found the name of the reporter, which, according to custom, was written on the margin. Then he requested that the young man bearing the name of Dickens should be immediately sent for. Dickens's father, all aglow with the prospect of probable promotion in the office, went immediately to his son's stopping-place in the country and brought him back to London. In telling the story, Dickens said: "I remember perfectly to this day the aspect of the room I was shown into, and the two persons in it, Mr. Stanley and his father. Both gentlemen were extremely courteous to me, but I noted their evident surprise at the appearance of so young a man. While we spoke together, I had taken a seat extended to me in the middle of the room. Mr. Stanley told me he wished to go over the whole speech and have it written out by me, and if I were ready he would begin now. Where would I like to sit? I told him I was very well where I was, and we could begin immediately. He tried to induce me to sit at a desk, but at that time in the House of Commons there was nothing but one's knees to write upon, and I had formed the habit of doing my work in that way. Without further pause he began and went rapidly on, hour after hour, to the end, often becoming very much excited and frequently bringing down his hand with great violence upon the desk near which he stood."

I have before me, as I write, an unpublished autograph letter of young Dickens, which he sent off to his employer in November, 1835, while he was on a reporting expedition for the Morning Chronicle. At that early stage of his career he seems to have had that unfailing accuracy of statement so marked in after years when he became famous. The letter was given to me several years ago by one of Dickens's brother reporters. Thus it runs: —

GEORGE AND PELICAN, NEWBURY, Sunday Morning.

DEAR FRASER: In conjunction with The Herald we have arranged for a Horse Express from Marlborough to London on Tuesday night, to go the whole distance at the rate of thirteen miles an hour, for six guineas: half has been paid, but, to insure despatch, the remainder is withheld until the boy arrives at the office, when he will produce a paper with a copy of the agreement on one side, and an order for three guineas (signed by myself) on the other. Will you take care that it is duly honored? A Boy from The Herald will be in waiting at our office for their copy; and Lyons begs me to remind you most strongly that it is an indispensable part of our agreement *that he should not be detained one instant.*

We go to Bristol to-day, and if we are equally fortunate in laying the chaise-horses, I hope the packet will reach town by seven. As all the papers have arranged to leave Bristol the moment Russell is down, we have determined on adopting the same plan, — one of us will go to Marlborough in the chaise with one Herald man, and the other remain at Bristol with the second Herald man to conclude the account for the next day. The Times has ordered a chaise and four the whole distance, so there is every probability of our beating them hollow. From all we hear, we think the Herald, relying on the packet reaching town early, intends publishing the report in their first Edition. This is however, of course, mere speculation on our parts, as we have no direct means of ascertaining their intention.

I think I have now given you all needful information. I have only in conclusion to impress upon you the necessity of having all the compositors ready, at a very early hour, for if Russell be down by half past eight, we hope to have his speech in town at six.

Believe me (for self and Beard) very truly yours,
CHARLES DICKENS.

Nov., 1835.

THOMAS FRASER, ESQ., Morning Chronicle Office.

No writer ever lived whose method was more exact, whose industry was more constant, and whose punctuality was more marked, than those of Charles Dickens. He never shirked labor, mental or bodily. He rarely declined, if the object were a good one, taking the chair at a public meeting, or accepting a charitable trust. Many widows and orphans of deceased literary men have for years been benefited by his wise trusteeship or counsel, and he spent a great portion of his time personally looking after the property of the poor whose interests were under his control. He was, as has been intimated, one of the most industrious of men, and marvellous stories are told (not by himself) of what he has accomplished in a given time in literary and social matters. His studies were all from nature and life, and his habits of observation were untiring. If he contemplated writing "Hard Times," he arranged with the master of Astley's circus to spend many hours behind the scenes with the riders and among the horses; and if the composition of the "Tale of Two Cities" were occupying his thoughts, he could banish himself to France for two years to prepare for that great work. Hogarth pencilled on his thumb-nail a striking face in a crowd that he wished to preserve; Dickens with his transcendent memory chronicled in his mind whatever of interest met his eye or reached his ear, any time or anywhere. Speaking of memory one day, he said the memory of children was prodigious; it was a mistake to fancy children ever forgot anything. When he was delineating the character of Mrs. Pipchin, he had in his mind an old lodging-house keeper in an English watering-place where he was living with his father and mother when he was but two years old. After the book was written he sent it to his sister, who wrote back at once: "Good heavens! what does this mean? you have painted our lodging-house keeper, and you were but two years old at that time!" Characters and incidents crowded the chambers of his brain, all ready for use when occasion required. No subject of human interest was ever indifferent to him, and never a day went by that did not afford him some suggestion to be utilized in the future.

His favorite mode of exercise was walking; and when in America, scarcely a day passed, no matter what the weather, that he did not accomplish his eight or ten miles. It was on these expeditions that he liked to recount to the companion of his rambles stories and incidents of his early life; and when he was in the mood, his fun and humor knew no bounds. He would then frequently discuss the numerous characters in his delightful books, and would act out, on the road, dramatic situations, where Nickleby or Copperfield or Swiveller would play distinguished parts. I remember he said, on one of these occasions, that during the composition of his first stories he could never entirely dismiss the characters about whom he happened to be writing; that while the "Old Curiosity Shop" was in process of composition Little Nell followed him about everywhere; that while he was writing "Oliver Twist" Fagin the Jew would never let him rest, even in his most retired moments; that at midnight and in the morning, on the sea and on the land, Tiny Tim and Little Bob Cratchit were ever tugging at his coat-sleeve, as if impatient for him to get back to his desk and continue the story of their lives. But he said after he had published several books, and saw what serious demands his characters were accustomed to make for the constant attention of his already overtasked brain, he resolved that the phantom individuals should no longer intrude on his hours of recreation and rest, but that when he closed the door of his study he would shut them all in, and only meet them again when he came back to resume his task. That force of will with which he was so pre-eminently endowed enabled him to ignore these manifold existences till he chose to renew their acquaintance. He said, also, that when the children of his brain had once been launched, free and clear of him, into the world, they would sometimes turn up in the most unexpected manner to look their father in the face.

Sometimes he would pull my arm while we were walking together and whisper, "Let us avoid Mr. Pumblechook, who is crossing the street to meet us"; or, "Mr. Micawber is coming; let us turn down this alley to get out of his way." He always seemed to enjoy the fun of his comic people, and had unceasing mirth over Mr. Pickwick's misadventures. In answer one day to a question, prompted by psychological curiosity, if he ever dreamed of any of his characters, his reply was, "Never; and I am convinced that no writer (judging from my own experience, which cannot be altogether singular, but must be a type of the experience of others) has ever dreamed of the creatures of his own imagination. It would," he went on to say, "be like a man's dreaming of meeting himself, which is clearly an impossibility. Things exterior to one's self must always be the basis of dreams." The growing up of characters in his mind never lost for him a sense of the marvellous. "What an unfathomable mystery there is in it all!" he said one day. Taking up a wineglass, he continued: "Suppose I choose to call this a *character*, fancy it a man, endue it with certain qualities; and soon the fine filmy webs of thought, almost impalpable, coming from every direction, we know not whence, spin and weave about it, until it assumes form and beauty, and becomes instinct with life."

In society Dickens rarely referred to the traits and characteristics of people he had known; but during a long walk in the country he delighted to recall and describe the peculiarities, eccentric and otherwise, of dead and gone as well as living friends. Then Sydney Smith and Jeffrey and Christopher North and Talfourd and Hood and Rogers seemed to live over again in his vivid reproductions, made so impressive by his marvellous memory and imagination. As he walked rapidly along the road, he appeared to enjoy the keen zest of his companion in the numerous impersonations with which he was indulging him.

He always had much to say of animals as well as of men, and there were certain dogs and horses he had met and known intimately which it was specially interesting to him to remember and picture. There was a particular dog in Washington which he was never tired of delineating. The first night Dickens read in the Capital this dog attracted his attention. "He came into the hall by himself," said he, "got a good place before the reading began, and paid strict attention throughout. He came the second night, and was ignominiously shown out by one of the check-takers. On the third night he appeared again with another dog, which he had evidently promised to pass in free; but you see," continued Dickens, "upon the imposition being unmasked, the other dog apologized by a howl and withdrew. His intentions, no doubt, were of the best, but he afterwards rose to explain outside, with such inconvenient eloquence to the reader and his audience, that they were obliged to put him down stairs."

He was such a firm believer in the mental faculties of animals, that it would have gone hard with a companion with whom he was talking, if a doubt were thrown, however inadvertently, on the mental intelligence of any four-footed friend that chanced to be at the time the subject of conversation. All animals which he took under his especial patronage seemed to have a marked affection for him. Quite a colony of dogs has always been a feature at Gad's Hill.

In many walks and talks with Dickens, his conversation, now, alas! so imperfectly recalled, frequently ran on the habits of birds, the raven, of course, interesting him particularly. He always liked to have a raven hopping about his grounds, and whoever has read the new Preface to "Barnaby Rudge" must remember several of his old friends in that line. He had quite a fund of canary-bird anecdotes, and the pert ways of birds that picked up worms for a living afforded him infinite amusement. He would give a capital imitation of the way a robin-redbreast cocks his head on one side preliminary to a dash forward in the direction of a wriggling victim. There is a small grave at Gad's Hill to which Dickens would occasionally take a friend, and it was quite a privilege to stand with him beside the burial-place of little Dick, the family's favorite canary.

What a treat it was to go with him to the London Zoölogical Gardens, a place he greatly delighted in at all times! He knew the zoölogical address of every animal, bird, and fish of any distinction; and he could, without the slightest hesitation, on entering the grounds, proceed straightway to the celebrities of claw or foot or fin. The delight he took in the hippopotamus family was most exhilarating. He entered familiarly into conversation with the huge, unwieldy creatures, and they seemed to understand him. Indeed, he spoke to all the unphilological inhabitants with a directness and tact which went home to them at once. He chaffed with the monkeys, coaxed the tigers, and bamboozled the snakes, with a dexterity unapproachable. All the keepers knew him, he was such a loyal visitor, and I noticed they came up to him in a friendly way, with the feeling that they had a sympathetic listener always in Charles Dickens.

There were certain books of which Dickens liked to talk during his walks. Among his especial favorites were the writings of Cobbett, DeQuincey, the Lectures on Moral Philosophy by Sydney Smith, and Carlyle's French Revolution. Of this latter Dickens said it was the book of all others which he read perpetually and of which he never tired, — the book which always appeared more imaginative in proportion to the fresh imagination he brought to it, a book for inexhaustibleness to be placed before every other book. When writing the "Tale of Two Cities," he asked Carlyle if he might see one of the works to which he referred in his history; whereupon Carlyle packed up and sent down to Gad's Hill *all* his reference volumes, and Dickens read them faithfully. But the more he read the more he was astonished to find how the facts had passed through the alembic of Carlyle's brain and had come out and fitted themselves, each as a part of one great whole, making a compact result, indestructible and unrivalled; and he always found himself turning away from the books of reference, and re-reading with increased wonder this marvellous new growth. There were certain books particularly hateful to him, and of which he never spoke except in terms of most ludicrous raillery. Mr. Barlow, in "Sandford and Merton," he said was the favorite enemy of his boyhood and his first experience of a bore. He had an almost supernatural hatred for Barlow, "because he was so very *instructive*, and always hinting doubts with regard to the veracity of 'Sindbad the Sailor,' and had no belief whatever in 'The Wonderful Lamp' or 'The Enchanted Horse.'" Dickens rattling his mental cane over the head of Mr. Barlow was as much better than any play as can be well imagined. He gloried in many of Hood's poems, especially in that biting Ode to Rae Wilson, and he would gesticulate with a fine fervor the lines,

> ". . . . the hypocrites who ope Heaven's door
> Obsequious to the sinful man of riches, —
> But put the wicked, naked, bare-legged poor
> In parish *stocks* instead of *breeches*."

One of his favorite books was Pepys's Diary, the curious discovery of the key to which, and the odd characteristics of its writer, were a never-failing source of interest and amusement to him. The vision of Pepys hanging round the door of the theatre, hoping for an invitation to go in, not being able to keep away in spite of a promise he had made to himself that he would spend no more money foolishly, delighted him. Speaking one day of Gray, the author of the Elegy, he said: "No poet ever came walking down to posterity with so *small* a book under his arm." He preferred Smollett to Fielding, putting "Peregrine Pickle" above "Tom Jones." Of the best novels by his contemporaries he always spoke with warm commendation, and "Griffith Gaunt" he thought a production of very high merit. He was "hospitable to the thought" of all writers who were really in earnest, but at the first exhibition of floundering or inexactness he became an unbeliever. People with dislocated understandings he had no tolerance for.

He was passionately fond of the theatre, loved the lights and music and flowers, and the happy faces of the audience; he was accustomed to say that his love of the theatre never failed, and, no matter how dull the play, he was always careful while he sat in the box to make no sound which could hurt the feelings of the actors, or show any lack of attention. His genuine enthusiasm for Mr. Fechter's acting was most interesting. He loved to describe seeing him first, quite by accident, in Paris, having strolled into a little theatre there one night. "He was making love to a woman," Dickens said, "and he so elevated her as well as himself by the sentiment in which he enveloped her, that they trod in a purer ether, and in another sphere, quite lifted out of the present. 'By heavens!' I said to myself, 'a man who can do this can do anything.' I never saw two people more purely and instantly elevated by the power of love. The manner, also," he continued, " in which he presses the hem of the dress of Lucy in the Bride of Lammermoor is something wonderful. The man has genius in him which is unmistakable."

Life behind the scenes was always a fascinating study to Dickens. "One of the oddest sights a green-room can present," he said one day, " is when they are collecting children for a pantomime. For this purpose the prompter calls together all the women in the ballet, and begins giving out their names in order, while they press about him eager for the chance of increasing their poor pay by the extra pittance their children will receive. ' Mrs. Johnson, how many?' 'Two, sir.' 'What ages?' 'Seven and ten.' ' Mrs. B., how many?' and so on, until the required number is made up. The people who go upon the stage, however poor their pay or hard their lot, love it too well ever to adopt another vocation of their free-will. A mother will frequently be in the wardrobe, children in the pantomime, elder sisters in the ballet, etc."

Dickens's habits as a speaker differed from those of most orators. He gave no thought to the composition of the speech he was to make till the day before he was to deliver it. No matter whether the effort was to be a long or a short one, he never wrote down a word of what he was going to say; but when the proper time arrived for him to consider his subject, he took a walk into the country and the thing was done. When he returned he was all ready for his task.

He liked to talk about the audiences that came to hear him read, and he gave the palm to his Parisian one, saying it was the quickest to catch his meaning. Although he said there were many always present in his room in

Paris who did not fully understand English, yet the French eye is so quick to detect expression that it never failed instantly to understand what he meant by a look or an act. "Thus, for instance," he said, "when I was impersonating Steerforth in "David Copperfield," and gave that peculiar grip of the hand to Emily's lover, the French audience burst into cheers and rounds of applause." He said with reference to the preparation of his readings, that it was three months' hard labor to get up one of his own stories for public recitation, and he thought he had greatly improved his presentation of the "Christmas Carol" while in this country. He considered the storm scene in "David Copperfield" one of the most effective of his readings. The character of Jack Hopkins in "Bob Sawyer's Party" he took great delight in representing, and as Jack was a prime favorite of mine, he brought him forward whenever the occasion prompted. He always spoke of Hopkins as my particular friend, and he was constantly quoting him, taking on the peculiar voice and turn of the head which he gave Jack in the public reading.

It gave him a natural pleasure when he heard quotations from his own books introduced without effort into conversation. He did not always remember, when his own words were quoted, that he was himself the author of them, and appeared astounded at the memory of others in this regard. He said Mr. Secretary Stanton had a most extraordinary knowledge of his books and a power of taking the text up at any point, which he supposed to belong to only one person, and that person not himself.

It was said of Garrick that he was the *cheerfullest* man of his age. This can be as truly said of Charles Dickens. In his presence there was perpetual sunshine, and gloom was banished as having no sort of relationship with him. No man suffered more keenly or sympathized more fully than he did with want and misery; but his motto was, "Don't stand and cry; press forward and help remove the difficulty." The speed with which he was accustomed to make the deed follow his yet speedier sympathy was seen pleasantly on the day of his visit to the School-ship in Boston Harbor. He said, previously to going on board that ship, nothing would tempt him to make a speech, for he should always be obliged to do it on similar occasions, if he broke through his rule so early in his reading tour. But Judge Russell had no sooner finished his simple talk, to which the boys listened, as they always do, with eager faces, than Dickens rose as if he could not help it, and with a few words so magnetized them that they wore their hearts in their eyes as if they meant to keep the words forever. An enthusiastic critic once said of John Ruskin, "that he could discover the Apocalypse in a daisy." As noble a discovery may be claimed for Dickens. He found all the fair humanities blooming in the lowliest hovel. He never *put on* the good Samaritan: that character was native to him. Once while in this country, on a bitter, freezing afternoon, — night coming down in a drifting snow-storm, — he was returning with me from a long walk in the country. The wind and baffling sleet were so furious that the street in which we happened to be fighting our way was quite deserted; it was almost impossible to see across it, the air was so thick with the tempest; all conversation between us had ceased, for it was only possible to breast the storm by devoting our whole energies to keeping on our feet; we seemed to be walking in a different atmosphere from any we had ever before encountered. All at once I missed Dickens from my side. What had become of him? Had he gone down in the drift, utterly exhausted, and was the snow burying him out of sight? Very soon the sound of his cheery voice was heard on the other side of the way.

With great difficulty, over the piled-up snow, I struggled across the street, and there found him lifting up, almost by main force, a blind old man who had got bewildered by the storm, and had fallen down unnoticed, quite unable to proceed. Dickens, a long distance away from him, with that tender, sensitive, and penetrating vision, ever on the alert for suffering in any form, had rushed at once to the rescue, comprehending at a glance the situation of the sightless man. To help him to his feet and aid him homeward in the most natural and simple way afforded Dickens such a pleasure as only the benevolent by intuition can understand.

Throughout his life Dickens was continually receiving tributes from those he had benefited, either by his books or by his friendship. There is an odd and very pretty story (vouched for here as true) connected with the influence he so widely exerted. In the winter of 1869, soon after he came up to London to reside for a few months, he received a letter from a man telling him that he had begun life in the most humble way possible, and that he considered he owed his subsequent great success and such education as he had given himself entirely to the encouragement and cheering influence he had derived from Dickens's books, of which he had been a constant reader from his childhood. He had been made a partner in his master's business, and when the head of the house died, the other day, it was found he had left the whole of his large property to this man. As soon as he came into possession of this fortune, his mind turned to Dickens, whom he looked upon as his benefactor and teacher, and his first desire was to tender him some testimonial of gratitude and veneration. He then begged Dickens to accept a large sum of money. Dickens declined to receive the money, but his unknown friend sent him instead two silver table ornaments of great intrinsic value bearing this inscription: "To Charles Dickens, from one who has been cheered and stimulated by his writings, and held the author amongst his first Remembrances when he became prosperous." One of these silver ornaments was supported by three figures, representing three seasons. In the original design there were, of course, four, but the donor was so averse to associating the idea of Winter in any sense with Dickens that he caused the workman to alter the design and leave only the *cheerful* seasons. No event in the great author's career was ever more gratifying and pleasant to him.

His friendly notes were exquisitely turned, and are among his most charming compositions. They abound in felicities only like himself. In 1860 he wrote to me while I was sojourning in Italy: "I should like to have a walk through Rome with you this bright morning (for it really *is* bright in London), and convey you over some favorite ground of mine. I used to go up the street of Tombs, past the tomb of Cecilia Metella, away out upon the wild campagna, and by the old Appian Road (easily tracked out among the ruins and primroses), to Albano. There, at a very dirty inn, I used to have a very dirty lunch, generally with the family's dirty linen lying in a corner, and inveigle some very dirty Vetturino in sheep-skin to take me back to Rome."

In a little note in answer to one I had written consulting him about the purchase of some old furniture in London he wrote: "There is a chair (without a bottom) at a shop near the office, which I think would suit you. It cannot stand of itself, but will almost seat somebody, if you put it in a corner, and prop one leg up with two wedges and cut another leg off. The proprietor asks £20, but says he admires literature and would take £18. He is of republican principles and I think would take £17 19 *s.* 6 *d.* from a cousin; shall I secure this prize? It is very ugly and wormy, and it is related, but without proof, that on one occasion Washington declined to sit down in it."

Here are the last two missives I ever received from his dear, kind hand: —

5 HYDE PARK PLACE, LONDON, W., Friday, January 14, 1870.

MY DEAR FIELDS: We live here (opposite the Marble Arch) in a charming house until the 1st of June, and then return to Gad's. The Conservatory is completed, and is a brilliant success; — but an expensive one!

I read this afternoon at three, — a beastly proceeding which I particularly hate, — and again this day week at three. These morning readings particularly disturb me at my book-work; nevertheless I hope, please God, to lose no way on their account. An evening reading once a week is nothing. By the by, I recommenced last Tuesday evening with the greatest brilliancy.

I should be quite ashamed of not having written to you and my dear Mrs. Fields before now, if I did n't know that you will both understand how occupied I am, and how naturally, when I put my papers away for the day, I get up and fly. I have a large room here, with three fine windows, overlooking the Park, — unsurpassable for airiness and cheerfulness.

You saw the announcement of the death of poor dear Harness. The circumstances are curious. He wrote to his old friend the Dean of Battle saying he would come to visit him on that day (the day of his death). The Dean wrote back: "Come next day, instead, as we are obliged to go out to dinner, and you will be alone." Harness told his sister a little impatiently that he *must* go on the first-named day, — that he had made up his mind to go, and MUST. He had been getting himself ready for dinner, and came to a part of the staircase whence two doors opened, — one, upon another level passage; one, upon a flight of stone steps. He opened the wrong door, fell down the steps, injured himself very severely, and died in a few hours.

You will know — *I* don't — what Fechter's success is in America at the time of this present writing. In his farewell performances at the Princess's he acted very finely. I thought the three first acts of his Hamlet very much better than I had ever thought them before, — and I always thought very highly of them. We gave him a foaming stirrup cup at Gad's Hill.

Forster (who has been ill with his bronchitis again) thinks No. 2 of the new book (Edwin Drood) a clincher, — I mean that word (as his own expression) for *Clincher*. There is a curious interest steadily working up to No. 5, which requires a great deal of art and self-denial. I think also, apart from character and picturesqueness, that the young people are placed in a very novel situation. So I hope — at Nos. 5 and 6 the story will turn upon an interest suspended until the end.

I can't believe it, and don't, and won't, but they say Harry's twenty-first birthday is next Sunday. I have entered him at the Temple just now; and if he don't get a fellowship at Trinity Hall when his time comes, I shall be disappointed, if in the present disappointed state of existence.

I hope you may have met with the little touch of Radicalism I gave them at Birmingham in the words of Buckle? With pride I observe that it makes the regular political traders, of all sorts, perfectly mad. Sich was my intentions, as a grateful acknowledgment of having been misrepresented.

I think Mrs. ——'s prose very admirable, but I don't believe it! No, I do *not*. My conviction is that those Islanders get frightfully bored by the Islands, and wish they had never set eyes upon them!

Charley Collins has done a charming cover for the monthly part of the new book. At the very earnest representations of Millais (and after having seen a great number of his drawings) I am going to engage with a new man; retaining, of course, C. C.'s cover aforesaid. K—— has made some more capital portraits, and is always improving.

My dear Mrs. Fields, if "He" (made proud by chairs and bloated by pictures) does not give you my dear love, let us conspire against him when you find him out, and exclude him from all future confidences. Until then

Ever affectionately yours and his,

C. D.

5 Hyde Park Place, London, W., Monday, April 18, 1870.

My dear Fields: I have been hard at work all day until post time, and have only leisure to acknowledge the receipt, the day before yesterday, of your note containing such good news of Fechter and to assure you of my undiminished regard and affection.

We have been doing wonders with No. 1 of Edwin Drood. *It has very, very far outstripped every one of its predecessors.*

Ever your affectionate friend,

Charles Dickens.

Bright colors were a constant delight to him; and the gay hues of flowers were those most welcome to his eye. When the rhododendrons were in bloom in Cobham Park, the seat of his friend and neighbor, Lord Darnley, he always counted on taking his guests there to enjoy the magnificent show. He delighted to turn out for the delectation of his Transatlantic cousins a couple of postilions in the old red jackets of the old red royal Dover road, making the ride as much as possible like a holiday drive in England fifty years ago.

When in the mood for humorous characterization, Dickens's hilarity was most amazing. To hear him tell a ghost story with a very florid imitation of a very pallid ghost, or hear him sing an old-time stage song, such as he used to enjoy in his youth at a cheap London theatre, to see him imitate a lion in a menagerie-cage, or the clown in a pantomime when he flops and folds himself up like a jack-knife, or to join with him in some mirthful game of his own composing, was to become acquainted with one of the most delightful and original companions in the world.

On one occasion, during a walk with me, he chose to run into the wildest of vagaries about *conversation*. The ludicrous vein he indulged in during that two hours' stretch can never be forgotten. Among other things, he said he had often thought how restricted one's conversation must become when one was visiting a man who was to be hanged in half an hour. He went on in a most surprising manner to imagine all sorts of difficulties in the way of becoming interesting to the poor fellow. "Suppose," said he, "it should be a rainy morning while you are making the call, you could not possibly indulge in the remark, 'We shall have fine weather to-morrow, sir,' for what would that be to him? For my part, I think," said he, "I should confine my observations to the days of Julius Cæsar or King Alfred."

At another time when speaking of what was constantly said about him in certain newspapers, he observed: "I notice that about once in every seven years I become the victim of a paragraph disease. It breaks out in England, travels to India by the overland route, gets to America per Cunard line, strikes the base of the Rocky Mountains, and, rebounding back to Europe, mostly perishes on the steppes of Russia from inanition and extreme cold." When he felt he was not under observation, and that tomfoolery would not be frowned upon or gazed at with astonishment, he gave himself up without reserve to healthy amusement and strengthening mirth. It was his mission to make people happy. Words of good cheer were native to his lips, and he was always doing what he could to lighten the lot of all who came into his beautiful presence. His talk was simple, natural, and direct, never dropping into circumlocution nor elocution. Now that he is gone, whoever has known him intimately for any considerable period of time will linger over his tender regard for, and his engaging manner with, children; his cheery "Good Day" to poor people he happened to be passing in the road; his trustful and earnest "Please God," when he was promising himself any special pleasure, like rejoining an old friend or returning again to scenes he loved. At such times his voice had an irresistible pathos in it, and his smile diffused a sensation like music. When he came into the presence of squalid or degraded persons, such as one sometimes encounters in almshouses or prisons, he had such soothing words to scatter here and there, that those who had been "most hurt by the archers" listened gladly, and loved him without knowing who it was that found it in his heart to speak so kindly to them.

Oftentimes during long walks in the streets and by-ways of London, or through the pleasant Kentish lanes, or among the localities he has rendered forever famous in his books, I have recalled the sweet words in which Shakespeare has embalmed one of the characters in Love's Labor's Lost: —

> "A merrier man,
> Within the limit of becoming mirth,
> I never spent an hour's talk withal:
> His eye begets occasion for his wit;
> For every object that the one doth catch
> The other turns to a mirth-moving jest,
> Which his fair tongue, conceit's expositor,
> Delivers in such apt and gracious words
> That aged ears play truant at his tales,
> And younger hearings are quite ravishéd;
> So sweet and voluble is his discourse."

Twenty years ago Daniel Webster said that Dickens had already done more to ameliorate the condition of the English poor than all the statesmen Great Britain had sent into Parliament. During the unceasing demands upon his time and thought, he found opportunities of visiting personally those haunts of suffering in London which needed the keen eye and sympathetic heart to bring them before the public for relief. Whoever has accompanied him, as I have, on his midnight walks into the cheap lodging-houses provided for London's lowest poor, cannot have failed to learn lessons never to be forgotten. Newgate and Smithfield were lifted out of their abominations by his eloquent pen, and many a hospital is to-day all the better charity for having been visited and watched by Charles Dickens. To use his own words, through his whole life he did what he could "to lighten the lot of those rejected ones whom the world has too long forgotten and too often misused."

These inadequate, and, of necessity, hastily written, records must stand for what they are worth as personal recollections of the great author who has made so many millions happy by his inestimable genius and sympathy. His life will no doubt be written out in full by some competent hand in England; but however numerous the volumes of his biography, the half can hardly be told of the good deeds he has accomplished for his fellow-men.

And who could ever tell, if those volumes were written, of the subtle qualities of insight and sympathy which rendered him capable of friendship above most men, — which enabled him to reinstate its ideal, and made his presence a perpetual joy, and separation from him an ineffaceable sorrow?

WORDSWORTH.

"*His mind is, as it were, coeval with the primary forms of things; his imagination holds immediately from nature, and 'owes no allegiance' but 'to the elements.' . . . . He sees all things in himself.*" — HAZLITT.

V.

WORDSWORTH.

THAT portrait looking down so calmly from the wall is an original picture of the poet Wordsworth, drawn in crayon a few years before he died. He went up to London on purpose to sit for it, at the request of Moxon, his publisher, and his friends in England always considered it a perfect likeness of the poet. After the head was engraved, the artist's family disposed of the drawing, and through the watchful kindness of my dear old friend, Mary Russell Mitford, the portrait came across the Atlantic to this house. Miss Mitford said America ought to have on view such a perfect representation of the great poet, and she used all her successful influence in my behalf. So there the picture hangs for anybody's inspection at any hour of the day.

I once made a pilgrimage to the small market-town of Hawkshead, in the valley of Esthwaite, where Wordsworth went to school in his ninth year. The thoughtful boy was lodged in the house of Dame Anne Tyson in 1788; and I had the good fortune to meet a lady in the village street who conducted me at once to the room which the lad occupied while he was a scholar under the Rev. William Taylor, whom he loved and venerated so much. I went into the chamber which he afterwards described in The Prelude, where he

> "Had lain awake on summer nights to watch
> The moon in splendor couched among the leaves
> Of a tall ash, that near our cottage stood";

and I visited many of the beautiful spots which tradition points out as the favorite haunts of his childhood.

It was true Lake-country weather when I knocked at Wordsworth's cottage door, three years before he died, and found myself shaking hands with the poet at the threshold. His daughter Dora had been dead only a few months, and the sorrow that had so recently fallen upon the house was still dominant there. I thought there was something prophet-like in the tones of his voice, as well as in his whole appearance, and there was a noble tranquillity about him that almost awed one, at first, into silence. As the day was cold and wet, he proposed we should sit down together in the only room in the house where there was a fire, and he led the way to what seemed a common sitting or dining room. It was a plain apartment, the rafters visible, and no attempt at decoration noticeable. Mrs. Wordsworth sat knitting at the fireside, and she rose with a sweet expression of courtesy and welcome as we entered the apartment. As I had just left Paris, which was in a state of commotion, Wordsworth was eager in his inquiries about the state of things on the other side of the Channel. As our talk ran in the direction of French revolutions, he soon became eloquent and vehement, as one can easily imagine, on such a theme. There was a deep and solemn meaning in all he had to say about France, which I recall now with added interest. The subject deeply moved him, of course, and he sat looking into the fire, discoursing in a low monotone, sometimes quite forgetful that he was not alone and soliloquizing. I noticed that Mrs. Wordsworth listened as if she were hearing him speak for the first time in her life, and the work on which she was engaged lay idle in her lap, while she watched intently every movement of her husband's face. I also was absorbed in the man and in his speech. I thought of the long years he had lived

W Wordsworth

in communion with nature in that lonely but lovely region. The story of his life was familiar to me, and I sat as if under the influence of a spell. Soon he turned and plied me with questions about the prominent men in Paris whom I had recently seen and heard in the Chamber of Deputies. "How did Guizot bear himself? What part was De Tocqueville taking in the fray? Had I noticed George Lafayette especially?" America did not seem to concern him much, and I waited for him to introduce the subject, if he chose to do so. He seemed pleased that a youth from a far-away country should find his way to Rydal cottage to worship at the shrine of an old poet.

By and by we fell into talk about those who had been his friends and neighbors among the hills in former years. "And so," he said, "you read Charles Lamb in America?" "Yes," I replied, "and *love* him too." "Do you hear that, Mary?" he eagerly inquired, turning round to Mrs. Wordsworth. "Yes, William, and no wonder, for he was one to be loved everywhere," she quickly answered. Then we spoke of Hazlitt, whom he ranked very high as a prose-writer; and when I quoted a fine passage from Hazlitt's essay on Jeremy Taylor, he seemed pleased at my remembrance of it.

He asked about Inman, the American artist, who had painted his portrait, having been sent on a special mission to Rydal by Professor Henry Reed of Philadelphia, to procure the likeness. The painter's daughter, who accompanied her father, made a marked impression on Wordsworth, and both he and his wife joined in the question, "Are all the girls in America as pretty as she?" I thought it an honor Mary Inman might well be proud of to be so complimented by the old bard. In speaking of Henry Reed, his manner was affectionate and tender.

Now and then I stole a glance at the gentle lady, the

poet's wife, as she sat knitting silently by the fireside. This, then, was the Mary whom in 1802 he had brought home to be his loving companion through so many years. I could not help remembering too, as we all sat there together, that when children they had "practised reading and spelling under the same old dame at Penrith," and that they had always been lovers. There sat the woman, now gray-haired and bent, to whom the poet had addressed those undying poems, " She was a phantom of delight," " Let other bards of angels sing," " Yes, thou art fair," and " O, dearer far than life and light are dear." I recalled, too, the " Lines written after Thirty-six Years of Wedded Life," commemorating her whose

> "Morn into noon did pass, noon into eve,
> And the old day was welcome as the young,
> As welcome, and as beautiful, — in sooth
> More beautiful, as being a thing more holy."

When she raised her eyes to his, which I noticed she did frequently, they seemed overflowing with tenderness.

When I rose to go, for I felt that I must not intrude longer on one for whom I had such reverence, Wordsworth said, "I must show you my library, and some tributes that have been sent to me from the friends of my verse." His son John now came in, and we all proceeded to a large room in front of the house, containing his books. Seeing that I had an interest in such things, he seemed to take a real pleasure in showing me the presentation copies of works by distinguished authors. We read together, from many a well-worn old volume, notes in the handwriting of Coleridge and Charles Lamb. I thought he did not praise easily those whose names are indissolubly connected with his own in the history of literature. It was languid praise, at least, and I observed he hesitated for mild terms which he could apply to names almost as great as his own. I believe a duplicate of the portrait which Inman had painted for Reed hung in the room; at any rate a picture of himself was there, and he seemed to regard it with veneration as we stood before it. As we moved about the apartment, Mrs. Wordsworth quietly followed us, and listened as eagerly as I did to everything her husband had to say. Her spare little figure flitted about noiselessly, pausing as we paused, and always walking slowly behind us as we went from object to object in the room. John Wordsworth, too, seemed deeply interested to watch and listen to his father. "And now," said Wordsworth, "I must show you one of my latest presents." Leading us up to a corner of the room, we all stood before a beautiful statuette which a young sculptor had just sent to him, illustrating a passage in "The Excursion." Turning to me, Wordsworth asked, "Do you know the meaning of this figure?" I saw at a glance that it was

> "A curious child, who dwelt upon a tract
> Of inland ground, applying to his ear
> The convolutions of a smooth-lipped shell,"

and I quoted the lines. My recollection of the words pleased the old man; and as we stood there in front of the figure he began to recite the whole passage from "The Excursion," and it sounded very grand from the poet's own lips. He repeated some fifty lines, and I could not help thinking afterwards, when I came to hear Tennyson read his own poetry, that the younger Laureate had caught something of the strange, mysterious tone of the elder bard. It was a sort of chant, deep and earnest, which conveyed the impression that the reciter had the highest opinion of the poetry.

Although it was raining still, Wordsworth proposed to show me Lady Fleming's grounds, and some other spots of interest near his cottage. Our walk was a wet one; but as he did not seem incommoded by it, I was only too glad to hold the umbrella over his venerable head. As we went on, he added now and then a sonnet to the scenery, telling me precisely the circumstances under which it had been composed. It is many years since my memorable walk with the author of "The Excursion," but I can call up his figure and the very tones of his voice so vividly that I enjoy my interview over again any time I choose. He was then nearly eighty, but he seemed hale and quite as able to walk up and down the hills as ever. He always led back the conversation that day to his own writings, and it seemed the most natural thing in the world for him to do so. All his most celebrated poems seemed to live in his memory, and it was easy to start him off by quoting the first line of any of his pieces. Speaking of the vastness of London, he quoted the whole of his sonnet describing the great city, as seen in the morning from Westminster Bridge. When I parted with him at the foot of Rydal Hill, he gave me messages to Rogers and other friends of his whom I was to see in London. As we were shaking hands I said, "How glad your many readers in America would be to see you on our side of the water!" "Ah," he replied, "I shall never see your country, — that is impossible now; but" (laying his hand on his son's shoulder) "John shall go, please God, some day." I watched the aged man as he went slowly up the hill, and saw him disappear through the little gate that led to his cottage door. The ode on "Intimations of Immortality" kept sounding in my brain as I came down the road, long after he had left me.

Since I sat, a little child, in "a woman's school," Wordsworth's poems had been familiar to me. Here is my first school-book, with a name written on the cover by dear old "Marm Sloper," setting forth that the owner thereof is "aged 5." As I went musing along in Westmoreland that rainy morning, so many years ago, little

RYDAL MOUNT: WORDSWORTH'S HOME

figures seemed to accompany me, and childish voices filled the air as I trudged through the wet grass. My small ghostly companions seemed to carry in their little hands quaint-looking dog's-eared books, some of them covered with cloth of various colors. None of these phantom children looked to be over six years old, and all were bareheaded, and some of the girls wore old-fashioned pinafores. They were the schoolmates of my childhood, and many of them must have come out of their graves to run by my side that morning in Rydal. I had not thought of them for years. Little Emily R—— read from her book with a chirping lisp:—

> "O, what's the matter? what's the matter?
> What is't that ails young Harry Gill?"

Mary B—— began:—

> "Oft I had heard of Lucy Grey";

Nancy C—— piped up:—

> "'How many are you, then,' said I,
> 'If there are two in heaven?'
> The little maiden did reply,
> 'O master! we are seven.'"

Among the group I seemed to recognize poor pale little Charley F——, who they told me years ago was laid in St. John's Churchyard after they took him out of the pond, near the mill-stream, that terrible Saturday afternoon. He too read from his well-worn, green-baize-covered book, —

> "The dew was falling fast, the stars began to blink."

Other white-headed little urchins trotted along *very near* me all the way, and kept saying over and over their "spirit ditties of no tone" till I reached the village inn, and sat down as if in a dream of long-past years.

Two years ago I stood by Wordsworth's grave in the

churchyard at Grasmere, and my companion wove a chaplet of flowers and placed it on the headstone. Afterwards we went into the old church and sat down in the poet's pew. "They are all dead and gone now," sighed the gray-headed sexton; "but I can remember when the seats used to be filled by the family from Rydal Mount. Now they are all outside there in yon grass."

MISS MITFORD.

"*I care not, Fortune, what you me deny:
You cannot rob me of free Nature's grace;
You cannot shut the windows of the sky,
Through which Aurora shows her brightening face;
You cannot bar my constant feet to trace
The woods and lawns, by living streams at eve:
Let health my nerves and finer fibres brace,
And I their toys to the great children leave:
Of fancy, reason, virtue, naught can me bereave.*"

THOMSON.

VI.

MISS MITFORD.

THAT portrait hanging near Wordsworth's is next to seeing Mary Russell Mitford herself as I first saw her, twenty-three years ago, in her geranium-planted cottage at Three-Mile Cross. She sat to John Lucas for the picture in her serene old age, and the likeness is faultless. She had proposed to herself to leave the portrait, as it was her own property, to me in her will; but as I happened to be in England during the latter part of her life, she altered her determination, and gave it to me from her own hands.

Sydney Smith said of a certain quarrelsome person, that his very face was a breach of the peace. The face of that portrait opposite to us is a very different one from Sydney's fighter. Everything that belongs to the beauty of old age one will find recorded in that charming countenance. Serene cheerfulness most abounds, and that is a quality as rare as it is commendable. It will be observed that the dress of Miss Mitford in the picture before us is quaint and somewhat antiquated even for the time when it was painted, but a pleasant face is never out of fashion.

An observer of how old age is neglected in America said to me the other day, "It seems an impertinence to be alive after sixty on this side of the globe"; and I have often thought how much we lose by not cultivating fine old-fashioned ladies and gentlemen. Our aged relatives and friends seem to be tucked away, nowadays, into neglected corners, as though it were the correct thing to give them a long preparation for still narrower quarters. For my own part, comely and debonair old age is most attractive; and when I see the "thick silver-white hair lying on a serious and weather-worn face, like moonlight on a stout old tower," I have a strong tendency to lift my hat, whether I know the person or not.

"No spring nor summer beauty hath such grace
As I have seen in an autumnal face."

It was a fortunate hour for me when kind-hearted John Kenyon said, as I was leaving his hospitable door in London one summer midnight in 1847, "You must know my friend, Miss Mitford. She lives directly on the line of your route to Oxford, and you must call with my card and make her acquaintance." I had lately been talking with Wordsworth and Christopher North and old Samuel Rogers, but my hunger at that time to stand face to face with the distinguished persons in English literature was not satisfied. So it was during my first "tourification" in England that I came to know Miss Mitford. The day selected for my call at her cottage door happened to be a perfect one on which to begin an acquaintance with the lady of "Our Village." She was then living at Three-Mile Cross, having removed there from Bertram House in 1820. The cottage where I found her was situated on the high road between Basingstoke and Reading; and the village street on which she was then living contained the public-house and several small shops near by. There was also close at hand the village pond full of ducks and geese, and I noticed several young rogues on their way to school were occupied in worrying their feathered friends. The windows of the cottage were filled with flowers, and cowslips and violets were plentifully scattered about the little garden. Miss Mitford liked to have one dog, at least, at her heels, and this day her pet seemed to be constantly under foot. I remember the room into which I was shown was sanded, and a quaint old clock behind the door was marking off the hour in small but very loud pieces. The cheerful old lady called to me from the head of the stairs to come up into her sitting-room. I sat down by the open window to converse with her, and it was pleasant to see how the village children, as they went by, stopped to bow and curtsey. One curly-headed urchin made bold to take off his well-worn cap, and wait to be recognized as " little Johnny " " No great scholar," said the kind-hearted old lady to me, " but a sad rogue among our flock of geese. Only yesterday the young marauder was detected by my maid with a plump gosling stuffed half-way into his pocket!" While she was thus discoursing of Johnny's peccadilloes, the little fellow looked up with a knowing expression, and very soon caught in his cap a gingerbread dog, which the old lady threw to him from the window. " I wish he loved his book as well as he relishes sweetcake," sighed she, as the boy kicked up his heels and disappeared down the lane.

Her conversation that afternoon, full of anecdote, ran on in a perpetual flow of good-humor, and I was shocked, on looking at my watch, to find I had stayed so long, and had barely time to reach the railway-station in season to arrive at Oxford that night. We parted with the mutual determination and understanding to keep our friendship warm by correspondence, and I promised never to come to England again without finding my way to Three-Mile Cross.

During the conversation that day, Miss Mitford had many inquiries to make concerning her American friends, Miss Catherine Sedgwick, Daniel Webster, and Dr. Channing. Her voice had a peculiar ringing sweetness in it, rippling out sometimes like a beautiful chime of silver bells; and when she told a comic story, hitting off some one of her acquaintances, she joined in with the laugh at the end with great heartiness and *naïveté*. When listening to anything that interested her, she had a way of coming into the narrative with " Dear me, dear me, dear me," three times repeated, which it was very pleasant to hear.

From that summer day our friendship continued, and during other visits to England I saw her frequently, driving about the country with her in her pony-chaise, and spending many happy hours in the new cottage which she afterwards occupied at Swallowfield. Her health had broken down years before, from too constant attendance on her invalid parents, and she was never certain of a well day. When her father died, in 1842, shamefully in debt (for he had squandered two fortunes not exactly his own, and was always one of the most improvident of men, belonging to that class of impecunious individuals who seem to have been born insolvent), she said, " Everybody shall be paid, if I sell the gown off my back or pledge my little pension." And putting her shoulder to the domestic wheel, she never flagged for an instant, or gave way to despondency.

She was always cheerful, and her talk is delightful to remember. From girlhood she had known and had been intimate with most of the prominent writers of her time, and her observations and reminiscences were so shrewd and pertinent that I have scarcely known her equal.

Carlyle tells us " nothing so lifts a man from all his mean imprisonments, were it but for moments, as true admiration"; and Miss Mitford admired to such an extent that she must have been lifted in this way nearly all her lifetime. Indeed she erred, if she erred at all, on this side, and over-praised and over-admired everything and everybody whom she regarded. When she spoke of Beranger or Dumas or Hazlitt or Holmes, she exhausted every term of worship and panegyric. Louis Napoleon was one of her most

M. R. Mitford

potent crazes, and I fully believe, if she had been alive during the days of his downfall, she would have died of grief. When she talked of Munden and Bannister and Fawcett and Emery, those delightful old actors for whom she had had such an exquisite relish, she said they had made comedy to her a living art full of laughter and tears. How often have I heard her describe John Kemble, Mrs. Siddons, Miss O'Neil, and Edmund Kean, as they were wont to electrify the town in her girlhood! With what gusto she reproduced Elliston, who was one of her prime favorites, and tried to make me, through her representation of him, feel what a spirit there was in the man. Although she had been prostrated by the hard work and increasing anxieties of forty years of authorship, when I saw her she was as fresh and independent as a skylark. She was a good hater as well as a good praiser, and she left nothing worth saving in an obnoxious reputation.

I well remember, one autumn evening, when half a dozen friends were sitting in her library after dinner, talking with her of Tom Taylor's Life of Haydon, then lately published, how graphically she described to us the eccentric painter, whose genius she was among the foremost to recognize. The flavor of her discourse I cannot reproduce; but I was too much interested in what she was saying to forget the main incidents she drew for our edification, during those pleasant hours now far away in the past.

"I am a terrible forgetter of dates," she used to say, when any one asked her of the *time when;* but for the *manner how* she was never at a loss. "Poor Haydon!" she began. "He was an old friend of mine, and I am indebted to Sir William Elford, one of my dear father's correspondents during my girlhood, for a suggestion which sent me to look at a picture then on exhibition in London, and thus was brought about my knowledge of the painter's existence. He, Sir William, had taken a fancy to me, and I became his child-correspondent. Few things contribute more to that indirect after-education, which is worth all the formal lessons of the school-room a thousand times told, than such good-humored condescension from a clever man of the world to a girl almost young enough to be his granddaughter. I owe much to that correspondence, and, amongst other debts, the acquaintance of Haydon. Sir William's own letters were most charming, — full of old-fashioned courtesy, of quaint humor, and of pleasant and genial criticism on literature and on art. An amateur-painter himself, painting interested him particularly, and he often spoke much and warmly of the young man from Plymouth, whose picture of the 'Judgment of Solomon' was then on exhibition in London. 'You must see it,' said he, 'even if you come to town on purpose.'" — The reader of Haydon's Life will remember that Sir William Elford, in conjunction with a Plymouth banker named Tingecombe, ultimately purchased the picture. The poor artist was overwhelmed with astonishment and joy when he walked into the exhibition-room and read the label, " Sold," which had been attached to his picture that morning before he arrived. " My first impulse," he says in his Autobiography, " was gratitude to God."

"It so happened," continued Miss Mitford, "that I merely passed through London that season, and, being detained by some of the thousand and one nothings which are so apt to detain women in the great city, I arrived at the exhibition, in company with a still younger friend, so near the period of closing, that more punctual visitors were moving out, and the doorkeeper actually turned us and our money back. I persisted, however, assuring him that I only wished to look at one picture, and promising not to detain him long. Whether my entreaties would have carried the point or not, I cannot tell; but half a crown did; so we stood admiringly before the 'Judgment of Solomon.' I am no great judge of painting; but that picture impressed me then, as it does now, as excellent in composition, in color, and in that great quality of telling a story which appeals at once to every mind. Our delight was sincerely felt, and most enthusiastically expressed, as we kept gazing at the picture, and seemed, unaccountably to us at first, to give much pleasure to the only gentleman who had remained in the room,—a young and very distinguished-looking person, who had watched with evident amusement our negotiation with the doorkeeper. Beyond indicating the best position to look at the picture, he had no conversation with us; but I soon surmised that we were seeing the painter, as well as his painting; and when, two or three years afterwards, a friend took me by appointment to view the 'Entry into Jerusalem,' Haydon's next great picture, then near its completion, I found I had not been mistaken.

"Haydon was, at that period, a remarkable person to look at and listen to. Perhaps your American word *bright* expresses better than any other his appearance and manner. His figure, short, slight, elastic, and vigorous, looked still more light and youthful from the little sailor's-jacket and snowy trousers which formed his painting costume. His complexion was clear and healthful. His forehead, broad and high, out of all proportion to the lower part of his face, gave an unmistakable character of intellect to the finely placed head. Indeed, he liked to observe that the gods of the Greek sculptors owed much of their elevation to being similarly out of drawing! The lower features were terse, succinct, and powerful,— from the bold, decided jaw, to the large, firm, ugly, good-humored mouth. His very spectacles aided the general expression; they had a look of the man. But how shall

I attempt to tell you of his brilliant conversation, of his rapid, energetic manner, of his quick turns of thought, as he flew on from topic to topic, dashing his brush here and there upon the canvas? Slow and quiet persons were a good deal startled by this suddenness and mobility. He left such people far behind, mentally and bodily. But his talk was so rich and varied, so earnest and glowing, his anecdotes so racy, his perception of character so shrewd, and the whole tone so spontaneous and natural, that the want of repose was rather recalled afterwards than felt at the time. The alloy to this charm was a slight coarseness of voice and accent, which contrasted somewhat strangely with his constant courtesy and high breeding. Perhaps this was characteristic. A defect of some sort pervades his pictures. Their great want is equality and congruity, — that perfect union of qualities which we call *taste*. His apartment, especially at that period when he lived in his painting-room, was in itself a study of the most picturesque kind. Besides the great picture itself, for which there seemed hardly space between the walls, it was crowded with casts, lay figures, arms, tripods, vases, draperies, and costumes of all ages, weapons of all nations, books in all tongues. These cumbered the floor; whilst around hung smaller pictures, sketches, and drawings, replete with originality and force. With chalk he could do what he chose. I remember he once drew for me a head of hair with nine of his sweeping, vigorous strokes! Among the studies I remarked that day in his apartment was one of a mother who had just lost her only child, — a most masterly rendering of an unspeakable grief. A sonnet, which I could not help writing on this sketch, gave rise to our long correspondence, and to a friendship which never flagged. Everybody feels that his life, as told by Mr. Taylor, with its terrible catastrophe, is a stern lesson to young artists, an awful warning that cannot be set aside. Let us not forget that amongst his many faults are qualities which hold out a bright example. His devotion to his noble art, his conscientious pursuit of every study connected with it, his unwearied industry, his love of beauty and of excellence, his warm family affection, his patriotism, his courage, and his piety, will not easily be surpassed. Thinking of them, let us speak tenderly of the ardent spirit whose violence would have been softened by better fortune, and who, if more successful, would have been more gentle and more humble."

And so with her vigilant and appreciative eye she saw, and thus in her own charming way she talked of, the man whose name, says Taylor, as a popularizer of art, stands without a rival among his brethren.

She loathed mere dandies, and there were no epithets too hot for her contempts in that direction. Old beaux she heartily despised, and, speaking of one whom she had known, I remember she quoted with a fine scorn this appropriate passage from Dickens: "Ancient, dandified men, those crippled *invalides* from the campaign of vanity, where the only powder was hair-powder, and the only bullets fancy balls."

There was no half-way with her, and she never could have said with M—— S——, when a certain visitor left the room one day after a call, "If we did not *love* our dear friend Mr. —— so much, should n't we hate him tremendously!" Her neighbor, John Ruskin, she thought as eloquent a prose-writer as Jeremy Taylor, and I have heard her go on in her fine way, giving preferences to certain modern poems far above the works of the great masters of song. Pascal says that "the heart has reasons that reason does not know"; and Miss Mitford was a charming exemplification of this wise saying.

Her dogs and her geraniums were her great glories. She used to write me long letters about Fanchon, a dog whose personal acquaintance I had made some time before, while on a visit to her cottage. Every virtue under heaven she attributed to that canine individual; and I was obliged to allow in my return letters, that, since our planet began to spin, nothing comparable to Fanchon had ever run on four legs. I had also known Flush, the ancestor of Fanchon, intimately, and had been accustomed to hear wonderful things of that dog; but Fanchon had graces and genius unique. Miss Mitford would have joined with Hamerton in his gratitude for canine companionship, when he says, "I humbly thank Divine Providence for having invented dogs, and I regard that man with wondering pity who can lead a dogless life."

Her fondness for rural life, one may well imagine, was almost unparalleled. I have often been with her among the wooded lanes of her pretty country, listening for the nightingales, and on such occasions she would discourse so eloquently of the sights and sounds about us, that her talk seemed to me "far above singing." She had fallen in love with nature when a little child, and had studied the landscape till she knew familiarly every flower and leaf which grows on English soil. She delighted in rural vagabonds of every sort, especially in gypsies; and as they flourished in her part of the country, she knew all their ways, and had charming stories to tell of their pranks and thievings. She called them "the commoners of nature"; and once I remember she pointed out to me on the road a villanous-looking youth on whom she smiled as we passed, as if he had been Virtue itself in footpad disguise. She knew all the literature of rural life, and her memory was stored with delightful eulogies of forests and meadows. When she repeated or read aloud the poetry she loved, her accents were

"Like flowers' voices, if they could but speak."

She *understood* how to enjoy rural occupations and rural

Walter Savage Landor Æt 29.

From a Painting by Dance, RA.

existence, and she had no patience with her friend Charles Lamb, who preferred the town. Walter Savage Landor addressed these lines to her a few months before she died, and they seem to me very perfect and lovely in their application : —

> "The hay is carried ; and the hours
> Snatch, as they pass, the linden flow'rs ;
> And children leap to pluck a spray
> Bent earthward, and then run away.
> Park-keeper! catch me those grave thieves
> About whose frocks the fragrant leaves,
> Sticking and fluttering here and there,
> No false nor faltering witness bear.
>
> "I never view such scenes as these
> In grassy meadow girt with trees,
> But comes a thought of her who now
> Sits with serenely patient brow
> Amid deep sufferings : none hath told
> More pleasant tales to young and old.
> Fondest was she of Father Thames,
> But rambled to Hellenic streams ;
> Nor even there could any tell
> The country's purer charms so well
> As Mary Mitford.
>   Verse ! go forth
> And breathe o'er gentle breasts her worth.
> Needless the task . . . . but should she see
> One hearty wish from you and me,
> A moment's pain it may assuage, —
> A rose-leaf on the couch of Age."

And Harriet Martineau pays her respects to my friend in this wise : "Miss Mitford's descriptions of scenery, brutes, and human beings have such singular merit, that she may be regarded as the founder of a new style ; and if the freshness wore off with time, there was much more than a compensation in the fine spirit of resignation and cheerfulness which breathed through everything she wrote, and endeared her as a suffering friend to thousands who formerly regarded her only as a most entertaining stranger."

What lovely drives about England I have enjoyed with

Miss Mitford as my companion and guide! We used to arrange with her trusty Sam for a day now and then in the open air. He would have everything in readiness at the appointed hour, and be at his post with that careful, kind-hearted little maid, the "hemmer of flounces," all prepared to give the old lady a fair start on her day's expedition. Both those excellent servants delighted to make their mistress happy, and she greatly rejoiced in their devotion and care. Perhaps we had made our plans to visit Upton Court, a charming old house where Pope's Arabella Fermor had passed many years of her married life. On the way thither we would talk over "The Rape of the Lock" and the heroine, Belinda, who was no other than Arabella herself. Arriving on the lawn in front of the decaying mansion, we would stop in the shade of a gigantic oak, and gossip about the times of Queen Elizabeth, for it was then the old house was built, no doubt.

Once I remember Miss Mitford carried me on a pilgrimage to a grand old village church with a tower half covered with ivy. We came to it through laurel hedges, and passed on the way a magnificent cedar of Lebanon. It was a superb pile, rich in painted glass windows and carved oak ornaments. Here Miss Mitford ordered the man to stop, and, turning to me with great enthusiasm, said, "This is Shiplake Church, where Alfred Tennyson was married!" Then we rode on a little farther, and she called my attention to some of the finest wych-elms I had ever seen.

Another day we drove along the valley of the Loddon, and she pointed out the Duke of Wellington's seat of Strathfieldsaye. As our pony trotted leisurely over the charming road, she told many amusing stories of the Duke's economical habits, and she rated him soundly for his money-saving propensities. The furniture in the house she said was a disgrace to the great man, and she described a certain old carpet that had done service so many years in the establishment that no one could tell what the original colors were.

But the mansion most dear to her in that neighborhood was the residence of her kind friends the Russells of Swallowfield Park. It is indeed a beautiful old place, full of historical and literary associations, for there Lord Clarendon wrote his story of the Great Rebellion. Miss Mitford never ceased to be thankful that her declining years were passing in the society of such neighbors as the Russells. If she were unusually ill, they were the first to know of it and come at once to her aid. Little attentions, so grateful to old age, they were always on the alert to offer; and she frequently told me that their affectionate kindness had helped her over the dark places of life more than once, where without their succor she must have dropped by the way.

As a letter-writer, Miss Mitford has rarely been surpassed. Her "Life, as told by herself in Letters to her Friends," is admirably done in every particular. Few letters in the English language are superior to hers, and I think they will come to be regarded as among the choicest specimens of epistolary literature. When her friend, the Rev. William Harness, was about to collect from Miss Mitford's correspondents, for publication, the letters she had written to them, he applied to me among others. I was obliged to withhold the correspondence for a reason that existed then; but I am no longer restrained from printing it now. Miss Mitford's first letter to me was written in 1847, and her last one came only a few weeks before she died, in 1855. I am inclined to think that her correspondence, so full of point in allusions, so full of anecdote and recollections, will be considered among her finest writings. Her criticisms, not always the wisest, were always piquant and readable. She had such a charming humor, and her style was so delightful, that her friendly notes had a relish about them quite their own. In reading some of them here collected one will see that she overrated my little services as she did those of many of her personal friends. I shall have hard work to place the dates properly, for the good lady rarely took the trouble to put either month or year at the head of her paper.

She began her correspondence with me before I left England after making her acquaintance, and, true to the instincts of her kind heart, the object of her first letter was to press upon my notice the poems of a young friend of hers, and she was constantly saying good words for unfledged authors who were struggling forward to gain recognition. No one ever lent such a helping hand as she did to the young writers of her country.

The recognition which America, very early in the career of Miss Mitford, awarded her, she never forgot, and she used to say, "It takes ten years to make a literary reputation in England, but America is wiser and bolder, and dares say at once, 'This is fine.'"

Sweetness of temper and brightness of mind, her never-failing characteristics, accompanied her to the last; and she passed on in her usual cheerful and affectionate mood, her sympathies uncontracted by age, narrow fortune, and pain.

A plain substantial cross marks the spot in the old churchyard at Swallowfield, where, according to her own wish, Mary Mitford lies sleeping. It is proposed to erect a memorial in the old parish church to her memory, and her admirers in England have determined, if a sufficient sum can be raised, to build what shall be known as "The Mitford Aisle," to afford accommodation for the poor people who are not able to pay for seats. Several of Miss Mitford's American friends will join in this beautiful object, and a tablet will be put up in the old church commemorating the fact that England and America united in the tribute.

LETTERS, 1848-1849.

Three-Mile Cross, December 4, 1848.

Dear Mr. Fields: My silence has been caused by severe illness. For more than a twelvemonth my health has been so impaired as to leave me a very poor creature, almost incapable of any exertion at all times, and frequently suffering severe pain besides. So that I have to entreat the friends who are good enough to care for me never to be displeased if a long time elapses between my letters. My correspondents being so numerous, and I myself so utterly alone, without any one even to fold or seal a letter, that the very physical part of the task sometimes becomes more fatiguing than I can bear. I am not, generally speaking, confined to my room, or even to the house; but the loss of power is so great that after the short drive or shorter walk which my very skilful medical adviser orders, I am too often compelled to retire immediately to bed, and I have not once been well enough to go out of an evening during the year 1848. Before its expiration I shall have completed my sixty-first year; but it is not age that has so prostrated me, but the hard work and increasing anxiety of thirty years of authorship, during which my poor labors were all that my dear father and mother had to look to, besides which for the greater part of that time I was constantly called upon to attend to the sick-bed, first of one aged parent and then of another. Few women could stand this, and I have only to be intensely thankful that the power of exertion did not fail until the necessity of such exertion was removed. Now my poor life is (beyond mere friendly feeling) of value to no one. I have, too, many alleviations, — in the general kindness of the neighborhood, the particular goodness of many admirable friends, the affectionate attention of a most attached and intelligent old servant, and above all in my continued interest in books and delight in reading. I love poetry and people as well at sixty as I did at sixteen, and can never be sufficiently grateful to God for having permitted me to retain the two joy-giving faculties of admiration and sympathy, by which we are enabled to escape from the consciousness of our own infirmities into the great works of all ages and the joys and sorrows of our immediate friends. Among the books which I have been reading with the greatest interest is the Life of Dr. Channing, and I can hardly tell you the glow of gratification with which I found my own name mentioned, as one of the writers in whose works that great man had taken pleasure. The approbation of Dr. Channing is something worth toiling for. I know no individual suffrage that could have given me more delight. Besides this selfish pleasure and the intense interest with which I followed that admirable thinker through the whole course of his pure and blameless life, I have derived another and a different satisfaction from that work, — I mean from its reception in England. I know nothing that shows a greater improvement in liberality in the least liberal part of the English public, a greater sweeping away of prejudice whether national or sectarian, than the manner in which even the High Church and Tory party have spoken of Dr. Channing. They really seem to cast aside their usual intolerance in his case, and to look upon a Unitarian with feelings of Christian fellowship. God grant that this spirit may continue! Is American literature rich in native biography? Just have the goodness to mention to me any lives of Americans, whether illustrious or not, that are graphic, minute, and outspoken. I delight in French memoirs and English lives, especially such as are either autobiography or made out by diaries and letters; and America, a young country with manners as picturesque and unhackneyed as the scenery, ought to be full of such works. We have had two volumes lately that will interest your countrymen: Mr. Milnes's Life of John Keats, that wonderful youth whose early death was, I think, the greatest loss that English poetry ever experienced. Some of the letters are very striking as developments of character, and the richness of diction in the poetical fragments is exquisite. Mrs. Browning is still at Florence with her husband. She sees more Americans than English.

Books here are sadly depreciated. Mr. Dyce's admirable edition of Beaumont and Fletcher, brought out two years ago at £6 12 s. is now offered at £2 17 s.

Adieu, dear Mr. Fields; forgive my seeming neglect, and believe me always most faithfully yours,

M. R. MITFORD.

(No date, 1849.)

DEAR MR. FIELDS: I cannot tell you how vexed I am at this mistake about letters, which must have made you think me careless of your correspondence and ungrateful for your kindness. The same thing has happened to me before, I may say often, with American letters, — with Professor Norton, Mrs. Sigourney, the Sedgwicks, — in short, I always feel an insecurity in writing to America which I never experience in corresponding with friends on the Continent; France, Germany, Italy, even Poland and Russia, are comparatively certain. Whether it be the agents in London who lose letters, or some fault in the post-office, I cannot tell, but I have twenty times experienced the vexation, and it casts a certain discouragement over one's communications. However, I hope that this letter will reach you, and that you will be assured that the fault does not lie at my door.

During the last year or two my health has been declining much, and I am just now thinking of taking a journey to Paris. My friend, Henry Chorley of the Athenæum, the first musical critic of Europe, is going thither next month to assist at the production of Meyerbeer's Prophète at the French Opera, and another friend will accompany me and my little maid to take care of us; so that I have just hopes that the excursion, erenow much facilitated by railways, may do me good. I have always been a great admirer of the great Emperor, and to see the heir of Napoleon at the Elysée seems to me a real piece of poetical justice. I know many of his friends in England, who all speak of him most highly; one of them says, "He is the very impersonation of calm and simple honesty." I hope the nation will be true to him, but, as Mirabeau says, "there are no such words as 'jamais' or 'toujours' with the French public."

10th of June, 1849.

I have been waiting to answer your most kind and interesting letter, dear Mr. Fields, until I could announce to you a publication that Mr. Colburn has been meditating and pressing me for, but which, chiefly I believe from my own fault in not going to town, and not liking to give him or Mr. Shoberl the trouble of coming here, is now probably adjourned to the autumn. The fact is that I have been and still am very poorly. We are stricken in our vanities, and the only things that I recollect having ever been immoderately proud of — my garden and my personal activity — have both now turned into causes of shame and pity; the garden, declining from one bad gardener to worse, has become a ploughed field, — and I myself, from a severe attack of rheumatism, and since then a terrible fright in a pony-chaise, am now little better than a cripple. However, if there be punishment here below, there are likewise consolations, — everybody is kind to me; I retain the vivid love of reading, which is one of the highest pleasures of life; and very interesting persons come to see me sometimes, from both sides of the water, — witness, dear Mr. Fields, our present correspondence. One such person arrived yesterday in the shape of Doctor ———, who has been working musical miracles in Scotland, (think of making singing teachers of children of four or five years of age!) and is now on his way to Paris, where, having been during seven years one of the editors of the National, he will find most of his colleagues of the newspaper filling the highest posts in the government. What is the American opinion of that great experiment; or, rather, what is yours? I wish it success from the bottom of my heart, but I am a little afraid, from their total want of political economy (we have not a school-girl so ignorant of the commonest principles of demand and supply as the whole of the countrymen of Turgot from the executive government downwards), and from a certain warlike tendency which seems to me to pierce through all their declarations of peace. We hear the flourish of trumpets through all the fine phrases of the orators, and indeed it is difficult to imagine what they will do with their *soi-disant ouvriers*, — workmen who have lost the habit of labor, — unless they make soldiers of them. In the mean time some friends of mine are about to accompany your countryman Mr. Elihu Burritt as a deputation, and doubtless M. de Lamartine will give them as eloquent an answer as heart can desire, — no doubt he will keep peace if he can, — but the government have certainly not hitherto shown firmness or vigor enough to make one rely upon them, if the question becomes pressing and personal. In Italy matters seem to be very promising. We have here one of the Silvio Pellico exiles, — Count Carpinetta, — whose story is quite a romance. He is just returned from Turin, where he was received with enthusiasm, might have been returned as Deputy for two places, and did recover some of his property, confiscated years ago by the Austrians. It does one's heart good to see a piece of poetical justice transferred to real life. *Apropos* of public events, all London is talking of the prediction of an old theological writer of the name of Fleming, who in or about the year 1700 prophesied a revolution in France in 1794 (only one year wrong), and the fall of papacy in 1848 at all events.

Ever yours,   M. R. M.

(No date, 1849.)

DEAR MR. FIELDS: I must have seemed very ungrateful in being so long silent. But your magnificent present of books, beautiful in every sense of the word, has come dropping in volume by volume, and only arrived complete (Mr. Longfellow's striking book being the last) about a fortnight ago, and then it found me keeping my room, as I am still doing, with a tremendous attack of neuralgia on the left side of the face. I am getting better now by dint of blisters and tonic medicine; but I can answer for that disease well deserving its bad eminence of "painful." It is however, blessed be God! more manageable than it used to be; and my medical friend, a man of singular skill, promises me a cure.

I have seen things of Longfellow's as fine as anything in Campbell or Coleridge or Tennyson or Hood. After all, our great lyrical poets are great only for half a volume. Look at Gray and Collins, at your own edition of the man whom one song immortalized, at Gerald Griffin, whom you perhaps do not know, and at Wordsworth, who, greatest of the great for about a hundred pages, is drowned in the flood of his own wordiness in his longer works. To be sure, there are giants who are rich to overflowing through a whole shelf of books, — Shakespeare, the mutual ancestor of Englishmen and Americans, above all, — and I think the much that they did, and did well, will be the great hold on posterity of Scott and of Byron. Have you happened to see Bulwer's King Arthur? It astonished me very much. I had a full persuasion that, with great merit in a certain way, he would never be a poet. Indeed, he is beginning poetry just at the age when Scott, Southey, and a host of others, left it off. But he is a strange person, full of the powerful quality called *will*, and has produced a work which, although it is not at all in the fashionable vein and has made little noise, has yet extraordinary merit. When I say that it is more like Ariosto than any other English poem that I know, I certainly give it no mean praise.

Everybody is impatient for Mr. George Ticknor's work. The subject seems to me full of interest. Lord Holland made a charming book of Lope de Vega years ago, and Mr. Ticknor, with equal qualifications and a much wider field, will hardly fail of delighting England and America. Will you remember me to him most gratefully and respectfully? He is a man whom no one can forget. As to Mr. Prescott, I know no author now, except perhaps Mr. Macaulay, whose works command so much attention and give so much delight. I am ashamed to send you so little news, but I live in the country and see few people. The day I caught my terrible Tic I spent with the great capitalist, Mr. Goldsmidt, and Mr. Cobden and his pretty wife. He is a very different person from what one expects, — graceful, tasteful, playful, simple, and refined, and looking absolutely young. I suspect that much of his power springs from his genial character. I heard last week from Mrs. Browning; she and her husband are at the Baths of Lucca. Mr. Kenyon's graceful

book is out, and I must not forget to tell you that "Our Village" has been printed by Mr. Bohn in two volumes, which include the whole five. It is beautifully got up and very cheap, that is to say, for 3 s. 6 d. a volume. Did Mr. Whittier send his works, or do I owe them wholly to your kindness? If he sent them, I will write by the first opportunity. Say everything for me to your young friend, and believe me ever, dear Mr. F—— most faithfully and gratefully yours,
M. R. M.

1850.
(No date.)

I have to thank you very earnestly, dear Mr. Fields, for two very interesting books. The "Leaves from Margaret Smith's Journal" are, I suppose, a sort of Lady Willoughby's Diary, so well executed that they read like one of the imitations of Defoe, — his "Memoirs of a Cavalier," for instance, which always seemed to me quite as true as if they had been actually written seventy years before. Thank you over and over again for these admirable books and for your great kindness and attention. What a perfectly American name Peabody is! And how strange it is that there should be in the United States so many persons of English descent whose names have entirely disappeared from the land of their fathers. Did you get my last unworthy letter? I hope you did. It would at all events show that there was on my part no intentional neglect, that I certainly had written in reply to the last letter that I received, although doubtless a letter had been lost on one side or the other. I live so entirely in the quiet country that I have little to tell you that can be interesting. Two things indeed, not generally known, I may mention: that Stanfield Hall, the scene of the horrible murder of which you have doubtless read, was the actual birthplace of Amy Robsart, — of whose tragic end, by the way, there is at last an authentic account, both in the new edition of Pepys and the first volume of the "Romance of the Peerage"; and that a friend of mine saw the other day in the window of a London bookseller a copy of Hume, ticketed "An Excellent Introduction to Macaulay." The great man was much amused at this practical compliment, as well he might be. I have been reading the autobiographies of Lamartine and Chateaubriand, as well as Raphael, which, although not avowed, is of course and most certainly a continuation of "Les Confiances." What strange beings these Frenchmen are! Here is M. de Lamartine at sixty, poet, orator, historian, and statesman, writing the stories of two ladies — one of them married — who died for love of him!

Think if Mr. Macaulay should announce himself as a lady-killer, and put the details not merely into a book, but into a feuilleton!

The Brownings are living quite quietly at Florence, seeing, I suspect, more Americans than English. Mrs. Trollope has lost her only remaining daughter; arrived in England only time enough to see her die.

Adieu, dear Mr. Fields; say everything for me to Mr. and Mrs. Ticknor, and Mr. and Mrs. Norton. How much I should like to see you!

Ever faithfully yours, M. R. M.

(February, 1850.)

You will have thought me either dead or dying, my dear Mr. Fields, for ungrateful I hope you could not think me to such a friend as yourself, but in truth I have been in too much trouble and anxiety to write. This is the story: I live alone, and my servants become, as they are in France, and ought, I think, always to be, really and truly part of my family. A most sensible young woman, my own maid, who waits upon me and walks out with me, (we have another to do the drudgery of our cottage,) has a little fatherless boy who is the pet of the house. I wonder whether you saw him during the glimpse we had of you! He is a fair-haired child of six years old, singularly quick in intellect, and as bright in mind and heart and temper as a fountain in the sun. He is at school in Reading, and, the small-pox raging there like a pestilence, they sent him home to us to be out of the way. The very next week my man-servant was seized with it, after vaccination of course. Our medical friend advised me to send him away, but that was, in my view of things, out of the question; so we did the best we could, — my own maid, who is a perfect Sister of Charity in all cases of illness, sitting up with him for seven nights following, for one or two were requisite during the delirium, and we could not get a nurse for love or money, and when he became better, then, as we had dreaded, our poor little boy was struck down. However, it has pleased God to spare him, and, after a long struggle, he is safe from the disorder and almost restored to his former health. But we are still under a sort of quarantine, for, although people pretend to believe in vaccination, they avoid the house as if the plague were in it, and stop their carriages at the end of the village and send inquiries and cards, and in my mind they are right. To say nothing of Reading, there have been above thirty severe cases, after vaccination, in our immediate neighborhood, five of them fatal. I had been inoculated after the old style, my maid had had the small-pox the natural way, and the only one who escaped was a young girl who had been vaccinated three times, the last two years ago. Forgive this long story; it was necessary to excuse my most unthankful silence, and may serve as an illustration of the way a disease, supposed to be all but exterminated, is making head again in England.

Thank you a thousand and a thousand times for your most delightful books. Mr. Whipple's Lectures are magnificent, and your own Boston Book could not, I think, be beaten by a London Book, certainly not approached by the collected works of any other British city, — Edinburgh, for example.

Mr. Bennett is most grateful for your kindness, and Mrs. Browning will be no less enchanted at the honor done her husband. It is most creditable to America that they think more of our thoughtful poets than the English do themselves.

Two female friends of mine — Mrs. Acton Tindal, a young beauty as well as a woman of genius, and a Miss Julia Day, whom I have never seen, but whose verses show extraordinary purity of thought, feeling, and expression — have been putting forth books. Julia Day's second series she has done me the honor to inscribe to me, notwithstanding which I venture to say how very much I admire it, and so I think would you. Henry Chorley is going to be a happy man. All his life long he has been dying to have a play acted, and now he has one coming out at the Surrey Theatre, over Blackfriars Bridge. He lives much among fine people, and likes the notion of a Faubourg audience. Perhaps he is right. I am not at all afraid of the play, which is very beautiful, — a blank-verse comedy full of truth and feeling. I don't know if you know Henry Chorley. He is the friend of Robert Browning, and the especial favorite of John Kenyon, and has always been a sort of adopted nephew of mine. Poor Mrs. Hemans loved him well; so did a very different person, Lady Blessington, — so that altogether you may fancy him a very likeable person; but he is much more, — generous, unselfish, loyal, and as true as steel, worth all his writings a thousand times over. If my house be in such condition as to allow of my getting to London to see "Old Love and New Fortune," I shall consult with Mr. Lucas about the time of sitting to him for a portrait, as I have promised to do; for, although there be several extant, not one is passably like. John Lucas is a man of so much taste that he will make a real old woman's picture of it, just with my every-day look and dress.

Will you make my most grateful thanks to Mr. Whipple, and

also to the author of "Greenwood Leaves," which I read with great pleasure, and say all that is kindest and most respectful for me to Mr. and Mrs. George Ticknor. I shall indeed expect great delight from his book.

Ever, dear Mr. Fields, most gratefully yours,

M. R. M.

We have had a Mr. Richmond here, lecturing and so forth. Do you know him? I can fancy what Mr. Webster would be on the Hungarian question. To hear Mr. Cobden talk of it was like the sound of a trumpet.

THREE-MILE CROSS, November 25, 1850.

I have been waiting day after day, dear Mr. Fields, to send you two books, — one new, the other old, — one by my friend, Mr. Bennett; the other a volume [her Dramatic Poems] long out of print in England, and never, I think, known in America. I had great difficulty in procuring the shabby copy which I send you, but I think you will like it because it is mine, and comes to you from friend to friend, and because there is more of myself, that is, of my own inner feelings and fancies, than one ever ventures to put into prose. Mr. Bennett's volume, which is from himself as well as from me, I am sure you will like; most thoroughly would like each other if ever you met. He has the poet's heart and the poet's mind, large, truthful, generous, and full of true refinement, delightful as a companion, and invaluable as a man.

After eight years' absolute cessation of composition, Henry Chorley, of the Athenæum, coaxed me last summer into writing for a Lady's Journal, which he was editing for Messrs. Bradbury and Evans, certain Readings of Poetry, old and new, which will, I suppose, form two or three separate volumes when collected, buried as they now are amongst all the trash and crochet-work and millinery. They will be quite as good as MS., and, indeed, every paper will be enlarged and above as many again added. One pleasure will be the doing what justice I can to certain American poets, — Mr. Whittier, for instance, whose "Massachusetts to Virginia" is amongst the finest things ever written. I gave one copy to a most intelligent Quaker lady, and have another in the house at this moment for Mrs. Walter, widow and mother of the two John Walters, father and son, so well known as proprietors of the Times. I shall cause my book to be immediately forwarded to you, but I don't think it will be ready for a twelvemonth. There is a good deal in it of my own prose, and it takes a wider range than usual of poetry, including much that has never appeared in any of the specimen books. Of course, dear friend, this is strictly between you and me, because it would greatly damage the work to have the few fragments that have appeared as yet brought forward without revision and completion in their present detached and crude form.

This England of ours is all alight and aflame with Protestant indignation against popery; the Church of England being likely to rekindle the fires of 1780, by way of vindicating the right of private judgment. I, who hold perfect freedom of thought and of conscience the most precious of all possessions, have of course my own hatred to these things. Cardinal Wiseman has taken advantage of the attack to put forth one of the most brilliant appeals that has appeared in my time; of course you will see it in America.

Professor Longfellow has won a station in England such as no American poet ever held before, and assuredly he deserves it. Except Beranger and Tennyson, I do not know any living man who has written things so beautiful. I think I like his Nuremburg best of all. Mr. Ticknor's great work, too, has won golden opinions, especially from those whose applause is fame; and I foresee that day by day our literature will become more mingled with rich, bright novelties from America, not reflections of European brightness, but gems all colored with your own skies and woods and waters. Lord Carlisle, the most accomplished of our ministers and the most amiable of our nobles, is giving this very week to the Leeds Mechanics' Institute a lecture on his travels in the United States, and another on the poetry of Pope.

May I ask you to transmit the accompanying letter to Mrs. H——? She has sent to me for titles and dates, and fifty things in which I can give her little help; but what I do know about my works I have sent her. Only, as, except that I believe her to live in Philadelphia, I really am as ignorant of her address as I am of the year which brought forth the first volume of "Our Village," I am compelled to go to you for help in forwarding my reply.

Ever, my dear Mr. Fields, most gratefully and faithfully yours,
M. R. MITFORD.

Is not Louis Napoleon the most graceful of our European chiefs? I have always had a weakness for the Emperor, and am delighted to find the heir of his name turning out so well.

1851.

February 10, 1851.

I cannot tell you, my dear Mr. Fields, how much I thank you for your most kind letter and parcel, which, after sending three or four emissaries all over London to seek, (Mr. —— having ignored the matter to my first messenger,) was at last sent to me by the Great Western Railway, — I suspect by the aforesaid Mr. ——, because, although the name of the London bookseller was dashed out, a *long-tailed* letter was left just where the " p " would come in ——, and as neither Bohn's nor Whittaker's name boasts such a grace, I suspect that, in spite of his assurance, the packet was in the Strand, and neither in Ave Maria Lane nor in Henrietta Street, to both houses I sent. Thank you a thousand times for all your kindness. The orations are very striking. But I was delighted with Dr. Holmes's poems for their individuality. How charming a person he must be! And how truly the portrait represents the mind, the lofty brow full of thought, and the wrinkle of humor in the eye! (Between ourselves, I always have a little doubt of genius where there is no humor; certainly in the very highest poetry the two go together, — Scott, Shakespeare, Fletcher, Burns.) Another charming thing in Dr. Holmes is, that every succeeding poem is better than the last. Is he a widower, or a bachelor, or a married man? At all events, he is a true poet, and I like him all the better for being a physician, — the one truly noble profession. There are noble men in all professions, but in medicine only are the great mass, almost the whole, generous, liberal, self-denying, living to advance science and to help mankind. If I had been a man I should certainly have followed that profession. I rejoice to hear of another Romance by the author of "The Scarlet Letter." That is a real work of genius. Have you seen "Alton Locke"? No novel has made so much noise for a long time; but it is, like "The Saint's Tragedy," inconclusive. Between ourselves, I suspect that the latter part was written with the fear of the Bishop before his eyes (the author, Mr. Kingsley, is a clergyman of the Church of England), which makes the one volume almost a contradiction of the others. Mrs. Browning is still at Florence, where she sees scarcely any English, a few Italians, and many Americans.

Ever most gratefully yours,

M. R. M.

(No date.)

DEAR MR. FIELDS: I sent you a packet last week, but I have just received your two charming books, and I cannot suffer a post to pass without thanking you for them. Mr. Whittier's volume is quite what might have been expected from the greatest of Quaker writers, the worthy compeer of Longfellow, and will give me other extracts to go with "From Massachusetts to Virginia" and "Cassandra Southwick" in my own book, where one of my pleasures will be trying to do justice to American poetry, and Dr. Holmes's fine "Astræa." We have nothing like that nowadays in England. Nobody writes now in the glorious resonant metre of Dryden, and very few ever did write as Dr. Holmes does. I see there is another volume of his poetry, but the name was new to me. How much I owe to you, my dear Mr. Fields! That great romance, "The Scarlet Letter," and these fine poets, — for true poetry, not at all imitative, is rare in England, common as elegant imitative verse may be, — and that charming edition of Robert Browning. Shall you republish his wife's new edition? I cannot tell you how much I thank you. I read an extract from the Times, containing a report of Lord Carlisle's lecture on America, chiefly because he and Dr. Holmes say the same thing touching the slavish regard to opinion which prevails in America. Lord Carlisle is by many degrees the most accomplished of our nobles. Another accomplished and cultivated nobleman, a friend of my own, we have just lost, — Lord Nugent, — liberal, too, against the views of his family.

You must make my earnest and very sincere congratulations to your friend. In publishing Gray, he shows the refinement of taste to be expected in your companion. I went over all his haunts two years ago, and have commemorated them in the book you will see by and by, — the book that is to be, — and there I have put on record the bride-cake, and the finding by you on my table your own edition of Motherwell. You are not angry, are you? If your father and mother in law ever come again to England, I shall rejoice to see them, and shall be sure to do so, if they will drop me a line. God bless you, dear Mr. Fields.

Ever faithfully and gratefully yours,   M. R. M.

THREE-MILE CROSS, July 20, 1851.

You will have thought me most ungrateful, dear Mr. Fields, in being so long your debtor for a most kind and charming letter; but first I waited for the "House of the Seven Gables," and then when it arrived, only a week ago, I waited to read it a second time. At sixty-four life gets too short to allow us to read every book once and again; but it is not so with Mr. Hawthorne's. The first time one sketches them (to borrow Dr. Holmes's excellent word), and

Robert Browning.

cannot put them down for the vivid interest; the next, one lingers over the beauty with a calmer enjoyment. Very beautiful this book is! I thank you for it again and again. The legendary part is all the better for being vague and dim and shadowy, all pervading, yet never tangible; and the living people have a charm about them which is as lifelike and real as the legendary folks are ghostly and remote. Phœbe, for instance, is a creation which, not to speak it profanely, is almost Shakespearian. I know no modern heroine to compare with her, except it be Eugene Sue's Rigolette, who shines forth amidst the iniquities of "Les Mystères de Paris" like some rich, bright, fresh cottage rose thrown by evil chance upon a dunghill. Tell me, please, about Mr. Hawthorne, as you were so good as to do about that charming person, Dr. Holmes. Is he young? I think he *is*, and I hope so for the sake of books to come. And is he of any profession? Does he depend altogether upon literature, as too many writers do here? At all events, he is one of the glories of your most glorious part of great America. Tell me, too, what is become of Mr. Cooper, that other great novelist? I think I heard from you, or from some other Transatlantic friend, that he was less genial and less beloved than so many other of your notabilities have been. Indeed, one sees that in many of his recent works; but I have been reading many of his earlier books again, with ever-increased admiration, especially I should say "The Pioneers"; and one cannot help hoping that the mind that has given so much pleasure to so many readers will adjust itself so as to admit of its own happiness, — for very clearly the discomfort was his own fault, and he is too clever a person for one not to wish him well.

I think that the most distinguished of our own *young* writers are, the one a dear friend of mine, John Ruskin; the other, one who will shortly be so near a neighbor that we must know each other. It is quite wonderful that we don't now, for we are only twelve miles apart, and have scores of friends in common. This last is the Rev. Charles Kingsley, author of "Alton Locke" and "Yeast" and "The Saint's Tragedy." All these books are full of world-wide truths, and yet, taken as a whole, they are unsatisfactory and inconclusive, knocking down without building up. Perhaps that is the fault of the social system that he lays bare, perhaps of the organization of the man, perhaps a little of both. You will have heard probably that he, with other benevolent persons, established a sort of socialist community (Christian socialism) for journeymen tailors, he himself being their chaplain. The evil was very great, for of twenty-one thousand of that class in London, fifteen thousand were ill-paid and only half-employed. For a while, that is, as long as the subscription lasted, all went well; but I fear this week that the money has come to an end, and so very likely will the experiment. Have you republished "Alton Locke" in America? It has one character, an old Scotchman, equal to anything in Scott. The writer is still quite a young man, but out of health. I have heard (but this is between ourselves) that ——'s brain is suffering, — the terrible malady by which so many of our great mental laborers (Scott and Southey, above all) have fallen. Dr. Buckland is now dying of it. I am afraid —— may be so lost to the world and his friends, not merely because his health is going, but because certain peculiarities have come to my knowledge which look like it. A brother clergyman saw him the other day, upon a common near his own house, spouting, singing, and reciting verse at the top of his voice at one o'clock in the morning. Upon inquiring what was the matter, the poet said that he never went to bed till two or three o'clock, and frequently went out in that way to exercise his lungs. My informant, an orderly person of a very different stamp, set him down for mad at once; but he is much beloved among his parishioners, and if the escapade above mentioned do not indicate disease of the brain, I can only say it would be good for the country if we had more madmen of the same sort. As to John Ruskin, I would not answer for quiet people not taking him for crazy too. He is an enthusiast in art, often right, often wrong, — "in the right very stark, in the wrong very sturdy," — bigoted, perverse, provoking, as ever man was; but good and kind and charming beyond the common lot of mortals. There are some pages of his prose that seem to me more eloquent than anything out of Jeremy Taylor, and I should think a selection of his works would answer to reprint. Their sale here is something wonderful, considering their dearness, in this age of cheap literature, and the want of attraction in the subject, although the illustrations of the "Stones of Venice," executed by himself from his own drawings, are almost as exquisite as the writings. By the way, he does not say what I heard the other day from another friend, just returned from the city of the sea, that Taglioni has purchased four of the finest palaces, and is restoring them with great taste, by way of investment, intending to let them to Russian and English noblemen. She was a very graceful dancer once, was Taglioni; but still it rather depoetizes the place, which of all others was richest in associations.

Mrs. Browning has got as near to England as Paris, and holds out enough of hope of coming to London to keep me from visiting it until I know her decision. I have not seen the great Exhibition, and, unless she arrives, most probably shall not see it. My lameness, which has now lasted five months, is the reason I give to myself for not going, chairs being only admitted for an hour or two on Saturday mornings. But I suspect that my curiosity has hardly reached the fever-heat needful to encounter the crowd and the fatigue. It is amusing to find how people are cooling down about it. We always were a nation of idolaters, and always had the trick of avenging ourselves upon our poor idols for the sin of our own idolatry. Many an overrated, and then underrated, poet can bear witness to this. I remember when my friend Mr. Milnes was called *the* poet, although Scott and Byron were in their glory, and Wordsworth had written all of his works that will live. We make gods of wood and stone, and then we knock them to pieces; and so figuratively, if not literally, shall we do by the Exhibition. Next month I am going to move to a cottage at Swallowfield, — so called, I suppose, because those migratory birds meet by millions every autumn in the park there, now belonging to some friends of mine, and still famous as the place where Lord Clarendon wrote his history. That place is still almost a palace; mine an humble but very prettily placed cottage. O, how proud and glad I should be, if ever I could receive Mr. and Mrs. Fields within its walls for more than a poor hour! I shall have tired you with this long letter, but you have made me reckon you among my friends, — ay, one of the best and kindest, — and must take the consequence.

Ever yours,   M. R. M.

SWALLOWFIELD, Saturday Night.

I write you two notes at once, my dear friend, whilst the recollection of your conversation is still in my head and the feeling of your kindness warm on my heart. To write, to thank you for a visit which has given me so much pleasure, is an impulse not to be resisted. Pray tell Mr. and Mrs. Bennoch how delighted I am to make their acquaintance and how earnestly I hope we may meet often. They are charming people.

Another motive that I had for writing at once is to tell you that the more I think of the title of the forthcoming book, the less I like it; and I care more for it, now that you are concerned in the matter, than I did before. "Personal Reminiscences" sounds like a bad title for an autobiography. Now this is nothing of the sort. It is literally a book made up of favorite scraps of poetry and prose; the bits of my own writing are partly critical, and partly have been interwoven to please Henry Chorley and give something of novelty, and as it were individuality, to a mere selection, to take off the dryness and triteness of extracts, and give the pen something to say in the work as well as the scissors. Still, it is a book founded on other books, and since it pleased Mr. Bentley to object to "Readings of Poetry," because he said nobody in England bought poetry, why "Recollections of Books," as suggested by Mr. Bennett, approved by me, and as I believed (till this very day) adopted by Mr. Bentley, seemed to meet exactly the truth of the case, and to be quite concession enough to the exigencies of the trade. By the other title we exposed ourselves, in my mind, to all manner of danger. I shall write this by this same post to Mr. Bennett, and get the announcement changed, if possible; for it seems to me a trick of the worst sort. I shall write a list of the subjects, and I only wish that I had duplicates, and I would send you the articles, for I am most uncomfortable at the notion of your being taken in to purchase a book that may, through this misnomer, lose its reputation in England; for of course it will be attacked as an unworthy attempt to make it pass for what it is not. . . . .

Now if you dislike it, or if Mr. Bentley keep that odious title, why, give it up at once. Don't pray, pray lose money by me. It would grieve me far more than it would you. A good many of these are about books quite forgotten, as the "Pleader's Guide" (an exquisite pleasantry), "Holcroft's Memoirs," and "Richardson's Correspondence." Much on Darley and the Irish Poets, unknown in England; and I think myself that the book will contain, as in the last article, much exquisite poetry and curious prose, as in the forgotten murder (of Toole, the author's uncle) in the State Trials. But it should be called by its right name, as everything should in this world. God bless you!

Ever faithfully yours,
M. R. M.

P. S. First will come the Preface, then the story of the book (without Henry Chorley's name; it is to be dedicated to him), noticing the coincidence of "Our Village" having first appeared in the Lady's Magazine, and saying something like what I wrote to you last night. I think this will take off the danger of provoking apprehension on one side and disappointment on the other; because after all, although anecdote be not the style of the book, it does contain some.

May I put in the story of Washington's ghost? without your

name, of course; it would be very interesting, and I am ten times more desirous of making the book as good as I can, since I have reason to believe you will be interested in it. Pray, forgive me for having worried you last night and now again. I am a terribly nervous person, and hate and dread literary scrapes, or indeed disputes of any sort. But I ought not to have worried you. Just tell me if you think this sort of preface will take the sting from the title, for I dare say Mr. Bentley won't change it.

Adieu, dear friend. All peace and comfort to you in your journey; amusement you are sure of. I write also to dear Mr. Bennett, whom I fear I have also worried.

Ever most faithfully yours,

M. R. M.

1852.

January 5.

Mr. Bennoch has just had the very great kindness, dear Mr. Fields, to let me know of your safe arrival at Genoa, and of your enjoyment of your journey. Thank God for it! We heard so much about commotions in the South of France that I had become fidgety about you, the rather that it is the best who go, and that I for one cannot afford to lose you.

Now let me thank you for all your munificence, — that beautiful Longfellow with the hundred illustrations, and that other book of Professor Longfellow's, beautiful in another way, the "Golden Legend." I hope I shall be only one among the multitude who think this the greatest and best thing he has done yet, so racy, so full of character, of what the French call local color, so, in its best and highest sense, original. Moreover, I like the happy ending. Then those charming volumes of De Quincey and Sprague and Grace Greenwood. (Is that her real name?) And dear Mr. Hawthorne, and the two new poets, who, if also young poets, will be fresh glories for America. How can I thank you enough for all these enjoyments? And you must come back to England, and add to my obligations by giving me as much as you can of your company in the merry month of May. I have fallen in with Mr. Kingsley, and a most charming person he is, certainly the least like an Englishman of letters, and the most like an accomplished, high-toned English gentleman, that I have ever met with. You must know Mr. Kingsley. He is very young too, really young, for it is characteristic of our "young poets" that they generally turn out middle-aged and very often elderly. My book is out at last, hurried through the press in a fortnight, — a process which half killed me, and has left the volumes, no doubt, full of errata, — and you, I mean your house, have not got it. I am keeping a copy for you personally. People say that they like it. I think you will, because it will remind you of this pretty country, and of an old Englishwoman who loves you well. Mrs. Browning was delighted with your visit. She is a Bonapartiste; so am I. I always adored the Emperor, and I think his nephew is a great man, full of ability, energy, and courage, who put an end to an untenable situation and got quit of a set of unrepresenting representatives. The Times newspaper, right as it seems to me about Kossuth, is dangerously wrong about Louis Napoleon, since it is trying to stimulate the nation to a war for which France is more than prepared, is ready, and England is not. London might be taken with far less trouble and fewer men than it took to accomplish the *coup d'état*. Ah! I suspect very different politics will enclose this wee bit notie, if dear Mr. Bennoch contrives to fold it up in a letter of his own; but to agree to differ is part of the privileges of friendship; besides, I think you and I generally agree.

Ever yours, M. R. M.

P. S. All this time I have not said a word of "The Wonder Book." Thanks again and again. Who was the Mr. Blackstone mentioned in "The Scarlet Letter" as riding like a myth in New England History, and what his arms? A grandson of Judge Blackstone, a friend of mine, wishes to know.

(March, 1852.)

I can never enough thank you, dearest Mr. Fields, for your kind recollection of me in such a place as the Eternal City. But you never forget any whom you make happy in your friendship, for that is the word; and therefore here in Europe or across the Atlantic, you will always remain . . . . Your anecdote of the —— is most characteristic. I am very much afraid that he is only a poet, and although I fear the last person in the world to deny that that is much, I think that to be a really great man needs something more. I am sure that you would not have sympathized with Wordsworth. I do hope that you will see Beranger when in Paris. He is the one man in France (always excepting Louis Napoleon, to whom I confess the interest that all women feel in strength and courage) whom I should earnestly desire to know well. In the first place, I think him by far the greatest of living poets, the one who unites most completely those two rare things, impulse and finish. In the next,

I admire his admirable independence and consistency, and his generous feeling for fallen greatness. Ah, what a truth he told, when he said that Napoleon was the greatest poet of modern days! I should like to have the description of Beranger from your lips. Mrs. Browning . . . . has made acquaintance with Madame Sand, of whom her account is most striking and interesting. But George Sand is George Sand, and Beranger is Beranger.

Thank you, dear friend, for your kind interest in my book. It has found far more favor than I expected, and I think, ever since the week after its publication, I have received a dozen of letters daily about it, from friends and strangers, — mostly strangers, — some of very high accomplishments, who will certainly be friends. This is encouragement to write again, and we will have a talk about it when you come. I should like your advice. One thing is certain, that this work has succeeded, and that the people who like it best are precisely those whom one wishes to like it best, the lovers of literature. Amongst other things, I have received countless volumes of poetry and prose, — one little volume of poetry written under the name of Mary Maynard, of the greatest beauty, with the vividness and picturesqueness of the new school, combined with infinite correctness and clearness, that rarest of all merits nowadays. Her real name I don't know, she has only thought it right to tell me that Mary Maynard was not the true appellation (this is between ourselves). Her own family know nothing of the publication, which seems to have been suggested by her and my friend, John Ruskin. Of course, she must have her probation, but I know of no young writer so likely to rival your new American school. I sent your gift-books of Hawthorne, yesterday, to the Walters of Bearwood, who had never heard of them! Tell him that I have had the honor of poking him into the den of the Times, the only civilized place in England where they were barbarous enough not to be acquainted with "The Scarlet Letter." I wonder what they 'll think of it. It will make them stare. They come to see me, for it is full two months since I have been in the pony-chaise. I was low, if you remember, when you were here, but thought myself getting better, *was* getting better. About Christmas, very damp weather came on, or rather very wet weather, and the damp seized my knee and ankles and brought back such an attack of rheumatism that I cannot stand upright, walk quite double, and am often obliged to be lifted from step to step up stairs. My medical adviser (a very clever man) says that I shall get much better when warm weather comes, but for weeks and weeks we have had east-winds and frost. No violets, no primroses, no token of spring. A little flock of ewes and lambs, with a pretty boy commonly holding a lamb in his arms, who drives his flock to water at the pond opposite my window, is the only thing that gives token of the season. I am quite mortified at this on your account, for April, in general a month of great beauty here, will be as desolate as winter. Nevertheless you must come and see me, you and Mr. and Mrs. Bennoch, and perhaps *you* can continue to stay a day or two, or to come more than once. I want to see as much of you as I can, and I must change much, if I be in any condition to go to London, even upon the only condition on which I ever do go, that is, into lodgings, for I never stay anywhere; and if I were to go, even to one dear and warm-hearted friend, I should affront the very many other friends whose invitations I have refused for so many years. I hope to get at Mr. Kingsley; but I have seen little of him this winter. We are five miles asunder; his wife has been ill; and my fear of an open carriage, or rather the medical injunction not to enter one, has been a most insuperable objection. We are, as we both said, summer neighbors. However, I will try that you should see him. He is well worth knowing. Thank you about Mr. Blackstone. He is worth knowing too, in a different way, a very learned and very clever man (you will find half Dr. Arnold's letters addressed to him), as full of crotchets as an egg is full of meat, fond of disputing and contradicting, a clergyman living in the house where Mrs. Trollope *was raised*, and very kind after his own fashion. One thing that I should especially like would be that you should see your first nightingale amongst our woody lanes. To be sure, these winds can never last till then. Mr. —— is coming here on Sunday. He always brings rain or snow, and that will change the weather. You are a person who ought to bring sunshine, and I suppose you do more than metaphorically; for I remember that both times I have had the happiness to see you — a summer day and a winter day — were glorious. Heaven bless you, dear friend! May all the pleasure . . . . return upon your own head! Even my little world is charmed at the prospect of seeing you again. If you come to Reading by the Great Western you could return later and make a longer day, and yet be no longer from home.

Ever faithfully yours,   M. R. M.

SWALLOWFIELD, April 27, 1852.

How can I thank you half enough, dearest Mr. Fields, for all your goodness! To write to me the very day after reaching Paris, to think of me so kindly! It is what I never can repay. I write now not to trouble you for another letter, but to remind you that, as soon as possible after your return to England, I hope to see you and Mr. and Mrs. Bennoch here. Heaven grant the spring may come to meet you! At present I am writing in an east-wind, which has continued two months and gives no sign of cessation. Professor Airy says it will continue five weeks longer. Not a drop of rain has fallen in all that time. We have frosts every night, the hedges are as bare as at Christmas, flowers forget to blow, or if they put forth miserable, infrequent, reluctant blossoms, have no heart, and I have only once heard the nightingale in this place where they abound, and not yet seen a swallow in the spot which takes name from their gatherings. It follows, of course, that the rheumatism, covered by a glut of wet weather, just upon the coming in of the new year, is fifty times increased by the bitter season, — a season which has no parallel in my recollection. I can hardly sit down when standing, or rise from my chair without assistance, walk quite double, and am lifted up stairs step by step by my man-servant. I thought, two years ago, I could walk fifteen or sixteen miles a day! O, I was too proud of my activity! I am sure we are smitten in our vanities. However, you will bring the summer, which is, they say, to do me good; and even if that should fail, it will do me some good to see you, that is quite certain. Thank you for telling me about the Galignani, and about the kind American reception of my book; some one sent me a New York paper (the Tribune, I think), full of kindness, and I do assure you that to be so heartily greeted by my kinsmen across the Atlantic is very precious to me. From the first American has there come nothing but good-will. However, the general kindness here has taken me quite by surprise. The only fault found was with the title, which, as you know, was no doing of mine; and the number of private letters, books, verses, (commendatory verses, as the old poets have it), and tributes of all sorts, and from all manner of persons, that I receive every day is something quite astonishing.

Our great portrait-painter, John Lucas, certainly the first painter of female portraits now alive, has been down here to take a portrait for engraving. He has been most successful. It is looking better, I suppose, than I ever do look; but not better than under certain circumstances — listening to a favorite friend, for example — I perhaps might look. The picture is to go to-morrow into the engraver's hands, and I hope the print will be completed before your departure; also they are engraving, or are about to engrave, a miniature taken of me when I was a little girl between three and four years old. They are to be placed side by side, the young child and the old withered woman, — a skull and cross-bones could hardly be a more significant *memento mori!* I have lost my near neighbor and most accomplished friend, Sir Henry Russell, and many other friends, for Death has been very busy this winter, and Mr. Ware is gone! He had sent me his "Zenobia," "from the author," and for that very reason, I suppose, some one had stolen it; but I had replaced both that and the letters from Rome, and sent them to Mr. Kingsley as models for his "Hypatia." He has them still. He had never heard of them till I named them to him. They seem to me very fine and classical, just like the best translations from some great Latin writer. And I have been most struck with Edgar Poe, who has been republished, prose and poetry, in a shilling volume called "Readable Books." What a deplorable history it was! — I mean his own, — the most unredeemed vice that I have met with in the annals of genius. But he was a very remarkable writer, and must have a niche if I write again; so must your two poets, Stoddard and Taylor. I am very sorry you missed Mrs. Trollope; she is a most remarkable woman, and you would have liked her, I am sure, for her warm heart and her many accomplishments. I had a sure way to Beranger, one of my dear friends being a dear friend of his; but on inquiring for him last week, that friend also is gone to heaven. Do pick up for me all you can about Louis Napoleon, my one real abiding enthusiasm, — the enthusiasm of my whole life, — for it began with the Emperor and has passed quite undiminished to the present great, bold, and able ruler of France. Mrs. Browning shares it, I think; only she calls herself cool, which I don't; and another still more remarkable co-religionist in the L. N. faith is old Lady Shirley (of Alderley), the writer of that most interesting letter to Gibbon, dated 1792, published by her father, Lord Sheffield, in his edition of the great historian's posthumous works. She is eighty-two now, and as active and vigorous in body and mind, as sixty years ago.

Make my most affectionate love to my friend in the Avenue des Champs Elysées, and believe me ever, my dear Mr. Fields, most gratefully and affectionately yours,   M. R. M.

(No date.)

Ah, my dearest Mr. Fields, how inimitably good and kind you are to me! Your account of Rachel is most delightful, the rather that it confirms a preconceived notion which two of my friends had taken pains to change. Henry Chorley, not only by his own opinion, but by that of Scribe, who told him that there was no comparison between her and Viardot. Now if Viardot, even in that one famous part of Fides, excels Rachel, she must be much the finer actress, having the horrible drawback of the music to get over. My other friend told me a story of her, in the modern play of Virginie; she declared that when in her father's arms she pointed to the butcher's knife, telling him what to do, and completely reversing that loveliest story; but I hold to your version of her genius, even admitting that she did commit the Virginie iniquity, which would be intensely characteristic of her calling, — all actors and actresses having a desire to play the whole play themselves, speaking every speech, producing every effect in their own person. No doubt she is a great actress, and still more assuredly is Louis Napoleon a great man, a man of genius, which includes in my mind both sensibility and charm. There are little bits of his writing from Ham, one where he speaks of "le repos de ma prison," another long and most eloquent passage on exile, which ends (I forget the exact words) with a sentiment full of truth and sensibility. He is speaking of the treatment shown to an exile in a foreign land, of the mistiness and coldness of some, of the blandness and smoothness of others, and he goes on to say, "He must be a man of ten thousand who behaves to an exile just as he would behave to another person." If I could trust you to perform a commission for me, and let me pay you the money you spent upon it, I would ask you to bring me a cheap but comprehensive life of him, with his works and speeches, and a portrait as like him as possible. I asked an English friend to do this for me, and fancy his sending me a book dated on the outside 1847!!!! Did I ever tell you a pretty story of him, when he was in England after Strasburg and before Boulogne, and which I know to be true? He spent a twelvemonth at Leamington, living in the quietest manner. One of the principal persons there is Mr. Hampden, a descendant of John Hampden, and the elder brother of the Bishop. Mr. Hampden, himself a very liberal and accomplished man, made a point of showing every attention in his power to the Prince, and they soon became very intimate. There was in the town an old officer of the Emperor's Polish Legion who, compelled to leave France after Waterloo, had taken refuge in England, and, having the national talent for languages, maintained himself by teaching French, Italian, and German in different families. The old exile and the young one found each other out, and the language master was soon an habitual guest at the Prince's table, and treated by him with the most affectionate attention. At last Louis Napoleon wearied of a country town and repaired to London; but before he went he called on Mr. Hampden to take leave. After warm thanks for all the pleasure he had experienced in his society, he said: "I am about to prove to you my entire reliance upon your unfailing kindness by leaving you a legacy. I want to ask you to transfer to my poor old friend the goodness you have lavished upon me. His health is failing, his means are small. Will you call upon him sometimes? and will you see that those lodging-house people do not neglect him? and will you, above all, do for him what he will not do for himself, draw upon me for what may be wanting for his needs or for his comforts?" Mr. Hampden promised. The prophecy proved true; the poor old man grew worse and worse, and finally died. Mr. Hampden, as he had promised, replaced the Prince in his kind attentions to his old friend, and finally defrayed the charges of his illness and of his funeral. "I would willingly have paid them myself," said he, "but I knew that that would have offended and grieved the Prince, so I honestly divided the expenses with him, and I found that full provision had been made at his banker's to answer my drafts to a much larger amount." Now I have full faith in such a nature. Let me add that he never forgot Mr. Hampden's kindness, sending him his different brochures and the kindest messages, both from Ham and the Elysée. If one did not admire Louis Napoleon, I should like to know upon whom one could, as a public man, fix one's admiration! Just look at our English statesmen! And see the state to which self-government brings everything! Look at London with all its sanitary questions just in the same state as ten years ago; look at all our acts of Parliament, one half of a session passed in amending the mismanagement of the other. For my own part, I really believe that there is nothing like one mind, one wise and good ruler; and I verily believe that the President of France is that man. My only doubt being whether the people are worthy of him, fickle as they are, like all great masses, — the French people, in particular. By the way, if a most vilely translated book, called the "Prisoner of Ham," be extant in French, I should like to possess it. The account of the escape looks true, and is most interesting.

I have been exceedingly struck, since I last wrote to you, by some extracts from Edgar Poe's writings; I mean a book called "The Readable Library," composed of selections from his works, prose and verse. The famous ones are, I find, The Maelstrom and The Raven; without denying their high merits, I prefer that fine poem on The Bells, quite as fine as Schiller's, and those remarkable bits of stories on circumstantial evidence.

I am lower, dear friend, than ever, and what is worse, in supporting myself on my hand I have strained my right side and can hardly turn in bed. But if we cannot walk round Swallowfield, we can drive, and the very sight of you will do me good. If Mr. Bentley send me only one copy of that engraving, it shall be for you. You know I have a copy for you of the book. There are no words to tell the letters and books I receive about it, so I suppose it is popular. I have lost, as you know, my most accomplished and admirable neighbor, Sir Henry Russell, the worthy successor of the great Lord Clarendon. His eldest daughter is my favorite young friend, a most lovely creature, the ideal of a poet. I hope you will see Beranger. Heaven bless you!

Ever yours, M. R. M.

Saturday Night.

Ah, my very dear friend, how can I ever thank you? But I don't want to thank you. There are some persons (very few, though) to whom it is a happiness to be indebted, and you are one of them. The books and the busts are arrived. Poor dear Louis Napoleon with his head off — Heaven avert the omen! Of course *that* head can be replaced, I mean stuck on again upon its proper shoulders. Beranger is a beautiful old man, just what one fancies him and loves to fancy him. I hope you saw him. To my mind, he is the very greatest poet now alive, perhaps the greatest man, the truest and best type of perfect independence. Thanks a thousand and a thousand times for those charming busts and for the books. Mrs. Browning had mentioned to me Mr. Read. If I live to write another book, I shall put him and Mr. Taylor and Mr. Stoddard together, and try to do justice to Poe. I have a good right to love America and the Americans. My Mr. Lucas tells me to go, and says he has a mind to go. I want you to know John Lucas, not only the finest portrait-painter, but about the very finest mind that I know in the world. He might be . . . . for talent and manner and heart; and, if you like, you shall, when I am dead, have the portrait he has just taken of me. I make the reserve, instead of giving it to you now, because it is possible that he might wish (I know he does) to paint one for himself, and if I be dead before sitting to him again, the present one would serve him to copy. Mr. Bentley wanted to purchase it, and many have wanted it, but it shall be for you.

Now, my very dear friend, I am afraid that Mr. —— has said or done something that would make you rather come here alone. His last letter to me, after a month's silence, was *odd*. There was no fixing upon line or word; still it was not like his other letters, and I suppose the air of —— is not genial, and yet dear Mr. Bennoch breathes it often! You must know that I never could have meant for one instant to impose him upon you as a companion. Only in the autumn there had been a talk of his joining your party. He knows Mr. Bennoch. . . . . He has been very kind and attentive to me, and is, I verily believe, an excellent and true-hearted person; and so I was willing that, if all fell out well, he should have the pleasure of your society here, — the rather that I am sometimes so poorly, and always so helpless now, that one who knows the place might be of use. But to think that for one moment I would make your time or your wishes bend to his is out of the question. Come at your own time, as soon and as often as you can. I should say this to any one going away three thousand miles off, much more to you, and forgive my having even hinted at his coming too. I only did it thinking it might fix you and suit you. In this view I wrote to him yesterday, to tell him that on Wednesday next there would be a cricket-match at Bramshill, one of the finest old mansions in England, a Tudor Manor House, altered by Inigo Jones, and formerly the residence of Prince Henry, the elder son of James the First. In the grand old park belonging to that grand old place, there will be on that afternoon a cricket-match. I thought you would like to see our national game in a scene so perfectly well adapted to show it to advantage. Being in Mr. Kingsley's parish, and he very intimate with the owner, it is most likely, too, that he will be there; so that altogether it seemed to me something that you and dear Mr. and Mrs. Bennoch might like to see. My poor little pony could take you from hence, but not to fetch or carry you, and if the dear Bennochs come, it would be advisable to let the flymen know the place of destination, because, Sir William Cope being a new-comer, I am not sure whether he (like his predecessor, whom I knew) allows horses and carriages to be put up there. I should like you to look on for half an hour at a cricket-match in Bramshill Park, and to be with you at a scene so English and so beautiful. We could dine here afterwards, the Great Western allowing till a quarter before nine in the evening. Contrive this if you can, and let me know by return of post, and forgive my *mal addresse* about Mr. ——. There certainly has something come across him, — not about you, but about me; one thing is, I think, his extreme politics. I always find these violent Radicals very unwilling to allow in others the unlimited freedom of thought that they claim for themselves. He can't forgive my love for the President. Now I must tell you a story I know to be true. A lady of rank was placed next the Prince a year or two ago. He was very gentle and courteous, but very silent, and she wanted to make him talk. At last she remembered that, having been in Switzerland twenty years before, she had received some kindness from the Queen Hortense, and had spent a day at Arenenburg. She told him so, speaking with warm admiration of the Queen. "Ah, madame, vous avez connu ma mère!" exclaimed Louis Napoleon, turning to her eagerly and talking of the place and the people as a school-boy talks of home. She spent some months in Paris, receiving from the Prince every attention which his position enabled him to show; and when she thanked him for such kindness, his answer was always: "Ah, madame, vous avez connu ma mère!" Is it in woman's heart not to love such a man? And then look at the purchase of the Murillo the other day, and the thousand really great things that he is doing. Mr. —— is a goose.

I send this letter to the post to-morrow, when I send other letters, — a vile, puritanical post-office arrangement not permitting us to send letters in the afternoon, unless we send straight to Reading (six miles) on purpose, — so perhaps this may cross an answer from Mr. —— or from you about Bramshill; perhaps, on the other hand, I may have to write again. At all events, you will understand that *this* is written on Saturday night. God bless you, my very dear and kind friend.

Ever faithfully yours,   M. R. M.

May 24, 1852.

Ah, dearest Mr. Fields, how much too good and kind you are to me always! .... I wish I were better, that I might go to town and see more of you; but I am more lame than ever, and having, in my weight and my shortness and my extreme helplessness, caught at tables and chairs and dragged myself along that fashion, I have now so strained the upper part of the body that I cannot turn in bed, and am full of muscular pains which are worse than the rheumatism and more disabling, so that I seem to cumber the earth. They say that summer, when it comes, will do me good. How much more sure that the sight of you will do me good, and I trust that, when your business will let you, you will give me that happiness. In the mean while will you take the trouble to send the enclosed and my answer, if it be fit and proper and properly addressed? I give you this office, because really the kindness seems so large and unlimited, that, if the letter had not come enclosed in one from

Mr. Kenyon, one could hardly have believed it to be serious, and yet I am well used to kindness, too. I thank over and over again your glorious poets for their kindness, and tell Mr. Hawthorne I shall prize a letter from him beyond all the worlds one has to give. I rejoice to hear of the new work, and can answer for its excellence.

I trust that the English edition of Dr. Holmes will contain the "Astræa," and the "Morning Visit," and the "Cambridge Address." I am not sure, in my secret soul, that I do not prefer him to any American poet. Besides his inimitable word-painting, the charity is so large and the scale so fine. How kind in you to like my book, — some people do like it. I am afraid to tell you what John Ruskin says of it from Venice, and I get letters, from ten to twenty a day. You know how little I dreamt of this! Mrs. Trollope has sent me a most affectionate letter, bemoaning her ill-fortune in missing you. I thank you for the Galignani edition, and the presidential kindness, and all your goodness of every sort. I have nothing to give you but as large a share of my poor affection as I think any human being has. You know a copy of the book from me has been waiting for you these three months. Adieu, my dear friend.

Ever yours,

M. R. M.

(July 6, 1852.) Monday Night, or, rather, 2 o'clock Tuesday Morning.

Having just finished Mr. Hawthorne's book, dear Mr. Fields, I shall get K —— to put it up and direct it so that it may be ready the first time Sam has occasion to go to Reading, at which time this letter will be put in the post; so that when you read this, you may be assured that the precious volumes are arrived at the Paddington Station, whence I hope they may be immediately transmitted to you. If not, send for them. They will have your full direction, carriage paid. I say this, because the much vaunted Great Western is like all other railways, most uncertain and irregular, and we have lost a packet of plants this very week, sent to us, announced by letter and never arrived. Thank you heartily for the perusal of the book. I shall not name it in a letter which I mean to enclose to Mr. Hawthorne, not knowing that you mean to tell him, and having plenty of other things to say to him besides. To you, and only to you, I shall speak quite frankly what I think. It is full of beauty and of power, but I agree with —— that it would not have made a reputation as the other two books did, and I have some doubts whether it will not be a disappointment, but one that will soon be redeemed by a fresh and happier effort. It seems to me too long, too slow, and the personages are to my mind ill chosen. Zenobia puts one in mind of Fanny Wright and Margaret Fuller and other unsexed authorities, and Hollingsworth will, I fear, recall, to English people at least, a most horrible man who went about preaching peace. I heard him lecture once, and shall never forget his presumption, his ignorance, or his vulgarity. He is said to know many languages. I can answer for his not knowing his own, for I never, even upon the platform, the native home of bad English, heard so much in so short a time. The mesmeric lecturer and the sickly girl are almost equally disagreeable. In short, the only likeable person in the book is honest Silas Foster, who alone gives one the notion of a man of flesh and blood. In my mind, dear Mr. Hawthorne mistakes exceedingly when he thinks that fiction should be based upon, or rather seen through, some ideal medium. The greatest fictions of the world are the truest. Look at the "Vicar of Wakefield," look at the "Simple Story," look at Scott, look at Jane Austen, greater because truer than all, look at the best works of your own Cooper. It is precisely the want of reality in his smaller stories which has delayed Mr. Hawthorne's fame so long, and will prevent its extension if he do not resolutely throw himself into truth, which is as great a thing in my mind in art as in morals, the foundation of all excellence in both. The fine parts of this book, at least the finest, are the truest, — that magnificent search for the body, which is as perfect as the search for the exciseman in Guy Mannering, and the burst of passion in Eliot's pulpit. The plot, too, is very finely constructed, and doubtless I have been a too critical reader, because, from the moment you and I parted, I have been suffering from fever, and have never left the bed, in which I am now writing. Don't fancy, dear friend, that you had anything to do with this. The complaint had fixed itself and would have run its course, even although your . . . . society has not roused and excited the good spirits, which will, I think, fail only with my life. I think I am going to get better. Love to all.

Ever most affectionately yours, M. R. M.

Tuesday. (No date.)

MY DEAR FRIEND: Being fit for nothing but lying in bed and reading novels, I have just finished Mr. Field's and Mr. Jones's "Adrien," and as you certainly will not have time to look at it, and may like to hear my opinion, I will tell it to you. Mr. Field, from the Preface, is of New York. The thing that has diverted me most is the love-plot of the book. A young gentleman, whose father came and settled in America and made a competence there, is third or fourth cousin to an English lord. He falls in love with a fisherman's daughter (the story appears to be about fifty years back). This fisherman's daughter is a most ethereal personage, speaking and reading Italian, and possessing in the fishing-cottage a pianoforte and a collection of books; nevertheless, she one day hears her husband say something about a person being "well born and well bred," and forthwith goes away from him, in order to set him free from the misery entailed upon him, as she supposes, by a disproportionate marriage. Is not this curious in your republic? We in England certainly should not play such pranks. A man having married a wife, his wife stays by him. This dilemma is got over by the fisherman's turning out to be himself fifth or sixth cousin of another English lord. But, having lived really as a fisherman ever since his daughter's birth, he knew nothing of his aristocratic descent. I think this is the most remarkable thing in the book. There are certain flings at the New England character (the scene is laid beside the waters of your Bay) which seem to foretell a not very remote migration on the part of Mr. Jones, though they may come from his partner; nothing very bad, only such hits as this: "He was simple, humble, affectionate, three qualities rare anywhere, but perhaps more rare in that part of the world than anywhere else." For the rest the book is far inferior to the best even of Mr. James's recent productions, such as "Henry Smeaton." These two authors speak of the corpse of a drowned man as beautified by death, and retaining all the look of life. You remember what Mr. Hawthorne says of the appearance of his drowned heroine, — which is right? I have had the most delightful letter possible (you shall see it when you come) from dear Dr. Holmes, and venture to trouble you with the enclosed answer. Yesterday, Mr. Harness, who had heard a bad account of me (for I have been very ill, and, although much better now, I gather from everybody that I am thought to be breaking down fast), so like the dear kind old friend that he is, came to see me. It was a great pleasure. We talked much of you, and I think he will call upon you. Whether he call or not, do go to see him. He is fully prepared for you as Mr. Dyce's friend and Mr. Rogers's friend, and my very dear friend. Do go; you will find him charming, so different from the author people that Mr. Kenyon collects. I am sure of your liking each other. Surely by next week I may be well enough to see you. You and Mrs. W—— would do me nothing but good. Say everything to her, and to our dear kind friends, the Bennochs. I ought to have written to them, but I get as much scolded for writing as talking.

Ever yours, M. R. M.

(No date.)

How good and kind you are to me, dearest Mr. Fields! kindest of all, I think, in writing me those . . . . One comfort is, that if London lose you this year I do think you will not suffer many to elapse before revisiting it. Ah, you will hardly find your poor old friend next time! Not that I expect to die just now, but there is such a want of strength, of the power that shakes off disease, which is no good sign for the constitution. Yesterday I got up for a little while, for the first time since I saw you; but, having let in too many people, the fever came on again at night, and I am only just now shaking off the attack, and feel that I must submit to perfect quietness for the present. Still the attack was less violent than the last, and unattended by sickness, so that I am really better and hope in a week or so to be able to get out with you under the trees, perhaps as far as Upton.

One of my yesterday's visitors was a glorious old lady of seventy-six, who has lived in Paris for the last thirty years, and I do believe came to England very much for the purpose of seeing me. She had known my father before his marriage. He had taken her in his hand (he was always fond of children) one day to see my mother; she had been present at their wedding, and remembered the old housekeeper and the pretty nursery-maid and the great dog too, and had won with great difficulty (she being then eleven years old) the privilege of having the baby to hold. Her descriptions of all these things and places were most graphic, and you may imagine how much she must have been struck with my book when it met her eye in Paris, and how much I (knowing all about her family) was struck on my part by all these details, given with the spirit and fire of an enthusiastic woman of twenty. We had certainly never met. I left Alresford at three years old. She made an appointment to spend a day here next year, having with her a daughter, apparently by a first husband. Also she had the same host of recollections of Louis Napoleon, remembered the Emperor as Premier Consul, and La Reine Hortense as Mlle. de Beauharnais. Her account of the Prince is favorable. She says that it is a most real popularity, and that, if anything like durability can ever be predicated of the French, it will prove a lasting one.

I had a letter from Mrs. Browning to-day, talking of the "Facts of the Times," of which she said some gentlemen were speaking with the same supreme contempt and disbelief that I profess for every paragraph in that collection of falsehoods. For my own part, I hold a wise despotism, like the Prince President's, the only rule to live under. Only look at the figure our *soi-disant* statesmen cut, — Whig and Tory, — and then glance your eye across the Atlantic to your "own dear people," as Dr. Holmes says, and their doings in the Presidential line. Apropos to Dr. Holmes, you'll see him read and quoted when —— and his doings are as dead as Henry the Eighth. —— has no feeling for finish or polish or delicacy, and doubtless dismisses Pope and Goldsmith with supreme contempt. She never mentions that horrid trial, to my great comfort. Did I tell you that I had been reading Louis Napoleon's most charming three volumes full?

Among my visitors yesterday was Miss Percy, the heiress of Guy's Cliff, one of the richest in England, and, what is odd, the translator of "Emilie Carlen's Birthright," the only Swedish novel I have ever got fairly through, because Miss Percy really does her work well, and I can't read ——'s English. Miss Percy, who, besides being very clever and agreeable, is also pretty, has refused some scores of offers, and declares she'll never marry; she has a dread of being sought for her money. . . . .

God bless you, dearest, kindest friend. Say everything for me to your companions.

Ever most faithfully yours,   M. R. M.

(No date.)

Yes, dearest Mr. Fields, I continue to get better and better, and shall be delighted to see you and Mr. and Mrs. W—— on Friday. I even went in to surprise Mr. May on Saturday, so, weather permitting, we shall get up to Upton together. I want you to see that relique of Protestant bigotry. No doubt many of my dear countrymen would play just the same pranks now, if the spirit of the age would permit; the will is not wanting, witness our courts of law.

I have been reading the "Life of Margaret Fuller." What a tragedy from first to last! She must have been odious in Boston in spite of her power and her strong sense of duty, with which I always sympathize; but at New York, where she dwindled from a sibyl to a "lionne," one begins to like her better, and in England and Paris, where she was not even that, better still; so that one is prepared for the deep interest of the last half-volume. Of course her example must have done much injury to the girls of her train. Of course, also, she is the Zenobia of dear Mr. Hawthorne. One wonders what her book would have been like.

Mr. Bennett has sent me the " Nile Notes." We must talk about that, which I have not read yet, not delighting much in Eastern travels, or, rather, being tired of them. Ah, how sad it will be when I cannot say " We will talk "! Surely Mr. Webster does not mean to get up a dispute with England! That would be an affliction; for what nations should be friends if ours should not? What our ministers mean, nobody can tell, — hardly, I suppose, themselves. My hope was in Mr. Webster. Well, this is for talking. God bless you, dear friend.

Ever most affectionately yours,   M. R. M.

August 7, 1852.

Hurrah! dear and kind friend, I have found the line without any other person's aid or suggestion. Last night it occurred to me that it was in some prologue or epilogue, and my little book-room being very rich in the drama, I have looked through many hundreds of those bits of rhyme, and at last made a discovery which, if it have no other good effect, will at least have "emptied my head of Corsica," as Johnson said to Boswell; for never was the great biographer more haunted by the thought of Paoli than I by that line. It occurs in an epilogue by Garrick on quitting the stage, June, 1776, when the performance was for the benefit of sick and aged actors.

> A veteran see! whose last act on the stage
> Entreats your smiles for sickness and for age;
> Their cause I plead, plead it in heart and mind,
> *A fellow-feeling makes one wondrous kind.*"

Not finding it quoted in Johnson convinced me that it would probably have been written after the publication of the Dictionary, and ultimately guided me to the right place. It is singular that epilogues were just dismissed at the first representation of one of my plays, " Foscari," and prologues at another, " Rienzi."

I have but a moment to answer your most kind letter, because I have been engaged with company, or rather interrupted by company, ever since I got up, but you will pardon me. Nothing ever did me so much good as your visit. My only comfort is the hope of your return in the spring. Then I hope to be well enough to show Mr Hawthorne all the holes and corners my own self. Tell him so. I am already about to study the State Trials, and make myself perfect in all that can assist the romance. It will be a labor of love to do for him the small and humble part of collecting facts and books, and making ready the palette for the great painter.

Talking of *artists*, one was here on Sunday who was going to Upton yesterday. His object was to sketch every place mentioned in my book. Many of the places (as those round Taplow) he had taken, and K—— says he took this house and the stick and Fanchon and probably herself. I was unluckily gone to take home the dear visitors who cheer me daily and whom I so wish you to see.

God bless you all, dear friends.

Ever most affectionately yours, M. R. M.

SWALLOWFIELD, September 24, 1852.

MY VERY DEAR MR. FIELDS: I am beginning to get very fidgety about you, and thinking rather too often, not only of the breadth of the Atlantic, but of its dangers. However I must hear soon, and I write now because I am expecting a fellow-townsman of yours, Mr. Thompson, an American artist, who expected to find you still in England, and who is welcomed, as I suppose all Boston would be . . . . People do not love you the less, dear friend, for missing you.

I write to you this morning, because I have something to say and something to ask. In the first place, I am better. Mr. Harness, who, God bless him, left that Temple of Art, the Deepdene, and Mr. Hope's delightful conversation, to come and take care of me, stayed at Swallowfield three weeks. He found out a tidy lodging, which he has retained, and he promises to come back in November; at present he is again at the Deepdene. Nothing could be so judicious as his way of going on; he came at two o'clock to my cottage and we drove out together; then he went to his lodgings to dinner, to give me three hours of perfect quiet; at eight he and the Russells met here to tea, and he read Shakespeare (there is no such reader in the world) till bedtime. Under his treatment no wonder that I improved, but the low-fever is not far off; doing a little too much, I fell back even before his departure, and have been worse since. However, on the whole, I am much better.

Now to my request. You perhaps remember my speaking to you of a copy of my "Recollections," which was in course of illustration in the winter. Mr. Holloway, a great print-seller of Bedford Street, Covent Garden, has been engaged upon it ever since, and brought me the first volume to look at on Tuesday. It would have rejoiced the soul of dear Dr. Holmes. My book is to be set into six or seven or eight volumes, quarto, as the case may be; and although not unfamiliar with the luxuries of the library, I could not have believed in the number and richness of the pearls which have been strung upon so slender a thread. The rarest and finest portraits, often many of one person and always the choicest and the best, — ranging from magnificent heads of the great old poets, from the Charleses and Cromwells, to Sprat and George Faulkner of Dublin, of whom it was thought none existed, until this print turned up unexpectedly in a supplementary volume of Lord Chesterfield; nothing is too odd for Mr. Holloway. There is a colored print of George the Third, — a full length which really brings the old king to life again, so striking is the resemblance, and quantities of theatrical people, Munden and Elliston and the Kembles. There are two portraits of "glorious John" in Penruddock. Then the curious old prints of old houses. They have not only one two hundred years old of Dorrington Castle, but the actual drawing from which that engraving was made; and they are rich beyond anything in exquisite drawings of scenery by modern artists sent on purpose to the different spots mentioned. Besides which there are all sorts of characteristic autographs (a capital one of Pope); in short, nothing is wanting that the most unlimited expense (Mr. Holloway told me that his employer, a great city merchant of unbounded riches, constantly urged him to spare no expense to procure everything that money would buy), added to taste, skill, and experience, could accomplish. Of course the number of proper names and names of places have been one motive for conferring upon my book an honor of which I never dreamt; but there is, besides, an enthusiasm for my writings on the part of Mrs. Dillon, the lady of the possessor, for whom it is destined as a birthday gift. Now what I have to ask of you is to procure for Mr. Holloway as many autographs and portraits as you can of the American writers whom I have named, — dear Dr. Holmes, Hawthorne, Longfellow, Whittier, Prescott, Ticknor. If any of them would add a line or two of their writing to their names, it would be a favor, and if, being about it, they would send two other plain autographs, for I have heard of two other copies in course of illustration, and expect to be applied to by their proprietors every day. Mr. Holloway wrote to some trade connection in Philadelphia, but probably because he applied to the wrong place and the wrong person, and because he limited his correspondent to time, obtained no results. If there be a print of Professor Longfellow's house, so much the better, or any other autographs of Americans named in my book. Forgive this trouble, dear friend. You will probably see the work when you come to London in the spring, and then you will understand the interest that I take in it as a great book of art. Also my dear old friend, Lady Morley (Gibbon's correspondent), who at the age of eighty-three is caught by new books and is as enthusiastic as a girl, has commissioned me to inquire about your new authoress, the writer of ——, who she is and all about her. For my part, I have not finished the book yet, and never shall. Besides my own utter dislike to its painfulness, its one-sidedness, and its exaggeration, I observe that the sort of popularity which it has obtained in England, and probably in America, is decidedly *bad*, of the sort which cannot and does not last, — a cry which is always essentially one-sided and commonly wrong.....

Ever most faithfully and affectionately yours,
M. R. M.

October 5, 1852.

DEAREST MR. FIELDS: You will think that I persecute you, but I find that Mr. Dillon, for whom Mr. Holloway is illustrating my Recollections so splendidly, means to send the volumes to the binder on the 1st of November. I write therefore to beg, in case of your not having yet sent off the American autographs and portraits, that they may be forwarded direct to Mr. Holloway, 25 Bedford Street, Covent Garden, London. It is very foolish not to wait until all the materials are collected, but it is meant as an offering to Mrs. Dillon, and I suppose there is some anniversary in the way. Mr. Dillon is a great lover and preserver of fine engravings; his collection, one of the finest private collections in the world, is estimated at sixty thousand pounds. He is a friend of dear Mr. Bennoch's, who, when I told him the compliment that had been paid to my work by a great city man, immediately said it could be nobody but Mr. Dillon. I have twice seen Mr. Bennoch within the last ten days, once with Mr. Johnson and Mr. Thompson, your own Boston artist, whom I liked much, and who gave me the great pleasure of talking of you and of dear Mr. and Mrs. W——, last time with his own good and charming wife and ——. Only think of ——'s saying that Shakespeare, if he had lived now, would have been thought nothing of, and this rather as a compliment to the age than not! But, if you remember, he printed amended words to the air of "Drink to me only." Ah, dear me, I suspect that both William Shakespeare and Ben Jonson will survive him; don't you? Nevertheless he is better than might be predicated from that observation.

All my domestic news is bad enough. My poor pretty pony keeps his bed in the stable, with a violent attack of influenza, and

Sam and Fanchon spend three parts of their time in nursing him. Moreover we have had such rains here that the Lodden has overflowed its banks, and is now covering the water meadows, and almost covering the lower parts of the lanes. Adieu, dearest friend.
Ever most faithfully yours, M. R. M.

SWALLOWFIELD, October 13, 1852.

More than one letter of mine, dearest friend, crossed yours, for which I cannot sufficiently thank you. Nobody can better understand than I do, how very, very glad your own people, and all the good city, must feel to get you back again, — I trust not to keep; for in spite of sea-sickness, that misery which during the summer I have contrived to feel on land, I still hope that we shall have you here again in the spring. I am impatiently waiting the arrival of portraits and autographs, and if they do not come in time to bind, I shall charge Mr. Holloway to contrive that they may be pasted with the copy of my Recollections to which Mr. Dillon is paying so high and so costly a compliment. Now I must tell you some news.

First let me say that there is an admirable criticism in one of the numbers of the Nonconformist, edited by Edward Miall, one of the new members of Parliament, and certainly the most able of the dissenting organs, on our favorite poet, Dr. Holmes. Also I have a letter from Dr. Robert Dickson, of Hertford Street, May Fair, one of the highest and most fashionable London physicians, respecting my book, liking Dr. Holmes better than anybody for the very qualities for which he would himself choose to be preferred, originality and justness of thought, admirable fineness and propriety of diction, and a power of painting by words, very rare in any age, and rarest of the rare in *this*, when vagueness and obscurity mar so much that is high and pure. I shall keep this letter to *show* Dr. Holmes, tell him with my affectionate love. If it were not written on the thickest paper ever seen, and as huge as it is thick, I would send it; but I'll keep it for him against he comes to claim it. The description of spring is, Dr. Dickson says, remarkable for originality and truth. He thanks me for those poems of Dr. Holmes as if I had written them. Now be free to tell him all this. Of course you have told Mr. Hawthorne of the highly eulogistic critique on the "Blithedale Romance" in the Times, written, I believe, by Mr. Willmott, to whom I lent the veritable copy received from the author. Another thing let me say, that I have been reading with the greatest pleasure some letters on African trees copied from the New York Tribune into Bentley's Miscellany, and no doubt by Mr. Bayard Taylor. Our chief London news is that Mrs. Browning's cough came on so violently, in consequence of the sudden setting in of cold weather, that they are off for a week or two to Paris, then to Florence, Rome, and Naples, and back here in the summer. Her father still refuses to open a letter or to hear her name. Mrs. Southey, suffering also from chest-complaint, has shut herself up till June. Poor Anne Hatton, who was betrothed to Thomas Davis, and was supposed to be in a consumption, is recovering, they say, under the advice of a clairvoyante. Most likely a broken vessel has healed on the lungs, or perhaps an abscess. Be what it may, the consequence is happy, for she is a lovely creature and the only joy of a fond mother. Alfred Tennyson's boy was christened the other day by the name of Hallam Tennyson, Mr. Hallam standing to it in person. This is just as it should be on all sides, only that Arthur Hallam would have been a prettier name. You know that Arthur Hallam was the lost friend of the "In Memoriam," and engaged to Tennyson's sister, and that after his death, and even after her marrying another man, Mr. Hallam makes her a large allowance.

We have just escaped a signal misfortune; my dear pretty pony has been upon the point of death with influenza. Would not you have been sorry if that pony had died? He has, however, recovered under Sam's care and skill, and the first symptom of convalescence was his neighing to Sam through the window. You will have found out that I too am better. I trust to be stronger when you come again, well enough to introduce you to Mr. Harness, whom we are expecting here next month. God bless you, my dear and kind friend. I send this through dear Mr. Bennoch, whom I like better and better; so I do Mrs. Bennoch, and everybody who knows and loves you. Ever, my dear Mr. Fields,

Your faithful and affectionate friend, M. R. M.

P. S. — October 17. I have kept this letter open till now, and I am glad I did so. Acting upon the hint you gave of Mr. De Quincey's kind feeling, I wrote to him, and yesterday I had a charming letter from his daughter, saying how much her father was gratified by mine, that he had already written an answer, amounting to a good-sized pamphlet, but that when it would be finished was doubtful, so she sent hers as a precursor.

SWALLOWFIELD, November 11, 1852.

I write, dearest friend, and although the packet which you had the infinite goodness to send, has not reached me yet, and may not

Oliver Wendell Holmes.

possibly before my letter goes, — so uncertain is our railway, — yet I will write because our excellent friend, Mr. Bennoch, says that he has sent it off. . . . . You will understand that I am even more obliged by your goodness about Mr. Dillon's book than by any of the thousand obligations to myself only. Besides my personal interest, as so great a compliment to my own work, Mr. Dillon appears to be a most interesting person. He is a friend of Mr. Bennoch's, from whom I had his history, one most honorable to him, and he has written to me since I wrote to you and proposes to come and see me. *You* must see him when you come to England, and must see his collection of engravings. Would not dear Dr. Holmes have a sympathy with Mr. Dillon? Have you such fancies in America? They are not common even here; but Miss Skerrett (the Queen's factotum) tells me that the most remarkable book in Windsor Castle is a De Grammont most richly and expensively illustrated by George the Fourth, who, with all his sins as a monarch, was the only sovereign since the Stuarts of any literary taste.

Here is your packet! O my dear, dear friend, how shall I thank you half enough! I shall send the parcels to-morrow morning, the very first thing, to Mr. Holloway. The work is at the binder's, but fly-leaves have been left for the American packet of which I felt so sure, although even I could hardly foresee its value. One or two duplicates I have kept. Tell Mr. Hawthorne that I shall make a dozen people rich and happy by his autograph, and tell Dr. Holmes I could not find it in my heart to part with the " Mary " stanza. Never was a writer who possessed more perfectly the art of doing great things greatly and small things gracefully. Love to Mr. Hawthorne and to him.

Poor Daniel Webster! or rather poor America! Rich as she is, she cannot afford the loss, the greatest the world has known since our Sir Robert. But what a death-bed, and what a funeral! How noble an end of that noble life! I feel it the more, hearing and reading so much about the Duke's funeral, which by dint of the delay will not cause the slightest real feeling, but will be attended just like every show, and yet as a show will be gloomy and poor. How much better to have laid him simply here at Strathfieldsaye, and left it as a place of pilgrimage, — as Strathfield will be, — although between the two men, in my mind, there was no comparison; the one was a genius, the other mere soldier, — pure physical force measured with intellect the richest and the proudest. I have twenty letters speaking of him as one of the greatest among the statesmen of the age. The Times only refuses to do him justice. But when did the Times do justice to any one? Look how it talks of our Emperor.

Your friend Bayard Taylor came to see me a fortnight ago, just before he sailed on his tour round the world. I told him the first of Bentley's reprinting his letters from the New York Tribune; he had not heard a word of it. He seemed an admirable person, and it is good to have such travellers to follow with one's heart and one's earnest good wishes.

Also I have had two packets, — one from Mrs. Sparks, with a nice letter, and some fresh and glorious autumnal flowers, and a collection of autumn leaves from your glorious forests. I have written to thank her. She seems full of heart, and she says that she drove into Boston on purpose to see you, but missed you. When you do meet, tell me about her. Also, I have through you, dear friend, a most interesting book from Mr. Ware. To him, also, I have written, but tell him how much I feel and prize his kindness, all the more welcome for coming from a kinsman of dear Mrs. W——. Tell her and her excellent husband that they cannot think of us oftener or more warmly than we think of them. O, how I should like to visit you at Boston! But I should have your malady by the way, and not your strength to stand it. . . . .

God bless you, my dear and excellent friend! I seem to have a thousand things to say to you, but the post is going, and a whole sheet of paper would not hold my thanks.

Ever yours, M. R. M.

SWALLOWFIELD, November 25, 1852.

MY DEAR FRIEND: Your most kind and welcome letter arrived to-day, two days after the papers, for which I thank you much. Still more do I thank you for that kind and charming letter, and for its enclosures. The anonymous poem [it was by Dr. T. W. Parsons] is far finer than anything that has been written on the death of the Duke of Wellington, as indeed it was a far finer subject. May I inquire the name of the writer? Mr. Everett's speech also is superb, and how very much I prefer the Marshfield funeral in its sublime simplicity to the tawdry pageantry here! I have had fifty letters from persons who saw the funeral in St. Paul's, and seen as many who saw that or the procession, and it is strange that the papers have omitted alike the great successes and the great failures. My young neighbor, a captain in the Grenadier Guards (the Duke's regiment), saw the uncovering the car which had been hidden by the drapery, and was to have been a great effect, and he says it was exactly what is sometimes seen in a theatre when one scene is drawn up too soon and the other is not ready. Carpenters and undertaker's men were on all parts of the car, and the draperies and ornaments were everywhere but in their places. Again, the procession waited upwards of an hour at the cathedral door, because the same people had made no provision for taking the coffin from the car; again, the sunlight was let into St. Paul's, mingling most discordantly with the gas, and the naked wood of screens and benches and board beams disfigured the grand entrance. In three months' interval they had not time! On the other hand, the strong points were the music, the effect of which is said to have been unrivalled; the actual performance of the service, — my friend Dean Milman is renowned for his manner of reading the funeral service, he officiated at the burial of Mrs. Lockhart (Sir Walter's favorite daughter), — and none who were present could speak of it without tears; the clerical part of the procession, which was a real and visible mourning pageant in its flowing robes of white with black bands and sashes; the living branches of laurel and cypress amongst the mere finery; and, above all, the hushed silence of the people, always most and best impressed by anything that appeals to the imagination or the heart.

I suppose you will have seen how England is flooded, and you will like to hear that this tiny speck has escaped. The Lodden is over the park, and turns the beautiful water meadows down to Strathfieldsaye into a no less beautiful lake, two or three times a week; but then it subsides as quickly as it rises, so there is none of the lying under water which results in all sorts of pestilential exhalations, and this cottage is lifted out of every bad influence, nay, a kind neighbor having had my lane scraped, I walk dry-shod every afternoon a mile and a half, which is more than I ever expected to compass again, and for which I am most thankful. But we have had our own troubles. K—— has lost her father. He was seized with paralysis and knew nobody, so they desired her not to come, and Sam went alone to the funeral. After all, *this* is her home, and she has pretty well got over her affliction, and the pony is well again, and strong enough to draw you and me in the spring, — for I am looking forward to good and happy days again when you shall return to England.

Your magnificent present for Mr. Dillon's book was quite in time, dear friend. I had warned them to leave room, and Mr. Holloway and the binders contrived it admirably. They are most grateful for your kindness, and most gratefully shall I receive the promised volumes. I have not yet got "the pamphlet," and am much afraid it is buried in what Miss De Quincey calls her "father's chaos"; but I have charming letters from her, and am heartily glad that I wrote. You have the way (like Mr. Bennoch) of making friends still better friends, and bringing together those who, without you, would have had no intercourse. It is the very finest of all the fine arts. Tell dear Dr. Holmes that the more I hear of him, the more I feel how inadequate has been all that I have said to express my own feelings; and tell President Sparks that his charming wife ought to have received a long letter from me at the same moment with yourself. Mr. Hawthorne's new work will be a real treat. Tell me if Mr. Bennoch has sent you some stanzas on Ireland, which have more of the very highest qualities of Beranger than I have ever seen in English verse. We who love him shall have to be very proud of dear Mr. Bennoch. Tell me, too, if our solution of the line, "A fellow-feeling makes us wondrous kind," was the first; and why the new President is at once called General and talked of as a civilian. The other President goes on nobly, does he not?

Say everything for me to dear Mr. and Mrs. W—— and all friends.

Ever yours,   M. R. M.

SWALLOWFIELD, December 14, 1852.

O my very dear friend, how much too kind you are to me, who have nothing to give you in return but affection and gratitude! Mr. Bennett brought me your beautiful book on Saturday, and you may think how heartily we wished that you had been here also. But you will come this spring, will you not? I earnestly hope nothing will come in the way of that happiness. Before leaving the subject of our good little friend, let me say that, talking over our own best authors and your De Quincey (N. B. The pamphlet has not arrived yet, I fear it is forever buried in De Quincey's "chaos"), — talking of these things, we both agreed that there was another author, probably little known in America, who would be quite worthy of a reprint, William Hazlitt. Is there any complete edition of his Lectures and Essays? I should think they would come out well, now that Thackeray is giving his Lectures. I know that Charles Lamb and Talfourd thought Hazlitt not only the most brilliant, but the soundest of all critics. Then his Life of Napoleon is capital, that is, capital for an English life; the only way really to know the great man is to read him in the *mémoires* of his own ministers, lieutenants, and servants; for *he was* a hero to his *valet de chambre*, the greatness was so real that it would bear close looking into. And our Emperor! I have just had a letter from Osborne, from Marianne Skerrett, describing the arrival of Count Walewski under a royal salute to receive the Queen's recognition of Napoleon III. She, Marianne, says, "How great a man that is, and how like a fairy tale the whole story!" She adds, that, seeing much of Louis Philippe, she never could abide him, he was so cunning and so false, not cunning enough to hide the falseness! Were not you charmed with the bits of sentiment and feeling that come out all through our hero's Southern progress? Always one finds in him traits of a gracious and graceful nature, far too frequent and too spontaneous to be the effect of calculation. It is a comfort to find, in spite of our delectable press, ministers are wise enough to understand that our policy is peace, and not only peace but cordiality. To quarrel with France would be almost as great a sin as to quarrel with America. What a set of fools our great ladies are! I had hoped better things of Lord Carlisle, but to find that long list at Stafford House in female parliament assembled, echoing the absurdities of Exeter Hall, leaving their own duties and the reserve which is the happy privilege of our sex to dictate to a great nation on a point which all the world knows to be its chief difficulty, is enough to make one ashamed of the title of Englishwoman. I know a great many of these committee ladies, and in most of them I trace that desire to follow the fashion, and concert with duchesses, which is one of the besetting sins of the literary circles in London. One name did surprise me, ———, considering that one of her husband's happiest bits, in the book of his that will live, was the subscription for sending flannel waistcoats to the negroes in the West Indies; and that in this present book a certain Mrs. Jellyby is doing just what his wife is doing at Stafford House!

Even if I had not had my earnest thanks to send you, I should have written this week to beg you to convey a message to Mr. Hawthorne. Mr. Chorley writes to me, "You will be interested to hear that a Russian literary man of eminence was so much attracted to the 'House of the Seven Gables' by the review in the Athenæum, as to have translated it into Russian and published it feuilletonwise in a newspaper." I know you will have the goodness to tell Mr. Hawthorne this, with my love. Mr. Chorley saw the entrance of the Empereur into the Tuileries. He looked radiant. The more I read that elegy on the death of Daniel Webster, the more I find to admire. It is as grand as a dirge upon an organ. Love to the dear W———s and to Dr. Holmes.

Ever, dearest Mr. Fields, most gratefully yours, M. R. M.

1853.

SWALLOWFIELD, January 5, 1853.

Your most welcome letter, my very dear friend, arrived to-day, and I write not only to acknowledge that, and your constant kindness, but because, if, as I believe, Mr. Bennoch has told you of my mischance, you will be glad to hear from my own hand that I am going on well. Last Monday fortnight I was thrown violently from my own pony-chaise upon the hard road in Lady Russell's park. No bones were broken, but the nerves of one side were so terribly bruised and lacerated, and the shock to the system was so great, that even at the end of ten days Mr. May could not satisfy himself, without a most minute re-examination, that neither fracture nor dislocation had taken place, and I am writing to you at this moment with my left arm bound tightly to my body and no power whatever of raising either foot from the ground. The only parts of me that have escaped uninjured are my head and my right hand, and this is much. Moreover Mr. May says that, although the cure will be tedious, he sees no cause to doubt my recovering altogether my former condition, so that we may still hope to drive about together when you come back to England. . . . .

I wrote I think, dearest friend, to thank you heartily for the beautiful and interesting book called "The Homes of American Authors." How comfortably they are housed, and how glad I am to find that, owing to Mr. Hawthorne's being so near the new President, and therefore keeping up the habit of friendship and intercourse, the want of which habit so frequently brings college friendship to an end, he is likely to enter into public life. It will be an excellent thing for his future books, — the fault of all his writings, in spite of their great beauty, being a want of reality, of the actual, healthy, every-day life which is a necessary element in literature. All the great poets have it, — Homer, Shakespeare, Scott. It will be the very best school for our pet poet.

Nobody under the sun has so much right as you have to see Mr. Dillon's book, which is in six quarto volumes, not one. Our dear friend Mr. Bennoch knows him, and tells me to-day that Mr. Dillon has invited him to go and look at it. He has just received it from the binders. Of course Mr. Bennoch will introduce you. I was so glad to read what looked like a renewed pledge of your return to England.

Mr. Bentley has sent me three several applications for a second series. At present Mr. May forbids all composition, but I suppose the thing will be done. I shall introduce some chapters on French poetry and literature. At this moment I am in full chase of Casimer Delavigne's *ballads*. He thought so little of them that he published very few in his Poésies, — one in a note, — and several of the very finest not at all. They are scattered about here and there. —— has reproduced two (which I had) in his Memories; but I want all that can be found, especially one of which the refrain is, "Chez l'Ambassadere de France." I was such a fool, when I read it six or seven years ago, as not to take a copy. Do you think Mr. Hector Bossange could help me to that, or to any others not printed in the Memories? . . . . Of course I shall devote one chapter to *our* Emperor. Ah, how much better is such a government as his than one which every four years causes a sort of moral earthquake; or one like ours, where whole sessions are passed in squabbling! The loss of his place has saved Disraeli's life, for everybody said he could not have survived three months' badgering in the House. A very intimate friend of his (Mr. Henry Drummond, the very odd, very clever member for Surrey) says that he had certainly broken a bloodvessel. One piece of news I have heard to-day from Miss Goldsmid, that the Jews are certain now to gain their point and be admitted to the House of Commons; for my part, I hold that every one has a claim to his civil rights, were he Mahometan or Hindoo, and I rejoice that poor old Sir Isaac, the real author of the movement, will probably live to see it accomplished. The thought of succeeding at last in the pursuit to which he has devoted half his life has quite revived him.

And now Heaven bless you, my very dear friend. None of the poems on Wellington are to be compared to that dirge on Webster. I rejoice that my article should have pleased his family. The only bit of my new book that I have written is a paper on Taylor and Stoddard. Say everything for me to the Ticknors and Nortons and your own people, the W——s.

Ever most faithfully and affectionately yours, M. R. M.

SWALLOWFIELD, February 1, 1853.

Ah, my dear friend! ask Dr. Holmes what these severe bruises and lacerations of the nerves of the principal joints are, and he will tell you that they are much more slow and difficult of cure, as well as more painful, than half a dozen broken bones. It is now above six weeks since that accident, and although the shoulder is going on favorably, there is still a total loss of muscular power in the lower limbs. I am just lifted out of bed and wheeled to the fireside, and then at night wheeled back and lifted into bed, — without the power of standing for a moment, or of putting one foot before the other, or of turning in bed. Mr. May says that warm weather will probably do much for me, but that till then I must be a prisoner to my room, for that if rheumatism supervenes upon my present inability, there will be no chance of getting rid of it. So "patience and shuffle the cards," as a good man, much in my state, the contented Marquess, says in Don Quixote. . . . . I assure you I am not out of spirits; indeed, people are so kind to me that it would be the basest of all ingratitude if I were not cheerful as well as thankful. I think that in a letter which you must have received by this time, I told you how it came about, and thanked you for the comely book which shows how cosily America lodges my brethren of the quill. Dr. Holmes ought to have been there, and Dr. Parsons, but their time will come and must. Nothing gratifies me more than to find how many strangers, writing to me of my Recollections, mention Dr. Holmes, classing him sometimes with Thomas Davis, sometimes with Praed. If I write another series of Recollections, as, when Mr. May will let me, I suppose I must, I shall certainly include Dr. Parsons. . . . .

Has anybody told you the terrible story of that boy, Lord Ockham, Lord Byron's grandson? I had it from Mr. Noel, Lady Byron's cousin-german and intimate friend. While his poor mother was dying her death of martyrdom from an inward cancer, — Mrs. Sartoris (Adelaide Kemble), who went to sing to her, saw her through the door, which was left open, crouching on a floor covered with mattresses, on her hands and knees, the only posture she could bear, — whilst she with the patience of an angel was enduring her long agony, her husband, engrossed by her, left this lad of seventeen to his sister and the governess. It was a dull life, and he ran away. Mr. Noel (my friend's brother, from whom he had the story) knew most of the youth, who had been for a long time staying at his house, and they begged him to undertake the search. Lord Ockham had sent a carpet-bag containing his gentleman's clothes to his father, Lord Lovelace, in London; he was therefore disguised, and from certain things he had said Mr. Noel suspected that he intended to go to America. Accordingly he went first to Bristol, then to Liverpool, leaving his description, a sort of written portrait of him, with the police at both places. At Liverpool he was found before long, and when Mr. Noel, summoned by the electric telegraph, reached that town, he found him dressed as a sailor-boy at a low public-house, surrounded by seamen of both nations, and enjoying, as much as possible, their sailor yarns. He had given his money, £36, to the landlord to keep; had desired him to inquire for a ship where he might be received as cabin-boy; and had entered into a shrewd bargain for his board, stipulating that he should have over and above his ordinary rations a pint of beer with his Sunday dinner. The landlord did not cheat him, but he postponed all engagements under the expectation — seeing that he was clearly a gentleman's son — that money would be offered for his recovery. The worst is that he (Lord Ockham) showed no regret for the sorrow and disgrace that he had brought upon his family at such a time. He has two tastes not often seen combined, — the love of money and of low company. One wonders how he will turn out. He is now in Paris, after which he is to re-enter in Green's ship (he had served in one before) for a twelvemonth, and to leave the service or remain in it as he may decide then. This is perfectly true; Mr. Noel had it from his brother the very day before he wrote it to me. He says that Lady Lovelace's funeral was too ostentatious. Escutcheons and silver coronals everywhere. Lord Lovelace's taste that, and not Lady Byron's, which is perfectly simple. You know that she was buried in the same vault with her father, whose coffin and the box containing his heart were in perfect preservation. Scott's only grandson, too, is just dead of sheer debauchery. Strange! As if one generation paid in vice and folly for the genius of the past. By the way, are you not charmed at the Emperor's marriage? To restore to princes honest love and healthy preference, instead of the conventional intermarriages which have brought epilepsy and idiotism and madness into half the royal families of Christendom! And then the beauty of that speech, with its fine appeals to the best sympathies of our common nature! I am proud of him. What a sad, sad catastrophe was that of young Pierce! I won't call his father general, and I hope he will leave it off. With us it is a real offence to give any man a higher rank than belongs to him, — to say captain, for instance, to a lieutenant, — and that is one of our usages which it would be well to copy. But we have follies enough, God knows; that duchess address, with all its tuft-hunting signatures, is a thing to make Englishwomen ashamed. Well, they caught it deservedly in an address from American women, written probably by some very clever American man. No, I have not seen Longfellow's lines on the Duke. One gets sick of the very name. Henry is exceedingly fond of his little sister. I remember that when he first saw the snow fall in large flakes, he would have it that it was a shower of white feathers. Love to all my dear friends, the W———s, Mrs. Sparks, Dr. Holmes, Mr. Hawthorne. Ever, dearest friend, most affectionately yours,

M. R. M.

(1st March, 1853.)

The numbers for the election of President of France in favor of Louis Napoleon were

for   against
7119791|1119

Look through the back of this against the candle, or the fire, or any light.

MY VERY DEAR FRIEND: Having a note to send to Mrs. Sparks, who has sent me, or rather whose husband has sent me, two answers to Lord Mahon, which, coming through a country bookseller, have, I suspect, been some months on the way, I cannot help sending it enclosed to you, that I may have a chat with you *en passant*, — the last, I hope, before your arrival. If you have not seen the above curious instance of figures forming into a word, and that word into a prophecy, I think it will amuse you, and I want besides to tell you some of the *on-dits* about the Empress. A Mr. Huddlestone, the head of one of our great Catholic houses, is in despair at the marriage. He had been desperately in love with her for two years in Spain, — had followed her to Paris, — was called back to England by his father's illness, and was on the point of crossing the Channel, after that father's death, to lay himself and £ 30,000 or £ 40,000 a year at her feet, when the Emperor stepped in and carried off the prize. To comfort himself he has got a portrait of her on horseback, which a friend of mine saw the other day at his house. Mrs. Browning writes me from Florence: "I wonder if the Empress pleases you as well as the Emperor. For my part, I approve altogether, and none the less that he has offended Austria by the mode of announcement. Every cut of the whip on the face of Austria is an especial compliment to me, or so I feel it. Let him heed the democracy, and do his duty to the world, and use to the utmost his great opportunities. Mr. Cobden and the peace societies are pleasing me infinitely just now in making head against the immorality — that 's the word — of the English press. The tone taken up towards France is immoral in the highest degree, and the invasion cry would be idiotic if it were not something worse. The Empress, I heard the other day from high authority, is charming and good at heart. She was brought up at a respectable school at Clifton, and is very English, which does not prevent her from shooting with pistols, leaping gates, driving four in hand, and upsetting the carriage if the frolic requires it, — as brave as a lion and as true as a dog. Her complexion is like marble, white, pale, and pure, — the hair light, rather sandy, they say, and she powders it with gold dust for effect; but there is less physical and more intellectual beauty than is generally attributed to her. She is a woman of very decided opinions. I like all that, don't you? and I like her letter to the press, as everybody must." Besides this, I have to-day a letter from a friend in Paris, who says that " everybody feels her charm," and that " the Emperor, when presenting her at the balcony on the wedding-day, looked radiant with happiness." My Parisian friend says that young Alexandre Dumas is amongst the people arrested for libel, — a thorough *mauvais sujet*. Lamartine is quite ruined, and forced to sell his estates. He was always, I believe, expensive, like all those French *littérateurs*. You don't happen to have in Boston — have you? — a copy of " Les Mémoires de Lally Tollendal" ? I think they are different publications in defence of his father, published, some in London during the Emigration, some in Paris after the Restoration. What I want is an account of the retreat from Pondicherie. I'll tell you why some day here. Mrs. Browning is most curious about your rappings, — of which I suppose you believe as much as I do of the Cock Lane Ghost, whose doings, by the way, they much resemble.

I liked Mrs. Tyler's letter; at least I liked it much better than the one to which it was an answer, although I hold it one of our best female privileges to have no act or part in such matters.

Now you will be sorry to have a very bad account of me. Three weeks ago frost and snow set in here, and ever since I have been unable to rise or stand, or put one foot before another, and the pain is much worse than at first. I suppose rheumatism has supervened upon the injured nerve. God bless you. Love to all.

Ever faithfully yours,   M. R. M.

SWALLOWFIELD, March 17, 1853.

MY DEAR FRIEND : I cannot enough thank you for your most kind and charming letter. Your letters, and the thoughts of you, and the hope that you will coax your partners into the hazardous experiment of letting you come to England, help to console me under this long confinement; for here I am at near Easter still a close prisoner from the consequences of the accident that took place before Christmas. I have only once left my room, and that only to the opposite chamber to have this cleaned, and I got such a chill that it brought back all the pain and increased all the weakness. But when fine weather — warm, genial, sunny weather — comes, I will get down in some way or other, and trust myself to that which never hurts any one, the honest open air. Spring, and even the approach of spring, has upon me something the effect that England has upon you. It sets me dreaming, — I see leafy hedges in my dreams, and flowery banks, and then I long to make the vision a reality. I remember that Fanchon's father, Flush, who was a famous sporting dog, used, at the approach of the covering season, to quest in his sleep, doubtless by the same instinct that works in me. So, as soon as the sun tells the same story with the primroses, I shall make a descent after some fashion, and no doubt, aided by Sam's stalwart arm, successfully. In the mean while I have one great pleasure in store, be the weather what it may; for next Saturday or the Saturday after I shall see dear Mr. Bennoch. We have not met since November, although he has written to me again and again. He will take this letter, and I trouble you with a note to kind Mrs. Sparks, who is about to send me, or rather who has sent me, some American cracknels, which have not yet arrived. To-day, too, I had a charming letter from Lasswade, — not *the* letter, the pamphlet one, but one full of kindness from father and daughter, written by Miss Margaret to ask after me with a reality of interest which one feels at once. It gave me pleasure in another way too; Mr. De Quincey is of my faith and delight in the Emperor! Is not that delightful? Also he holds in great abomination that blackest of iniquities ———, my heresy as to which nearly cost me an idolator t' other day, a lady from Essex, who came here to take a house in my neighborhood to be near me. She was so shocked that, if we had not met afterwards, when I regained my ground a little by certain congenialities, she certainly would have abjured me forever. Well! no offence to Mrs. ———. I had rather in a literary question agree with Thomas De Quincey than with her and Queen Victoria, who, always fond of strong not to say coarse excitements, is amongst ———'s warm admirers. I knew you would like the Emperor's marriage. I heard last week from a stiff English lady, who had been visiting one of the Empress's ladies of honor, that one day at St. Cloud she shot thirteen brace of partridges; "but," added the narrator, "she is so sweet and charming a creature that any man might fall in love with her notwithstanding." To be sure Mr. Thackeray liked you. How could he help it? Did not he also like Dr. Holmes? I hope so. How glad I should be to see him in England, and how glad I shall be to see Mr. Hawthorne! He will find all the best judges of English writing admiring him to his heart's content, warmly and discriminatingly; and a consulship in a bustling town will give him the cheerful reality, the healthy air of every-day life, which is his only want. Will you tell all these dear friends, especially Mr. and Mrs. W——, how deeply I feel their affectionate sympathy, and thank Mr. Whittier and Professor Longfellow over and over again for their kind condolence? Tell Mr. Whittier how much I shall prize his book. He has an earnest admirer in Buckingham Palace, Marianne Skerrett, known as the Queen's Miss Skerrett, the lady chiefly about her, and the only one to whom she talks of books. Miss Skerrett is herself a very clever woman, and holds Mr. Whittier to be not only the greatest, but the *one* poet of America; which last assertion the poet himself would, I suspect, be the very first to deny. Your promise of Dr. Parsons's poem is very delightful to me. I hold firm to my admiration of those stanzas on Webster. Nothing written on the Duke came within miles of it, and I have no doubt that the poem on Dante's bust is equally fine. .... Mr. Justice Talfourd has just printed a new tragedy. He sent it to me from Oxford, not from Reading, where he had passed four days and never gave a copy to any mortal, and told me, in a very affectionate letter which accompanied it, that "it was at present a very private sin, he having only given eight or ten copies in all." I suppose that it will be published, for I observe that the "not published" is written, not printed, and that Moxon's name is on the title-page. It is called "The Castilian," — is on the story of a revolt headed by Don John de Padilla in the early part of Charles the Fifth's reign, and is more like Ion than either of his other tragedies. I have just been reading a most interesting little book in manuscript, called "The Heart of Montrose." It is a versification in three ballads of a very striking letter in Napier's "Life and Times of Montrose," by the young lady who calls herself Mary Maynard. It is really a little book that ought to make a noise, not too long, full of grace and of interest, and she has adhered to the true story with excellent taste, that story being a very remarkable union of the romantic and the domestic. I am afraid that my other young poet, ——, is dying of consumption; those fine spirits often fall in that way. I have just corrected my book for a cheaper edition. Mr. Bentley is very urgent for a second series, and I suppose I must try. I shall get you to write for me to Mr. Hector Bossange when you come, for come you must. My eyes begin to feel the effects of this long confinement to one smoky and dusty room.

So far had I written, dearest friend, when this day (March 26) brought me your most kind and welcome letter enclosed in another from dear Mr. Bennoch. Am I to return Dr. Parsons's? or shall I keep it till you come to fetch it? Tell the writer how very much I prize his kindness, none the less that he likes (as I do) my tragedies, that is, one of them, the best of my poor doings. The lines on the Duchess are capital, and quite what she deserves; but I think those the worst who, in so true a spirit of what Carlyle would call flunkeyism, consent to sign any nonsense that their names may figure side by side with that of a duchess, and they themselves find (for once) an admittance to the gilded saloons of Stafford House. For my part, I well-nigh lost an admirer the other day by taking a common-sense view of the question. A lady (whose name I never heard till a week ago) came here to take a house to be near me. (N. B. There was none to be had.) Well, she was so provoked to find that I had stopped short of the one hundredth page of ——, and never intended to read another, that I do think, if we had not discovered some sympathies to counterbalance that grand difference — As I live, I have told you that story before! Ah! I am sixty-six, and I get older every day! So does little Henry, who is at home just now, and longing to put the clock forward that he may go to America. He is a boy of great promise, full of sound sense, and as good as good can be. I suppose that he never in his life told an untruth, or broke a promise, or disobeyed a command. He is very fond of his little sister; and not at all jealous either — to the great praise of that four-footed lady be it said — is Fanchon, who watches over the cradle, and is as fond of the baby in her way as Henry in his.

So far from paying me copyright money, all that I ever received from Mr. B—— was two copies of his edition of "Our Village," one of which I gave away, and of the other some chance visitor has taken one of the volumes. I really do think I shall ask him for a copy or two. How can I ever thank you enough for your infinite kindness in sending me books! Thank you again and again. Dear Mr. Bennoch has been making an admirable speech, in moving to present the thanks of the city to Mr. Layard. How one likes to feel proud of one's friends! God bless you!

Ever most faithfully yours, M. R. M.

Kind Mrs. Sparks's biscuits arrived quite safe. How droll some of the cookery is in "The Wide, Wide World"! It would try English stomachs by its over-richness. I wonder you are not all dead, if such be your *cuisine*.

SWALLOWFIELD, May 3, 1853.

How shall I thank you enough, dear and kind friend, for the copy of —— that arrived here yesterday! Very like, only it wanted what that great painter, the sun, will never arrive at giving, the actual look of life which is the one great charm of the human countenance. Strange that the very source of light should fail in giving that light of the face, the smile. However, all that can be given by that branch of art has been given. I never before saw so good a photographic portrait, and for one that gives more I must wait until John Lucas, or some American John Lucas, shall coax you into sitting. I sent you, ten days ago, a batch of notes, and a most unworthy letter of thanks for one of your parcels of gift-books; and I write the rather now to tell you I am better than then, and hope to be in a still better plight before July or August, when a most welcome letter from Mr. Tuckerman has bidden us to expect you to officiate as Master of the Ceremonies to Mr. Hawthorne, who, welcome for himself, will be trebly welcome for such an introducer.

Now let me say how much I like De Quincey's new volumes. The "Wreck of a Household" shows great power of narrative, if he would but take the trouble to be right as to details; the least and lowest part of the art, that of interesting you in his people, he has. And those "Last Days of Kant," how affecting they are, and how thoroughly in every line and in every thought, agree with him or not, (and in all that relates to Napoleon I differ from him, as in his overestimate of Wordsworth and of Coleridge), one always feels how thoroughly and completely he is a gentleman as well as a great writer; and so much has *that* to do with my admiration, that I have come to tracing personal character in books almost as a test of literary merit; Charles Boner's "Chamois-Hunting," for instance, owes a great part of its charm to the resolute truth of the writer, and a great drawback from the attraction of "My Novel" seems to me to be derived from the *blasé* feeling, the unclean mind from whence it springs, felt most when trying after moralities.

Amongst your bounties I was much amused with the New York magazines, the curious turning up of a new claimant to the Louis-the-Seventeenth pretension amongst the Red Indians, and the rappings and pencil-writings of the new Spiritualists. One should wonder most at the believers in these two branches of faith, if that particular class did not always seem to be provided most abundantly whenever a demand occurs. Only think of Mrs. Browning giving the most unlimited credence to every "rapping" story which anybody can tell her! Did I tell you that the work on which she is engaged is a fictitious autobiography in blank verse, the heroine a woman artist (I suppose singer or actress), and the tone intensely modern? You will see that "Colombe's Birthday" has been brought out at the Haymarket. Mr. Chorley (Robert Browning's most intimate friend) writes me word that Mrs. Martin (Helen Faucit, at whose persuasion it was acted) told him that it had gone off "better than she expected." Have you seen Alexander Smith's book, which is all the rage just now? I saw some extracts from his poems a year and a half ago, and the whole book is like a quantity of extracts put together without any sort of connection, a mass of powerful metaphor with scarce any lattice-work for the honeysuckles to climb upon. Keats was too much like this; but then Keats was the first. Now this book, admitting its merit in a certain way, is but the imitation of a school, and, in my mind, a bad school. One such poem as that on the bust of Dante is worth a whole wilderness of these new writers, the very best of them. Certainly nothing better than those two pages ever crossed the Atlantic.

God bless you, dear friend. Say everything for me to dear Mr. and Mrs. W——, to Dr. Holmes, to Dr. Parsons, to Mr. Whittier, (how powerful his new volume is!) to Mr. Stoddard, to Mrs. Sparks, to all my friends.

Ever most affectionately yours,   M. R. M.

I am writing on the 8th of May, but where is the May of the poets? Half the morning yesterday it snowed, at night there was ice as thick as a shilling, and to-day it is absolutely as cold as Christmas. Of course the leaves refuse to unfold, the nightingales can hardly be said to sing, even the hateful cuckoo holds his peace. I am hoping to see dear Mr. Bennoch soon to supply some glow and warmth.

SWALLOWFIELD, June 4, 1853.

I write at once, dearest friend, to acknowledge your most kind and welcome letter. I am better than when I wrote last, and get out almost every day for a very slow and quiet drive round our lovely lanes; far more lovely than last year, since the foliage is quite as thick again, and all the flowery trees, aloes, laburnums, horse-chestnuts, acacias, honeysuckles, azalias, rhododendrons, hawthorns, are one mass of blossoms, — literally the leaves are hardly visible, so that the color, whenever we come upon park, shrubbery, or plantation, is such as should be seen to be imagined. In my long life I never knew such a season of flowers; so the wet winter and the cold spring have their compensation. I get out in this way with Sam and K—— and the baby, and it gives me exquisite pleasure, and if you were here the pleasure would be multiplied a thousand fold by your society; but I do not gain strength in the least. Attempting to do a little more and take some young people to the gates of Whiteknights, which, without my presence, would be closed, proved too far and too rapid a movement, and for two days I could not stir for excessive soreness all over the body. I am still lifted down stairs step by step, and it is an operation of such time (it takes half an hour to get me down that one flight of cottage stairs), such pain, such fatigue, and such difficulty, that, unless to get out in the pony-chaise, I do not attempt to leave my room. I am still lifted into bed, and can neither turn nor move in any way when there, am wheeled from the stairs to the pony-carriage, cannot walk three steps, can hardly stand a moment, and in rising from my chair am sometimes ten minutes, often longer. So you see that I am very, very feeble and infirm. Still I feel sound at heart and clear in head, am quite as cheerful as ever, and, except that I get very much sooner exhausted, enjoy society as much as ever, so you must come if only to make me well. I do verily believe your coming would do me more good than anything.

I was much interested by your account of the poor English stage coachman. Ah, these are bad days for stage coachmen on both sides the Atlantic! Do you remember his name? and do you know whether he drove between London and Reading, or between Reading and Basingstoke? — a most useless branch railroad between the two latter places, constructed by the Great Western simply out of spite to the Southwestern, which I am happy to state has never yet paid its daily expenses, to say nothing of the cost of construction, and has taken everything off our road, which before abounded in coaches, carriers, and conveyances of all sorts. The vile railway does us no earthly good, we being above four miles from the nearest station, and you may imagine how much inconvenience the absence of stated communication with a market town causes to our small family, especially now that I can neither spare Sam nor the pony to go twelve miles. You must come to England and come often to see me, just to prove that there is any good whatever in railways, — a fact I am often inclined to doubt.

I shall send this letter to be forwarded to Mr. Bennett, and desire him to write to you himself. He is, as you say, an "excellent youth," although it is very generous in me to say so for I do believe that you came to see me since he has been. Dear Mr. Bennoch, with all his multifarious business, has been again and again. God bless him! . . . . To return to Mr Bennett. He has been engaged in a grand battle with the trustees of an old charity school, principally the vicar. His two brothers helped in the fight. They won a notable victory. They were quite right in the matter in dispute, and the "excellent youth" came out well in various letters. His opponent, the vicar, was Senior Wrangler at our Cambridge, the very highest University honor in England, and tutor to the present Lord Grey.

By the way, Mr. —— wrote to me the other day to ask that I would let him be here when Mr. Hawthorne comes to see me. I only answered this request by asking whether he did not intend to come to see *me* before that time, for certainly he might come to visit an old friend, especially a sick one, for her own sake, and not merely to meet a notability, and I am by no means sure that Mr. Hawthorne might not prefer to come alone or with dear Mr. Bennoch; at all events it ought to be left to *his* choice, and besides I have not lost the hope of your being the introducer of the great romancer, and then how little should I want anybody to come between us. Begin as they may, all my paragraphs slide into that refrain of Pray, pray come!

I have written to you about other kindnesses since that note full of hopes, but I do not think that I did write to thank you for dear Dr. Holmes's "Lecture on English Poetesses," or rather the analysis of a lecture which sins only by over-gallantry. Ah, there *is* a difference between the sexes, and the difference is the reverse way to that in which he puts it! Tell him I sent his charming stanzas on Moore to a leading member of the Irish committee for raising a monument to his memory, and that they were received with enthusiasm by the Irish friends of the poet. I have sent them to many persons in England worthy to be so honored, and the very cleverest woman whom I have ever known (Miss Goldsmid) wrote to me only yesterday to thank me for sending her that exquisite poem, adding, "I think the stanza 'If on his cheek, etc.,' contains one of the most beautiful similes to be found in the whole domain of poetry." I also told Mrs. Browning what dear Dr. Holmes said of her. The American poets whom she prefers are Lowell and Emerson. Now I know something of Lowell and of Emerson, but I hold that those lines on Dante's bust are amongst the finest ever written in the language, whether by American or Englishman; don't you? And what a grand Dead March is the poem on Webster! .... Also Mrs. Browning believes in spirit-rapping stories, — all, — and tells me that Robert Owen has been converted by them to a belief in a future state. Everybody everywhere is turning tables. The young Russells, who are surcharged with electricity, set them spinning in

J. M. Lowell.

ten minutes. In general, you know, it is usual to take off all articles of metal. They, the other night, took a fancy to remove their rings and bracelets, and, having done so, the table, which had paused for a moment, began whirling again as fast as ever the contrary way. This is a fact, and a curious one.

I have lent three volumes of your "De Quincey" to my young friend, James Payn, a poet of very high promise, who has verified the Green story, and taken the books with him to the Lakes. God grant, my dear friend, that you may not lose by "Our Village"; that is what I care for.

Ever faithfully yours,   M. R. M.

SWALLOWFIELD, June 23, 1853.

Ah, my very dear friend, we shall not see you this summer, I am sure. For the first time I clearly perceive the obstacle, and I feel that unless some chance should detain Mr. Ticknor, we must give up the great happiness of seeing you till next year. I wonder whether your poor old friend will be alive to greet you then! Well, that is as God pleases; in the mean time be assured that you have been one of the chief comforts and blessings of these latter years of my life, not only in your own friendship and your thousand kindnesses, but in the kindness and friendship of dear Mr. Bennoch, which, in the first instance, I mainly owe to you. I am in somewhat better trim, although the getting out of doors and into the pony-carriage, from which Mr. May hoped such great things, has hardly answered his expectations. I am not stronger, and I am so nervous that I can only bear to be driven, or more ignominiously still to be led, at a foot's pace through the lanes. I am still unable to stand or walk, unless supported by Sam's strong hands lifting me up on each side, still obliged to be lifted into bed, and unable to turn or move when there, the worst grievance of all. However, I am in as good spirits as ever, and just at this moment most comfortably seated under the acacia-tree at the corner of my house, — the beautiful acacia literally loaded with its snowy chains (the flowering trees this summer, lilacs, laburnums, rhododendrons, azalias, have been one mass of blossoms, and none are so graceful as this waving acacia); on one side a syringa, smelling and looking like an orange-tree; a jar of roses on the table before me, — fresh-gathered roses, the pride of Sam's heart; and little Fanchon at my feet, too idle to eat the biscuits with which I am trying to tempt her, — biscuits from Boston, sent to me by Mrs. Sparks, whose kindness is really indefatigable, and which Fanchon ought to like upon that principle if upon no other, but you know her laziness of old, and she improves in it every day. Well, that is a picture of the Swallowfield cottage at this moment, and I wish that you and the Bennochs and the W——s and Mr. Whipple were here to add to its life and comfort. You must come next year, and come in May, that you and dear Mr. Bennoch may hear the nightingales together. He has never heard them, and this year they have been faint and feeble (as indeed they were last) compared with their usual song. Now they are over, and although I expect him next week, it will be too late.

Precious fooling that has been at Stafford House! And our —— who delights in strong, not to say worse, emotions, whose chief pleasure it was to see the lions fed in Van Amburgh's time, who went seven times to see the Ghost in the "Corsican Brothers," and has every sort of natural curiosity (not to say wonder) brought to her at Buckingham Palace, was in a state of exceeding misery because she could not, consistently with her amicable relations with the United States, receive Mrs. —— there. (Ah! our dear Emperor has better taste. Heaven bless him!) From Lord Shaftesbury one looks for unmitigated cant, but I did expect better things of Lord Carlisle. How many names that both you and I know went there merely because the owner of the house was a fashionable Duchess,—the Wilmers ("though they are my friends"), the P——s and ——! For my part, I have never read beyond the first one hundred pages, and have a certain malicious pleasure in so saying. Let me add that almost all the clever men whom I have seen are of the same faction; they took up the book and laid it down again. Do you ever reprint French books, or ever get them translated? By very far the most delightful work that I have read for many years is Sainte-Beuve's "Causeries du Lundi," or his weekly feuilletons in the "Constitutionnel." I am sure they would sell if there be any taste for French literature. It is so curious, so various, so healthy, so catholic in its biography and criticism; but it must be well done by some one who writes good English prose and knows well the literary history of France. Don't trust women; they, especially the authoresses, are as ignorant as dirt. Just as I had got to this point, Mr. Willmot came to spend the evening, and very singularly consulted me about undertaking a series of English Portraits Littéraires, like Sainte-Beuve's former works. He will do it well, and I commended him to the charming "Causeries," and advised him to make that a weekly article, as no doubt he could. It would only tell the better for the wide diffusion. He does, you know, the best criticism of The Times. I have most charming letters from Dr. Parsons and dear Mr. Whittier. His cordiality is delightful. God bless you.

Ever yours,

M. R. M.

(No date.)

Never, my dear friend, did I expect to like so well a man who came in your place, as I do like Mr. Ticknor. He is an admirable person, very like his cousin in mind and manners, unmistakably good. It is delightful to hear him talk of you, and to feel that the sort of elder brotherhood which a senior partner must exercise in a firm is in such hands. He was very kind to little Harry, and Harry likes him *next* to you. You know he had been stanch in resisting all the advances of dear Mr. ——, who had asked him if he would not come to him, to which he had responded by a sturdy "no!" He (Mr. Ticknor) came here on Saturday with the dear Bennochs (N. B. I love him better than ever), and the Kingsleys met him. Mr. Hawthorne was to have come, but could not leave Liverpool so soon, so that is a pleasure to come. He will tell you that all is arranged for printing with Colburn's successors, Hurst and Blackett, two separate works, the plays and dramatic scenes forming one, the stories to be headed by a long tale, of which I have always had the idea in my head, to form almost a novel. God grant me strength to do myself and my publishers justice in that story! This whole affair springs from the fancy which Mr. Bennoch has taken to have the plays printed in a collected form during my lifetime, for I had always felt that they would be so printed after my death, so that their coming out now seems to me a sort of anachronism. The one certain pleasure that I shall derive from this arrangement will be, having my name and yours joined together in the American edition, for we reserve the early sheets. Nothing ever vexed me so much as the other book not being in your hands. That was Mr. ——'s fault, for, stiff as Bentley is, Mr. Bennoch would have managed him. . . . . Of a certainty my first strong interest in American poetry sprang from dear Dr. Holmes's exquisite little piece of scenery painting, which he delivered where his father had been educated. You sent me that, and thus made the friendship between Dr. Holmes and me ; and now you are yourself — you, my dearest American friend — delivering an address at the greatest American University. It is a great honor, and one . . . .

I suppose Mr. Ticknor tells you the book-news? The most striking work for years is "Haydon's Life." I hope you have reprinted it, for it is sure, not only of a run, but of a durable success. You know that the family wanted me to edit the book. I shrank from a task that required so much knowledge which could only be possessed by one living in the artist world *now*, to know who was dead and who alive, and Mr. Tom Taylor has done it admirably. I read the book twice over, so profound was my interest in it. In his early days, I used to be a sort of safety-valve to that ardent spirit, most like Benvenuto Cellini both in pen and tongue and person. Our dear Mr. Bennoch was the providence of his later years. They tell me that that powerful work has entirely stopped the sale of Moore's Life, which, all tinsel and tawdry rags, might have been written by a court newsman or a court milliner. I wonder whether they will print the other six volumes; for the four out they have given Mrs. Moore three thousand pounds. A bad account Mr. Tupper gives of ———. Fancy his conceit! When Mr. Tupper praised a passage in one of his poems, he said, "If I had known you liked it, I would have omitted that passage in my new edition," and he has done so by passages praised by persons of taste, cut them out bodily and left the sentences before and after to join themselves how they could. What a bad figure your President and Mr. ——— cut at the opening of your Exhibition! I am sorry for ———, for, although he has quite forgotten me since his aunt's book came out, he once stayed three weeks with us, and I liked him. Well, so many of his countrymen are over-good to me, that I may well forgive one solitary instance of forgetfulness! Make my love to all my dear friends at Boston and Cambridge. Tell Mrs. Sparks how dearly I should have liked to have been at her side on *the* Thursday. Tell Dr. Holmes that his kind approbation of Rienzi is one of my encouragements in this new edition. I had a long talk about him with Mr. Ticknor, and rejoice to find him so young. Thank Mr. Whipple again and again for his kindness.

Ever yours,   M. R. M.

(No date.)

MY VERY DEAR FRIEND: Mr. Hillard (whom I shall be delighted to see if he come to England and will let me know when he can get here) — Mr. Hillard has just put into verse my own feelings about you. It is the one comfort belonging to the hard work of these *two* books (for besides the Dramatic Works in two thick volumes, there are prose stories in two also, and I have one long tale, almost a novel, to write), — it is the one comfort of this labor that *I* shall see our names together on one page. I have just finished a long gossiping preface of thirty or forty pages to the Dramatic Works, which is much more an autobiography than the Recollections, and which I have tried to make as amusing as if it were ill-natured. *That* work is dedicated to our dear Mr. Bennoch, another consolation. I sent the dedication to dear Mr. Ticknor, but as his letter of adieu did not reach me till two or three days after it was written, and I am not quite sure that I recollected the number in Paternoster Row, I shall send it to you here. "To Francis Bennoch, Esq., who blends in his life great public services with the most genial private hospitality; who, munificent patron of poet and of painter, is the first to recognize every talent except his own, content to be beloved where others claim to be admired; to him, equally valued as companion and as friend, these volumes are most respectfully and affectionately inscribed by the author." I write from memory, but if this be not it, it is very like it, (and I beg you to believe that my preface is a little better English than this agglomeration of "its.")

Mr. Kingsley says that Alfred Tennyson says that Alexander Smith's poems show fancy, but not imagination; and on my repeating this to Mrs. Browning, she said it was exactly her impression. For my part I am struck by the extravagance and the total want of finish and of constructive power, and I am in hopes that ultimately good will come out of evil, for Mr. Kingsley has written, he tells me, a paper called "Alexander Pope and Alexander Smith," and Mr. Willmott, the powerful critic of The Times, takes the same view, he tells me, and will doubtless put it into print some day or other, so that the carrying this bad school to excess will work for good. By the way, Mr. ——, whose Imogen is so beautiful, sent me the other day a terrible wild affair in that style, and I wrote him a frank letter, which my sincere admiration for what he does well gives me some right to do. He has in him the making of a great poet; but, if he once take to these obscurities, he is lost. I hope I have not offended him, for I think it is a real talent, and I feel the strongest interest in him. My young friend, James Payn, went a fortnight or three weeks ago to Lasswade and spent an evening with Mr. De Quincey. He speaks of him just as you do, marvellously fine in point of conversation, looking like an old beggar, but with the manners of a prince, "if," adds James Payn, "we may understand by that all that is intelligent and courteous and charming." (I suppose he means such manners as our Emperor's.) He began by saying that his life was a mere misery to him from nerves, and that he could only render it endurable by a semi-inebriation with opium. (I always thought he had not left opium off.)....

On his return, James Payn again visited Harriet Martineau, who talked frankly about *the* book, exculpating Mr. Atkinson and taking all the blame to herself. She asked if I had read it, and on finding that I had not, said, "It was better so." There are fine points about Harriet Martineau. Mrs. Browning is positively crazy about the spirit-rappings. She believes every story, European or American, and says our Emperor consults the mediums, which I disbelieve.

The above was written yesterday. To-day has brought me a charming letter from Miss De Quincey. She has been very ill, but is now back at Lasswade, and longing most earnestly to persuade her father to return to Grasmere. Will she succeed? She sends me a charming message from a brother Francis, a young physician settled in India. She says that her sister told her her father was in bad spirits when talking to Mr. Payn, which perhaps accounts for his confessing to the continuing the opium-eating.

Mr. —— brought me some proofs of his new volume of poems. I think that if he will take pains he will be a real poet. But it is so difficult to get young men to believe that correcting and re-correcting is necessary, and he is a most charming person, and so gets spoiled. I spoil him myself, God forgive me! although I advise him to the best of my power. No signs of Mr. Hawthorne yet! Heaven bless you, my dear friend.

Ever faithfully yours,   M. R. M.

October, 1853.

My very dear Friend: I cannot thank you enough for the two charming books which you have sent me. I enclose a letter for the author of this very remarkable book of Italian travel, and I have written to dear Mr. Hawthorne myself.

Since I wrote to you, dear Mr. Bennoch sent to me to look out what letters I could find of poor Haydon's. I was half killed by the operation, all my sins came upon me; for, lulling my conscience by carelessness about bills and receipts, and by answering almost every letter the day it comes, I am in other respects utterly careless, and my great mass of correspondence goes where fate and K—— decree. We had five great chests and boxes, two huge hampers, fifteen or sixteen baskets, and more drawers than you would believe the house could hold, to look over, and at last disinterred sixty-five. I did not dare read them for fear of the dust, but I have no doubt they will be most valuable, for his letters were matchless for talent and spirit. I hope you have reprinted the Life; if so, of course you will publish the Correspondence. By the way, it is a curious specimen of the little care our highest people have for poetry of the —— school, that Vice-Chancellor Wood, one of the most accomplished men whom I have ever known, a bosom friend of Macaulay, was with me last week, and had never heard of Alexander Smith.

I continue terribly lame, and with no chance of amendment till the spring, when you will come and do me good. Besides the lameness, I am also miserably feeble, ten years older than when you saw me last. I am working as well as I can, but very slowly. I send you a proof of the Preface to the Dramatic Works (not knowing whether they have sent you the sheets, or when they mean to bring it out). The few who have seen this Introduction like it. It tells the truth about myself and says no ill of other people. God bless you, dear friend. Say everything for me to all friends, not forgetting Mr. Ticknor.

Ever yours,   M. R. M.

SWALLOWFIELD, November 8, 1853.

MY VERY DEAR FRIEND: Your letters are always delightful to me, even when they are dated Boston; think what they will be when they are dated London. In my last I sent you a very rough proof of my Preface (I think Mr. Hurst means to call it Introduction), which you will find autobiographical to your heart's content; I hope you will like it. To-day I enclose the first rough draft of an account of my first impression of Haydon. Don't print it, please, because I suppose they mean it for a part of the Correspondence when it shall be published. I looked out for those sixty-five long letters of Haydon's, — as long, perhaps, each, as half a dozen of mine to you, — and doubtless I have many more, but I was almost blinded by the dust in hunting up those, my eyes having been very tender since I was shut up in a smoky room for twenty-two weeks last winter. I find now that Messrs. Longman have postponed the publication of the Correspondence in the fear that it would injure the sale of the Memoirs, the book having had a great success here. By the enclosed, which is as true and as like as I could make it, you will see that he was a very brilliant and charming person. I believe that next to having been heart-broken by the committee and the heartlessness of his pupil ——, and enraged by the passion for that miserable little wretch, Tom Thumb, that the real cause of his suicide was to get his family provided for. It succeeded. By one way and another they had £ 440 a year between the four; but although the poor father never complained, you will see by his book what a selfish wretch that —— was. . . . .

My tragedies are printed, and the dramatic scenes, forming, with the preface, two volumes of above four hundred pages each. But I don't think they are to come out till the prose work, and that is not a quarter finished. I am always a most slow and laborious writer (that Preface was written three times over throughout, and many parts of it five or six), and of course my ill health does not improve my powers of composition. This wet summer and autumn have been terribly against me. I am lamer even than when Mr. Ticknor saw me, and sometimes cannot even dip the pen in the ink without holding it in my left hand. Thank God my head is spared, and my heart is, I think, as young as ever.

I had a letter to-day from Mr. Chorley; he has been staying all the autumn with Sir William Molesworth, now a Cabinet Minister, but he complains terribly about his own health, notwithstanding he has a play coming out at the Olympic, which Mr. Wigan has taken. Mrs. Kingsley, a most sweet person, has a cough which has forced them to send her to the sea. You shall be sure to see both him and Mr. Willmott if I can compass it; but we live, each of us, seven miles apart, and these country clergymen are so tied to their parish that they are difficult to catch. However, they both come to see me whenever they can, and we must contrive it. You will like both in different ways. Mr. Willmott is one of the most agreeable men in the world, and Mr. Kingsley is charming. I have another dear friend, not an author, whom I prefer to either, — Hugh Pearson. He made for himself a collection of De Quincey, when a lad at Oxford. You would like him, I think, better than anybody; but he too is a country clergyman, living eight miles off. Poor Mr. Norton! His letters were charming. He is connected in my mind with Mrs. Hemans, too, to whom he was so kind. You must say everything for me to dear Mrs. Sparks. I seem most ungrateful to her, but I really have little power of writing letters just now. Did I tell you that Mr. —— sent me a poem called ——, which I am very sorry that he ever wrote. It has shocked Mr. Bennoch even more than it did me. You must get him to write more poems like ——. A young friend of mine has brought out a little volume in which there is striking evidence of talent; but none of these young writers take pains. How very pretty is that scrap on a country church! Mrs. Browning is at Florence, but is going to Rome. She says that your countryman, Mr. Story, has made a charming statuette, I think of Beethoven, or else of Mendelssohn, which ought to make his reputation. She is crazy about mediums. She says (but I have not heard it elsewhere) that Thackeray and Dickens are to winter at Rome, and Alfred Tennyson at Florence. Mrs. Trollope has quite recovered, and receives as usual. How full of beauty Mr. Hillard's book is! thank him for it again and again. Did I tell you that they are going to engrave a portrait of me by Haydon, now belonging to Mr. Bennoch, for the Dramatic Works? God bless you, my very dear friend. Say everything for me to Mr. Ticknor and Dr. Holmes and Dr. Parsons, and all my friends in Boston. Little Henry grows a very sensible, intelligent boy, and is a great favorite at his school. He is getting on with French.

Once more, ever yours, M. R. M.

1854.

(January, 1854.)

MY BELOVED FRIEND: They who correspond with sick people must be content to receive such letters as are sent from hospitals. For many weeks I have been wholly shut up in my own room, getting with exceeding difficulty from the bed to the fireside, quite unable to stir either in the chair or in the bed, but much less miserable up than when in bed. The terrible cold of last summer did not allow me to gain any strength, so that although the fire in my room is kept up night and day, yet a severe attack of influenza came on and would have carried me off, had not Mr. May been so much alarmed at the state of the pulse and the general feebleness as to order me two tablespoonfuls of champagne in water once a day, and a teaspoonful of brandy also in water, at night, which undoubtedly saved my life. It is the only good argument for what is called teetotalism that it keeps more admirable medicines as medicine; for undoubtedly a wine-drinker, however moderate, would not have been brought round by the remedy which did me so much good. Miserably feeble I still am, and shall continue till May or June (if it please God to spare my life till then), when, if it be fine weather, Sam will lift me down stairs and into the pony-chaise, and I may get stronger. Well, in the midst of the terrible cough, which did not allow me to lie down in bed, and a weakness difficult to describe, I finished "Atherton." I did it against orders and against warning, because I had an impression that I should not live to complete it, and I sent it yesterday to London to dear Mr. Bennoch, so I suppose you will soon receive the sheets. Almost every line has been written three times over, and it is certainly the most cheerful and sunshiny story that was ever composed in such a state of helplessness, feebleness, and suffering; for the rheumatic pain in the chest not only rendered the cough terrible (that, thank God, is nearly gone now), but makes the position of writing one of misery. God grant you may like this story! I shall at least say in the Preface that it will give me one pleasure, that of having in the American title-page the names of dear friends united with mine. Mind I don't know whether the story be good or bad. I only answer for its having the youthfulness which you liked in the preface to the plays. Well, dearest friend, just when I was at the worst came your letter about the ducks and the ducks themselves. Never were birds so welcome. My friend, Mr. May, the cleverest and most admirable person whom I know in this neighborhood, refuses all fees of any sort, and comes twelve miles to see me, when torn to pieces by all the great folk round, from pure friendship. Think how glad I was to have such a dainty to offer him just when he had all his family gathered about him at Christmas. I thank you from the bottom of my heart for giving me this great pleasure, infinitely greater than eating it myself would have been. They were delicious. How very, very good you are to me!

Has Mrs. Craig written to you to tell you of her marriage? I will run the risk of repetition and tell you that it is the charming Margaret De Quincey, who has married the son of a Scotch neighbor. He has purchased land in Ireland, and they are about to live in Tipperary, — a district which Irish people tell me is losing its reputation for being the most disturbed in Ireland, but keeping that for superior fertility. They are trying to regain a reputation for literature in Edinburgh. John Ruskin has been giving a series of lectures on art there, and Mr. Kingsley four lectures on the schools of Alexandria.

Nothing out of Parliament has for very long made so strong a sensation as our dear Mr. Bennoch's evidence on the London Corporation. Three leading articles in The Times paid him the highest compliments, and you know what that implies. I have myself had several letters congratulating me on having such a friend. Ah! the public qualities make but a part of that fine and genial character, although I firmly believe that the strength is essential to the tenderness. I always put you and him together, and it is one of the compensations of my old age to have acquired such friends.

Have you seen Matthew Arnold's poems? They have fine bits. The author is a son of Dr. Arnold.

God bless you! Say everything for me to my dear American

friends, Drs. Holmes and Parsons, Mr. Longfellow, Mr. Whittier, Mrs. Sparks, Mr. Taylor, Mr. Whipple, Mr. and Mrs. Willard, and Mr. Ticknor. Many, very many happy years to them and to you.
Always most affectionately yours,   M. R. M.

P. S. I enclose some slips to be pasted into books for my different American friends. If I have sent too many, you will know which to omit. I must add to the American preface a line expressive of my pleasure in joining my name to yours. I will send one line here for fear of its not going. Mr. May says that those ducks were amongst the few things thoroughly deserving their reputation, holding the same place, as compared with our wild ducks, that the finest venison does to common mutton. I cannot tell you how much I thank you for enabling me to send such a treat to such a friend. You will send a copy of the prose book or the dramas, according to your own pleasure, only I should like the two dear doctors to have the plays.

SWALLOWFIELD, January 23, 1854.

I have always to thank you for some kindness, dearest Mr. Fields, generally for many. How clever those magazines are, especially Mr. Lowell's article, and Mr. Bayard Taylor's graceful stanzas! Just now I have to ask you to forward the enclosed to Mr. Whittier. He sent me a charming poem on Burns, full of tenderness and humanity, and the indulgence which the wise and good can so well afford, and which only the wisest and best can show to their erring brethren. I rejoice to hear that he is getting well again. I myself am weaker and more helpless every day, and the rheumatic pain in the chest increases so rapidly, and makes writing so difficult, even the writing such a note as this, that I cannot be thankful enough for having finished "Atherton," for I am sure I could not write it now. There is some chance of my getting better in the summer, if I can be got into the air, and that must be by being let down in a chair through a trap-door, like so much railway luggage, for there is not the slightest power of helping myself left in me, — nothing, indeed, but the good spirits which Shakespeare gave to Horatio, and Hamlet envied him. Dearest Mr. Bennoch has made me a superb present, — two portraits of our Emperor and his fair wife. He all intellect, — never was a brow so full of thought; she all sweetness, — such a mouth was never seen, it seems waiting to smile. The beauty is rather of expression than of feature, which is exactly what it ought to be. . . . .
M. R. M.

SWALLOWFIELD, May 2, 1854.

MY DEAR FRIEND : Long before this time, you will, I hope, have received the sheets of "Atherton." It has met with an enthusiastic reception from the English press, and certainly the friends who have written to me on the subject seem to prefer the tale which fills the first volume to anything that I have done. I hope you will like it, — I am sure you will not detect in it the gloom of a sick-chamber. Mr. May holds out hopes that the summer may do me good. As yet the spring has been most unfavorable to invalids, being one combined series of east-wind, so that instead of getting better I am every day weaker than the last, unable to see more than one person a day, and quite exhausted by half an hour's conversation. I hope to be a little better before your arrival, dearest friend, because I must see you; but any stranger — even Mr. Hawthorne — is quite out of the question.

You may imagine how kind dear Mr. Bennoch has been all through this long trial, next after John Ruskin and his admirable father the kindest of all my friends, and that is saying much.

God bless you. Love to all my friends, poets, prosers, and the dear ——, who are that most excellent thing, readers. I wonder if you ever received a list of people to whom to send one or other of my works? I wrote such with little words in my own hand, but writing is so painful and difficult, and I am always so uncertain of your getting my letters, that I cannot attempt to send another. There was one for Mrs. Sparks. I am sure of liking Dr. Parsons's book, — quite sure. Once again, God bless you! Little Henry grows a nice boy.

Ever most affectionately yours, M. R. M.

SWALLOWFIELD, July 12, 1854.

DEAREST MR. FIELDS : Our excellent friend Mr. Bennoch will have told you from how painful a state of anxiety your most welcome letter relieved us. You have done quite right, my beloved friend, in returning to Boston. The voyage, always so trying to you, would, with your health so deranged, have been most dangerous, and next year you will find all your friends, except one, as happy to see and to welcome you. Even if you had arrived now our meeting would have been limited to minutes. Dr. Parsons will tell you that fresh feebleness in a person so long tried and so aged (sixty-seven) must have a speedy termination. May Heaven prolong your valuable life, dear friend, and grant that you may be as happy yourself as you have always tried to render others!

Elmwood, 5th March,
1868.
O.S. 22nd Feby.

My dear Fields,

You know that there is a very considerable party in the world, headed by the Pope, that pagan full of pride, who wants cure all our ills by simply putting the world back, & this feat they would accomplish by putting back the hands of the clock. When I got home last night & reflected on the indecency of which I had been guilty in not answering your note, I was struck with the simplicity of this plan & especially with its adaptation to a difficulty like that in which I found myself. I at first thought of lengthening the pendulum of my clock & waiting patiently till it should have <u>lost time</u> enough to carry me back to where I wished to be. But on mature reflection, I found a swifter solution of my problem. I remembered that the Russians, a highly respectable & friendly nation, still adhered to the Old Style in their computation of time, thus always having twelve more days in their pockets than those spendthrift people who had allowed themselves to be cheated by the Pope out of that precious advantage. By our purchase of Alaska, I think we are entitled to share in this benefit of Calendar. On this computation I have not yet received, & shall not for a couple of days yet, the note you were so kind as to be going to write me day after tomorrow, 24th Feb O.S. Provided I do get it (for you may change your mind) I shall be very happy to come, but I will never join in a conspiracy to cheat Longfellow out of near a fortnight of his days — a very serious matter at sixty-one. If you should be going to send me me also some tickets for Dickens's readings of the 24th, 25th, 27th & 28th of Feb), as you kindly hint, I shall be extremely obliged to you. There can be no greater privilege than to hear a man of genius interpret his own creations. And a very delightful man of genius he is — simple, sweet, & natural, & so used to being a lion that he might lie down with Charles Lamb without scaring him. If Britannia could always have ruled her mane as quietly as he does, there would have been a kindlier feeling between us & her — I mean her & us, saving her presence.

I conclude a treaty with Miss Fields on Saturday, 5th terms of which you are to come & Eat roast pig with us & learn for the fitting time for the feast of these innocents. Shall arrive, which will be in about three weeks. I have a lovely brood, whose tails curl with eagerness for martyrdom, & who will be as Tertles a young informans

Yours always
J.R.L.

I rejoice to hear what you tell me of "Atherton." Here the reception has been most warm and cordial. Every page of it was written three times over, so that I spared no pains, but I was nearly killed by the terrible haste in which it was finished, and I do believe that many of the sheets were sent to me without ever being read in the office. I have corrected one copy for the third English edition, but I cannot undertake such an effort again, so, if (as I venture to believe) it be destined to be often reprinted by you, you must correct it from *that* edition. I hope you sent a copy to Mr. Whittier from me. I had hoped you would bring one to Mr. Hawthorne and Mr. De Quincey, but I must try what I can do with Mr. Hurst, and must depend on you for assuring these valued friends that it was not neglect or ingratitude on my part.

Mr. Boner, my dear and valued friend, wishes you and dear Mr. Ticknor to print his "Chamois-Hunting" from a second edition which Chapman and Hall are bringing out. I sent my copy of the work to Mr. Bennoch when we were expecting you, that you might see it. It is a really excellent book, full of interest, with admirable plates, which you could have, and, speaking in your interest, as much as in his, I firmly believe that it would answer to you in money as well as in credit to bring it out in America. Also Mrs. Browning (while in Italy) wrote to me to inquire if you would like to bring out a new poem by her, and a new work by her husband. I told her that I could not doubt it, but that she had better write duplicate letters to London and to Boston. Our poor little boy is here for his holidays. His excellent mother and step-father have nursed me rather as if they had been my children than my servants. Everybody has been most kind. The champagne, which I believe keeps me alive, is dear Mr. Bennoch's present; but you will understand how ill I am when I tell you that my breath is so much affected by the slightest exertion that I cannot bear even to be lifted into bed, but have spent the last eight nights sitting up, with my feet supported on a leg-rest. This from exhaustion, not from disease of the lungs.

Give the enclosed to Dr. Parsons. You know what I have always thought of his genius. In my mind no poems ever crossed the Atlantic which approached his stanzas on Dante and on the death of Webster, and yet you have great poets too. Think how glad and proud I am to hear of the honor he has done me. I wish you had transcribed the verses.

God bless you, my beloved friend! Say everything for me to all my dear friends, to Dr. Parsons, to Dr. Holmes, to Mr. Whittier, to

Professor Longfellow, to Mr. Taylor, to Mr. Stoddard, to Mrs. Sparks, and above all to the excellent Mr. Ticknor and the dear W——s.

Ever yours,   M. R. M.

SWALLOWFIELD, July 23, 1854.

MY VERY DEAR FRIEND: This is a sort of postscript to my last, written instantly on the receipt of yours and sent through Mr. ——. I hope you received it, for he is so impetuous that I always a little doubt his care; at least it was when sent through him that the loss of letters to and fro took place. However, I enjoined him to be careful this time, and he assured me that he was so.

The purport of this is to add the name of my friend, Mr. Willmott, to the authors who wish for the advantage of your firm as their American publishers. I have begged him to write to you himself, and I hope he has done so, or that he will do so. But he is staying at Richmond with sick relatives, and I am not sure. You know his works, of course. They are becoming more and more popular in England, and he is writing better and better. The best critical articles in The Times are by him. He is eminently a scholar, and yet full of anecdote of the most amusing sort, with a memory like Scott, and a charming habit of applying his knowledge. His writings become more and more like his talk, and I am confident that you would find his works not only most creditable, but most profitable. I would not recommend you to each other if it were not for your mutual advantage, so far as my poor judgment goes. On the 25th my Dramatic Works are to be published here. I hope they have sent you the sheets.

I have not heard yet from any American friend, except your delightful letter and one from Grace Greenwood, but I hope I shall. I prize the good word of such persons as Drs. Parsons and Holmes and Professor Longfellow and John Whittier and many others. I am still very ill.

The Brownings remain this year in Italy. If it be very hot, they will go for a month or two to the Baths of Lucca, but their home is Florence. She has taken a fancy to an American female sculptor, — a girl of twenty-two, — a pupil of Gibson's, who goes with the rest of the fraternity of the studio to breakfast and dine at a *café*, and yet keeps her character. Also she believes in all your rappings.

God be with you, my very dear friend. I trust you are quite recovered.

Always affectionately yours,   M. R. M.

SWALLOWFIELD, August 21, 1854.

MY DEAR MR. FIELDS: Mr. Bayard Taylor having sent me a most interesting letter, but no address, I trouble you with my reply. Read it, and you will perhaps understand that I am declining day by day; and that, humanly speaking, the end is very near. Perhaps there may yet be time for an answer to this. . . . .

I believe that one reason for your not quite understanding my illness is, that you, if you have seen long and great sickness at all, which is doubtful, have seen it with an utter prostration of the mind and the spirits, — that your women are languid and querulous, and never dream of bearing up against bodily evils by an effort of the mind. Even now, when half an hour's visit is utterly forbidden, and half that time leaves me panting and exhausted, I never mention (except forced into it by your evident disbelief) my own illness either in speaking or writing, — never, except to answer Mr. May's questions, or to join my beloved friend, Mr. Pearson, in thanking God for the visitation which I humbly hope was sent in his mercy to draw me nearer to him; may he grant me grace to use it! — for the rest, whilst the intelligence and the sympathy are vouchsafed to me, I will write of others, and give to my friends, as far as in me lies, the thoughts which would hardly be more worthily bestowed on my own miserable body.

You will be sorry to find that the poor Talfourds are likely to be very poor. A Reading attorney has run away, cheating half the town. He has carried off £4,000 belonging to Lady Talfourd, and she herself tells my friend, William Harness (one of her kindest friends), that that formed the principal part of the Judge's small savings, and, together with the sum for which he had insured his life (only £5,000), was all which they had. Now there are five young people, — his children, — the widow and an adopted niece, seven in all, accustomed to every sort of luxury and indulgence. The only glimpse of hope is, that the eldest son held a few briefs on circuit and went through them creditably; but it takes many years in England to win a barrister's reputation, and the poorer our young men are the more sure they are to marry. Add the strange fact that since the father's death (he having reserved his copyrights) not a single copy of any of his books has been sold! A fortnight ago I had a great fright respecting Miss Martineau, which still continues. James Payn, who is living at the Lakes, and to whom she has been most kind, says he fears she will be a great pecuniary sufferer by ———. I only hope that it is a definite sum, and no general security or partnership, — even that will be bad enough for a woman of her age, and so hard a worker, who intended to give herself rest; but observe these are only *fears*, I *know* nothing. The Brownings are detained in Italy, she tells me, for want of money, and cannot even get to Lucca. This is my bad news, — O, and it is very bad that sweet Mrs. Kingsley must stay two years in Devonshire and cannot come home. I expect to see him this week. John Ruskin is with his father and mother in Switzerland, constantly sending me tokens of friendship. Everybody writes or sends or comes; never was such kindness. The Bennochs are in Scotland. He sends me charming letters, having, I believe, at last discovered what every one else has known long. Remember me to Mr. Ticknor. Say everything to my Athenian friends all, especially to Dr. Holmes and Dr. Parsons.

Ever, dear friend, your affectionate

M. R. M.

September 26, 1854.

MY VERY DEAR FRIEND: Your most kind and interesting letter has just arrived, with one from our good friend, Mr. Bennoch, announcing the receipt of the £ 50 bill for "Atherton." More welcome even as a sign of the prosperity of the book in a country where I have so many friends and which I have always loved so well, than as money, although in that way it is a far greater comfort than you probably guess, this very long and very severe illness obliging me to keep a third maid-servant. I get no sleep, — not on an average an hour a night, — and require perpetual change of posture to prevent the skin giving way still more than it does, and forming what we emphatically call bed-sores, although I sit up night and day, and have no other relief than the being, to a slight extent, shifted from one position to another in the chair that I never quit. Besides this, there are many other expenses. I tell you this, dear friend, that Mr. Ticknor and yourself may have the satisfaction of knowing that, besides all that you have done for many years for my gratification, you have been of substantial use in this emergency. In spite of all this illness, after being so entirely given over that dear Mr. Pearson, leaving me a month ago to travel with Arthur Stanley for a month, took a final leave of me, I have yet revived greatly during these last three weeks. I owe this, under Providence, to my admirable friend, Mr. May, who, instead of abandoning the stranded ship, as is common in these cases, has continued, although six miles off, and driving four pair of horses a day, ay, and while himself hopeless of my case, to visit me constantly and to watch every symptom, and exhaust every resource of his great art, as if his own fame and fortune depended on the result. One kind but too sanguine friend, Mr. Bennoch, is rather over-hopeful about this amendment, for I am still in a state in which the slightest falling back would carry me off, and in which I can hardly think it possible to weather the winter. If that incredible contingency should arise, what a happiness it would be to see you in April! But I must content myself with the charming little portrait you have sent me, which is your very self. Thank you for it over and over. Thank you, too, for the batch of notices on "Atherton." . . . .

Dr. Parsons's address is very fine, and makes me still more desire to see his volume; and the letter from Dr. Holmes is charming, so clear, so kind, and so good. If I had been a boy, I would have followed their noble profession. Three such men as Mr. May, Dr. Parsons, and Dr. Holmes are enough to confirm the predilection that I have always had for the art of healing.

I have no good news to tell you of dear Mr. K——. His sweet wife (Mr. Ticknor will remember her) has been three times at death's door since he saw her here, and must spend at least two winters more at Torquay. But I don't believe that he could stay here even if she were well. Bramshill has fallen into the hands of a Puseyite parson, who, besides that craze, which is so flagrant as to have made dear Mr. K—— forbid him his pulpit, is subject to fits of raving madness, — one of those most dangerous lunatics whom an age (in which there is a great deal of false humanity) never shuts up until some terrible crime has been committed. (A celebrated mad-doctor said the other day of this very man, that he had "homicidal madness.") You may fancy what such a Squire, opposing him in every way, is to the rector of the parish. Mr. K—— told me last winter that he was driving him mad, and I am fully persuaded that he would make a large sacrifice of income to exchange his parish. To make up for this, he is working himself to death, and I greatly fear that his excess of tobacco is almost equal to the opium of Mr. De Quincey. With his temperament this is full of danger. He was only here for two or three days to settle a new curate, but he walked over to see me, and I will take care that he receives your message. His regard for me is, I really believe, sincere and very warm. Remember that all this is in strict confidence. The kindness that people show to me is something surprising. I have not deserved it, but I receive it most gratefully. It touches one's very heart. Will you say everything for me to my many kind friends, too many to name? I had a kind letter from Mrs. Sparks the other day. The poets I cling to while I can hold a pen. God bless you.

Ever yours,   M. R. M.

Can you contrive to send a copy of your edition of "Atherton" to Mr. Hawthorne? Pray, dear friend, do if you can.

October 12, 1854.

MY VERY DEAR FRIEND: I can hardly give you a greater proof of affection, than in telling you that your letter of yesterday affected me to tears, and that I thanked God for it last night in my prayers; so much a mercy does it seem to me to be still beloved by one whom I have always loved so much. I thank you a thousand times for that letter and for the book. I enclose you my own letter to dear Dr. Parsons. Read it before giving it to him. I could not help being amused at his having appended my name to a poem in some sort derogating from the fame of the only Frenchman who is worthy to be named after the present great monarch. I hope I have not done wrong in confessing my faith. Holding back an opinion is often as much a falsehood as the actual untruth itself, and so I think it would be here. Now we have the book, do you remember through whom you sent the notices? If you do, let me know. You will see by my letter to Dr. Parsons that —— dined here yesterday, under K——'s auspices. He invited himself for three days, — luckily I have Mr. Pearson to take care of him, — and still more luckily I told him frankly yesterday that three days would be too much, for I had nearly died last night of fatigue and exhaustion and their consequences. To-night I shall leave all to my charming friend. There is nobody like John Ruskin for refinement and eloquence. You will be glad to hear that he has asked me for a letter to dear Mr. Bennoch to help him in his schools of Art, — I mean with advice. This will, I hope, bring our dear friend out of the set he is in, and into that where I wish to see him, for John Ruskin must always fill the very highest position. God bless you all, dear friends!

Ever most affectionately yours,   M. R. M.

Love to all my friends.

You have given me a new motive for clinging to life by coming to England in April. Till this pull-back yesterday, I was better, although still afraid of being lifted into bed, and with small hope of getting alive through the winter. God bless you!

October 18, 1854.

MY VERY DEAR FRIEND: Another copy of dear Dr. Parsons's book has arrived, with a charming, most charming letter from him, and a copy of your edition of "Atherton." It is very nicely got up indeed, the portrait the best of any engraving that has been made of me, at least, any recent engraving. May I have a few copies of that engraving when you come to England? And if I should be gone, will you let poor K—— have one? The only thing I lament in the American "Atherton" is that a passage that I wrote to add to that edition has been omitted. It was to the purport of my having a peculiar pleasure in the prospect of that reprint, because few things could be so gratifying to me as to find my poor name conjoined with those of the great and liberal publishers, for one of whom I entertain so much respect and esteem, and for the other so true and so lively an affection. The little sentence was better turned much, but that was the meaning. No doubt it was in one of my many missing letters. I even think I sent it twice, — I should greatly have liked that little paragraph to be there. May I ask you to give the enclosed to dear Dr. Parsons? There are noble lines in his book, which gains much by being known. Dear John Ruskin was here when it arrived, and much pleased with it on turning over the leaves, and he is the most fastidious of men. I must give him the copy. His praise is indeed worth having. I am as when I wrote last. God bless you, beloved friend.

Ever yours, M. R. M.

December 23, 1854.

Your dear affectionate letter, dearest and kindest friend, would have given me unmingled pleasure had it conveyed a better account of your business prospects. Here, from what I can gather, and from the sure sign of all works of importance being postponed, the trade is in a similar state of depression, caused, they say, by this war, which but for the wretched imbecility of our ministers could never have assumed so alarming an appearance. Whether we shall recover from it, God only knows. My hope is in Louis Napoleon; but that America will rally seems certain enough. She has elbow-room, and, moreover, she is not unused to rapid transitions from high prosperity to temporary difficulty, and so back again. Moreover, dear friend, I have faith in you. . . . . God bless you, my dear friend! May he send to both of you health and happiness and length of days, and so much of this world's goods as is needful to prevent anxiety and insure comfort. I have known many rich people in my time, and the result has convinced me that with great wealth some deep black shadow is as sure to walk, as it is to follow the bright sunshine. So I never pray for more than the blessed enough for those whom I love best.

And very dearly do I love my American friends, — you best of all, — but all very dearly, as I have cause. Say this, please, to Dr. Parsons and Dr. Holmes (admiring their poems is a sort of touchstone of taste with me, and very, very many stand the test well), and dear Bayard Taylor, a man soundest and sweetest the nearer one gets to the kernel, and good, kind John Whittier, who has the fervor of the poet ingrafted into the tough old Quaker stock, and Mr. Stoddard, and Mrs. Lippincott, and Mrs. Sparks, and the Philadelphia Poetess, and dear Mr. and Mrs. W——, and your capital critics and orators. Remember me to all who think of me; but keep the choicest tenderness for yourself and your wife.

Do you know those books which pretend to have been written from one hundred to two hundred years ago, — "Mary Powell" (Milton's Courtship), "Cherry and Violet," and the rest? Their fault is that they are too much alike. The authoress (a Miss Manning) sent me some of them last winter, with some most interesting letters. Then for many months I ceased to hear from her, but a few weeks ago she sent me her new Christmas book, — "The Old Chelsea Bun House," — and told me she was dying of a frightful internal complaint. She suffers martyrdom, but bears it like a saint, and her letters are better than all the sermons in the world. May God grant me the same cheerful submission! I try for it and pray that it be granted, but I have none of the enthusiastic glow of devotion, so real and so beautiful in Miss Manning. My faith is humble and lowly, — not that I have the slightest doubt, — but I cannot get her rapturous assurance of acceptance. My friend, William Harness, got me to employ our kind little friend, Mr. ——, to procure for him Judge Edmonds's "Spiritualism." What an odious book it is! there is neither respect for the dead nor the living. Mrs. Browning believes it all; so does Bulwer, who is surrounded by mediums who summon his dead daughter. It is too frightful to talk about. Mr. May and Mr. Pearson both asked me to send it away, for fear of its seizing upon my nerves. I get weaker and weaker, and am become a mere skeleton. Ah, dear friend, come when you may, you will find only a grave at Swallowfield. Once again, God bless you and yours!

Ever yours,   M. R. M.

"BARRY CORNWALL"
AND SOME OF HIS FRIENDS.

"*All, all are gone, the old familiar faces.*"
CHARLES LAMB.

"*Old Acquaintance, shall the nights
You and I once talked together,
Be forgot like common things?*"

"*His thoughts half hid in golden dreams,
Which make thrice fair the songs and streams
Of Air and Earth.*"

"*Song should breathe of scents and flowers;
Song should like a river flow;
Song should bring back scenes and hours
That we loved, — ah, long ago!*"
BARRY CORNWALL.

VII.

"BARRY CORNWALL"
AND SOME OF HIS FRIENDS.

THERE is no portrait in my possession more satisfactory than the small one of Barry Cornwall, made purposely for me in England, from life. It is a thoroughly honest resemblance.

I first saw the poet five-and-twenty years ago, in his own house in London, at No. 13 Upper Harley Street, Cavendish Square. He was then declining into the vale of years, but his mind was still vigorous and young. My letter of introduction to him was written by Charles Sumner, and it proved sufficient for the beginning of a friendship which existed through a quarter of a century. My last interview with him occurred in 1869. I found him then quite feeble, but full of his old kindness and geniality. His speech was somewhat difficult to follow, for he had been slightly paralyzed not long before; but after listening to him for half an hour, it was easy to understand nearly every word he uttered. He spoke with warm feeling of Longfellow, who had been in London during that season, and had called to see his venerable friend before proceeding to the Continent. "Was n't it good of him," said the old man, in his tremulous voice, "to think of *me* before he had been in town twenty-four hours?" He also spoke of his dear companion, John Kenyon, at whose house we had often met in years past, and he called to mind a breakfast party there, saying with deep feeling, "And you and I are the only ones now alive of all who came together that happy morning!"

A few months ago,* at the great age of eighty-seven, Bryan Waller Procter, familiarly and honorably known in English literature for sixty years past as "Barry Cornwall," calmly "fell on sleep." The schoolmate of Lord Byron and Sir Robert Peel at Harrow, the friend and companion of Keats, Lamb, Shelley, Coleridge, Landor, Hunt, Talfourd, and Rogers, the man to whom Thackeray "affectionately dedicated" his "Vanity Fair," one of the kindest souls that ever gladdened earth, has now joined the great majority of England's hallowed sons of song. No poet ever left behind him more fragrant memories, and he will always be thought of as one whom his contemporaries loved and honored. No harsh word will ever be spoken by those who have known him of the author of "Marcian Colonna," "Mirandola," "The Broken Heart," and those charming lyrics which rank the poet among the first of his class. His songs will be sung so long as music wedded to beautiful poetry is a requisition anywhere. His verses have gone into the Book of Fame, and such pieces as "Touch us gently, Time," "Send down thy winged Angel, God," "King Death," "The Sea," and "Belshazzar is King," will long keep his memory green. Who that ever came habitually into his presence can forget the tones of his voice, the tenderness in his gray retrospective eyes, or the touch of his sympathetic hand laid on the shoulder of a friend! The elements were indeed so kindly mixed in him that no bitterness or rancor or jealousy had part or lot in his composition. No distinguished person was ever more ready to help forward the rising and as yet nameless literary man or woman who asked his counsel and warm-hearted suffrage.

* October, 1874.

His mere presence was sunshine to a new-comer into the world of letters and criticism, for he was always quick to encourage, and slow to disparage anybody. Indeed, to be *human* only entitled any one who came near him to receive the gracious bounty of his goodness and courtesy. He made it the happiness of his life never to miss, whenever opportunity occurred, the chance of conferring pleasure and gladness on those who needed kind words and substantial aid.

His equals in literature venerated and loved him. Dickens and Thackeray never ceased to regard him with the deepest feeling, and such men as Browning and Tennyson and Carlyle and Forster rallied about him to the last. He was the delight of all those interesting men and women who habitually gathered around Rogers's famous table in the olden time, for his manner had in it all the courtesy of genius, without any of that chance asperity so common in some literary circles. The shyness of a scholar brooded continually over him and made him reticent, but he was never silent from ill-humor. His was that true modesty so excellent in ability, and so rare in celebrities petted for a long time in society. His was also that happy alchemy of mind which transmutes disagreeable things into golden and ruby colors like the dawn. His temperament was the exact reverse of Fuseli's, who complained that "*nature* put him out." A beautiful spirit has indeed passed away, and the name of "Barry Cornwall," beloved in both hemispheres, is now sanctified afresh by the seal of eternity so recently stamped upon it.

It was indeed a privilege for a young American, on his first travels abroad, to have "Barry Cornwall" for his host in London. As I recall the memorable days and nights of that long-ago period, I wonder at the good fortune which brought me into such relations with him, and

I linger with profound gratitude over his many acts of unmerited kindness. One of the most intimate rambles I ever took with him was in 1851, when we started one morning from a book-shop in Piccadilly, where we met accidentally. I had been in London only a couple of days, and had not yet called upon him for lack of time. Several years had elapsed since we had met, but he began to talk as if we had parted only a few hours before. At first I thought his mind was impaired by age, and that he had forgotten how long it was since we had spoken together. I imagined it possible that he mistook me for some one else; but very soon I found that his memory was not at fault, for in a few minutes he began to question me about old friends in America, and to ask for information concerning the probable sea-sick horrors of an Atlantic voyage. "I suppose," said he, "knowing your infirmity, you found it hard work to stand on your immaterial legs, as Hood used to call Lamb's quivering limbs." Sauntering out into the street, he went on in a quaintly humorous way to imagine what a rough voyage must be to a real sufferer, and thus walking gayly along, we came into Leadenhall Street. There he pointed out the office where his old friend and fellow-magazinist, "Elia," spent so many years of hard work from ten until four o'clock of every day. Being in a mood for reminiscence, he described the Wednesday evenings he used to spend with "Charles and Mary" and their friends around the old "mahogany-tree" in Russell Street. I remember he tried to give me an idea of how Lamb looked and dressed, and how he stood bending forward to welcome his guests as they arrived in his humble lodgings. Procter thought nothing unimportant that might serve in any way to illustrate character, and so he seemed to wish that I might get an exact idea of the charming person both of us prized so ardently and he had known so intimately.

CHARLES AND MARY LAMB

Speaking of Lamb's habits, he said he had never known his friend to drink immoderately except upon one occasion, and he observed that "Elia," like Dickens, was a small and delicate eater. With faltering voice he told me of Lamb's "givings away" to needy, impoverished friends whose necessities were yet greater than his own. His secret charities were constant and unfailing, and no one ever suffered hunger when he was by. He could not endure to see a fellow-creature in want if he had the means to feed him. Thinking, from a depression of spirits which Procter in his young manhood was once laboring under, that perhaps he was in want of money, Lamb looked him earnestly in the face as they were walking one day in the country together, and blurted out, in his stammering way, "My dear boy, I have a hundred-pound note in my desk that I really don't know what to do with: oblige me by taking it and getting the confounded thing out of my keeping." "I was in no need of money," said Procter, "and I declined the gift; but it was hard work to make Lamb believe that I was not in an impecunious condition."

Speaking of Lamb's sister Mary, Procter quoted Hazlitt's saying that "Mary Lamb was the most rational and wisest woman he had ever been acquainted with." As we went along some of the more retired streets in the old city, we had also, I remember, much gossip about Coleridge and his manner of reciting his poetry, especially when "Elia" happened to be among the listeners, for the philosopher put a high estimate upon Lamb's critical judgment. The author of "The Ancient Mariner" always had an excuse for any bad habit to which he was himself addicted, and he told Procter one day that perhaps snuff was the final cause of the human nose. In connection with Coleridge we had much reminiscence of such interesting persons as the Novellos, Martin Burney, Talfourd, and Crabb Robinson, and a store of anecdotes in which Haydon, Manning, Dyer, and Godwin figured at full length. In course of conversation I asked my companion if he thought Lamb had ever been really in love, and he told me interesting things of Hester Savory, a young Quaker girl of Pentonville, who inspired the poem embalming the name of Hester forever, and of Fanny Kelly, the actress with "the divine plain face," who will always live in one of "Elia's" most exquisite essays. "He had a *reverence* for the sex," said Procter, "and there were tender spots in his heart that time could never entirely cover up or conceal."

During our walk we stepped into Christ's Hospital, and turned to the page on its record book where together we read this entry: "October 9, 1782, Charles Lamb, aged seven years, son of John Lamb, scrivener, and Elizabeth his wife."

It was a lucky morning when I dropped in to bid "good morrow" to the poet as I was passing his house one day, for it was then he took from among his treasures and gave to me an autograph letter addressed to himself by Charles Lamb in 1829. I found the dear old man alone and in his library, sitting at his books, with the windows wide open, letting in the spring odors. Quoting, as I entered, some lines from Wordsworth embalming May mornings, he began to talk of the older poets who had worshipped nature with the ardor of lovers, and his eyes lighted up with pleasure when I happened to remember some almost forgotten stanza from England's "Helicon." It was an easy transition from the old bards to "Elia," and he soon went on in his fine enthusiastic way to relate several anecdotes of his eccentric friend. As I rose to take leave he said, —

"Have I ever given you one of Lamb's letters to carry home to America?"

"No," I replied, "and you must not part with the least scrap of a note in 'Elia's' handwriting. Such things are too precious to be risked on a sea-voyage to another hemisphere."

"America ought to share with England in these things," he rejoined; and leading me up to a sort of cabinet in the library, he unlocked a drawer and got out a package of time-stained papers. "Ah," said he, as he turned over the golden leaves, "here is something you will like to handle." I unfolded the sheet, and lo! it was in Keats's handwriting, the sonnet on first looking into Chapman's Homer. "Keats gave it to me," said Procter, "many, many years ago," and then he proceeded to read, in tones tremulous with delight, these undying lines:—

> "Much have I travelled in the realms of gold,
> And many goodly states and kingdoms seen;
> Round many Western islands have I been
> Which bards in fealty to Apollo hold.
> Oft of one wide expanse had I been told
> That deep-browed Homer ruled as his demesne;
> Yet did I never breathe its pure serene
> Till I heard Chapman speak out loud and bold:
> Then felt I like some watcher of the skies
> When a new planet swims into his ken,
> Or like stout Cortez when with eagle eyes
> He stared at the Pacific — and all his men
> Looked at each other with a wild surmise —
> Silent, upon a peak in Darien."

I sat gazing at the man who had looked on Keats in the flush of his young genius, and wondered at my good fortune. As the living poet folded up again the faded manuscript of the illustrious dead one, and laid it reverently in its place, I felt grateful for the honor thus vouchsafed to a wandering stranger in a foreign land, and wished that other and worthier votaries of English letters might have been present to share with me the boon of such an interview. Presently my hospitable friend, still rummaging among the past, drew out a letter, which was the one, he said, he had been looking after. "Cram it into your pocket," he cried, "for I hear —— coming down stairs, and perhaps she won't let you carry it off!" The letter is addressed to B. W. Procter, Esq., 10 Lincoln's Inn, New Square. I give the entire epistle here just as it stands in the original which Procter handed me that memorable May morning. He told me that the law question raised in this epistle was a sheer fabrication of Lamb's, gotten up by him to puzzle his young correspondent, the conveyancer. The coolness referred to between himself and Robinson and Talfourd, Procter said, was also a fiction invented by Lamb to carry out his legal mystification.

"*Jan'y* 19, 1829.

"MY DEAR PROCTER, — I am ashamed to have not taken the drift of your pleasant letter, which I find to have been pure invention. But jokes are not suspected in Bœotian Enfield. We are plain people, and our talk is of corn, and cattle, and Waltham markets. Besides I was a little out of sorts when I received it. The fact is, I am involved in a case which has fretted me to death, and I have no reliance except on you to extricate me. I am sure you will give me your best legal advice, having no professional friend besides but Robinson and Talfourd, with neither of whom at present I am on the best terms. My brother's widow left a will, made during the lifetime of my brother, in which I am named sole Executor, by which she bequeaths forty acres of arable property, which it seems she held under Covert Baron, unknown to my Brother, to the heirs of the body of Elizabeth Dowden, her married daughter by her first husband, in fee simple, recoverable by fine — invested property, mind, for there is the difficulty — subject to leet and quit rent — in short, worded in the most guarded terms, to shut out the property from Isaac Dowden the husband. Intelligence has just come of the death of this person in India, where he made a will, entailing this property (which seem'd entangled enough already) to the heirs of his body, that should not be born of his wife; for it seems by the Law in India natural children can recover. They have put the cause into Exchequer Process here, removed by Certiorari from the Native Courts, and the question is whether I should as Executor, try

B. W. Procter

the cause here, or again re-remove to the Supreme Sessions at Bangalore, which I understand I can, or plead a hearing before the Privy Council here. As it involves all the little property of Elizabeth Dowden, I am anxious to take the fittest steps, and what may be the least expensive. For God's sake assist me, for the case is so embarrassed that it deprives me of sleep and appetite. M. Burney thinks there is a Case like it in Chapt. 170 Sect. 5 in Fearn's *Contingent Remainders*. Pray read it over with him dispassionately, and let me have the result. The complexity lies in the questionable power of the husband to alienate in usum enfeoffments whereof he was only collaterally seized, etc."

[On the leaf at this place there are some words in another hand. — F.]

"The above is some of M. Burney's memoranda, which he has left here, and you may cut out and give him. I had another favour to beg, which is the beggarliest of beggings. A few lines of verse for a young friend's Album (six will be enough). M. Burney will tell you who she is I want 'em for. A girl of gold. Six lines — make 'em eight — signed Barry C——. They need not be very good, as I chiefly want 'em as a foil to mine. But I shall be seriously obliged by any refuse scrap. We are in the last ages of the world, when St. Paul prophesied that women should be 'headstrong, lovers of their own wills, having Albums.' I fled hither to escape the Albumean persecution, and had not been in my new house 24 hours, when the Daughter of the next house came in with a friend's Album to beg a contribution, and the following day intimated she had one of her own. Two more have sprung up since. If I take the wings of the morning and fly unto the uttermost parts of the earth, there will Albums be. New Holland has Albums. But the age is to be complied with. M. B. will tell you the sort of girl I request the ten lines for. Somewhat of a pensive cast what you admire. The lines may come before the Law question, as that cannot be determined before Hilary Term, and I wish your deliberate judgment on that. The other may be flimsy and superficial. And if you have not burnt your returned letter pray re-send it me as a monumental token of my stupidity. 'T was a little unthinking of you to touch upon a sore subject. Why, by dabbling in those accursed Annuals I have become a by-word of infamy all over the kingdom. I have sicken'd decent women for asking me to write in Albums. There be 'dark jests' abroad, Master Cornwall, and some riddles may live to be clear'd up. And 't is n't every saddle is put on the right steed. And forgeries and false Gospels are not peculiar to the age following the Apostles. And some tubs don't stand on their right bottom. Which is all I wish to say in these ticklish Times — and so your servant,

"CHS. LAMB."

At the age of seventy-seven Procter was invited to print his recollections of Charles Lamb, and his volume was welcomed in both hemispheres as a pleasant addition to "Eliana." During the last eighteen years of Lamb's life Procter knew him most intimately, and his chronicles of visits to the little gamboge-colored house in Enfield are charming pencillings of memory. When Lamb and his sister, tired of housekeeping, went into lodging and boarding with T—— W——, their sometime next-door neighbor, — who, Lamb said, had one joke and forty pounds a year, upon which he retired in a green old age, — Procter still kept up his friendly visits to his old associate. And after the brother and sister moved to their last earthly retreat in Edmonton, where Charles died in 1834, Procter still paid them regular visits of love and kindness. And after Charles's death, when Mary went to live at a house in St. John's Wood, her unfailing friend kept up his cheering calls there till she set out "for that unknown and silent shore," on the 20th of May, in 1847.

Procter's conversation was full of endless delight to his friends. His "asides" were sometimes full of exquisite touches. I remember one evening when Carlyle was present and rattling on against American institutions, half comic and half serious, Procter, who sat near me, kept up a constant underbreath of commentary, taking exactly the other side. Carlyle was full of horse-play over the character of George Washington, whom he never vouchsafed to call anything but George. He said our first President was a good surveyor, and knew how to measure timber, and that was about all. Procter kept whispering to me all the while Carlyle was discoursing, and going over Washington's fine traits to the disparagement of everything Carlyle was laying down as gospel. I was listening to both these distinguished men at the same time, and it was one of the most curious experiences in conversation I ever happened to enjoy.

I was once present when a loud-voiced person of quality, ignorant and supercilious, was inveighing against the want of taste commonly exhibited by artists when they chose their wives, saying they almost always selected inferior women. Procter, sitting next to me, put his hand on my shoulder, and, with a look expressive of ludicrous pity and contempt for the idiotic speaker, whispered, "And yet Vandyck married the daughter of Earl Gower, poor fellow!" The mock solemnity of Procter's manner was irresistible. It had a wink in it that really embodied the genius of fun and sarcasm.

Talking of the ocean with him one day, he revealed this curious fact: although he is the author of one of the most stirring and popular sea-songs in the language, —

"The sea, the sea, the open sea!" —

he said he had rarely been upon the tossing element, having a great fear of being made ill by it. I think he told me he had never dared to cross the Channel even, and so had never seen Paris. He said, like many others, he delighted to gaze upon the waters from a safe place on land, but had a horror of living on it even for a few hours. I recalled to his recollection his own lines, —

"I'm on the sea! I'm on the sea!
I am where I would ever be,"—

and he shook his head, and laughingly declared I must have misquoted his words, or that Dibdin had written the piece and put "Barry Cornwall's" signature to it. We had, I remember, a great deal of fun over the poetical lies, as he called them, which bards in all ages had perpetrated in their verse, and he told me some stories of English poets, over which we made merry as we sat together in pleasant Cavendish Square that summer evening.

His world-renowned song of "The Sea" he afterward gave me in his own handwriting, and it is still among my autographic treasures.

It was Procter who first in my hearing, twenty-five years ago, put such an estimate on the poetry of Robert Browning that I could not delay any longer to make acquaintance with his writings. I remember to have been startled at hearing the man who in his day had known so many poets declare that Browning was the peer of any one who had written in this century, and that, on the whole, his genius had not been excelled in his (Procter's) time. "Mind what I say," insisted Procter; "Browning will make an enduring name, and add another supremely great poet to England."

Procter could sometimes be prompted into describing that brilliant set of men and women who were in the habit of congregating at Lady Blessington's, and I well recollect his description of young N. P. Willis as he first appeared in her *salon*. "The young traveller came among us," said Procter, "enthusiastic, handsome, and good-natured, and took his place beside D'Orsay, Bulwer, Disraeli, and the other dandies as naturally as if he had been for years a London man about town. He was full of fresh talk concerning his own country, and we all admired his cleverness in compassing so aptly all the little newnesses of the situation. He was ready on all occasions, a little too ready, some of the *habitués* of the *salon* thought, and they could not understand his cool and quiet-at-home manners. He became a favorite at first trial, and laid himself out determined to please and be pleased. His ever kind and thoughtful attention to others won him troops of friends, and I never can forget his unwearied goodness to a sick child of mine, with whom, night after night, he would sit by the bedside and watch, thus relieving the worn-out family in a way that was very tender and self-sacrificing."

Of Lady Blessington's tact, kindness, and remarkable beauty Procter always spoke with ardor, and abated nothing from the popular idea of that fascinating person. He thought she had done more in her time to institute good feeling and social intercourse among men of letters than any other lady in England, and he gave her eminent credit for bringing forward the rising talent of the metropolis without waiting to be prompted by a public verdict. As the poet described her to me as she moved through her exquisite apartments, surrounded by all the luxuries that naturally connect themselves with one of her commanding position in literature and art, her radiant and exceptional beauty of person, her frank and cordial manners, the wit, wisdom, and grace of her speech, I thought of the fair Giovanna of Naples as painted in "Bianca Visconti":—

> "Gods! what a light enveloped her!
> . . . . Her beauty
> Was of that order that the universe
> Seemed governed by her motion. . . . .
> The pomp, the music, the bright sun in heaven,
> Seemed glorious by her leave."

One of the most agreeable men in London literary society during Procter's time was the companionable and ever kind-hearted John Kenyon. He was a man compacted of all the best qualities of an incomparable good-nature. His friends used to call him "the apostle of cheerfulness." He could not endure a long face under his roof, and declined to see the dark side of anything. He wrote verses almost like a poet, but no one surpassed him in genuine admiration for whatever was excellent in others. No happiness was so great to him as the conferring of happiness on others, and I am glad to write myself his eternal debtor for much of my enjoyment in England, for he introduced me to many lifelong friendships, and he inaugurated for me much of that felicity which springs from intercourse with men and women whose books are the solace of our lifelong existence.

Kenyon was Mrs. Browning's cousin, and in 1856 she dedicates "Aurora Leigh" to him in these affectionate terms: —

> "The words 'cousin' and 'friend' are constantly recurring in this poem, the last pages of which have been finished under the hospitality of your roof, my own dearest cousin and friend; — cousin and friend, in a sense of less equality and greater disinterestedness than Romney's. . . . . I venture to leave in your hands this book, the most mature of my works, and the one into which my highest convictions upon Life and Art have entered; that as, through my various efforts in literature and steps in life, you have believed in me, borne with me, and been generous to me, far beyond the common uses of mere relationship or sympathy of mind, so you may kindly accept, in sight of the public, this poor sign of esteem, gratitude, and affection from your unforgetting
>
> "E. B. B."

How often have I seen Kenyon and Procter chirping together over an old quarto that had floated down from an early century, or rejoicing together over a well-worn letter in a family portfolio of treasures! They were a pair of veteran brothers, and there was never a flaw in their long and loving intercourse. In a letter which Procter wrote to me in March, 1857, he thus refers to his old friend, then lately dead: "Everybody seems to be dying hereabouts, — one of my colleagues, one of my relations, one of my servants, three of them in one week, the last one in my own house. And now I seem fit for little else myself. My dear old friend Kenyon is dead. There never was a man, take him for all in all, with more amiable, attractive qualities. A kind friend, a good master,

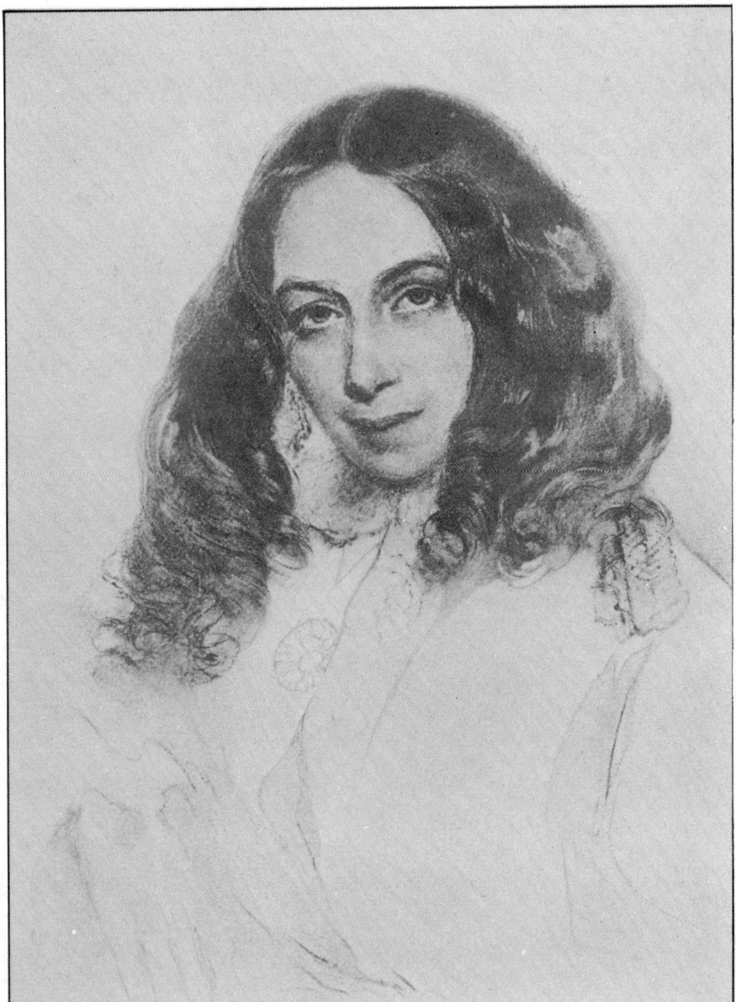

Elizabeth Barrett Browning

a generous and judicious dispenser of his wealth, honorable, sweet-tempered, and serene, and genial as a summer's day. It is true that he has left me a solid mark of his friendship. I did not expect anything; but if to like a man sincerely deserved such a mark of his regard, I deserved it. I doubt if he has left one person who really liked him more than I did. Yes, one — I think one — a woman. .... I get old and weak and stupid. That pleasant journey to Niagara, that dip into your Indian summer, all such thoughts are over. I shall never see Italy; I shall never see Paris. My future is before me, — a very limited landscape, with scarcely one old friend left in it. I see a smallish room, with a bow-window looking south, a bookcase full of books, three or four drawings, and a library chair and table (once the property of my old friend Kenyon — I am writing on the table now), and you have the greater part of the vision before you. Is this the end of all things? I believe it is pretty much like most scenes in the fifth act, when the green (or black) curtain is about to drop and tell you that the play of *Hamlet* or of John Smith is over. But wait a little. There will be another piece, in which John Smith the younger will figure, and quite eclipse his old, stupid, wrinkled, useless, time-slaughtered parent. The king is dead, — long live the king!"

Kenyon was very fond of Americans, Professor Ticknor and Mr. George S. Hillard being especially dear to him. I remember hearing him say one day that the "best prepared" young foreigner he had ever met, who had come to see Europe, was Mr. Hillard. One day at his dinner-table, in the presence of Mrs. Jameson, Mr. and Mrs. Carlyle, Walter Savage Landor, Mr. and Mrs. Robert Browning, and the Procters, I heard him declare that one of the best talkers on any subject that might be started at the social board was the author of "Six Months in Italy."

It was at a breakfast in Kenyon's house that I first met Walter Savage Landor, whose writings are full of verbal legacies to posterity. As I entered the room with Procter, Landor was in the midst of an eloquent harangue on the high art of portraiture. Procter had been lately sitting to a daguerreotypist for a picture, and Mrs. Jameson, who was very fond of the poet, had arranged the camera for that occasion. Landor was holding the picture in his hand, declaring that it had never been surpassed as a specimen of that particular art. The grand-looking author of "Pericles and Aspasia" was standing in the middle of the room when we entered, and his voice sounded like an explosion of first-class artillery. Seeing Procter enter, he immediately began to address him compliments in high-sounding Latin. Poor modest Procter pretended to stop his ears that he might not listen to Landor's eulogistic phrases. Kenyon came to the rescue by declaring the breakfast had been waiting half an hour. When we arrived at the table Landor asked Procter to join him on an expedition into Spain which he was then contemplating. "No," said Procter, "for I cannot even 'walk Spanish,' and having never crossed the Channel, I do not intend to begin now."

"Never crossed the Channel!" roared Landor,—"never saw Napoleon Bonaparte!" He then began to tell us how the young Corsican looked when he first saw him, saying that he had the olive complexion and roundness of face of a Greek girl; that the consul's voice was deep and melodious, but untruthful in tone. While we were eating breakfast he went on to describe his Italian travels in early youth, telling us that he once saw Shelley and Byron meet in the doorway of a hotel in Pisa. Landor had lived in Italy many years, for he detested the climate of his native country, and used to say "one could only live comfortably in England who was rich enough to have a solar system of his own."

The Prince of Carpi said of Erasmus he was so thin-skinned that a fly would draw blood from him. The author of the "Imaginary Conversations" had the same infirmity. A very little thing would disturb him for hours, and his friends were never sure of his equanimity. I was present once when a blundering friend trod unwittingly on his favorite prejudice, and Landor went off instanter like a blaspheming torpedo. There were three things in the world which received no quarter at his hands, and when in the slightest degree he scented *hypocrisy*, *pharisaism*, or *tyranny*, straightway he became furious, and laid about him like a mad giant.

Procter told me that when Landor got into a passion, his rage was sometimes uncontrollable. The fiery spirit knew his weakness, but his anger quite overmastered him in spite of himself. "Keep your temper, Landor," somebody said to him one day when he was raging. "That is just what I don't wish to keep," he cried; "I wish to be rid of such an infamous, ungovernable thing. I don't wish to *keep* my temper." Whoever wishes to get a good look at Landor will not seek for it alone in John Forster's interesting life of the old man, admirable as it is, but will turn to Dickens's "Bleak House" for side glances at the great author. In that vivid story Dickens has made his friend Landor sit for the portrait of Lawrence Boythorn. The very laugh that made the whole house vibrate, the roundness and fulness of voice, the fury of superlatives, are all given in Dickens's best manner, and no one who has ever seen Landor for half an hour could possibly mistake Boythorn for anybody else. Talking the matter over once with Dickens, he said, "Landor always took that presentation of himself in hearty good-humor, and seemed rather proud of the picture." This is Dickens's portrait: "He was not only a very handsome old gentleman, upright and stalwart, with a massive gray head, a fine composure of face when silent, a figure that might have become corpulent but for his being so continually in earnest that he gave it no rest, and a chin that might have subsided into a double chin but for the vehement emphasis in which it was constantly required to assist; but he was such a true gentleman in his manner, so chivalrously polite, his face was lighted by a smile of so much sweetness and tenderness, and it seemed so plain that he had nothing to hide, that really I could not help looking at him with equal pleasure, whether he smilingly conversed with Ada and me, or was led by Mr. Jarndyce into some great volley of superlatives, or threw up his head like a bloodhound, and gave out that tremendous Ha! ha! ha!"

Landor's energetic gravity, when he was proposing some colossal impossibility, the observant novelist would naturally seize on, for Dickens was always on the lookout for exaggerations in human language and conduct. It was at Procter's table I heard Dickens describe a scene which transpired after the publication of the "Old Curiosity Shop." It seems that the first idea of Little Nell occurred to Dickens when he was on a birthday visit to Landor, then living in Bath. The old man was residing in lodgings in St. James Square, in that city, and ever after connected Little Nell with that particular spot. No character in prose fiction was a greater favorite with Landor, and one day, years after the story was published, he burst out with a tremendous emphasis, and declared the one mistake of his life was that he had not purchased the house in Bath, and then and there burned it to the ground, so that no meaner association should ever desecrate the birthplace of Little Nell!

It was Procter's old schoolmaster (Dr. Drury, headmaster of Harrow) who was the means of introducing Edmund Kean, the great actor, on the London stage.

Procter delighted to recall the many theatrical triumphs of the eccentric tragedian, and the memoir which he printed of Kean will always be read with interest. I heard the poet one evening describe the player most graphically as he appeared in Sir Giles Overreach in 1816 at Drury Lane, when he produced such an effect on Lord Byron, who sat that night in a stage-box with Tom Moore. His lordship was so overcome by Kean's magnificent acting that he fell forward in a convulsive fit, and it was some time before he regained his wonted composure. Douglas Jerrold said that Kean's appearance in Shakespeare's Jew was like a chapter out of Genesis, and all who have seen the incomparable actor speak of his tiger-like power and infinite grace as unrivalled.

At Procter's house the best of England's celebrated men and women assembled, and it was a kind of enchantment to converse with the ladies one met there. It was indeed a privilege to be received by the hostess herself, for Mrs. Procter was not only sure to be the most brilliant person among her guests, but she practised habitually that exquisite courtesy toward all which renders even a stranger, unwonted to London drawing-rooms, free from awkwardness and that constraint which are almost inseparable from a first appearance.

Among the persons I have seen at that house of urbanity in London I distinctly recall old Mrs. Montague, the mother of Mrs. Procter. She had met Robert Burns in Edinburgh when he first came up to that city to bring out his volume of poems. "I have seen many a handsome man in my time," said the old lady one day to us at dinner, "but never such a pair of eyes as young Robbie Burns kept flashing from under his beautiful brow." Mrs. Montague was much interested in Charles Sumner, and predicted for him all the eminence of his after-position. With a certain other American visitor she had no patience, and spoke of him to me as a "note of interrogation, too curious to be comfortable."

I distinctly recall Adelaide Procter as I first saw her on one of my early visits to her father's house. She was a shy, bright girl, and the poet drew my attention to her as she sat reading in a corner of the library. Looking at the young maiden, intent on her book, I remembered that exquisite sonnet in her father's volume, bearing date November, 1825, addressed to the infant just a month after her birth: —

> "Child of my heart! My sweet, beloved First-born!
> Thou dove who tidings bring'st of calmer hours!
> Thou rainbow who dost shine when all the showers
> Are past or passing! Rose which hath no thorn,
> No spot, no blemish, — pure and unforlorn,
> Untouched, untainted! O my Flower of flowers!
> More welcome than to bees are summer bowers,
> To stranded seamen life-assuring morn!
> Welcome, a thousand welcomes! Care, who clings
> Round all, seems loosening now its serpent fold:
> New hope springs upward; and the bright world seems
> Cast back into a youth of endless springs!
> Sweet mother, is it so? or grow I old,
> Bewildered in divine Elysian dreams?"

I whispered in the poet's ear my admiration of the sonnet and the beautiful subject of it as we sat looking at her absorbed in the volume on her knees. Procter, in response, murmured some words expressive of his joy at having such a gift from God to gladden his affectionate heart, and he told me afterward what a comfort Adelaide had always been to his household. He described to me a visit Wordsworth made to his house one day, and how gentle the old man's aspect was when he looked at the children. "He took the hand of my dear Adelaide in his," said Procter, "and spoke some words to her, the recollection of which helped, perhaps, with other things, to incline her to poetry." When a little child "the golden-tressed Adelaide," as the poet calls her in one of his songs, must often have heard her father read aloud his own poems as they came fresh from the fount of song, and the impression no doubt wrought upon her young imagination a spell she could not resist. On a sensitive mind like hers such a piece as the "Petition to Time" could not fail of producing its full effect, and no girl of her temperament would be unmoved by the music of words like these: —

>"Touch us gently, Time!
> Let us glide adown thy stream
>Gently, as we sometimes glide
> Through a quiet dream.
>Humble voyagers are we,
>Husband, wife, and children three.
>(One is lost, an angel, fled
>To the azure overhead.)

>"Touch us gently, Time!
> We 've not proud nor soaring wings:
>*Our* ambition, *our* content,
> Lie in simple things.
>Humble voyagers are we,
>O'er Life's dim unsounded sea,
>Seeking only some calm clime:
>Touch us *gently*, gentle Time!"

Adelaide Procter's name will always be sweet in the annals of English poetry. Her place was assured from the time when she made her modest advent, in 1853, in the columns of Dickens's "Household Words," and everything she wrote from that period onward until she died gave evidence of striking and peculiar talent. I have heard Dickens describe how she first began to proffer contributions to his columns over a feigned name, that of Miss Mary Berwick; how he came to think that his unknown correspondent must be a governess; how, as time went on, he learned to value his new contributor for her self-reliance and punctuality, — qualities upon which

Dickens always placed a high value; how at last, going to dine one day with his old friends the Procters, he launched enthusiastically out in praise of Mary Berwick (the writer herself, Adelaide Procter, sitting at the table); and how the delighted mother, being in the secret, revealed, with tears of joy, the real name of the young aspirant. Although Dickens has told the whole story most feelingly in an introduction to Miss Procter's "Legends and Lyrics," issued after her death, to hear it from his own lips and sympathetic heart, as I have done, was, as may be imagined, something better even than reading his pathetic words on the printed page.

One of the most interesting ladies in London literary society in the period of which I am writing was Mrs. Jameson, the dear and honored friend of Procter and his family. During many years of her later life she stood in the relation of consoler to her sex in England. Women in mental anguish needing consolation and counsel fled to her as to a convent for protection and guidance. Her published writings established such a claim upon her sympathy in the hearts of her readers that much of her time for twenty years before she died was spent in helping others, by correspondence and personal contact, to submit to the sorrows God had cast upon them. She believed, with Milton, that it is miserable enough to be blind, but still more miserable not to be able to bear blindness. Her own earlier life had been darkened by griefs, and she knew from a deep experience what it was to enter the cloud and stand waiting and hoping in the shadows. In her instructive and delightful society I spent many an hour twenty years ago in the houses of Procter and Rogers and Kenyon. Procter, knowing my admiration of the Kemble family, frequently led the conversation up to that regal line which included so many men and women of genius. Mrs. Jameson was never

Anna Jameson

weary of being questioned as to the legitimate supremacy of Mrs. Siddons and her nieces, Fanny and Adelaide Kemble. While Rogers talked of Garrick, and Procter of Kean, she had no enthusiasms that were not bounded in by those fine spirits whom she had watched and worshipped from her earliest years.

Now and then in the garden of life we get that special bite out of the sunny side of a peach. One of my own memorable experiences in that way came in this wise. I had heard, long before I went abroad, so much of the singing of the youngest child of the "Olympian dynasty," Adelaide Kemble, so much of a brief career crowded with triumphs on the lyric stage, that I longed, if it might be possible, to listen to the "true daughter of her race." The rest of her family for years had been, as it were, "nourished on Shakespeare," and achieved greatness in that high walk of genius; but now came one who could interpret Mozart, Bellini, and Mercadante, one who could equal what Pasta and Malibran and Persiani and Grisi had taught the world to understand and worship. "Ah!" said a friend, "if you could only hear *her* sing 'Casta Diva'!" "Yes," said another, "and 'Auld Robin Gray'!" No wonder, I thought, at the universal enthusiasm for a vocal and lyrical artist who can alternate with equal power from "Casta Diva" to "Auld Robin Gray." I *must* hear her! She had left the stage, after a brief glory upon it, but as Madame Sartoris she sometimes sang at home to her guests.

"We are invited to hear some music, this evening," said Procter to me one day, "and you must go with us." I went, and our hostess was the once magnificent *prima donna!* At intervals throughout the evening, with a voice

"That crowds and hurries and precipitates
With thick fast warble its delicious notes,"

she poured out her full soul in melody. We all know her now as the author of that exquisite "Week in a French Country-House," and her fascinating book somehow always mingles itself in my memory with the enchanted evening when I heard her sing. As she sat at the piano in all her majestic beauty, I imagined her a sort of later St. Cecilia, and could have wished for another Raphael to paint her worthily. Henry Chorley, who was present on that memorable evening, seemed to be in a kind of nervous rapture at hearing again the supreme and willing singer. Procter moved away into a dim corner of the room, and held his tremulous hand over his eyes. The old poet's sensitive spirit seemed at times to be going out on the breath of the glorious artist who was thrilling us all with her power. Mrs. Jameson bent forward to watch every motion of her idol, looking applause at every noble passage. Another lady, whom I did not know, was tremulous with excitement, and I could well imagine what might have taken place when the "impassioned chantress" sang and enacted Semiramide as I have heard it described. Every one present was inspired by her fine mien, as well as by her transcendent voice. Mozart, Rossini, Bellini, Cherubini, — how she flung herself that night, with all her gifts, into their highest compositions! As she rose and was walking away from the piano, after singing an air from the "Medea" with a pathos that no musically uneducated pen like mine can or ought to attempt a description of, some one intercepted her and whispered a request. Again she turned, and walked toward the instrument like a queen among her admiring court. A flash of lightning, followed by a peal of thunder that jarred the house, stopped her for a moment on her way to the piano. A sudden summer tempest was gathering, and crash after crash made it impossible for her to begin. As she stood waiting for the "elemental fury" to subside, her attitude was quite worthy of the niece of Mrs. Siddons. When the thunder had grown less frequent, she threw back her beautiful classic head and touched the keys. The air she had been called upon to sing was so wild and weird, a dead silence fell upon the room, and an influence as of terror pervaded the whole assembly. It was a song by Dessauer, which he had composed for her voice, the words by Tennyson. No one who was present that evening can forget how she broke the silence with

"We were two daughters of one race,"

or how she uttered the words,

"The wind is roaring in turret and tree."

It was like a scene in a great tragedy, and then I fully understood the worship she had won as belonging only to those consummate artists who have arisen to dignify and ennoble the lyric stage. As we left the house Procter said, "You are in great luck to-night. I never heard her sing more divinely."

The Poet frequently spoke to me of the old days when he was contributing to the "London Magazine," which fifty years ago was deservedly so popular in Great Britain. All the "best talent" (to use a modern advertisement phrase) wrote for it. Carlyle sent his papers on Schiller to be printed in it; De Quincey's "Confessions of an English Opium-Eater" appeared in its pages; and the essays of "Elia" came out first in that potent periodical; Landor, Keats, and John Bowring contributed to it; and to have printed a prose or poetical article in the "London" entitled a man to be asked to dine out anywhere in society in those days. In 1821 the proprietors began to give dinners in Waterloo Place once a month to their contributors, who, after the cloth was removed, were expected to talk over the prospects of the magazine, and lay out the contents for next month. Procter described to me the authors of his generation as they sat round the old "mahogany-tree" of that period. "Very social and expansive hours they passed in that pleasant room half a century ago. Thither came stalwart Allan Cunningham, with his Scotch face shining with good-nature; Charles Lamb, 'a Diogenes with the heart of a St. John'; Hamilton Reynolds, whose good temper and vivacity were like condiments at a feast; John Clare, the peasant-poet, simple as a daisy; Tom Hood, young, silent, and grave, but who nevertheless now and then shot out a pun that damaged the shaking sides of the whole company; De Quincey, self-involved and courteous, rolling out his periods with a pomp and splendor suited, perhaps, to a high Roman festival; and with these sons of fame gathered certain nameless folk whose contributions to the great 'London' are now under the protection of that tremendous power which men call *Oblivion*."

It was a vivid pleasure to hear Procter describe Edward Irving, the eccentric preacher, who made such a deep impression on the spirit of his time. He is now dislimned into space, but he was, according to all his thoughtful contemporaries, a "son of thunder," a "giant force of activity." Procter fully indorsed all that Carlyle has so nobly written of the eloquent man who, dying at forty-two, has stamped his strong personal vitality on the age in which he lived.

Procter, in his younger days, was evidently much impressed by that clever rascal who, under the name of "Janus Weathercock," scintillated at intervals in the old "London Magazine." Wainwright — for that was his real name — was so brilliant, he made friends for a time among many of the first-class contributors to that once famous periodical; but the Ten Commandments ruined all his prospects for life. A murderer, a forger, a thief,

— in short, a sinner in general, — he came to grief rather early in his wicked career, and suffered penalties of the law accordingly, but never to the full extent of his remarkable deserts. I have heard Procter describe his personal appearance as he came sparkling into the room, clad in undress military costume. His smart conversation deceived those about him into the belief that he had been an officer in the dragoons, that he had spent a large fortune, and now condescended to take a part in periodical literature with the culture of a gentleman and the grace of an amateur. How this vapid charlatan in a braided surtout and prismatic necktie could so long veil his real character from, and retain the regard of, such men as Procter and Talfourd and Coleridge is amazing. Lamb calls him the "kind and light-hearted Janus," and thought he liked him. The contributors often spoke of his guileless nature at the festal monthly board of the magazine, and no one dreamed that this gay and mock-smiling London cavalier was about to begin a career so foul and monstrous that the annals of crime for centuries have no blacker pages inscribed on them. To secure the means of luxurious living without labor, and to pamper his dandy tastes, this lounging, lazy *littérateur* resolved to become a murderer on a large scale, and accompany his cruel poisonings with forgeries whenever they were most convenient. His custom for years was to effect policies of insurance on the lives of his relations, and then at the proper time administer strychnine to his victims. The heart sickens at the recital of his brutal crimes. On the life of a beautiful young girl named Abercrombie this fiendish wretch effected an insurance at various offices for £18,000 before he sent her to her account with the rest of his poisoned too-confiding relatives. So many heavily insured ladies dying in violent convulsions drew attention to the gentleman who always called to collect the money. But why this consumate crimminal was not brought to justice and hung, my Lord Abinger never satisfactorily divulged. At last this polished Sybarite, who boasted that he always drank the richest Montepulciano, who could not sit long in a room that was not garlanded with flowers, who said he felt lonely in an apartment without a fine cast of the Venus de' Medici in it, — this self-indulgent voluptuary at last committed several forgeries on the Bank of England, and the Old Bailey sessions of July, 1837, sentenced him to transportation for life. While he was lying in Newgate prior to his departure, with other convicts, to New South Wales, where he died, Dickens went with a former acquaintance of the prisoner to see him. They found him still possessed with a morbid self-esteem and a poor and empty vanity. All other feelings and interests were overwhelmed by an excessive idolatry of self, and he claimed (I now quote his own words to Dickens) a soul whose nutriment is love, and its offspring art, music, divine song, and still holier philosophy. To the last this super-refined creature seemed undisturbed by remorse. What place can we fancy for such a reptile, and what do we learn from such a career? Talfourd has so wisely summed up the whole case for us that I leave the dark tragedy with the recital of this solemn sentence from a paper on the culprit in the "Final Memorials of Charles Lamb": "Wainwright's vanity, nurtured by selfishness and unchecked by religion, became a disease, amounting perhaps to monomania, and yielding one lesson to repay the world for his existence, viz. that there is no state of the soul so dangerous as that in which the vices of the sensualist are envenomed by the grovelling intellect of the scorner."

One of the men best worth meeting in London, under any circumstances, was Leigh Hunt, but it was a special boon to find him and Procter together. I remember a

meantime I send to said "kindly reader"
some verses which I translated once from
Marot, and which, I believe, are not in the
American edition of my poems; though I begin
to think, they might as well have been there as
some others.

   To a Lady who wished to see him.
    (From the French of Marot).

     I.
  She loved me, as she read my books,
   And wish'd to see my face;
  Grey was my beard, and dark my looks;
   They lost me not her grace.

 2. | 3.
O gentle heart, O noble brow, | Those eyes of thine found hope & youth,
 Full rightly didst thou see: | And vigour in my page;
For this poor body, failing now, | And saw me better there, in truth,
 Is but my jail, not me. | Than through the mists of age.

Thus you see, my dear Sir, you must still name your day
of coming here without waiting for arrangement. Pray make no ceremony
with me of any kind, but treat me as in every respect an old friend; for so
    I am indeed. Very sincerely yours, Leigh Hunt

day in the summer of 1859 when Procter had a party of friends at dinner to meet Hawthorne, who was then on a brief visit to London. Among the guests were the Countess of ——, Kinglake, the author of "Eothen," Charles Sumner, then on his way to Paris, and Leigh Hunt, the mercurial qualities of whose blood were even then perceptible in his manner.

Adelaide Procter did not reach home in season to begin the dinner with us, but she came later in the evening, and sat for some time in earnest talk with Hawthorne. It was a "goodly companie," long to be remembered. Hunt and Procter were in a mood for gossip over the ruddy port. As the twilight deepened around the table, which was exquisitely decorated with flowers, the author of "Rimini" recalled to Procter's recollection other memorable tables where they used to meet in vanished days with Lamb, Coleridge, and others of their set long since passed away. As they talked on in rather low tones, I saw the two old poets take hands more than once at the mention of dead and beloved names. I recollect they had a good deal of fine talk over the great singers whose voices had delighted them in bygone days; speaking with rapture of Pasta, whose tones in opera they thought incomparably the grandest musical utterances they had ever heard. Procter's tribute in verse to this

"Queen and wonder of the enchanted world of sound"

is one of his best lyrics, and never was singer more divinely complimented by poet. At the dinner I am describing he declared that she walked on the stage like an empress, "and when she sang," said he, "I held my breath." Leigh Hunt, in one of his letters to Procter in 1831, says: "As to Pasta, I love her, for she makes the ground firm under my feet, and the sky blue over my head."

I cannot remember all the good things I heard that day, but some of them live in my recollection still. Hunt quoted Hartley Coleridge, who said, "No boy ever imagined himself a poet while he was reading Shakespeare or Milton." And speaking of Landor's oaths, he said, "They are so rich, they are really nutritious." Talking of criticism, he said he did not believe in spiteful imps, but in kindly elves who would "nod to him and do him courtesies." He laughed at Bishop Berkeley's attempt to destroy the world in one octavo volume. His doctrine to mankind always was, "Enlarge your tastes, that you may enlarge your hearts." He believed in reversing original propensities by education, — as Spallanzani brought up eagles on bread and milk, and fed doves on raw meat. "Don't let us demand too much of human nature," was a line in his creed; and he believed in Hood's advice, that gentleness in a case of wrong direction is always better than vituperation.

> "Mid light, and by degrees, should be the plan
> To cure the dark and erring mind;
> But who would rush at a benighted man
> And give him two black eyes for being blind?"

I recollect there was much converse that day on the love of reading in old age, and Leigh Hunt observed that Sir Robert Walpole, seeing Mr. Fox busy in the library at Houghton, said to him: "And you can read! Ah, how I envy you! I totally neglected the *habit* of reading when I was young, and now in my old age I cannot read a single page." Hunt himself was a man who could be "penetrated by a book." It was inspiring to hear him dilate over "Plutarch's Morals," and quote passages from that delightful essay on "The Tranquillity of the Soul." He had such reverence for the wisdom folded up on his library shelves, he declared that the very perusal of the *backs of his books* was "a discipline of humanity."

Whenever and wherever I met this charming person, I learned a lesson of gentleness and patience; for, steeped to the lips in poverty as he was, he was ever the most cheerful, the most genial companion and friend. He never left his good-nature outside the family circle, as a Mussulman leaves his slippers outside a mosque, but he always brought a smiling face into the house with him. T—— A——, whose fine floating wit has never yet quite condensed itself into a star, said one day of a Boston man that he was "east-wind made flesh." Leigh Hunt was exactly the opposite of this; he was compact of all the spicy breezes that blow. In his bare cottage at Hammersmith the temperament of his fine spirit heaped up such riches of fancy that kings, if wise ones, might envy his magic power.

"Onward in faith, and leave the rest to Heaven,"

was a line he often quoted. There was about him such a modest fortitude in want and poverty, such an inborn mental superiority to low and uncomfortable circumstances, that he rose without effort into a region encompassed with felicities, untroubled by a care or sorrow. He always reminded me of that favorite child of the genii who carried an amulet in his bosom by which all the gold and jewels of the Sultan's halls were no sooner beheld than they became his own. If he sat down companionless to a solitary chop, his imagination transformed it straightway into a fine shoulder of mutton. When he looked out of his dingy old windows on the four bleak elms in front of his dwelling, he saw, or thought he saw, a vast forest, and he could hear in the note of one poor sparrow even the silvery voices of a hundred nightingales. Such a man might often be cold and hungry, but he had the wit never to be aware of it.

Hunt's love for Procter was deep and tender, and in

one of his notes to me he says, referring to the meeting my memory has been trying to describe, "I have reasons for liking our dear friend Procter's wine beyond what you saw when we dined together at his table the other day." Procter prefixed a memoir of the life and writings of Ben Jonson to the great dramatist's works printed by Moxon in 1838. I happen to be the lucky owner of a copy of this edition that once belonged to Leigh Hunt, who has enriched it and perfumed the pages, as it were, by his annotations. The memoir abounds in felicities of expression, and is the best brief chronicle yet made of rare Ben and his poetry. Leigh Hunt has filled the margins with his own neat handwriting, and as I turn over the leaves, thus companioned, I seem to meet those two loving brothers in modern song, and have again the benefit of their sweet society, — a society redolent of

> "The love of learning, the sequestered nooks,
> And all the sweet serenity of books."

I shall not soon forget the first morning I walked with Procter and Kenyon to the famous house No. 22 St. James Place, overlooking the Green Park, to a breakfast with Samuel Rogers. Mixed up with this matutinal rite was much that belongs to the modern literary and political history of England. Fox, Burke, Talleyrand, Grattan, Walter Scott, and many other great ones have sat there and held converse on divers matters with the banker-poet. For more than half a century the wits and the wise men honored that unpretending mansion with their presence. On my way thither for the first time my companions related anecdote after anecdote of the "ancient bard," as they called our host, telling me also how all his life long the poet of Memory had been giving substantial aid to poor authors; how he had befriended Sheridan, and how good he had been to Campbell in his sorest needs.

Intellectual or artistic excellence was a sure passport to his *salon*, and his door never turned on reluctant hinges to admit the unfriended man of letters who needed his aid and counsel.

We arrived in quite an expectant mood, to find our host already seated at the head of his table, and his good man Edmund standing behind his chair. As we entered the room, and I saw Rogers sitting there so venerable and strange, I was reminded of that line of Wordsworth's,

"The oldest man he seemed that ever wore gray hair."

But old as he was, he seemed full of *verve*, vivacity, and decision. Knowing his homage for Ben Franklin, I had brought to him as a gift from America an old volume issued by the patriot printer in 1741. He was delighted with my little present, and began at once to say how much he thought of Franklin's prose. He considered the style admirable, and declared that it might be studied now for improvement in the art of composition. One of the guests that morning was the Rev. Alexander Dyce, the scholarly editor of Beaumont and Fletcher, and he very soon drew Rogers out on the subject of Warren Hastings's trial. It seemed ghostly enough to hear that famous event depicted by one who sat in the great hall of William Rufus; who day after day had looked on and listened to the eloquence of Fox and Sheridan; who had heard Edmund Burke raise his voice till the old arches of Irish oak resounded, and impeach Warren Hastings, "in the name of both sexes, in the name of every age, in the name of every rank, as the common enemy and oppressor of all." It thrilled me to hear Rogers say, "As I walked up Parliament Street with Mrs. Siddons, after hearing Sheridan's great speech, we both agreed that never before could human lips have uttered more eloquent words." That morning Rogers described to us the appearance of

Grattan as he first saw and heard him when he made his first speech in Parliament. "Some of us were inclined to laugh," said he, "at the orator's Irish brogue when he began his speech that day, but after he had been on his legs five minutes nobody dared to laugh any more." Then followed personal anecdotes of Madame De Staël, the Duke of Wellington, Walter Scott, Tom Moore, and Sydney Smith, all exquisitely told. Both our host and his friend Procter had known or entertained most of the celebrities of their day. Procter soon led the conversation up to matters connected with the stage, and thinking of John Kemble and Edmund Kean, I ventured to ask Rogers who of all the great actors he had seen bore away the palm. "I have looked upon a magnificent procession of them," he said, "in my time, and I never saw any one superior to *David Garrick*." He then repeated Hannah More's couplet on receiving as a gift from Mrs. Garrick the shoe-buckles which once belonged to the great actor: —

> "Thy buckles, O Garrick, another may use,
> But none shall be found who can tread in thy shoes."

We applauded his memory and his manner of reciting the lines, which seemed to please him. "How much can sometimes be put into an epigram!" he said to Procter, and asked him if he remembered the lines about Earl Grey and the Kaffir war. Procter did not recall them, and Rogers set off again: —

> "A dispute has arisen of late at the Cape,
> As touching the devil, his color and shape;
> While some folks contend that the devil is white,
> The others aver that he's black as midnight;
> But now 't is decided quite right in this way,
> And all are convinced that the devil is *Grey*."

We asked him if he remembered the theatrical excitement in London when Garrick and his troublesome contemporary, Barry, were playing King Lear at rival houses, and dividing the final opinion of the critics. "Yes," said he, "perfectly. I saw both those wonderful actors, and fully agreed at the time with the admirable epigram that ran like wildfire into every nook and corner of society." "Did the epigram still live in his memory?" we asked. The old man seemed looking across the misty valley of time for a few moments, and then gave it without a pause:—

> "The town have chosen different ways
> To praise their different Lears;
> To Barry they give loud applause,
> To Garrick only tears.
>
> "A king! ay, every inch a king,
> Such Barry doth appear;
> But Garrick's quite another thing, —
> He's every inch *King Lear!*"

Among other things which Rogers told us that morning, I remember he had much to say of Byron's *forgetfulness* as to all manner of things. As an evidence of his inaccuracy, Rogers related how the noble bard had once quoted to him some lines on Venice as Southey's, "which he wanted me to admire," said Rogers; "and as I wrote them myself, I had no hesitation in doing so. The lines are in my poem on Italy, and begin,

> "'There is a glorious city in the sea.'"

Samuel Lawrence had recently painted in oils a portrait of Rogers, and we asked to see it; so Edmund was sent up stairs to get it, and bring it to the table. Rogers himself wished to compare it with his own face, and had a looking-glass held before him. We sat by in silence as he regarded the picture attentively, and waited for his criticism. Soon he burst out with, "Is my nose so d——y sharp as that?" We all exclaimed, "No! no! the artist is at fault there, sir." "I thought so," he cried;

"he has painted the face of a dead man, d—n him!" Some one said, "The portrait is too hard." "I won't be painted as a hard man," rejoined Rogers. "I am not a hard man, am I, Procter?" asked the old poet. Procter deprecated with energy such an idea as that. Looking at the portrait again, Rogers said, with great feeling, "Children would run away from that face, and they never ran away from me!" Notwithstanding all he had to say against the portrait, I thought it a wonderful likeness, and a painting of great value. Moxon, the publisher, who was present, asked for a certain portfolio of engraved heads which had been made from time to time of Rogers, and this was brought and opened for our examination of its contents. Rogers insisted upon looking over the portraits, and he amused us by his cutting comments on each one as it came out of the portfolio. "This," said he, holding one up, "is the head of a cunning fellow, and this the face of a debauched clergyman, and this the visage of a shameless drunkard!" After a comic discussion of the pictures of himself, which went on for half an hour, he said, "It is time to change the topic, and set aside the little man for a very great one. Bring me my collection of Washington portraits." These were brought in, and he had much to say of American matters. He remembered being told, when a boy, by his father one day, that "a fight had recently occurred at a place called Bunker Hill, in America." He then inquired about Webster and the monument. He had met Webster in England, and greatly admired him. Now and then his memory was at fault, and he spoke occasionally of events as still existing which had happened half a century before. I remember what a shock it gave me when he asked me if Alexander Hamilton had printed any new pamphlets lately, and begged me to send him anything that distinguished man might publish after I got home to America.

Saml Rogers.

I recollect how delighted I was when Rogers sent me an invitation the second time to breakfast with him. On that occasion the poet spoke of being in Paris on a pleasure-tour with Daniel Webster, and he grew eloquent over the great American orator's genius. He also referred with enthusiasm to Bryant's poetry, and quoted with deep feeling the first three verses of "The Future Life." When he pronounced the lines: —

> "My name on earth was ever in thy prayer,
> And must thou never utter it in heaven?"

his voice trembled, and he faltered out, "I cannot go on: there is something in that poem which breaks me down, and I must never try again to recite verses so full of tenderness and undying love."

For Longfellow's poems, then just published in England, he expressed the warmest admiration, and thought the author of "Voices of the Night" one of the most perfect artists in English verse who had ever lived.

Rogers's reminiscences of Holland House that morning were a series of delightful pictures painted by an artist who left out none of the salient features, but gave to everything he touched a graphic reality. In his narrations the eloquent men, the fine ladies, he had seen there assembled again around their noble host and hostess, and one listened in the pleasant breakfast-room in St. James Place to the wit and wisdom of that brilliant company which met fifty years ago in the great *salon* of that princely mansion, which will always be famous in the literary and political history of England.

Rogers talked that morning with inimitable finish and grace of expression. A light seemed to play over his faded features when he recalled some happy past experience, and his eye would sometimes fill as he glanced back among his kindred, all now dead save one, his sister, who also lived to a great age. His head was very fine, and I never could quite understand the satirical sayings about his personal appearance which have crept into the literary gossip of his time. He was by no means the vivacious spectre some of his contemporaries have represented him, and I never thought of connecting him with that terrible line in "The Mirror of Magistrates," —

"His withered fist still striking at Death's door."

His dome of brain was one of the amplest and most perfectly shaped I ever saw, and his countenance was very far from unpleasant. His faculties to enjoy had not perished with age. He certainly looked like a well-seasoned author, but not dropping to pieces yet. His turn of thought was characteristic, and in the main just, for he loved the best, and was naturally impatient of what was low and mean in conduct and intellect. He had always lived in an atmosphere of art, and his reminiscences of painters and sculptors were never wearisome or dull. He had a store of pleasant anecdotes of Chantrey, whom he had employed as a wood-carver long before he became a modeller in clay; and he had also much to tell us of Sir Joshua Reynolds, whose lectures he had attended, and whose studio-talk had been familiar to him while he was a young man and studying art himself as an amateur. It was impossible almost to make Rogers seem a real being as we used to surround his table during those mornings and sometimes deep into the afternoons. We were listening to one who had talked with Boswell about Dr. Johnson; who had sat hours with Mrs. Piozzi; who read the "Vicar of Wakefield" the day it was published; who had heard Haydn, the composer, playing at a concert, "dressed out with a sword"; who had listened to Talleyrand's best sayings from his own lips; who had seen John Wesley lying dead in his coffin, "an old man, with the countenance of a little child"; who had been with Beckford at Fonthill; who had seen Porson slink back into the dining-room after the company had left it and drain what was left in the wineglasses; who had crossed the Apennines with Byron; who had seen Beau Nash in the height of his career dancing minuets at Bath; who had known Lady Hamilton in her days of beauty, and seen her often with Lord Nelson; who was in Fox's room when that great man lay dying; and who could describe Pitt from personal observation, speaking always as if his mouth was "full of worsted." It was unreal as a dream to sit there in St. James Place and hear that old man talk by the hour of what one had been reading about all one's life. One thing, I must confess, somewhat shocked me, — I was not prepared for the feeble manner in which some of Rogers's best stories were received by the gentlemen who had gathered at his table on those Tuesday mornings. But when Procter told me in explanation afterward that they had all "heard the same anecdotes every week, perhaps, for half a century from the same lips," I no longer wondered at the seeming apathy I had witnessed. It was a great treat to me, however, the talk I heard at Rogers's hospitable table, and my three visits there cannot be erased from the pleasantest tablets of memory. There is only one regret connected with them, but that loss still haunts me. On one of those memorable mornings I was obliged to leave earlier than the rest of the company on account of an engagement out of London, and Lady Beecher (formerly Miss O'Neil), the great actress of other days, came in and read an hour to the old poet and his guests. Procter told me afterward that among other things she read, at Rogers's request, the 14th chapter of Isaiah, and that her voice and manner seemed like inspiration.

Seeing and talking with Rogers was, indeed, like living

in the past: and one may imagine how weird it seemed to a raw Yankee youth, thus facing the man who might have shaken hands with Dr. Johnson. I ventured to ask him one day if he had ever seen the doctor. "No," said he; "but I went down to Bolt Court in 1782 with the intention of making Dr. Johnson's acquaintance. I raised the knocker tremblingly, and hearing the shuffling footsteps as of an old man in the entry, my heart failed me, and I put down the knocker softly again, and crept back into Fleet Street without seeing the vision I was not bold enough to encounter." I thought it was something to have heard the footsteps of old Sam Johnson stirring about in that ancient entry, and for my own part I was glad to look upon the man whose ears had been so strangely privileged.

Rogers drew about him all the musical as well as the literary talent of London. Grisi and Jenny Lind often came of a morning to sing their best *arias* to him when he became too old to attend the opera; and both Adelaide and Fanny Kemble brought to him frequently the rich tributes of their genius in art.

It was my good fortune, through the friendship of Procter, to make the acquaintance, at Rogers's table, of Leslie, the artist,— a warm friend of the old poet,— and to be taken round by him and shown all the principal private galleries in London. He first drew my attention to the pictures by Constable, and pointed out their quiet beauty to my uneducated eye, thus instructing me to hate all those intemperate landscapes and lurid compositions which abound in the shambles of modern art. In the company of Leslie I saw my first Titians and Vandycks, and felt, as Northcote says, on my good behavior in the presence of portraits so lifelike and inspiring. It was Leslie who inoculated me with a love of Gainsborough, before whose perfect pictures a spectator involuntarily raises his hat and stands uncovered. (And just here let me advise every art lover who goes to England to visit the little Dulwich Gallery, only a few miles from London, and there to spend an hour or two among the exquisite Gainsboroughs. No small collection in Europe is better worth a visit, and the place itself in summer-time is enchanting with greenery.)

As Rogers's dining-room abounded in only first-rate works of art, Leslie used to take round the guests and make us admire the Raphaels and Correggios. Inserted in the walls on each side of the mantel-piece, like tiles, were several of Turner's original oil and water-color drawings, which that supreme artist had designed to illustrate Rogers's "Poems" and "Italy." Long before Ruskin made those sketches world-famous in his "Modern Painters," I have heard Leslie point out their beauties with as fine an enthusiasm. He used to say that they purified the whole atmosphere round St. James Place!

Procter had a genuine regard for Count d'Orsay, and he pointed him out to me one day sitting in the window of his club, near Gore House, looking out on Piccadilly. The count seemed a little past his prime, but was still the handsomest man in London. Procter described him as a brilliant person, of special ability, and by no means a mere dandy.

I first saw Procter's friend, John Forster, the biographer of Goldsmith and Dickens, in his pleasant rooms, No. 58 Lincoln's Inn Fields. He was then in his prime, and looked brimful of energy. His age might have been forty, or a trifle onward from that mile-stone, and his whole manner announced a determination to assert that nobody need prompt *him*. His voice rang loud and clear, up stairs and down, everywhere throughout his premises. When he walked over the uncarpeted floor, you *heard* him walk, and he meant you should. When *he* spoke, nobody required an ear-trumpet; the deaf never lost a syllable of his manly utterances. Procter and he were in the same Commission, and were on excellent terms, the younger officer always regarding the elder with a kind of leonine deference.

It was to John Forster these charming lines were addressed by Barry Cornwall, when the poet sent his old friend a present of Shakespeare's Works. A more exquisite compliment was never conveyed in verse so modest and so perfect in simple grace: —

> "I do not know a man who better reads
> Or weighs the great thoughts of the book I send, —
> Better than he whom I have called my friend
> For twenty years and upwards. He who feeds
> Upon Shakesperian pastures never needs
> The humbler food which springs from plains below;
> Yet may he love the little flowers that blow,
> And him excuse who for their beauty pleads.
>
> "Take then my Shakespeare to some sylvan nook;
> And pray thee, in the name of Days of old,
> Good-will and friendship, never bought or sold,
> Give me assurance thou wilt always look
> With kindness still on Spirits of humbler mould;
> Kept firm by resting on that wondrous book,
> Wherein the Dream of Life is all unrolled."

Forster's library was filled with treasures, and he brought to the dinner-table, the day I was first with him, such rare and costly manuscripts and annotated volumes to show us, that one's appetite for "made dishes" was quite taken away. The excellent lady whom he afterward married was one of the guests, and among the gentlemen present I remember the brilliant author of "The Bachelor of the Albany," a book that was then the Novel sensation in London. Forster flew from one topic to another with admirable skill, and entertained us with anecdotes of Wellington and Rogers, gilding the time with

Wm. Forster

capital imitations of his celebrated contemporaries in literature and on the stage. A touch about Edmund Kean made us all start from our chairs and demand a mimetic repetition. Forster must have been an excellent private actor, for he had power and skill quite exceptional in that way. His force carried him along wherever he chose to go, and when he played "Kitely," his ability must have been strikingly apparent. After his marriage, and when he removed from Lincoln's Inn to his fine residence at "Palace-Gate House," he gave frequent readings, evincing remarkable natural and acquired talents. For Dickens he had a love amounting to jealousy. He never quite relished anybody else whom the great novelist had a fondness for, and I have heard droll stories touching this weakness. For Professor Felton he had unbounded regard, which had grown up by correspondence and through report from Dickens. He had never met Felton, and when the professor arrived in London, Dickens, with his love of fun, arranged a bit of cajolery, which was never quite forgotten, though wholly forgiven. Knowing how highly Forster esteemed Felton, through his writings and his letters, Dickens resolved to take Felton at once to Forster's house and introduce him as *Professor Stowe*, the *port* of both these gentlemen being pretty nearly equal. The Stowes were then in England on their triumphant tour, and this made the attempt at deception an easy one. So, Felton being in the secret, he and Dickens proceed to Forster's house and are shown in. Down comes Forster into the library, and is presented forthwith to "*Professor Stowe.*" "Uncle Tom's Cabin" is at once referred to, and the talk goes on in that direction for some time. At last both Dickens and Felton fell into such a paroxysm of laughter at Forster's dogged determination to be complimentary to the world-renowned novel, that they could no longer hold out; and Forster, becoming almost insane with wonder at the hilarious conduct of his two visitors, Dickens revealed their wickedness, and a right jolly day the happy trio made of it.

Talfourd informs us that Forster had become to Charles Lamb as one of his oldest companions, and that Mary also cherished a strong regard for him. It is surely a proof of his admirable qualities that the love of so many of England's best and greatest was secured to him by so lasting a tenure. To have the friendship of Landor, Dickens, and Procter through long years; to have Carlyle for a constant votary, and to be mourned by him with an abiding sorrow, — these are no slight tributes to purity of purpose.

Forster had that genuine sympathy with men of letters which entitled him to be their biographer, and all his works in that department have a special charm, habitually gained only by a subtle and earnest intellect.

It is a singular coincidence that the writers of two of the most brilliant records of travel of their time should have been law students in Barry Cornwall's office. Kinglake, the author of "Eothen," and Warburton, the author of "The Crescent and the Cross," were at one period both engaged as pupils in their profession under the guidance of Mr. Procter. He frequently spoke with pride of his two law students, and when Warburton perished at sea, his grief for his brilliant friend was deep and abiding. Kinglake's later literary fame was always a pleasure to the historian's old master, and no one in England loved better to point out the fine passages in the "History of the Invasion of the Crimea" than the old poet in Weymouth Street.

"Blackwood" and the "Quarterly Review" railed at Procter and his author friends for a long period; but how true is the saying of Macaulay, "that the place of books in the public estimation is fixed, not by what is written *about* them, but by what is written in them!" No man was more decried in his day than Procter's friend, William Hazlitt. The poet had for the critic a genuine admiration; and I have heard him dilate with a kind of rapture over the critic's fine sayings, quoting abundant passages from the essays. Procter would never hear any disparagement of his friend's ability and keenness. I recall his earnest but restrained indignation one day, when some person compared Hazlitt with a diffusive modern writer of notes on the theatre, and I remember with what contempt, in his sweet forgivable way, the old man spoke of much that passes nowadays for criticism. He said Hazlitt was exactly the opposite of Lord Chesterfield, who advised his son, if he could not get at a thing in a straight line, to try the serpentine one. There were no crooked pathways in Hazlitt's intellect. His style is brilliant, but never cloyed with ornamentation. Hazlitt's paper on Gifford was thought by Procter to be as pungent a bit of writing as had appeared in his day, and he quoted this paragraph as a sample of its biting justice: "Mr. Gifford is admirably qualified for the situation he has held for many years as editor of the 'Quarterly' by a happy combination of defects, natural and acquired." In one of his letters to me Procter writes, "I despair of the age that has forgotten to read Hazlitt."

Procter was a delightful prose writer, as well as a charming poet. Having met in old magazines and annuals several of his essays and stories, and admiring their style and spirit, I induced him, after much persuasion, to collect and publish in America his prose works. The result was a couple of volumes, which were brought out in Boston in 1853. In them there are perhaps no "thoughts that wander through eternity," but they abound in fancies which the reader will recognize as agile

"Daughters of the earth and sun."

In them there is nothing loud or painful, and whoever really loves "a good book," and knows it to be such on trial, will find Barry Cornwall's "Essays and Tales in Prose" most delectable reading. "Imparadised," as Milton hath the word, on a summer hillside, or tented by the cool salt wave, no better afternoon literature can be selected. One will never meet with distorted metaphor or tawdry rhetoric in Barry's thoughtful pages, but will find a calm philosophy and a beautiful faith, very precious and profitable in these days of doubt and insecurity of intellect. There is a respite and a sympathy in this fine spirit, and so I commend him heartily in times so full of turmoil and suspicion as these. One of the stories in the first volume of these prose writings, called "The Man-Hunter," is quite equal in power to any of the graphic pieces of a similar character ever written by De Quincey or Dickens, but the tone in these books is commonly more tender and inclining to melancholy. What, for instance, could be more heart-moving than these passages of his on the death of little children?

"I scarcely know how it is, but the deaths of children seem to me always less premature than those of elder persons. Not that they are in fact so; but it is because they themselves have little or no relation to time or maturity. Life seems a race which they have yet to run entirely. They have made no progress toward the goal. They are born — nothing further. But it seems hard, when a man has toiled high up the steep hill of knowledge, that he should be cast like Sisyphus, downward in a moment; that he who has worn the day and wasted the night in gathering the gold of science should be, with all his wealth of learning, all his accumulations, made bankrupt at once. What becomes of all the riches of the soul, the piles and pyramids of precious thoughts which men heap together? Where are Shakespeare's imagination, Bacon's learning, Galileo's dream? Where is the sweet fancy of Sidney, the airy spirit of Fletcher, and Milton's thought severe? Methinks such things should not die and dissipate, when a hair can live for centuries, and a brick of Egypt will last three thousand years! I am content to believe that the mind of man survives (somewhere or other) his clay.

"I was once present at the death of a little child. I will not pain the reader by portraying its agonies; but when its breath was gone, its *life*, (nothing more than a cloud of smoke!) and it lay like a waxen image before me, I turned my eyes to its moaning mother, and sighed out my few words of comfort. But I am a beggar in grief. I can feel and sigh and look kindly, I think; but I have nothing to give. My tongue deserts me. I know the inutility of too soon comforting. I know that *I* should weep were I the loser, and I let the tears have their way. Sometimes a word or two I can muster: a 'Sigh no more!' and 'Dear lady, do not grieve!' but further I am mute and useless."

I have many letters and kind little notes which Procter used to write me during the years I knew him best. His tricksy fancies peeped out in his correspondence, and several of his old friends in England thought no literary man of his time had a better epistolary style. His neat elegant chirography on the back of a letter was always a delightful foretaste of something good inside, and I never received one of his welcome missives that did not contain, no matter how brief it happened to be, welcome passages of wit or affectionate interest.

In one of his early letters to me he says:—

"There is no one rising hereabouts in literature. I suppose our national genius is taking a mechanical turn. And, in truth, it is much better to make a good steam-engine than to manufacture a bad poem. 'Building the lofty rhyme' is a good thing, but our present buildings are of a low order, and seldom reach the Attic. This piece of wit will scarcely throw you into a fit, I imagine, your risible muscles being doubtless kept in good order."

In another he writes:—

"I see you have some capital names in the 'Atlantic Monthly.' If they will only put forth their strength, there is no doubt as to the result, but the misfortune is that persons who write anonymously *don't* put forth their strength, in general. I was a magazine writer for no less than a dozen years, and I felt that no personal credit or responsibility attached to my literary trifling, and although I sometimes did pretty well (for me), yet I never did my best."

As I read over again the portfolio of his letters to me, bearing date from 1848 to 1866, I find many passages of interest, but most of them are too personal for type. A few extracts, however, I cannot resist copying. Some of his epistles are enriched with a song or a sonnet, then just written, and there are also frequent references in them to American editions of his poetical and prose works, which he collected at the request of his Boston publishers.

In June, 1851, he writes: —

"I have encountered a good many of your countrymen here lately, but have been introduced only to a few. I found Mr. Norton, who has returned to you, and Mr. Dwight, who is still here, I believe, very intelligent and agreeable.

"If all Americans were like them and yourself, and if all Englishmen were like Kenyon and (so far as regards a desire to judge fairly) myself, I think there would be little or no quarrelling between our small island and your great continent.

"Our glass palace is a perpetual theme for small-talk. It usurps the place of the weather, which is turned adrift, or laid up in ordinary for future use. Nevertheless it (I mean the palace) is a remarkable achievement, after all; and I speak sincerely when I say, 'All honor and glory to Paxton!' If the strings of my poor little lyre were not rusty and overworn, I think I should try to sing some of my nonsense verses before his image, and add to the idolatry already existing.

"If you have hotter weather in America than that which is at present burning and blistering us here, you are entitled to pity. If it continue much longer, I shall be held in solution for the remainder of my days, and shall be remarkable as 'Oxygen, the poet' (reduced to his natural weakness and simplicity by the hot summer of 1851), instead of   Your very sincere and obliged
"B. W. PROCTER."

Here is a brief reference to Judd's remarkable novel, forming part of a note written to me in 1852: —

"Thanks for 'Margaret' (the book, *not* the woman), that you have sent me. When will you want it back? and who is the author? There is a great deal of clever writing in it, — great observation of nature, and also of character among a certain class of persons. But it is almost too minute, and for me decidedly too theological. You see what irreligious people we are here. I shall come over to one of your camp-meetings and *try* to be converted. What will they administer in such a case? brimstone or brandy? I shall try the latter first."

Here is a letter bearing date "Thursday night, November 25, 1852," in which he refers to his own writings, and copies a charming song: —

"Your letter, announcing the arrival of the little preface, reached me last night. I shall look out for the book in about three weeks hence, as you tell me that they are all printed. You Americans are a rapid race. When I thought you were in Scotland, lo, you had touched the soil of Boston; and when I thought you were unpacking my poor MS., tumbling it out of your great trunk, behold! it is arranged — it is in the printer's hands — it is *printed* — published — it is — ah! would I could add, SOLD! That, after all, is the grand triumph in Boston as well as London.

"Well, since it is not sold yet, let us be generous and give a few copies away. Indeed, such is my weakness, that I would sometimes rather give than sell. In the present instance you will do me the kindness to send a copy each to Mr. Charles Sumner, Mr. Hillard, Mr. Norton: but no — my wife requests to be the donor to Mr. Norton, so you must, if you please, write his name in the first leaf and state that it comes from '*Mrs*. Procter.' I liked him very much when I met him in London, and I should wish him to be reminded of his English acquaintance.

"I am writing to you at eleven o'clock at night, after a long and busy day, and I write *now* rather than wait for a little inspiration, because the mail, I believe, starts to-morrow. The unwilling Minerva is at my elbow, and I feel that every sentence I write, were it pounded ten times in a mortar, would come out again unleavened and heavy. Braying some people in a mortar, you know, is but a weary and unprofitable process.

"You speak of London as a delightful place. I don't know how it may be in the white-bait season, but at present it is foggy, rainy, cold, dull. Half of us are unwell and the other half dissatisfied. Some are apprehensive of an invasion, — not an impossible event; some writing odes to the Duke of Wellington; and I am putting my good friend to sleep with the flattest prose that ever dropped from an English pen. I wish that it were better; I wish that it were even worse; but it is the most undeniable twaddle. I must go to bed, and invoke the Muses in the morning. At present, I cannot touch one of their petticoats.

"A SLEEPY SONG.

"Sing! sing me to sleep!
    With gentle words, in some sweet slumberous measure,
Such as lone poet on some shady steep
    Sings to the silence in his noonday leisure.

"Sing! as the river sings,
    When gently it flows between soft banks of flowers,
And the bee murmurs, and the cuckoo brings
    His faint May music, 'tween the golden showers.

"Sing! O divinest tone!
    I sink beneath some wizard's charming wand;
I yield, I move, by soothing breezes blown,
    O'er twilight shores, into the Dreaming Land!

"I read the above to you when you were in London. It will appear in an Annual edited by Miss Power (Lady Blessington's niece).

"*Friday Morning.*

"The wind blowing down the chimney; the rain sprinkling my windows. The English Apollo hides his head — you can scarcely see him on the 'misty mountain-tops' (those brick ones which you remember in Portland Place).

"My friend Thackeray is gone to America, and I hope is, by this time, in the United States. He goes to New York, and afterward I *suppose* (but I don't know) to Boston and Philadelphia. Have you seen *Esmond?* There are parts of it charmingly written. His pathos is to me very touching. I believe that the best mode of making one's way to a person's head is — through his heart.

"I hope that your literary men will like some of my little prose matters. I know that they will *try* to like them; but the papers have been written so long, and all, or almost all, written so hastily, that I have my misgivings. However, they must take their chance.

"Had I leisure to complete something that I began two or three years ago, and in which I have written a chapter or two, I should reckon more surely on success; but I shall probably never finish the thing, although I contemplated only one volume.

"(If you cannot read this letter apply to the printer's devil. — Hibernicus.)

"Farewell. All good be with you. My wife desires to be kindly remembered by you.
"Always yours, very sincerely,
"B. W. PROCTER."

"P. S. — Can you contrive to send Mr. Willis a copy of the prose book? If so, pray do."

In February, 1853, he writes: —

"Those famous volumes, the advent of which was some time since announced by the great transatlantic trumpet, have duly arrived. My wife is properly grateful for her copy, which, indeed, impresses both of us with respect for the American skill in binding. Neither too gay to be gaudy, nor too grave, so as to affect the theological, it hits that happy medium which agrees with the tastes of most people and disgusts none. We should flatter ourselves that it is intended to represent the matter within, but that we are afraid of incurring the sin of vanity, and the indiscretion of taking appearances too much upon trust. We suspend our conjectures on this very interesting subject. The whole getting up of the book is excellent.

"For the little scraps of (critical) sugar enclosed in your letter, due thanks. These will sweeten our imagination for some time to come.

"I have been obliged to give all the copies you sent me away. I dare say you will not grudge me four or five copies more, to be sent at your convenience, of course. Let me hear from you at the same time. You can give me one of those frequent quarters of an hour which I know you now devote to a meditation on 'things in general.'

"I am glad that you like Thackeray. He is well worth your liking. I trust to his making both friends and money in America, and to his *keeping* both. I am not so sure of the money, however, for he has a liberal hand. I should have liked to have been at one of the dinners you speak of. When shall you begin that *bridge*? You seem to be a long time about it. It will, I dare say, be a bridge of boats, after all. . . . .

"I was reading (rather re-reading) the other evening the introductory chapter to the 'Scarlet Letter.' It is admirably written. Not having any great sympathy with a custom-house, — nor, indeed, with Salem, except that it seems to be Hawthorne's birthplace, — all my attention was concentrated on the *style*, which seems to me excellent.

"The most striking book which has been recently published here is 'Villette,' by the authoress of 'Jane Eyre,' who, as you know, is a Miss Brontë. The book does not give one the most pleasing notion of the authoress, perhaps, but it is very clever, graphic, vigorous. It is 'man's meat,' and not the whipped syllabub, which is *all* froth, without any jam at the bottom. The scene of the drama is Brussels.

"I was sorry to hear of poor Willis. Our critics here were too severe upon him. . . . .

"The Frost King (vulg. Jack Frost) has come down upon us with all his might. Banished from the pleasant shores of Boston, he has come with his cold scythe and ice pincers to our undefended little island, and is tyrannizing in every corner and over every part of every person. Nothing is too great for him, nothing too mean. He condescends even to lay hold of the nose (an offence for which any one below the dignity of a King — or a President — would be kicked.) As for me I have taken refuge in

"A SONG WITH A MORAL.

"When the winter bloweth loud,
And the earth is in a shroud,
Frozen rain or sleety snow
Dimming every dream below, —
  There is e'er a spot of green
  Whence the heavens may be seen.

"When our purse is shrinking fast,
And our friend is lost, (the last!)
And the world doth pour its pain,
Sharper than the frozen rain, —
  There is still a spot of green
  Whence the heavens may be seen.

"Let us never meet despair
While the little spot is there;
Winter brighteneth into May,
And sullen night to sunny day, —
  Seek we then the spot of green
  Whence the heavens may be seen.

"I have left myself little space for more small-talk. I must, therefore, conclude with wishing that your English dreams may continue bright, and that when they begin to fade you will come and *relume* at one of the white-bait dinners of which you used to talk in such terms of rapture.

"Have I space to say that I am very truly yours?

"B. W. PROCTER."

A few months later, in the same year (1853), he sits by his open window in London, on a morning of spring, and sends off the following pleasant words: —

"You also must now be in the first burst and sunshine of spring. Your spear-grass is showing its points, your succulent grass its richness, even your little plant [?] (so useful for certain invalids) is seen here and there; primroses are peeping out in your neighborhood, and you are looking for cowslips to come. I say nothing of your hawthorns (from the common May to the classic Nathaniel), except that I trust they are thriving, and like to put forth a world of blossoms soon.

'With all this wealth, present and future,
The yellow cowslip and the pale primrose,'

you will doubtless feel disposed to scatter your small coins abroad on the poor, and, among other things, to forward to your humble correspondent those copies of B—— C——'s prose works which you promised I know not how long ago. 'He who gives *speedily*,' they say, 'gives twice.' I quote, as you see, from the Latins.

"I have just got the two additional volumes of De Quincey, for which — thanks! I have not seen Mr. Parker, who brought them, and who left his card here yesterday, but I have asked if he will come and breakfast with me on Sunday, — my only certain leisure day. Your De Quincey is a man of a good deal of reading, and has thought on divers and sundry matters; but he is evidently so thoroughly well pleased with the Sieur 'Thomas De Quincey' that his self-sufficiency spoils even his best works. Then some of his facts are, I hear, *quasi* facts only, not unfrequently. He has his moments when he sleeps, and becomes oblivious of all but the aforesaid 'Thomas,' who pervades both his sleeping and waking visions. I, like all authors, am glad to have a little praise now and then (it is my hydromel), but it must be dispensed by others. I do not think it decent to manufacture the sweet liquor myself, and I hate a coxcomb, whether in dress or print.

"We have little or no literary news here. Our poets are all going to the poorhouse (except Tennyson), and our prose writers are piling up their works for the next 5th of November, when there will be a great bonfire. It is deuced lucky that my immortal (ah! I am De Quinceying) — I mean my humble — performances were printed in America, so that they will escape. By the by, are they on foolscap? for I forgot to caution you on that head.

"I have been spending a week at Liverpool, where I rejoiced to hear that Hawthorne's appointment was settled, and that it was a valuable post; but I hear that it lasts for three years only. This is melancholy. I hope, however, that he will 'realize' (as you transatlantics say) as much as he can during his consulate, and that your next President will have the good taste and the good sense to renew his lease for three years more.

"I have not seen Mrs. Stowe. I shall probably meet her somewhere or other when she comes to London.

"I dare not ask after Mr. Longfellow. He was kind enough to write me a very agreeable letter some time ago, which I ought to have answered. I dare say he has forgotten it, but my conscience is a serpent that gives me a bite or a sting every now and then when I think of him. The first time I am in fit condition (I mean in point of brightness) to reply to so famous a correspondent, I shall try what an English pen and ink will enable me to say. In the mean time, God be thanked for all things!

"My wife heard from Thackeray about ten days ago. He speaks gratefully of the kindness that he has met with in America. Among other things, it appears that he has seen something of your slaves, whom he represents as leading a very easy life, and as being fat, cheerful, and happy. Nevertheless, *I* (for one) would rather be a free man, — such is the singularity of my opinions. If my prosings should ever in the course of the next twenty years require to be reprinted, pray take note of the above opinion.

"And now I have no more paper; I have scarcely room left to say that I hope you are well, and to remind you that for your ten lines of writing I have sent you back a hundred. Give my best compliments to all whom I know, personally or otherwise. God be with you!

"Yours, very sincerely,
"B. W. PROCTER."

Procter always seemed to be astounded at the travelling spirit of Americans, and in his letters he makes frequent reference to our "national propensity," as he calls it.

"Half an hour ago," he writes in July, 1853, "we had three of your countrymen here to lunch, — countrymen I mean, Hibernically, for two of them wore petticoats. They are all going to Switzerland, France, Italy, Egypt, and Syria. What an adventurous race you are, you Americans! Here the women go merely 'from the blue bed to the brown,' and think that they have travelled and seen the world. I myself should not care much to be confined to a circle reaching six or seven miles round London. There are the fresh winds and wild thyme on Hampstead Heath, and from Richmond you may survey the Naiades. Highgate, where Coleridge lived, Enfield, where Charles Lamb dwelt, are not far off. Turning eastward, there is the river Lea, in which Izaak Walton fished; and farther on — ha! what do I see? What are those little fish frisking in the batter (the great Naval Hospital close by), which fixed the affections of the enamored American while he resided in London, and have been floating in his dreams ever since? They are said by the naturalists to be of the species *Blandamentum album*, and are by vulgar aldermen spoken carelessly of as *white-bait*.

"London is full of carriages, full of strangers, full of parties feasting on strawberries and ices and other things intended to allay the heat of summer; but the Summer herself (fickle virgin) keeps back, or has been stopped somewhere or other, — perhaps at the Liverpool custom-house, where the very brains of men (their books) are held in durance, as I know to my cost.

"Thackeray is about to publish a new work in numbers, — a serial, as the newspapers call it. Thomas Carlyle is publishing (a sixpenny matter) in favor of the slave-trade. Novelists of all shades are plying their trades. Husbands are killing their wives in every day's newspaper. Burglars are peaching against each other; there is no longer honor among thieves. I am starting for Leicester on a week's expedition amidst the mad people; and the Emperor of Russia has crossed the Pruth, and intends to make a tour of Turkey.

"All this appears to me little better than idle, restless vanity. O my friend, what a fuss and a pother we are all making, we little flies who are going round on the great wheel of time! To-day we are flickering and buzzing about, our little bits of wings glittering in the sunshine, and to-morrow we are safe enough in the little crevice at the back of the fireplace, or hid in the folds of the old curtain, shut up, stiff and torpid, for the long winter. What do you say to that profound reflection?

"I struggle against the lassitude which besets me, and strive in vain to be either sensible or jocose. I had better say farewell."

On Christmas day, 1854, he writes in rather flagging spirits, induced by ill health: —

"I have owed you a letter for these many months, my good friend. I am afraid to think *how* long, lest the interest on the debt should have exceeded the capital, and be beyond my power to pay.

"You must be good-natured and excuse me, for I have been ill — very frequently — and dispirited. A bodily complaint torments me, that has tormented me for the last two years. I no longer look at the world through a rose-colored glass. The prospect, I am sorry to say, is gray, grim, dull, barren, full of withered leaves, without flowers, or if there be any, all of them trampled down, soiled, discolored, and without fragrance. You see what a bit of half-smoked glass I am looking through. At all events, you must see how entirely I am disabled from returning, except in sober sentences, the lively and good-natured letters and other things which you have sent me from America. They were welcome, and I thank you for them now, in a few words, as you observe, but sincerely. I am somewhat brief, even in my gratitude. Had I been in braver spirits, I might have spurred my poor Pegasus, and sent you some lines on the Alma, or the Inkerman, — bloody battles, but exhibiting marks not to be mistaken of the old English heroism, which, after all is said about the enervating effects of luxury, is as grand and manifest as in the ancient fights which English history talks of so much. Even you, sternest of republicans, will, I think, be proud of the indomitable courage of Englishmen, and gladly refer to your old paternity. I, at least, should be proud of Americans fighting after the same fashion (and without doubt they *would* fight thus), just as old people exult in the brave conduct of their runaway sons. I cannot read of these later battles without the tears coming into my eyes. It is said by 'our correspondent' at *New York* that the folks there rejoice in the losses and disasters of the allies. This can never be the case, surely? No one whose opinion is worth a rap can rejoice at any success of the Czar, whose double-dealing and unscrupulous greediness must have rendered him an object of loathing to every well-thinking man. But what have I to do with politics, or you? Our 'pleasant object and serene employ' are books, books. Let us return to pacific thoughts.

"What a number of things have happened since I saw you! I looked for you in the last spring, little dreaming that so fat and flourishing a 'Statesman' could be overthrown by a little fever. I had even begun some doggerel, announcing to you the advent of the white-bait, which I imagined were likely to be all eaten up in your absence. My memory is so bad that I cannot recollect half a dozen lines, probably not one, as it originally stood.

"I was at Liverpool last June. After two or three attempts I contrived to seize on the famous Nathaniel Hawthorne. Need I say that I like him *very* much? He is very sensible, very genial, — a little shy, I think (for an American!) — and altogether extremely agreeable. I wish that I could see more of him, but our orbits are wide apart. Now and then — once in two years — I diverge into and cross his circle, but at other times we are separated by a space amounting to 210 miles. He has three children, and a nice little wife, who has good-humor engraved on her countenance.

"As to verse — yes, I have begun a dozen trifling things, which are in my drawer unfinished; poor rags with ink upon them, none of them, I am afraid, properly labelled for posterity. I was for six weeks at Ryde, in the Isle of Wight, this year, but so unwell that I could not write a line, scarcely read one; sitting out in the sun, eating, drinking, sleeping, and sometimes (poor soul!) imagining I was thinking. One Sunday I saw a magnificent steamer go by, and on placing my eye to the telescope I saw some Stars and Stripes (streaming from the mast-head) that carried me away to Boston. By the way, when *will* you finish the bridge?

"I hear strange hints of you all quarrelling about the slave question. Is it so? You are so happy and prosperous in America that you must be on the lookout for clouds, surely! When you see Emerson, Longfellow, Sumner, any one I know, pray bespeak for me a kind thought or word from them."

Procter was always on the lookout for Hawthorne, whom he greatly admired. In November, 1855, he says, in a brief letter:—

"I have not seen Hawthorne since I wrote to you. He came to London this summer, but, I am sorry to say, did not inquire for me. As it turned out, I was absent from town, but sent him (by Mrs. Russell Sturgis) a letter of introduction to Leigh Hunt, who was very much pleased with him. Poor Hunt! he is the most genial of men; and, now that his wife is confined to her bed by rheumatism, is recovering himself, and, I hope, doing well. He asked to come and see me the other day. I willingly assented, and when I saw him — grown old and sad and broken down in health — all my ancient liking for him revived.

"You ask me to send you some verse. I accordingly send you a scrap of recent manufacture, and you will observe that instead of forwarding my epic on Sevastopol, I select something that is fitter for these present vernal love days than the bluster of heroic verse:—

"SONG.

"Within the chambers of her breast
Love lives and makes his spicy nest,
Midst downy blooms and fragrant flowers,
And there he dreams away the hours —
  There let him rest!
Some time hence, when the cuckoo sings,
I'll come by night and bind his wings, —
Bind him that he shall not roam
From his warm white virgin home.

"Maiden of the summer season,
  Angel of the rosy time,
Come, unless some graver reason
  Bid thee scorn my rhyme;
Come from thy serener height,
On a golden cloud descending,
Come ere Love hath taken flight,
And let thy stay be like the light,
When its glory hath no ending
  In the Northern night!"

Now and then we get a glimpse of Thackeray in his letters. In one of them he says:—

"Thackeray came a few days ago and read one of his lectures at our house (that on George the Third), and we asked about a dozen persons to come and hear it, among the rest, your handsome countrywoman, Mrs. R—— S——. It was very pleasant, with that agreeable intermixture of tragedy and comedy that tells so well when judiciously managed. He will not print them for some time to come, intending to read them at some of the principal places in England, and perhaps Scotland.

"What are you doing in America? You are too happy and independent! 'O fortunatos Agricolas, sua si bona nôrint!' I am not quite sure of my Latin (which is rusty from old age), but I am sure of the sentiment, which is that when people are too happy, they don't know it, and so take to quarrelling to relieve the monotony

[Song.]

Within the chambers of her breast
Love lives, and makes his spicy nest,
'Midst downy blooms and fragrant flowers,
And there he dreams away the hours;—
— There let him rest!
Sometime hence, when the cuckoo sings,
I'll come by night and bind his wings,—
Bind him, that he shall not roam
From his warm, white, virgin home.

×

Maiden of the Summer season,—
Angel of the rosy time,,—
Come, unless some graver reason
Bid thee scorn my rhyme;
Come, from thy serener height
On a golden cloud descending,—
Come, ere Love hath taken flight,—
And let thy stay be like the light,
When its glory hath no ending
In the Northern night!

Yours very truly B. W. Procter.

of their blue sky. Some of these days you will split your great kingdom in two, I suppose, and then —

"My wife's mother, Mrs. Basil Montagu, is very ill, and we are apprehensive of a fatal result, which, in truth, the mere fact of her age (eighty-two or eighty-three) is enough to warrant. Ah, this terrible *age!* The young people, I dare say, think that we live too long. Yet how short it is to look back on life! Why, I saw the house the other day where I used to play with a wooden sword when I was five years old! It cannot surely be eighty years ago! What has occurred since? Why, nothing that is worth putting down on paper. A few nonsense verses, a flogging or two (richly deserved), and a few white-bait dinners, and the whole is reckoned up. Let us begin again." [Here he makes some big letters in a school-boy hand, which have a very pathetic look on the page.]

In a letter written in 1856 he gives me a graphic picture of sad times in India: —

"All our anxiety here at present is the Indian mutiny. We ourselves have great cause for trouble. Our son (the only son I have, indeed) escaped from Delhi lately. He is now at Meerut. He and four or five other officers, four women, and a child escaped. The men were obliged to drop the women a fearful height from the walls of the fort, amidst showers of bullets. A round shot passed within a yard of my son, and one of the ladies had a bullet through her shoulder. They were seven days and seven nights in the jungle, without money or meat, scarcely any clothes, no shoes. They forded rivers, lay on the wet ground at night, lapped water from the puddles, and finally reached Meerut. The lady (the mother of the three other ladies) had not her wound dressed, or seen, indeed, for upward of a week. Their feet were full of thorns. My son had nothing but a shirt, a pair of trousers, and a flannel waistcoat. How they contrived to *live* I don't know; I suppose from small gifts of rice, etc., from the natives.

"When I find any little thing now that disturbs my serenity, and which I might in former times have magnified into an evil, I think of what Europeans suffer from the vengeance of the Indians, and pass it by in quiet.

"I received Mr. Hillard's epitaph on my dear kind friend Kenyon. Thank him in my name for it. There are some copies to be reserved of a lithograph now in progress (a portrait of Kenyon) for his American friends. Should it be completed in time, Mr. Sumner will be asked to take them over. I have put down your name for one of those who would wish to have this little memento of a good kind man. . . . .

"I shall never visit America, be assured, or the continent of Europe, or any distant region. I have reached nearly to the length of my tether. I have grown old and apathetic and stupid. All I care for, in the way of personal enjoyment, is quiet, ease, — to have nothing to do, nothing to think of. My only glance is backward. There is so little before me that I would rather not look that way."

In a later letter he again speaks of his son and the war in India: —

"My son is *not* in the list of killed and wounded, thank God! He was before Delhi, having *volunteered* thither after his escape. We trust that he is at present safe, but every mail is pregnant with bloody tidings, and we do not find ourselves yet in a position to rejoice securely. What a terrible war this Indian war is! Are all people of black blood cruel, cowardly, and treacherous? If it were a case of great oppression on our part, I could understand and (almost) excuse it; but it is from the *spoiled* portion of the Hindostanees that the revengeful mutiny has arisen. One thing is quite clear, that whatever luxury and refinement have done for our race (for I include Americans with English), they have not diminished the courage and endurance and heroism for which I think we have formerly been famous. We are the same Saxons still. There has never been fiercer fighting than in some of the battles that have lately taken place in India. When I look back on the old history books, and see that *all* history consists of little else than the bloody feuds of nation with nation, I almost wonder that God has not extinguished the cruel, selfish animals that we dignify with the name of men. No — I cry forgiveness: let the women live, if they can, without the men. I used the word 'men' only."

Here is a pleasant paragraph about "Aurora Leigh": —

"The most successful book of the season has been Mrs. Browning's 'Aurora Leigh.' I could wish some things altered, I confess; but as it is, it is by far (a hundred times over) the finest poem ever written by a woman. We know little or nothing of Sappho, — nothing to induce comparison, — and all other wearers of petticoats must courtesy to the ground."

In several of his last letters to me there are frequent allusions to our civil war. Here is an extract from an epistle written in 1861: —

"We read with painful attention the accounts of your great quarrel in America. We know nothing beyond what we are told by the New York papers, and these are the stories of *one* of the combatants. I am afraid that, however you may mend the schism, you will never be so strong again. I hope, however, that something may arise to terminate the bloodshed; for, after all, fighting is an unsatisfactory way of coming at the truth. If you were to stand up at once (and finally) against the slave-trade, your band of soldiers would have a more decided *principle* to fight for. But —

"— But I really know little or nothing. I hope that at Boston you are comparatively peaceful, and I know that you are more abolitionist than in the more southern countries.

"There is nothing new doing here in the way of books. The last book I have seen is called 'Tannhäuser,' published by Chapman and Hall, — a poem under feigned names, but *really* written by Robert Lytton and Julian Fane. It is not good enough for the first, but (as I conjecture) too good for the last. The songs which decide the contest of the bards are the worst portions of the book.

"I read some time ago a novel which has not made much noise, but which is prodigiously clever, — 'City and Suburb.' The story hangs in parts, but it is full of weighty sentences. We have no poet *since* Tennyson except Robert Lytton, who, you know, calls himself Owen Meredith. Poetry in England is assuming a new character, and not a better character. It has a sort of pre-Raphaelite tendency which does not suit my aged feelings. I am for Love, or the World well lost. But I forget that, if I live beyond the 21st of next November, I shall be *seventy-four* years of age. I have been obliged to resign my Commissionership of Lunacy, not being able to bear the pain of travelling. By this I lose about £900 a year. I am, therefore, sufficiently poor, even for a poet. Browning, as you know, has lost his wife. He is coming with his little boy to live in England. I rejoice at this, for I think that the English should live in England, especially in their youth, when people learn things that they never forget afterward."

Near the close of 1864 he writes: —

"Since I last heard from you, nothing except what is melancholy seems to have taken place. You seem all busy killing each other in America. Some friends of yours and several friends of mine have died. Among the last I cannot help placing Nathaniel Hawthorne, for whom I had a sincere regard. . . . . He was about your best prose writer, I think, and intermingled with his humor was a great deal of tenderness. To die so soon!

"You are so easily affronted in America, if we (English) say anything about putting an end to your war, that I will not venture to hint at the subject. Nevertheless, I wish that you were all at peace again, for your own sakes and for the sake of human nature. I detest fighting now, although I was a great admirer of fighting in my youth. My youth? I wonder where it has gone. It has left me with gray hairs and rheumatism, and plenty of (too many other) infirmities. I stagger and stumble along, with almost seventy-six years on my head, upon failing limbs, which no longer enable me to walk half a mile. I see a great deal, all behind me (the Past), but the prospect before me is not cheerful. Sometimes I wish that I had tried harder for what is called Fame, but generally (as now) I care very little about it. After all, — unless one could be Shakespeare, which (clearly) is not an easy matter, — of what value is a little puff of smoke from a review? If we could settle permanently who is to be the Homer or Shakespeare of our time, it might be worth something; but we cannot. Is it Jones, or Smith, or —— ? Alas! I get short-sighted on this point, and cannot penetrate the impenetrable dark. Make my remembrances acceptable to Longfellow, to Lowell, to Emerson, and to any one else who remembers me.   Yours, ever sincerely,

"B. W. PROCTER."

And here are a few paragraphs from the last letter I ever received in Procter's loving hand: —

"Although I date this from Weymouth Street, yet I am writing 140 or 150 miles away from London. Perhaps this temporary retreat from our great, noisy, turbulent city reminds me that I have been very unmindful of your letter, received long ago. But I have been busy, and my writing now is not a simple matter, as it was fifty years ago. I have great difficulty in forming the letters, and you would be surprised to learn with what labor *this* task is performed. Then I have been incessantly occupied in writing (I refer to the *mechanical* part only) the 'Memoir of Charles Lamb.' It is not my book, — i. e. not my property, — but one which I was hired

Nov. 16.th 1876.

Queen Anne's Mansion. SW

My dear Mr Fields

I am about to publish the small sketch that your old friend and my dear husband left — as well as some papers describing his contemporaries. The sketch of his own life is very short — and ends at his 18.th or 20.th year. I am every day more gratified by your admirable description of him — I wish you could understand how well those who never knew him arrive after reading your little book at a true estimate of his character. —

I am anxious to place in my book the Portrait you have given in the Dramatic Scenes — Have you the Plate — and could you send it me? If so you will render me a great service. —

I hope the book will be out in Feb.y — It is unnecessary to say that

one of the first Copies will be sent to you.
I have been greatly amused by reading
M[rs] Fanny Kembles life in Harpers Magazine.
I suppose when it is completed it will appear
in one Volume.
I trust you and yours are all well.

Y[r] obliged & grateful old friend
Anne B. Procter

to write, and it forms my last earnings. You will have heard of the book (perhaps seen it) some time since. It has been very well received. I would not have engaged myself on anything else, but I had great regard for Charles Lamb, and so (somehow or other) I have contrived to reach the end.

"I *have* already (long ago) written something about Hazlitt, but I have received more than one application for it, in case I can manage to complete my essay. As in the case of Lamb, I am really the only person living who knew much about his daily life. I have not, however, quite the same incentive to carry me on. Indeed, I am not certain that I should be able to travel to the real Finis.

"My wife is very grateful for the copies of my dear Adelaide's poems which you sent her. She appears surprised to hear that I have not transmitted her thanks to you before.

"We get the 'Atlantic Monthly' regularly. I need not tell you how much better the poetry is than at its commencement. Very good is 'Released,' in the July number, and several of the stories; but they are in London, and I cannot particularize them.

"'We were very much pleased with Colonel Holmes, the son of your friend and contributor. He seems a very intelligent, modest young man; as little military as need be, and, like Coriolanus, not baring his wounds (if he has any) for public gaze. When you see Dr. Holmes, pray tell him how much I and my wife liked his son.

"We are at the present moment rusticating at Malvern Wells. We are on the side of a great hill (which you would call small in America), and our intercourse is only with the flowers and bees and swallows of the season. Sometimes we encounter a wasp, which I suppose comes from over seas!

"The Storys are living two or three miles off, and called upon us a few days ago. You have not seen *his* Sibyl, which I think very fine, and as containing a *very great* future. But the young poets generally disappoint us, and are too content with startling us into admiration of their first works, and then go to sleep.

"I wish that I had, when younger, made more notes about my contemporaries; for, being of no faction in politics, it happens that I have known far more literary men than any other person of my time. In counting up the names of persons known to me who were, in some way or other, *connected* with literature, I reckoned up more than one hundred. But then I have had more than sixty years to do this in. My first acquaintance of this sort was Bowles, the poet. This was about 1805.

"Although I can scarcely write, I am able to say, in conclusion, that I am

"Very sincerely yours,

"B. W. Procter."

Procter was an ardent student of the works of our older English dramatists, and he had a special fondness for such writers as Decker, Marlowe, Heywood, Webster, and Fletcher. Many of his own dramatic scenes are modelled on that passionate and romantic school. He had great relish for a good modern novel, too; and I recall the titles of several which he recommended warmly for my perusal and republication in America. When I first came to know him, the duties of his office as a Commissioner obliged him to travel about the kingdom, sometimes on long journeys, and he told me his pocket companion was a cheap reprint of Emerson's "Essays," which he found such agreeable reading that he never left home without it. Longfellow's "Hyperion" was another of his favorite books during the years he was on duty.

Among the last agreeable visits I made to the old poet was one with reference to a proposition of his own to omit several songs and other short poems from a new issue of his works then in press. I stoutly opposed the ignoring of certain old favorites of mine, and the poet's wife joined with me in deciding against the author in his proposal to cast aside so many beautiful songs, — songs as well worth saving as any in the volume. Procter argued that, being past seventy, he had now reached to years of discretion, and that his judgment ought to be followed without a murmur. I held out firm to the end of our discussion, and we settled the matter with this compromise: he was to expunge whatever he chose from the English edition, but I was to have my own way with the American one. So to this day the American reprint is the only complete collection of Barry Cornwall's earliest pieces, for I held on to all the old lyrics, without discarding a single line.

The poet's figure was short and full, and his voice had a low, veiled tone habitually in it, which made it sometimes difficult to hear distinctly what he was saying. When in conversation, he liked to be very near his listener, and thus stand, as it were, on confidential ground with him. His turn of thought was cheerful among his friends, and he proceeded readily into a vein of wit and nimble expression. Verbal felicity seemed natural to him, and his epithets, evidently unprepared, were always perfect. He disliked cant and hard ways of judging character. He praised easily. He had no wish to stand in anybody's shoes but his own, and he said, "There is no literary vice of a darker shade than envy." Talleyrand's recipe for perfect happiness was the opposite to his. He impressed every one who came near him as a born gentleman, chivalrous and generous in a marked degree, and it was the habit of those who knew him to have an affection for him. Altering a line of Pope, this counsel might have been safely tendered to all the authors of his day, —

"Disdain whatever *Procter's mind* disdains."